FORGETFUL MUSES: READING THE AUTHOR IN THE TEXT

IAN LANCASHIRE

Forgetful Muses

Reading the Author in the Text

UNIVERSITY OF TORONTO PRESS
Toronto Buffalo London

© University of Toronto Press Incorporated 2010
Toronto Buffalo London
www.utppublishing.com
Printed in Canada

ISBN 978-1-4426-4093-1

Printed on acid-free, 100% post-consumer recycled paper
with vegetable-based inks.

Library and Archives Canada Cataloguing in Publication

Lancashire, Ian
Forgetful muses : reading the author in the text / Ian Lancashire.

Includes bibliographical references and index.
ISBN 978-1-4426-4093-1

1. Authorship – Psychological aspects.   2. Style, Literary.   3. Creation
(Literary, artistic, etc.) – Psychological aspects.   4. Criticism –
Psychological aspects.   5. Psychology and literature.   I. Title.

PN171.P83L35 2010   801′.92   C2010-904477-0

This book has been published with the help of a grant from the
Humanities and Social Sciences Federation of Canada, through the Aid
to Scholarly Publications Program, using funds provided by the Social
Sciences and Humanities Research Council of Canada.

University of Toronto Press acknowledges the financial assistance to its
publishing program of the Canada Council for the Arts and the Ontario
Arts Council.

 Canada Council   Conseil des Arts
for the Arts   du Canada   ONTARIO ARTS COUNCIL
CONSEIL DES ARTS DE L'ONTARIO

University of Toronto Press acknowledges the financial support of the
Government of Canada through the Canada Book Fund for its publishing activities.

To my students

Returne forgetfull Muse, and straight redeeme,
In gentle numbers time so idely spent,
Sing to the eare that doth thy laies esteeme,
And giues thy pen both skill and argument.

Shakespeare, Sonnet 100

Can we someday say valid, simple, and important things about the working
of the mind in producing written text and other things as well?

John Pierce, *An Introduction to Information Theory*

The native speaker's ability to produce fluent and idiomatic stretches of
connected discourse, spontaneously and in real time, is a marvel and a
mystery.

Bengt Altenberg, 'Recurrent Verb-Complement Constructions
in the London-Lund Corpus'

Contents

Figures, Distribution Graphs, and Tables

Figures

Distribution Graphs and Tables

Preface

IBM Canada and the University of Toronto funded the Centre for Computing in the Humanities (CCH) that I founded in 1985 to see – my private hope – whether text-analysis systems could find evidence of the author in the text. I was cul-de-sacked for some years before turning to cognitive psychology, and the writers in *Representative Poetry Online* were my first subjects. Geoffrey Rockwell's initiative, the Text Analysis Portal for Research (TAPoR), gave me the research infrastructure I needed to persevere after my double term as CCH director ended. Two former students of mine, Raymond Siemens and Willard McCarty, nudged me repeatedly for talks and essays, I guess to bring some closure to my research on cognitive stylistics and cybertextuality. Others had tried before. My student Gary Shawver made something fine out of Chaucer's phrasal repetends. Donald Foster showed that authorship attribution could succeed. The late Harold Love referred to me as the theorist of authorship attribution, 'so far as it has one' (2002, 149), and told me that I should do something about it.

Let me thank those who gave me help: Anne, for four decades of encouragement; our three children, Susannah, David, and Ruth, all uniquely courageous; my big-hearted parents, Ernie and Betty; John Bradley, Michael Stairs, and Lidio Presutti, for making *CollGen* in *TACT*, and Alex Cheng for getting it to work in 2007; Susan Hockey, for collegial generosity; Carole Moore, Peter Clinton, Kent Weaver, and Sian Meikle, for a sunny research lab within Information Technology on the seventh floor of Robarts Library; for their example, Marshall McLuhan, who never knew me, and David Olson, who does; Jennifer Roberts Smith, for anecdotes; Michael Eberle-Sinatra, for encouragement; Angela Guardiani, for telling me about Margaret Atwood's papers;

Timothy Harrison and Anastasia Berdinskikh, for listening; Graeme
Hirst, Regina Jokel, and Xuan Le, for advancing the Agatha Christie
case and educating me; the late John Leyerle, my thesis supervisor, for
patience; fellow golfers Brian Merrilees, for twenty-four years of faith,
and Shelley Woolner and Greig Henderson, who read this book in typescript and saved me from many slips of mind and tongue; Jeff Heath
and Linda Hutcheon; authors Molly Peacock and Margaret Atwood;
Gordon De Wolfe, for suggesting Agatha Christie; Barbara Thomson,
for help with statistics; Jan Svartvik and Magnus Ljung and my other
friends at Lund and Stockholm universities during my visits in February 1991; Fergus Craik, Peter St George-Hyslop, David Tang-Wai, Craig
Chambers, and Susan Kemper for cautions (the remaining faults are
mine) and some brilliant suggestions; and the anonymous reviewers
of this book in manuscript, my editors, Suzanne Rancourt and Barbara
Porter, and my copy editor, Charles Stuart, for their high expectations. I
also acknowledge gratefully the generous support of the Social Sciences
and Humanities Research Council of Canada over several decades of
research in text analysis, and of the Canada Foundation for Innovation
for its support of the TAPoR node at Toronto, where I did my research
and writing.

I had the good fortune to teach and learn from excellent students in
undergraduate courses in authoring in 2008–9, and in four graduate
courses in cybertextuality and authoring since 2000.

To write this book also allowed me to know its hidden subject
and ultimate source, my own Anonymous, better than I had thought
possible.

Toronto
30 September 2009

Credits and Sources

FORGETFUL MUSES

Introduction: Finding the Author in the Text

> I am convinced that most writers, even some of the greatest, knew very little about what they were doing when they wrote and had much less conscious control over the final product than is commonly supposed.
>
> (Milic 1971, 87)

Is there an author in this book? Roland Barthes, in 'The Death of the Author' (1967), thought not. Only the reader assigns meaning to a work, he believed; a reader, as the 'site' of the text, supplies its interpretation from its nature as a 'fabric of quotations, resulting from a thousand sources of culture' (1989, 53–4). Many literary critics since have agreed – their own works excepted – and call readers who rely on authorial intention naive (de Beaugrande 1989). Barthes conceded a little ground for authorship attribution – the determination of who wrote a text by finding evidence of authorial characteristics in it – by alloting to each work an agent of language, a scriptor. This entity could be identified even if the author no longer existed. Michel Foucault (1977) further dignified authoring for research by arguing that we continually construct the 'author function,' whether as a corpus of writings ('Have you read any Foucault lately?'), as the owner of copyright, or as a writing subject whose biography can be analysed. Barthes and Foucault voiced a by-then huge consensus of scholarly opinion that E.D. Hirsch Jr, in his essay 'Objective Interpretation' (1960) and in subsequent books, was wrong to locate the interpretation of a work in the author. Barthes and Foucault truly valued the role of a human being in literary criticism, but William K. Wimsatt Jr and Monroe C. Beardsley (whom my student Angela affectionately calls 'Wimsley'), in their classic essays on the intentional and affective fallacy (1946, 1949), which bespeaks the common sense of their times, breathtakingly drive a stake into the author. It is an error, they argue, to believe what authors say about their intentions and to attribute to the author, not the text, any purposefulness that a reader experiences while attending to a literary work. They add that the 'psychological causes' of a work have no bearing on its success (1949, 31). According to them, we ought to judge a poem like a 'pudding or a machine': it works if everything in it is 'relevant' (1946, 469). Subsequent theoreticians like Kenneth Burke and phenomenologist Wolfgang Iser moderated this position. Burke, especially, asserted that meaning was always 'codetermined, the reader's horizon of expectation attempting to fuse with the author's.'[1]

Frustrated readers adopt sceptical literary paradigms of authorship for understandable reasons. In *The World on Paper* (1994), David Olson identified one downside of literacy: the loss of the author's 'illocutionary force' in his written texts. Readers go without the author's embodied utterance. Gesture, context, tone, facial expression, and emotional content would tell immediately an author's intentions in making a text. J.L. Austin coined this term to describe performative speech acts that render a verdict, exercise a right, assert a proposition, promise to do something, and undertake to apologize, congratulate, commend, commiserate, swear at, and challenge (1975, 151–2). Olson uses the term more generally to mean an expressive power without which readers must use an exegetical hermeneutics to discover the speaker's feelings. Knowing what words mean in dictionaries is not enough. Some authors disguise or expunge their intentions from their writing, leaving disoriented readers awash in doubt. Even novels with an omniscient narrator who tells us what he wants and thinks may be suffused with irony. Literary criticism in fact depends on authors for a steady supply of problematic novels, plays, and poems so that it can teach readers how to impose or deduce or problematize illocutionary force, that is, the paraphernalia of intention. Much criticism de-authors written works, transubstantiating[2] intention into a property of text.

Ordinary readers who apply their own illocutionary force to a work are re-authoring it. Cognitively, they embody language and invest it with the force of their own intentions and emotions. All readers understand words as 'embodied conceptualizations of the situations that language describes' (Niedenthal 2007, 1005). Unconsciously, we activate schemata in long-term memory when we comprehend many words. The associative neurological clusters that a word lights up extend to the stored sensations of how we execute or experience the action that word signifies. Word meaning is not just symbolic. For example, part of one recent experiment in cognitive psychology showed subjects a sequence of two pictures. The first was a baseball with the sentence, 'The shortstop hurled the ball at you,' and the second was an image of just the baseball, either smaller or larger than the first image. Then the experimenter asked the subjects to agree, or disagree, that the two images displayed the same object. When the second image was smaller, the quick sequencing thus suggesting movement away, the response 'yes' was slower than when the second image was 'bigger,' suggesting movement towards (Zwann, Madden, Yaxley, and Aveyard 2004, 616). When the two sequenced images appear to contradict the sentence, subjects were slow to respond. They experienced the phrase 'hurl at' in a bodily way.

Here is a literary example of my own. Molly Peacock is an exceptionally fine contemporary poet who makes poetry fans of ordinary readers. When she allowed me to select some of her poems for *Representative Poetry Online*, her 'A Favor of Love' (2002, 19–20) touched me. In plain vocabulary, with disarming cheerfulness, Molly describes how she saved a life. In Kim's market to buy some watercress, asparagus, garlic, pecans, and endive, Molly saw a girl choking and turning purple. A lollipop had got stuck in her throat. While her boyfriend shouted for the manager to call 911 for help, Molly raised her 'woollen arm, aiming for her / shoulder blades where I whack, whack her again.' We experience what Molly did by reading these words. We activate the sensory, motor, and emotional experiences in our long-term memory for lifting our arm and whacking something. I did not hear Molly read this poem, and so I had no access to her voice, tone, and bodily delivery of it, but she managed, somehow, to ensure that, distanced by print, I still felt the emotionally intense event that led her to write. Reading how the girl 'grabs' Molly 'in a bear hug' and 'shouts' 'Oh Mommy' and 'Thank you for saving my life!' stimulates much more than semantic memories. Molly chose words that embody the experience by lighting up sensory and motor neurons. If she had used metaphors, the passage would have fallen flat, in that action verbs like 'raise,' 'whack,' 'grab,' and 'shout' only 'evoke somatotropic activation of the motor cortex … when used as literal action verbs' (Willems and Hagoort 2007, 286). Most poignant for me is the girl's cry, 'Oh Mommy!' (which the amused poet frames with her mildly indignant reply, '*My name is Molly!*'). The phrase 'Oh Mommy!' aroused, at first unconsciously, my emotions as a child when something bad happened to me and in panic I sought my *Mommy*'s arms.[3] Few have not cried out once, as a child, 'Oh Mommy!' It is very different from saying, 'Oh Mother!' Molly Peacock avoids all metaphors, dead or new, and uses literal words that vividly save some of the author's 'illocutionary force' that Olson believes is lost. Non-literal language deactivates embodied responses such as Molly Peacock allows. No wonder readers often cannot find an author's feelings in florid writing.

Authorship attribution research tries to find the name – not the intentionality or the character – of the person who wrote a work. At first, researchers used similarities of thought and meaning between the works of a known author and those of an anonymous writer, but different authors can express the same themes, images, words, or thoughts. A better method situates anonymous texts historically, finds candidate authors who might have written them, and then searches for stylistic evidence with external historical witness about authorship. We look for an idiolect, that is, for Barthes's agent of language, and Foucault's author-function, the one who has a distinctive lexical style. Most authorship-attribution researchers today gather in the digital humanities and practise computational stylistics. They identify a configuration of language markers, each characterized by a distinctive frequency range, with the style of known and anonymous authors. We cannot read the frequencies of such stylistic markers as we read a book; they are intelligible only if we believe that words and word combinations exist cognitively in the author's mind, separate from the texts that devolve from them. To the cognitive paradigm of authorship, a text is a secondary phenomenon; it is only the author's mind that contains feelings and intentions.

Not all stylistic markers are useful in authorship naming. Stylistics focuses on lexical markers of which scriptors (transcribers, writers) are supposedly unconscious and, therefore, cannot deliberately imitate. Any marker or configuration of markers of which a writer can be conscious, so it is said, is untrustworthy if we are, by nature, suspicious of potential fraud. Scholars sometimes ignore the requirement of unconsciousness, maybe because no one has access to an author's mind and can tell what is conscious and what unconscious. In distinguishing the work of Fletcher from that of Beaumont, Cyrus Hoy (1956, 130) accordingly refers to markers as 'linguistic preferences.' He argues that, when only author A uses a feature x, among a large body of other authors who do not use it, x reliably marks A's work. Hoy does not insist that x be impossible for A to avoid using, or that it be unconsciously invoked; as a result, he implies that A can choose (prefer) to use or not to use x. If so, then other authors can also choose (prefer) to use and not use x; and thus the method fails in principle, even if in practice the results are instructive. David J. Lake (1975, 7) may share Hoy's views. Thomas B. Horton insists that a unique marker in A, clearly not found in any other author, is insufficient: that marker must be accompanied by evidence that it is substylistic and unconscious: 'Unfortunately the textual features that stand out to a literary scholar usually reflect a writer's conscious stylistic decisions and are thus open to imitation, deliberate or otherwise. Tests of authorship that are founded on subconscious habits are a desirable goal in most (if not all) applications' (1987, 9). If this is true, before we select any marker as reliable for purposes of identifying authorship, we must ask, 'What markers are unconsciously employed?' To answer that, we need a new author-function, not about idiolect, but about cognitivity. An author-function becomes a brain-function. As we will see, this in turn breaks down into three entities: languageless thought or reasoning; what I call the Writer's Own Anonymous, after E.M. Forster's remarkable description of the nameless inner voice that writers rely on to generate language for them; and the reader-editor, who is at least partly conscious.

The literary paradigm for authoring sees stylistic markers, and their frequencies, as accidental characteristics of text, not mind. They have no more significance than white noise in an art gallery. We must derive stylistic markers from brain functions to make a reasonable link between text and mind. We must understand how the brain produces language and what role unconsciousness plays in that production. Only then will we be able to distinguish those markers of which we are innately conscious all the time from those markers of which we have an uncontrollable neglect. How the brain utters language provides the context for selecting valuable authorship markers.

It seems absurd to say that I am unconscious of my own language. When I read a book or listen to someone talk, I am conscious of each sentence. I own grammars, rhetorics, dictionaries, style books, and a wide variety of tools to analyse linguistic features. I have memorized and can recall grammatical rules and lexical meanings. I know the experience of going under anaesthetic, and the sudden disorientation that accompanies emerging from unconsciousness in an unfamiliar place. As a speaker and a writer I experience no such break in consciousness, no later awakening. In no sense does giving a public talk, or writing a letter, anaesthetize my mind. I am not even exhibiting 'zombie behaviour' such as happens when I drive to work on a route I have used for decades and am thinking about something else. I am not sedated or absent-minded because I will immediately experience what I am saying. Freudian psychoanalysis hypothesizes the ego (one's conscious sense of oneself), the superego (one's partly conscious moral sense), and the id (the unconscious mind, holding both one's impulses and any repressions of thoughts or behaviour about which one conceivably might be conscious). Although Freud was very interested in slips of the tongue, as well as in dreams, for the insights they might yield of the id, he did not think of language itself as an unconscious drive. Yet we are unconscious of the uttering process.

Stylometry claims that many language markers are unconscious. In Shakespeare studies (a hotbed of authorship controversy), M.W.A. Smith's analysis of *Edward III*, until recently one of the Shakespeare apocrypha (but now securely accepted as his work), employs as markers 'the first word of speeches, all other words, and pairs of consecutive words, henceforth referred to as collocations' (1991, 166). In analysing the same play, Thomas Merriam instead uses 'counts of certain function-words such as "but," "by," "for," "no," "not," "so," "that," "the," "to," and "with"' (1993, 59). MacDonald P. Jackson first recommended these markers in 1979 and uses them still. Thomas Horton has his doubts because five of these function words are known to co-vary, in frequency, according to which genre Shakespeare is writing (1994, 324). Low or high occurrences need not be significant for authorship. Jonathan Hope (1994) focuses on the auxiliary 'do,' relatives ('who,' 'that,' 'which,' etc.), and 'thou' and 'you.' In the field of forensic linguistics, few mathematical statisticians write with greater authority than David Holmes. He says, of stylometry in the 1990s, that 'there is no consensus as to correct methodology or technique' (1998, 111). For every stylometrist whose research supports an attribution, there is another who can point out weaknesses in that research and cast doubt on the claim. To the literary reader and non-stylometrist, attributions of anonymous works to Shakespeare, and attributions of his undoubted works to others, resemble stock market predictions. These disagreements aside, most attribution researchers today believe that authors use some aspects of language unconsciously.

Attribution experts call such a marker 'substylistic.' They define it as habitual, unambiguous, and difficult for the author to observe, to edit in, and to cut. The author cannot deliberately select or avoid substylistic markers. Yet what are the grounds for believing them to be unconscious? What mental state corresponds to the writer's working unconscious, as conceived by stylometrists? And why should function words like 'but,' 'who,' and 'you,' for instance, be better unconscious markers than nouns or lexical verbs? Because frequency-based attribution methodology depends on a biological, not a conceptual, paradigm of authorship, we should look to cognitive psychology and the neurosciences to reopen the issue of unconscious creative process, something that is central to the humanities and the arts. We will find that *all* language, as it is spontaneously produced by the mind, happens unconsciously. Authorship attribution researchers do not need to select one kind of language over another. They only need to assure themselves that they are testing spontaneous text that has not been consciously edited on paper. They are looking to find utterances that precede what is always the first reading of a work, the authorial reading. These flow from the Writer's Own Anonymous.

Many fields of enquiry help us to understand authoring. Poets and novelists bear first-hand witness to how they compose. They give us a place to stand. Interviewers often ask writers what they experience during making (as Chaucer called it), less in the hope of illumination than respecting the curiosity of readers who do not know what the experience of authoring is like. Many writers make penetratingly accurate witnesses. Two formal disciplines, cognitive psychology and neuroscience, cast light on the mechanics of language production by experimenting on living subjects and by treating patients for lesions to the brain's language centres. These studies affirm the observations of many writers on how they author. Science tells us about cognitive constraints and procedures: the forms or channels of uttering rather than its content. One is George Miller's 'magical number' (1956), the amount of auditory language of which we can be conscious in working or short-term memory – it is now barely three or four words, or less than two seconds in length. Such fragments are called chunks. Cognitive and corpus linguistics, another pair of disciplines, model language structures as produced in actual usage by a non-innate or learned cognitive ability (Croft and Cruse 2004, 1). Cognitive linguistics focuses on variably sized constructs, which are chunks anatomized, and corpus linguistics on repeating phrases. Another three disciplines extract and analyse evidence from entire texts: computational linguistics, text analysis, and writing research. They make tools to disintegrate and rebuild complete texts. They find their repeated constituent parts, that is, lexical and syntactic patterns that are potential markers and formally resemble chunks and constructs; and they devise methods, tools, and software that can reassemble or create texts. Computational linguists do machine translation and text summarization, writing researchers make protocols, and text-analysis researchers extrapolate models.

Each field has its limitations. Authorial testimony is impressionistic. The patient is the last person whom doctors trust to make a diagnosis, but because every medical exam begins when the doctor asks the patient about his or her symptoms, we should pay attention. Human-subject experiments in cognitive psychology and neuroscience amass an extraordinary body of hard-won knowledge about language processing, but do they deal with texts? Corpus linguists describe language, especially oral conversation (the closest to the mind's inner speech), by assembling and analysing statistically the features of representative types of authentic speech and writing. These studies extract small samples of a writer's work, usually 1,500 words, and combine it with like excerpts from hundreds of other writers. Cognitive linguists develop non-generative theories of language by examining the segmentation of typical idiomatic expressions. Their research on how we comprehend texts resembles reception- and reader-response literary theories, but few scientists, aside from human-computer-interface designers, use technologies – such as keystroke and eye-movement analysis – that analyse complete texts by single authors. Computational linguists simulate authoring with logic-based processes. This field neglects human authors for language data. Text-analysis research in the humanities applies the interactive concordancer, a relatively straightforward indexing tool developed in the 1950s, to derive visual representations of meaning from the fundamental particles of an author's text. Jonathan Feinberg's *Wordle* (2008) is a good example. Yet it is impossible to read a word-cloud or a concordance listing as a text, or to find the author in these transforms. They work with trains of single strings, defined by the spaces that separate them; yet the mind does not compose with sequences of atomistic lexical units. Writing researchers analyse the processes used by writers and emphasize the last stage in uttering. They aim to help people write effectively.

These fields have differing strengths, but what matters is where they agree. They all tend to believe that we make sentences as a sequence of phrasal chunks, as if cognitive language production were a pulsing heart. They also theorize about what the author does in the planning and making stages of language production because, as far as they can tell, no one is conscious of those processes until an utterance reaches either inner and outer speech (as what can be heard) or the page and the screen. These theories take the form of simulations and models. Cognitive psychologists see this interaction of the unconscious and conscious creative selves in two parallel processes or functions (Evans 2003), the language maker and the self-monitor, which authors have historically perceived as the sending muse and the receiving editor. Authors who wake out of their flow to see what their Anonymous has uttered make their first reading of the text and proceed to edit. They disguise or remove habitual, unconsciously generated markers. They leave traces of intention. Cognitive and corpus linguistics assume a degree of language unconsciousness but are more interested in the shape of the language as a system than in the human minds that utter it. Text and writing analyses interrogate finished texts for their repeating phrases, or repetends, or their brief writing bursts. These phenomena beg for an explanation by cognitive disciplines.

Since the late 1980s, literary critics have devised a new neuro-cognitive theory and method that analyses texts as embodied by the author's or the reader's biological brain. Norman Holland, Mark Turner, Ellen Spolsky, Alan Richardson, David Miall, Mary Crane, Patrick Colm Hogan, Keith Oatley, and others have applied cognitive concepts to literary studies. They have also carried theory into interpretation of authors as diverse as Robert Frost, S.T. Coleridge, Shakespeare, and Samuel Richardson. A cognitive critical method, which has common ground to theories as different as deconstructionism (Spolsky 2002) and reader response, can bridge them. I build on their pioneering work and am no less idiosyncratic than they, but we all share a vital interest in understanding literature in the light of the cognitive sciences (Richardson and Spolsky 2004, 2).

I have endeavoured to write this book with two different audiences in mind. One is a well-educated general reader who wants to go behind the scenes to see how writers create. Punctuating the book, for this reason, are interventions of the Anonymous who partly authored it. Much of this book comes from consciously selecting and editing information from sources in external memory, but the one who shaped and interpreted that information has no name. I tried to observe him – a male voice, I think – and mostly failed. The other audience is the professional researcher and teacher. For this reader I included the analyses of authorial readings by writers from Cædmon to Margaret Atwood. I hope that both readerships are sufficiently interested in a writer's creative process that they will endure my subjective speculations and the technical analyses. What the sciences (cognitive, linguistic, and literary) say is sometimes boring but also astounding. You must know both cultures, as C.P. Snow says, to understand yourself. You also need to search your own mind when you speak and write. You are a good authority on your own uttering.

Chronologically, some years ago I started with Chaucer. His phrasal clusters reminded me then of associational-memory networks, and so I set myself to read cognitive psychology, where I discovered Alan Baddeley's phonological loop in working memory (1992). That had a small capacity, like a phrase. Chapters 2 and 3 began as a theory of cognitive stylistics. This in turn led me to look for corroborative testimony from authors, the germ of chapter 1. Last, because memory does not utter anything, but only records it, I needed to know more about the mind if I was going to understand what the cognitive mechanics of authoring left behind in texts. Espen Aarseth's book *Cybertext* (1997), which described mechanical texts (such as interactive fictions), got me thinking again about Norbert Wiener's cybernetics. I found in it the actions whose products are caught by Alan Baddeley's whimsically named phonological loop. Cybertextuality is a variant on a neologism that goes back to a Canadian computer firm in the 1980s (Koekebakker 1983), a science fiction writer (Bruce Boston) in 1991, and Espen Aarseth, who names a theory of how mind and print technologies manage word-packets or messages. This (the subject of chapter 3) came last, about half a dozen years ago.

Chapter 1 describes what many authors say about their creative process, their muses, often in interviews. Richard Eberhart and William Stafford go further, describing the genesis of two of their poems. They speak of a distinctive sense of flow, but their works show every sign of being stitched together chunkwise. If you enjoy this, chapters 4.III, 4.V, and 5.II and IV (about the impact of drug use, depression, and dementia on four well-known writers) and 5.III (a Canadian perspective) may be of most interest to you.

Chapter 2, for those who are not well read in cognitive psychology and neuroscience, summarizes current research in those fields. I give a plausible account of language production as many scientists perceive it to be at the beginning of the twenty-first century. If you do research in cognitivity, you will know this anyway. If not, persevere: you may be surprised by how much we believe we know about how the mind makes language. Of course, I give an English teacher's understanding of these things: the five, simultaneously cascading stages of uttering, the nature of chunks, the role that different types of memory play in sustaining them, embodiment, syntactic priming, the self-monitor, the default mode network, and the linked processes of reading and writing. These contentious issues, still long from resolved, still changing, are debated in scientific journals.

Chapter 3 poses a theory of authoring and composing that I call cybertextual. It is based on Norbert Wiener's theory of messages (1948), cybernetics, which offers a mathematical basis for describing how humans and machines communicate. This is not a computational theory of mind, but one that uses computer text analysis as a tool to formulate an empirically based explanation of how the author steers a text into being, and how we can read a text so to recover something of that authoring process. Authors make cybertexts (from the Greek words for 'to steer' and 'to weave') – that is, any oral, written, or digital utterance – cognitively with the help of a persistent cybernetic feedback received first from themselves. The unconscious mind generates text, and at least as soon as the utterance becomes speech (that is, is auditorily encoded), the mind's own equally inchoate self-monitor gives necessary corrections as feedback. The mind thus must model its own utterance in order to comprehend it. The author's mainly unconscious Anonymous does some tweaking before finally sounding the text out or writing it down. Once the inner self-monitor gives way to the writer as a conscious editor of his text, stored on the page or screen, another message-feedback system takes over. This is the moment of the authorial reading, the first reading that any work receives. Mechanically, by externalizing our cognitive memory systems as writing and media technologies, the author consciously shuttles between three states of being: thought itself (which seems different from language); an unconscious utterer; and a conscious reader-editor who gives feedback and who alters the text by resummoning that unconscious language-making process that launched the utterance. Our own cognitive limitations in language making have precipitated the speech-to-script, script-to-print, and print-to-digital-text revolutions. Cybertextuality studies how the dynamics of inner speech making shape both our utterances and the functionality of language technologies we employ to enhance (and sometimes degrade) our cognitive powers.

How does cybertextuality differ methodologically from literary studies? Consider an analogy: identifying the make of a car that lacked all identifying plates. A postmodernist might insist that the car could only be known by how its driver interpreted it: for a suburbanite, an errand-running city car; for teens, a race car; for a businessperson, a moving telephone booth. A literary editor would take the car apart, looking to date and identify the manufacturers of its parts. An authorship-attribution researcher who uses digital text analysis would melt the car down, measure the quantity of each kind of metal, plastic, and glass, and compare its table of elements against known specifications from car makers. A cybertextualist values all these approaches but takes a different tack. Cybertextuality reconstructs the mechanical process of making the car, looking for process features that would distinguish its making from that of other known assembly lines. All these methods complement one another, and sometimes they overlap. The cybertextualist's assembly line, the authorship attributor's table of elements, and the literary editor's catalogue of parts are all determined by the way the car's driver, the postmodernist's absent author, once used the car. Authoring, composing, and reading are one interrelated process.

Cybertextuality grew from my trying to understand the repeating patterns found in textual indexes. By co-developing two interactive concordancers in 1984 and 1989–96, *Micro-Text Analysis System* (*MTAS*) and *Text Analysis Computing Tools* (*TACT*), especially a procedure called *CollGen* (collocations generator), I learned that Chaucer and Shakespeare had phrasal vocabularies, not lexical ones. Word-frequency lists, a basic tool of stylistics, proved easy to do but deceptive. Key Word in Context (KWIC) software was made to index books, not minds; and we speak, listen, read, and write in word-packets, for which we have no name but chunks, which form clusters.

Cybertextually, authoring begins with the emotion-driven pulse in the flow of mind's dark conceptualizer. We need not utter and overhear words in order to think: we might, like Nabokov, see shapes.[4] A partly attended self-monitor, a mind-voice we overhear in silent speech when we attend to errors, responds to this flow. Since the birth of literacy, in any communications that are not oral, the Writer's Own Anonymous ceases when the literate composer begins – the one who reads text in visual chunks and uses writing, printing, and computing to extend the powers of the cognitive conceptualizer and self-monitor. Mind technologies like these respond to our mental frustrations and constraints. They transmute authoring into a cyborgic composing, enabled by human-made tools that midwife the birthing of its utterances. A composer, unlike an author, is a cyborg ('cybernetic-organism'), because tools extend his powers. Our communications tools have changed the toolmaker's own language. Millennia ago, we only authored works spontaneously, but now we also compose them over time, partnered with tools that mimic and supplement our native cognition, and that fundamentally transform what was once only uttered. Today, the partnership of the cognitive voice and the consciously composing mind thrives. We create texts far longer and more complex on screen and paper than we ever could with our unaided mind. Only in very unusual circumstances do compositional tools fail. In extreme cyborg literature such as output by poetry generators and chatbots (Lancashire 1991, 67–71), bordering on AI, the author does not exist at all except as a programmer of compositional tools. Barthes's language agent does, but it also can behave in a lobotomized manner.

With a theory and a nail, it is said, we have a nail. The hammer that makes something out of the theory (cybertextuality) and the nail (authored works) is a close reading of those texts. Can the theory be put to work? Chaper 1 analyses poems by Cædmon (the first named poet) and two modern American poets, Richard Eberhart and William Stafford. Chapter 4 has close readings of poets Geoffrey Chaucer (Middle English), Shakespeare (Early Modern English), S.T. Coleridge, W.B. Yeats, and T.S. Eliot. Chapter 5 has readings of novelists James Joyce, Agatha Christie, Iris Murdoch, and Margaret Atwood. Chapter 6 summarizes how to make an authorial reading. The close readings search for the author's brain-function in his text. What, exactly, are the unconscious markers that authorship attribution needs? Is an author who died three hundred years ago truly dead in his works, or can he be partly recognized in them? Are there texts that can never be attributed because they have been considerably altered during editing, losing so many distinctive features of their authors that only cyborgic assemblages remain?[5] And how can we distinguish the mind's unsupported authoring from a mind-digital hybrid, one crafted by hands that were directed by eyes to encode, visually, a mental-oral utterance by means of a symbol set? Unless holographic materials have survived, texts that have been composed – that is, revised by means of sentence-editing a paper copy over a period of time – will have deleted many signs of spontaneous uttering. Chapters 4, 5, and 6 serve the teacher and reader of mainstream classical literature. If my close readings remind you too much of an introductory course in English, enjoy the biographical anecdotes. Some numerical findings are secreted in already published essays and this book's appendix.

Chapter 4 begins with Geoffrey Chaucer, the phrasal basis of whose language shows how general constraints in mental authoring carry forward into the uttered work itself. The basic poetic lexicon of both Old English and Middle English has a phrasal beat. The well-known oral-formulaic vocabulary of Cædmon reveals that cognitive chunks, constructs stitched together by alliteration, pervade our earliest verse literature. Chaucer's *Canterbury Tales*, eight centuries later, are outwardly less formulaic, but so pervasive are their repeating phrases we appear to be able to date tales written at the same time by the overlap in their phrasal and collocational repertoires. The distribution of repeated phrases and collocations found in the General Prologue through the rest of the tales also suggests that many have a limited lifetime in a poet's mental lexicon. We see Chaucer's authorial readings in the character of little Geoffrey in *The House of Fame*, and in the pilgrim who told the Tale of Sir Thopas.

Shakespeare's 'Hand D' in the play *Sir Thomas More* reveals his two styles, the cognitive and the editorial. We can estimate his cognitive capacity or load, what I call the omega value: the maximum size that a complex thought can take in writing. Lexical entrainment and syntactic priming mark the boundary where one thought ends and another begins. The impulse to repeat words and phrases, made possible by Shakespeare's reading of what he has just written, may coincide with a sense of having exhausted a thought. The More fragment also reveals his partly unconscious self-monitor, correcting with such speed as he wrote that the impulse to amend came in mid-word.

The next two poets wrote notorious works, S.T. Coleridge 'Kubla Khan' and T.S. Eliot *The Waste Land*. Both poets were ill or psychologically upset, and both poems required considerable editing before publication. Coleridge was among the first authors to become alert to the mysterious voice within him. It was the lamp, as severe editorial reason was the mirror. Using Byron's words, Coleridge termed 'Kubla Khan' a 'psychological curiosity,' first claiming that he made it in an opium reverie and quickly wrote it down on rousing himself. He changed this story in 1816. Only the first part of the poem fits his story. Lexical entrainment and syntactic priming mark points at which he seems to have consciously extended the original. The history of the making of Eliot's poem, following the discovery of the manuscripts in the New York Public Library, is by now well known. It consists of fragments, sized at cognitive capacity, that he and Ezra Pound knitted together afterwards. Pound cut half the draft materials that Eliot had generated, including passages that parody Alexander Pope and James Joyce. What Pound let survive, and what Eliot declared afterwards to be the best lines in the work, was written in a flow state with few editorial corrections. The unconscious voice that uttered both poems produced very mixed work, both great and weak. Eliot's use of writing technology, handwriting and typing, released his Anonymous. Pound's editing tamed it. The last poet discussed here, W.B. Yeats, nimbly harvests the best work of both his Anonymous and its editor. All three poets witnessed their two authoring states, unconscious and flowing, and conscious and calculating.

Chapter 5 opens with a dissection of how the young James Joyce, fictionalized as Stephen Dedalus, created a villanelle on waking up one morning. The episode is Joyce's sympathetic but at times comic authorial reading of himself as a poet a decade before he published *A Portrait of the Artist as a Young Man* (1916). His perceptive description of the cognitive creative process reveals an author's shocked recognition of how much work he must do to repress and disguise his Anonymous. An examination of the second novelist, Agatha Christie, illustrates the effects of a healthy old age and, I believe, dementia on the process of authoring. Christie wrote scores of detective novels up into her eighties, but the last two, published in 1972–3, exhibit a severe drop in her vocabulary. She must have recognized this cognitive decline because *Elephants Can Remember* (1972) describes the confused forgetfulness of an aging writer of detective fiction. There is little question that this author remains in her work. Margaret Atwood also makes excellent use of her selves. The holograph and preliminary typed drafts of two parts of *The Handmaid's Tale* allow us to see Atwood's chunking Anonymous and her reader-editor working as a team. Her description of the three stages of writing – building schemata in long-term memory, untapping the flow, and then editing it closely – shows how authors tame unguarded flow. The fourth novelist, Iris Murdoch, lived with Alzheimer's disease as she tried to finish her last novel, *Jackson's Dilemma* (1995). An autopsy on her brain, and the results of straightforward concording of her text, have given us the equivalent of a Rosetta Stone that translates between the author's brain and her text. Peter Garrard et al. (2005) showed that this novel exhibits a severe reduction in vocabulary (in comparison to her previous works) that can only be explained as a consequence of advancing dementia.[6]

Chapter 6 offers some advice on authorial readings. These are the first reading an utterance has – the author's. The consequences of those readings determine whether or not we can find the Writer's Own Anonymous, an author's undisguised flow from the default mode network, in his final published texts. The inner voice, the muse, or what gives dictation truly characterizes the authoring mind at work, but it can only be seen if we strip away the conscious editorial additions and changes exacted on it before publication by the writer's non-anonymous compositional style. This second style, the editorial, resides in the cognitive control network: it makes calculated changes on the flow of its own Anonymous, which is constantly shifting and tends to be vulnerable to lapses of memory. Cognitive style grows with the author's schemata in long-term memory, like a chess grandmaster's, but it flows within established channels laid down by genetics and articulated in brain function. Constraints of many kinds, common to everyone, shape its utterances. This authoring architecture can be observed in authentic texts, that is, ones produced by people rather than artificial makers such as we see in chatterbots. However, the Writer's Own Anonymous is unstable, changing over time, as Chaucer's was when he wrote *The Canterbury Tales*, and as Iris Murdoch discovered. What youth and middle age developed can leave in old age. Unless authorship attribution carefully distinguishes not just the unconscious markers from the editorially manipulated ones, but the healthy styles from the diseased, naming the author-writer of any text will be problematic.

Authors differ by how they cope with the unconscious voice, the muse, within them. Iris Murdoch, Paul Auster, Agatha Christie, and James Joyce mistrusted their inner voice so much that, instead of relying on schemata (which have built over months and years in long-term memory) to feed the flow when the author at last sits down to write, they penned outlines, abstracts, summaries, and extensive notes of their stories in notebooks. Joyce and Auster frequently reversioned their manuscripts by extensive editing. Other authors, including E.M. Forster and Margaret Atwood, rest content with their long-term memory and start writing, not knowing where it will take them, but trusting that the mind will find a way. Some of these edit and revise fiercely. A few others, like Shakespeare, let the first spontaneous production stand.

Louis Milic some decades ago argued that stylistics must abandon impressionism and rely on quantitative measures. He believed that, because mental authoring is unconscious and cognitively unattended, we might be forgetful of the springs of authoring, like Shakespeare's muse. In reading a text *by the numbers,* by reference to the cognitive channels through which it flows, we can perceive these unconscious markers and patterns. Cybertextuality applies experimental findings and scientific models in brain function to illuminate literary making, to distinguish between texts devised spontaneously, with minimal editorial changes (like Shakespeare's part in *The Play of Sir Thomas More*), and texts whose cognitive features have been obliterated by a ruthless editorial process embarrassed by the repetitions it finds. Cognitive stylistics, once informed by cybertextuality, underlines how complex is authoring. It is hostage to the neural constraints of mental language processes; and because minds can only be indirectly analysed, stylistics as a discipline does research at the interface of cognitive sciences and corpus linguistics. Science and the testimony of authors tell us what to expect. Corpus and cognitive linguistics and writing research extract quantitative features of texts that can be analysed in terms of how they match what human sciences predict will be found. Close reading brings these two things together.

*   *   *   *   *

You're running down a road that materializes before you as your feet meet the ground and you can't see the road that's me but vaguely sense my opening word or phrase, and I don't need your say-so for what I'm doing so you hear me at about the same time as our friends do but are you hearing me or do you think it's you?

Want to see what I'm going to say, then just slow down then as if you've a headache or maybe a stroke ... unless that impression isn't one you'd want to make ... and you'll stop me in my tracks by looking.

Remember standing in front of the drugstore on Mortimer Street in Bloomsbury, your receipt and goods in hand, when you silently voiced, word by word, let's see ... here it is in long-term memory, because you memorized it (what a waste of time) ... 'I bought this electric haircutter here yesterday, new, but while trying it out the first time, blue smoke came out the handle and it stopped. Could I have my money back please?' well, you didn't trust me for that but, you know, I did it anyway! and the truth is, Ian, you've no place to recollect how I do so many things and you owe so much to me ... the next sentence, the feeling and drive to make it, and the draw that rides the wind into the centre of the fairway.

1 Experiencing the Muse

Why does my Muse only speak when she is unhappy?
She does not, I only listen when I am unhappy
When I am happy I live and despise writing
For my Muse this cannot but be dispiriting.

(Stevie Smith, 'My Muse')

I Sightings

The classical notion of the nine Muses represents our inner voice in creative process. We listen daily to our minds think in an auditory silence, and a few among us may hear a different voice, unfamiliar as our own. In classical myth the Muses (Sperduti 1950) were the divine daughters of Zeus and Mnemosyne and enabled a god to possess and use a human as a tool for prophecy. Frenzy, mania, and madness afflicted anyone seized for this reason. Later, poets like Hesiod and Homer associated the Muses not with possession but with gentler inspiration, validating the poets' wisdom. The nine are Calliope for epic poetry, Clio for history, Erato for erotic poetry, Euterpe for lyric song, Melpomene for tragedy, Polyhymnia for religious song, Terpsichore for dance, Thalia for bucolic poetry and comedy, and Urania for astronomy. No one Muse served all artistic purposes. Muses were sensitive to knowledge domain and expertise, just as most of us are. The most brilliant love poet may write poor tragedies. We do not expect great history from a dancer. None of the Muses treated a genre that relies on logic, requires mastery of encyclopedic information (such as other languages), uses mainly visual or material content (in painting, sculpture, and architecture), or documents news or administrivia in letters, technical documents, proclamations, and archival records. The classical Muses serve an autonomous, auditory, language-mediated imagination and communicate in speech, principally poetry and dramatic verse that flows even as it is segmented into measured units, normally small and regular, like lines.

About 430–440 BC the so-called Achilles Painter produced a striking full-length portrait of two unveiled women on a lekythos or vase (see figs. 1–2). One woman stands, left arm at her side, right arm bent at the elbow and pointing towards a bird on the ground, possibly a nightingale (which is associated with song). The bird looks leftwards to the standing woman, as if pointing at her. She faces another woman who sits playing a stringed instrument, a seven-string kithara. Both women look down at it solemnly and intently. The title identifies the rise on which the woman sits as Mount Helicon. She appears to be the muse Polyhymnia, except that both she and the standing woman share the same facial profile, have black hair tucked into a knot at the back (although the hair of the seated woman is bound by a cloth wrap or fillet), are barefoot and unveiled, and wear an undergarment (an ankle-length chiton) and a wrap or wraparound shawl (a himation) common to married women at home (Welters 2006, 244–5). The himation of the standing woman is draped from the left shoulder, freeing up her right arm; the one worn by the seated woman has fallen to her waist, evidently to free her arms for playing. The standing woman has also been taken to be a muse (Oakley 1997, 142), although she plays no instrument and carries no icon that would associate her with one. She stares intensely at the instrument played by the seated woman and, by the way she stands, her head slightly above the level of the player on the mount, assumes some authority in the scene. Neither exhibits any sign of being possessed. They look like married Greek women, unconcerned at showing their hair and feet.

The lekythos on which the two women appear was meant to hold oil, especially for anointing the dead, and so is associated with funerary rites. Some regard the seated woman as the deceased (*Lexicon* 1992, VI.1, 660); others do not believe that these two women are 'deceased maidens shown as Muses' (Oakley 1997, 65). However, they mirror one another in appearance as if they are the same married woman. The Achilles Painter presents both as wholly human and mortal, keeping company in the context of or after death as if they are one and the same person. If they depict the muse and the muse-inspired, the Achilles Painter anthropomorphizes an immortal servant of the gods. The Muse

Figure 1. Polyhymnia on Mount Helicon by the Achilles Painter (with the permission of the Staatliche Antikensammlungen und Glyptothek München; photograph by Renate Kühling)

Figure 2. Listener to Polyhymnia's music by the Achilles Painter (with the permission of the Staatliche Antikensammlungen und Glyptothek München; photograph by Renate Kühling)

and her inspired disciple also foreshadow, by centuries, our cognitive embodiment of the abstract, divine Muse as the heard inner voice in our mortal human brain. Muse and bemused die together today, although they can survive in the music that they have made.

The first muse experience in English poetry belongs to Cædmon. The Venerable Bede (673–735), a monk of Jarrow in Northumbria, tells Cædmon's story in Book IV, Chapter 24, of the *Historia Ecclesiastica Gentis Anglorum*, finished in 731. Cædmon was a brother of Strenæs-hale (Whitby) monastery (Magoun 1955, 49), situated about fifty miles south of Jarrow on the coast of Yorkshire. It was founded by Hild the abbess, who ruled it from 658 to 680. Hild admitted Cædmon to monastic life after he suddenly found, in a dream, the ability to turn scripture that was explained to him into secular verse. Before, Cædmon used to leave a communal feast when the harp being passed around the table neared him. He feared embarrassing himself by having to admit that he knew no songs. One night he got up from the feast table, as usual, and went out to the stable where he was to care for the animals. He fell asleep and in a dream 'saw a man standing beside him who called him by name. "Cædmon," he said, "sing me a song." "I don't know how to sing," he replied. "It is because I cannot sing that I left the feast and came here." The man who addressed him then said: "But you shall sing to me." "What should I sing about?" he replied. "Sing about the Creation of all things," the other answered. And Cædmon immediately began to sing verses in praise of God the Creator that he had never heard before' (Bede 250–3). What astounded Cædmon and others was the immediacy of composition. The verses came in his dream without work, and he could later recite them from memory. The man in his dream had acted as if he were an angel of God or a messenger who, like a classical muse, inspired Cædmon to compose. Bede describes the poem as God's gift or grace (Orchard 1996, 403), as later John Milton in blindness would do in attributing his *Paradise Lost* to a 'Heavenly Muse.' Yet as Bede tells the story, Cædmon only received a command to make verse, not the poem; and the command came from a man, not a god. This order, from someone like Cædmon, overcame the 'stage fright' that led him to leave the table at feasts. The grace was twofold: an invitation from an inner, entirely human male voice to sing, and a new-found ability to utter verse spontaneously. The man in the dream crystallized new desire in Cædmon: for the very first time, Cædmon in effect told himself to sing. The accompanying skill in versifying other scripture earned him a monastic living.

Seventeen manuscripts of Bede's history have Cædmon's poem in Anglo-Saxon. This is a Northumbrian version in the earliest, so-called Moore manuscript (Cambridge University Library MS. Kk 5.16, fol. 128v; Dobbie 1937, 13, 17), dated about 737:

1 Nu scylun hergan hefaenricaes uard   Now let me praise the keeper of Heaven's kingdom,
2 metudæs maecti end his modgidanc   the might of the Creator, and his thought,
3 uerc uuldurfadur sue he uundra
   gihuaes   the work of the Father of glory, how each of wonders
4 eci dryctin or astelidæ   the Eternal Lord established in the beginning.
5 he aerist scop aelda barnum   He first created for the sons of men
6 heben til hrofe haleg scepen.   Heaven as a roof, the holy Creator,
7 tha middungeard moncynnæs uard   then Middle-earth the keeper of mankind,
8 eci dryctin æfter tiadæ   the Eternal Lord, afterwards made,
9 firum foldu frea allmectig   the earth for men, the Almighty Lord.

The making of the poem is wholly believable. It emerges from the unconscious, segmented as a cognitive psychologist today would expect. The first segment is the half-line. Each line consists of two balanced phrases or chunks with four stressed syllables each, only three of which alliterate. A half-line fits neatly into our phonological working (short-term) memory, which holds less than two seconds of speech only before recycling (Lord 1979). Some half-lines are formulaic fixed phrases such as 'eci dryctin' ('the Eternal Lord'; lines 4 and 8), easily reused and remembered building blocks from long-term memory. These formulas, as found in other Old English poems, make up all but three half-lines of the poem (Magoun 1955, 54). Many half-lines succeed one another additively, linked by alliteration. In the first line, the word 'hergan' ('praise') calls up 'hefaenricæs' ('Heaven's kingdom'); and in the second line, 'metudæs maecti' ('the creator's might') links to 'modgidanc' ('thought'). One and the same word begins different half-lines, as with 'hefaenricæs' and 'heben til hrofe' (lines 1 and 6), or ends such lines, like 'uard' (lines 1 and 7) and 'maecti' (lines 2 and 9). Such verse, called 'oral formulaic,' might better be termed cognitively spontaneous. The second segment is possibly Cædmon's thought size-limit. The poem has just two sentences, which can be summarized: 'Let me now praise God the Creator' (lines 1–4), and 'God created Heaven, earth, and man' (lines 5–9). The object of the first sentence is the subject of the second sentence.

The human muse began to wither in the early nineteenth century. In his 'Defence of Poetry' (1821), Percy Bysshe Shelley was among the first to draw a total blank in searching for the origins of creativity in the poet's imagination. He writes that 'the mind in creation is as a fading coal which some invisible influence, like an inconstant wind, awakens to transitory brightness: this power arises from within, like the colour of a flower which fades and changes as it is developed, and the conscious portions of our nature are unprophetic either of its approach or its departure' (Shelley 1994, 70–1). This absolute frustration in observing how the inner voice speaks was arousing horror by last century. Giorgio de Chirico's oil painting *The Disquieting Muses* (1916), now in the University of Iowa Museum of Art (http://www.uiowa.edu/uima/collections/img/euramer/1968_12.html), is such a surrealist's bad dream (see fig. 3). Sylvia Plath makes famous, in her poem of the same name (first published in 1957), the unknowns before which Shelley felt awe. De Chirico's two Muses have 'heads like darning-eggs,' a 'Mouthless, eyeless … stitched bald head,' and 'gowns of stone' (75–6). In the background are factory chimneys and the Castello Estence in Ferrara. His standing Muse has its back to us and is at an angle from the seated one, which faces us. We can see a large black hole where the womb of the seated Muse should be, and her standing partner has medieval arrow slits in the back of its head. They are empty shells. To come under the influence of these lifeless, brainless, evacuated figures of stone disquietingly questions whether modern artists lack not only gods, but a mind itself. The painting elicits the distraught feelings that accompany recognition of our blindness to how our mind works.

Post-classical writers have obviously diminished the Muses. Sir Philip Sidney's Muse says to him, 'Foole … looke in thy heart and write' (Sidney 1591: b1r), as if she has nothing to do with his verse. Shakespeare in Sonnet 100 calls his Muse 'forgetful.' Robbie Burns finds his Muse in 'guid, auld Scotch Drink!' ('Scotch Drink,' line 7). The concept in modern times has receded into figures of speech, names for mistresses, and banter. Still and all, writers from time to time have experienced a Muse-like contact, as Paul Auster (1947–) did in writing his favourite novel, not the much-taught *New York Trilogy* (1990), but the post-apocalyptic *In the Country of Last Things* (1987), a novel that took him from 1970 to 1985 to finish. Postmodern prose fiction owes much to this self-conscious minimalist writer, who admits to rewriting sentences 'fifteen times on

Figure 3. Giorgio de Chirico's *The Disquieting Muses* 1947 (with permission of the University of Iowa Museum of Art; the Gift of Owen and Leone Elliott, 1968.12)

average' (Bigsby 2000–1, 2:24, 27). *Last Things* takes the form of a first-person letter by Anna Blume from a nameless city, very like New York, to her fiancé. Auster confesses having heard Anna's voice in his head from 1970 to the early 1980s, when it appeared 'in full force' and writing the book 'was like taking dictation. I *heard* her voice speaking to me – and that voice was utterly distinct from my own' (1995, 147). Auster does not use the term 'Muse' to describe Anna's persistent, uncharacteristic mental haunting. The word may have long since disappeared from his usual vocabulary.

There are no external Muses, heavenly or otherwise, whose existence we can substantiate. Yet we can understand why we have an inner voice begging for a name.

Cognitive psychologists say we can only remember how to do some things by doing them. This memory is procedural (to recall is to execute some act directly) rather than declarative (to detail its steps, item by item). That we have no mental capacity to declare a procedural memory like making a sentence does not mean that we cannot take apart sentences and put them together. Our long-term memory has retrievable information about words, their parts of speech, their inflectional endings, and syntactic rules for combining them. We can observe the sentence parts appear in our conscious short-term memory, and we can arrange them, but we cannot see how we draw on cognitive resources to put them there and rearrange them. Something constrains us mentally from examining the *process* of speech or writing as it occurs. To observe that assembling, while doing it, meets a built-in obstacle that is unscalable by an act of will. We have no senses to perceive this process and no memory function capacious enough to hold it. We can consciously launch probes into our long-term memory to retrieve information, but once we find what we have searched for, the process of uttering it remains blank.

Karl Lashley (a professor of psychology who showed that the brain acts holistically in learning activities), Louis Milic (an English professor who chaired a department that has taught thousands of undergraduates how to write), John R. Pierce (a mathematician whose account of information science remains the most readable after several decades), Mark Turner (a cognitive literary critic and theorist), and the great American novelist Saul Bellow all *believe in* something surprising: we do not know how we make sentences. No matter how we utter something, in mental silence, vocal speech, or writing, we cannot directly observe ourselves creating that utterance:

When we think in words, the thoughts come in grammatical form with subject, verb, object and modifying clauses falling into place without our having the slightest perception of how the sentence structure is produced. (Lashley 1958, 4)

Without for a moment denying the possibility that some part of a writer's style is conscious artistry or craftsmanship, I am convinced that most writers, even some of the greatest, knew very little about what they were doing when they wrote and had much less conscious control over the final product than is commonly supposed. (Milic 1971, 87)

Subjectively, in speaking or listening to a speaker one has a strong impression that sentences are generated largely from beginning to end. One also gets the impression that the person generating a sentence doesn't have a very elaborate pattern in his head at any one time but that he elaborates the pattern as he goes along. (Pierce 1961, 115)

All but the smallest fraction of our thought and our labor in performing acts of language and literature is unconscious and automatic. (Turner 1991, 39)

I suppose that all of us have a primitive prompter or commentator within, who from earliest years has been advising us, telling us what the real world is. There is such a commentator in me. I have to prepare the ground for him. From this source come words, phrases, syllables; sometimes only sounds, which I try to interpret, sometimes whole paragraphs, fully punctuated. When E.M. Forster said, 'How do I know what I think until I see what I say?' he was perhaps referring to his own prompter. (Bellow 2006, 95)

A deep need to supply a source and an explanation for his uttering, unconscious as Lashley, Milic, Pierce, and Turner believe, leads Bellow to postulate 'a primitive prompter or commentator.'

It is easy to see this constraint operating at first hand, but few of us ever realize that we generate language unconsciously, *because we consciously experience the utterances we make.* Somehow, that we hear or see our utterances as we make them deceives us into believing that we know how we make them. Like most essential cognitive services – the beating of our hearts, sensitivity to hot things, walking, feeling grief or joy – making natural language cannot be recalled non-procedurally. Why do our genes implement this self-blindness? Maybe it protects us from forgetting how to speak. People who suffer from general amnesia do not forget how to explain things, verbally or in writing, even if they cannot remember who they are (Squire 1987, 161, 171; Shimamura et al. 1992).

In moments of anxiety, when we must say something, our fear betrays that, at some level, we recognize that language production is beyond our direct control and, as such, may falter. Three typical experiences of faltering are fear of public speaking, the blanking of an actor's mind before walking onstage, and writer's block. Neurological processes, protected from declarative recollection so as to ensure reliable perform-ance of an essential skill, can have frightening and even disabling effects.

Stage fright will freeze people who are suddenly put in a situation where they must speak in public. Rather than just *letting go* and talk-ing, as if they were saying something to a friend, casually, victims of stage fright mentally probe their minds for something to say and only become more and more agitated when their searching comes up empty.

Recently one of my students, a professional actor, described an unnerv-ing experience she had midway through a theatrical run of Henrik Ibsen's *Enemy of the People*. As she stood, waiting to go onstage, she could not remember anything of what she was to say or do when performing her part. Yet once she walked onstage, she executed everything perfectly just in time. She then understood why other actors repeatedly feel a sickly dread just before going on. So ingrained had their experience of perform-ing become, over many weeks, that they could no longer summon the words or even the actions to conscious memory. The better we know something, the harder it is to declare how we do it: 'when one becomes an expert in any domain, one often cannot report how one performs the task. Much, if not most, of the information in memory cannot be directly accessed and communicated' (Kosslyn and Koenig 1992, 373).

Writer's block can arise from different causes. Anxiety that writing will result in unbearable consequences, such as rejection letters or caustic book reviews, can debilitate a writer who sits down to compose (Fla-herty 2004). Another factor in blockage is a writer's lack of a subject, the intense search for which can lead to mental self-observation. This confronts the writer with the mind's inability to start up, to tinker with, or to control the fount of language. Most of us converse fluently, with-out fear of drying up, because we have something we want to say, and listeners obliged to hear it. It rarely occurs to us to stop in mid-chat to wonder, where's that coming from and will more follow? In first-draft mode, many writers observe how easily, promptly, their sentences come, without prompting, without thought. The more adept we are at writing, the less conscious we appear to be of how we write (cf. Turner 1991, 39). A writer with a block resembles an actor who stands frozen in the wings, unable to step onstage. Both know too much.

Readers of literature, in awe of the works of great writers, often want to know how they write. This question regularly comes up in interviews, thousands of which have been published in special collections and in journals such as the *New York Quarterly* and the *Paris Review*. Writers' testimony on their own language production deserves to be taken more seriously than it has been. It clearly distinguishes between uttering and editing. Many authors agree with Lashley, Milic, Turner, Pierce, and Bellow that the primary creative process, uttering, is mysterious. The sentences we create come apparently out of nothing. The subsequent editing, begun once an utterance is text on paper or on computer screen, is very different: a highly self-conscious, problem-solving, and even social activity. Because the primary uttering itself is hidden from direct observation, authors use metaphors such as the Muse and the prompter to describe it.

Authors stress six features of the creative process. It is *mysterious* and, to the author, numinous. Its unknowability arises because it is *unconscious*. An *inner voice* thus appears to dictate language out of a void. The author falls into a trance-like state of mind that resembles *dreaming*. Words come in *small groups*, a bit, a phrase, a line, or a short passage. Yet one piece pulls out another evenly, and creating assumes a *flow*-like state.

Scrupulously honest or flummoxed writers admit that the source of their words is *unknowable* and beyond comprehension. They characterize uttering as a mystery. Even those playwrights who imitate ordinary speech and dialogue agree. The London novelist, playwright, and screenwriter Fay Weldon (b. 1931) read psychology at the University of St Andrews when she was young, and she underwent psychoanalysis in her thirties, experiences that may have inured her to mystery: 'Since I am writing largely out of my own unconscious much of the time I barely know at the beginning what I am going to say' (Winter 1978, 42). The American dramatist Edward Albee (b. 1928), best known for *Who's Afraid of Virginia Woolf?* admits that his plays take form in his 'unconscious without my being aware of it' and that he writes them down 'to get them out of my head': 'when I begin to write a play down ... I don't even know what the first two lines of dialogue are going to be until I start writing them down and hear what is going on in my head' (Bigsby 2000–1, 1:2). Albee gives the impression of being a tool employed by another entity entirely.

Many novelists other than Saul Bellow agree with him. Robert Louis Stevenson (1850–94) attributed his stories, particularly *The Strange Case of Dr Jekyll and Mr Hyde,* to the Little People, the Brownies,

> who do one-half my work for me while I am fast asleep, and in all human likelihood, do the rest for me as well, when I am wide awake and fondly suppose I do it for myself. That part which is done while I am sleeping is the Brownies' part beyond contention; but that which is done when I am up and about is by no means necessarily mine, since all goes to show the Brownies have a hand in it even then. Here is a doubt that much concerns my conscience. For myself – what I call I, my conscious ego, the denizen of the pineal gland unless he has changed his residence since Descartes, the man with the conscience and the variable bank-account, the man with the hat and the boots, and the privilege of voting and not carrying his candidate at the general elections – I am sometimes tempted to suppose he is no story-teller at all, but a creature as matter of fact as any cheese-monger or any cheese, and a realist bemired up to the ears in actuality; so that, by that account, the whole of my published fiction should be the single-handed product of some Brownie, some Familiar, some unseen col-laborator, whom I keep locked in a back garret, while I get all the praise and he but a share (which I cannot prevent him getting) of the pudding. I am an excellent adviser, something like Molière's servant; I pull back and I cut down; and I dress the whole in the best words and sentences that I can find and make; I hold the pen, too; and I do the sitting at the table, which is about the worst of it; and when all is done, I make up the manuscript and pay for the registration; so that, on the whole, I have some claim to share, though not so largely as I do, in the profits of our common enterprise. (Stevenson 1892, 30)

E.M. Forster (1879–1970), after publishing his sixth and finest novel, *A Passage to India* (1924), exposed his creative process in *Anonymity: An Enquiry* (1925) and *Aspects of the Novel* (1927) 'People will not realize how little conscious one is of these things; how one flounders about. They want us to be so much better informed than we are' (1958, 32). Elizabeth Hardwick (1916–2007) was a critic, essayist, fiction writer, and co-founder of the *New York Review of Books* who thrived in marriage to the poet Robert Lowell. Despite her intimate knowledge of writing, she had to say that 'I'm not sure I understand the process of writing. There is, I'm sure, something strange about imaginative concentration. The brain slowly begins to function in a different way, to make mysterious connections' (Plimpton 1989, 113). Robert Kotlowitz (b. 1924), a man-of-letters who published novels and was a contributing editor of *Atlantic Monthly* (1971–6), observed other writers as well as himself and came away puzzled: 'I can't describe the creative process – it's so mysterious. Nobody knows what it is but finally it takes hold of you and you let it happen. Sometimes the well runs dry and then you have to wait for it to fill up again' (Publishers Weekly 1997, 95).

Gore Vidal (b. 1925) had a great capacity for successful work: he published twenty-four novels, perhaps peaking with *Myra Breckinridge* (1968) and *Lincoln* (1984). His friend Judith Calvino described him 'as a man without an unconscious' (Deresiewicz 1999), and yet he attributed all his work to it: 'I never know what is coming next. The phrase that sounds in the head changes when it appears on the page. Then I start probing it with a pen, finding new meanings. Sometimes I burst out laughing at what is happening as I twist and turn sentences. Strange business, all in all. One never gets to the end of it. That's why I go on, I suppose. To see what the next sentences I write will be' (Plimpton 1989, 63). John Fowles (1926–2005), who wrote *The Collector* (1963), *The Magus* (1965), and *The French Lieutenant's Woman* (1969), was one with Forster: 'you don't understand the creative processes in your own mind. It's a total mystery to you' (1999, 128). Joyce Carol Oates (b. 1938) has 150 books to her credit, continues her prolific work at Princeton University today, and sees her literary works 'as if materializing out of the void … basically a mystery' (2006, 144, 148). Patricia Hampl (b. 1946), a highly accomplished Midwestern memoirist, chronicles lives but admits that 'It still comes as a shock to realize that I don't write about what I know: I write in order to find out what I know. Is it possible to convey to a reader the enormous degree of blankness, confusion, hunch and uncertainty lurking in the art of writing?' (1996, 205). Stephen King (1947–) loves and writes horror stories, and Paul Auster admires French literary theory and poetry, but both agree on composing: 'There is no Idea Dump, no Story Central, no Island of the Buried Bestsellers; good story ideas seem to come quite literally from nowhere, sailing at you right out of the empty sky: two previously unrelated ideas come together and make something new under the sun' (King 2000, 37). (They both also love baseball, Auster the New York teams, and King the Boston Red Sox.)

Almost all poets since Shelley adhere to his faith in the unconscious. John Ashbery (b. 1927) refers to making poems as 'some kind of instinctive thing' (Bigsby 2000–1, 2:2). In the early 1990s C.B. McCully sent out a questionnaire to British poets that asked them to give a talk on their creative process. According to McCully, almost all poets who contributed their lectures to *The Poet's Voice and Craft* (1994) agreed with Grevel Lindop, one of the group, that poems started with a 'few words which seem to be "given" and whose production is involuntary and unconscious' (42, 52). C.H. Sisson went further, saying that 'poems formed themselves, somewhere beyond the poet's control or awareness' (28). The translator of *Beowulf,* Edwin Morgan, attributed poems to 'the power of the subconscious mind to erupt ... into full consciousness' (61). While at pains to stress the 'hard work' in writing, Fleur Adcock admitted that most opening phrases are 'given' and that she has authored some 'haunted, middle-of-the-night pieces, arising directly from the subconscious' (148–9).

Writers also attribute creative uttering, the imagination that makes sentences, to someone else, a force, a life, an inner voice, a toneless pronouncer, an 'ancient presence,' or a Muse from whom words, sentences, and thoughts come mentally unsummoned. As early the eleventh century, Eadmer of Canterbury viewed writing as self-dictation (Clanchy 1979, 218). When the voice speaks, the author behaves as a secretary and takes dictation. These writers, interestingly, never say that they see words displayed on a moving billboard. The source expresses itself in an auditory way. The American imagist poet Amy Lowell (1874–1925) writes: 'I do not hear a voice, but I do hear words pronounced, only the pronouncing is toneless. The words seem to be pronounced in my head, but with nobody speaking them' (Ghiselin 1952, 110). Henry Miller (1891–1980), author of *Tropic of Cancer* (1934), agrees with her: 'it happens only at rare intervals, this dictation. Someone takes over and you just copy out what is being said' (1963, 171). François Mauriac (1885–1970), the French novelist and playwright who won the Nobel Prize for Literature in 1952, admits, 'I write with complete *naïveté*, spontaneously ... When I cease to be carried along, when I no longer feel as though I were taking dictation, I stop' (1958, 38, 40). Jean Cocteau (1889–1963), the French novelist and filmmaker, confesses: 'I feel myself inhabited by a force or being -- very little known to me. *It gives* the orders; I follow' (1989, 106). His *Les enfants terribles* (1929) is about two co-authors snared by their own game. Russell Hoban (b. 1925) is best known as the author of the dystopic science fiction novel *Riddley Walker* (1980), which he spent half a dozen years writing. For this he invented a unique dialect of English. Despite his extensive rewriting of drafts, Hoban describes the creative process as receiving a transmission: 'I never know precisely what I'm looking for when I start. I even make a point of trying *not* to know. (I never work from an outline, for instance.) I trust luck in the sense that I trust whatever gets me started. After that it's a matter of trying to place myself in a position of active receptivity … it's being as alert as I can be and doing what I can to bring in whatever it is that's trying to get said through me. That's what I mean by being an "active receptor". It's like tuning a radio' (1987, 141–4).

W.S. Merwin (b. 1925), the American poet, speaks about 'some really very ancient presence' (Merwin 1984, 176), and his compatriot Russell Edson (b. 1935) tells us that 'the mysterious *other* life begins to send its message' (Edson 1977, 91). John Fowles calls the self who did his drafts the 'wild man' and 'the Green Man in the wood,' as distinguished from the editor, who was 'a professor of literature' (Bigsby 2000–1, 2:70). Jonathan Raban (b. 1942), who lives in Seattle and maintains his own Web site today, is a man of letters, a writer of what he has called non-fiction novels on travel and politics. Although he believes that 'the word *fiction* doesn't come from some imaginary Latin verb meaning *I make things up as I go along*' (Weich 2000), he also takes dictation: 'All writers are in some sense secretaries to their own books, which emerge by a process of dictation. You start the thing off and on the first few pages you're in control, but if the book has any real life of its own, *it* begins to take control, *it* begins to demand certain things of you, which you may or may not live up to, and it imposes shapes and patterns on you; it calls forth the quality of experience it needs. Or that's what you hope happens. I don't just sit, making conscious decisions externally about how much of my experience I am going to use' (Wachtel 1993, 120). Gregory Orr (b. 1947), an American poet who teaches creative writing at the University of Virginia, says that 'The constant struggle is to believe that you can become more and more conscious and aware of the processes of your own mind and your own imagination, and yet at the same time when it comes time to write the poem all prayers go toward a total silence of your mind and a reception in which you hope you hear a voice inside you saying anything, saying some word whose meaning you don't know, that will begin to form a poem' (Orr 1989, 102). Julia Donaldson (b. 1948), a Scottish children's writer and author of *The Gruffalo* (1999), admits simply that 'the muse takes you' (Donaldson 2006, 57) and Steven Heighton (b. 1961), a Canadian poet and novelist, remarks cautiously that 'it seems you're not consciously working but instead playing secretary, taking shorthand from a more alert and vital version of yourself' (2002, 172). Far from being masters of the proceedings, these authors admit to being possessed, functioning as a host, or feeling disembodied. They register a loss of cognitive self-control.

Many writers characterize themselves in this unconscious state of making as dreaming, being entranced, or acting involuntarily, as if in the power of the other, that voice within.[1] Robert Louis Stevenson's Brownies is the first of many someones who lay down stories in the author's dreams. Typically, dreaming or being in a trance (unless it is 'lucid,' and no writer known to me says it is) takes place when an author feels unable to change the experience. Stephen King (b. 1947) refers to his muse and inspiration as 'a basement guy' who takes over when he himself falls into a 'creative sleep'; as a result, his stories 'pretty much make themselves' (King 2000, 144–5, 156–7, 163). The poet Richard Eberhart (1904–2005) likes 'the old word "inspiration" ... there is something magical or trancelike' (1977, 86–7). Nobel Prize–winning Irish poet Seamus Heaney says: 'I only write when I'm in the trance. It is a mystery of sorts. If you are possessed by a subject, if you have a subject in you ... the thing moves .... The poem *came, it came*. I didn't go and fetch it. To some extent you wait for it, you coax it in the door when it gets there. I prefer to think of myself as the host to the thing rather than a big-game hunter' (1981, 64, 72). John Hersey (1914–93), whose *Hiroshima* dramatically altered American attitudes to atomic weapons, said that creating was 'something like dreaming ... I don't know how to draw the line between the conscious management of what you're doing and this state' (Plimpton 1988, 126). The poet A.E. Housman took a biological perspective on the notion of dreaming poetry into existence: 'In short I think that the production of poetry, in its first stage, is less an active than a passive and involuntary process; and if I were obliged, not to define poetry, but to name the class of things to which it belongs, I should call it a secretion' (Housman in Ghiselin 1952, 91). Other writers, such as Michael Morpurgo (b. 1943) and Cynthia Ozick (b. 1928), have also attested to the dream-like experience of composing words:

[I] dream things out and trust to my instinct ... dream time (Morpurgo 2006, 130, 134)

I find when I write I am disembodied. I have no being. Sometimes I'm entranced in the sense of being in a trance, a condition that speaks, I think, for other writers as well. Sometimes I discover that I'm actually clawing the air looking for a handhold. The clawing can be for an idea, for a word. It can be reaching for the use of language, it can be reaching for the solution to something that's happening on the page, wresting out of nothingness what will happen next. But it's all disembodied ... I fear falling short. I probably also fear entering that other world; the struggle on the threshold of that disembodied state is pure terror. (Ozick in Wachtel 1993, 16, 18)

A few other authors sense the otherness of the source but identify an unusual feature of the gifts it offers for dictation: they come in small units, a line, a bit, or a passage.

I don't start writing until I have got a line or two in my head. Sitting with a bare piece of paper in front of me is a terrifying thought, but I don't do that; I wait until I have a bit in my mind and then a bit more will attach itself. (U.A. Fanthorpe [1929–2009] 2006, 78)

... you have that bit at the start when you get something for nothing: the inspiration that comes with the force of a miracle (Don Paterson [b. 1963] 2006, 157)

There are two theories of inspiration. One idea is that poetry can actually be dictated to you, like it was to William Blake. You are in a hallucinated state, and you hear a voice or you are in communication with something outside, like James Merrill's new poem, which he says is dictated through the Ouija board by Auden and other people. The other idea is Paul Valéry's, which he calls *une ligne donnée*, that you are given one line and you try to follow up this clue, pulling the whole poem out of it. (Stephen Spender [1909–95] in Plimpton 1989, 89)

I forget which of the great sonneteers said: 'One line in the fourteen comes from the ceiling; the others have to be adjusted around it.' Well, likewise there are passages in every novel whose first writing is pretty much the last. But it's the joint and cement, between those spontaneous passages, that take a great deal of rewriting. (Thornton Wilder [1897–1975] 1958, 96)

These very different authors tried to observe their creative process and found instead a veil of unknowability. That uttering was a mystery they attributed to an unconscious source whose inner voice dictates language segments, words and phrases, to them in a dream-like state. Despite their wealth of experience, they gained agreement on only one more characteristic: an accompanying *sense of flow*. James Dickey advises a poet to 'surrender himself and flow with the poem wherever it may go instead of trying to order it in the early stages' (1970, 91). Doris Lessing says, 'Actually, I think I write much better if I am flowing' (1988, 94). Mihaly Csikszentmihalyi (1996) characterizes flow as a peculiar state of consciousness, associated with losing a sense of elapsed time, in which someone is deeply absorbed in a successful activity. Susan Karen Perry (1996) undertook a study of how thirty-three poets and twenty-nine fiction writers entered this desirable 'altered state of consciousness' (2) that they usually thought of as losing conscious control over writing.

We could learn much by observing an author composing a work in a trance-like, dreaming flow-state, but (as far as I know) few audio records exist of such sessions, ones occurring without any benefit of writing or digital editing and storage tools. During editing on the page or screen, authors consciously delete and rearrange words within passages, adjust syntactic structure, re-sequence parts, and make word substitutions. These manipulations disguise telltale features of what Colin Martindale calls 'primary-process cognition,' that 'free-associative ... autistic ... thought of dreams and reveries' so unlike the mind's deliberative capability, which he refers to as 'secondary-process cognition' (1990, 56). Authors employ an artificial memory – the script – to make grammatical and lexical changes to what has been uttered on paper, and reworking text to meet standards of clarity and economy in problem solving. There is little 'to remember' in such editing; the effort is made unnecessary by the writing on the page. Although authors edit and correct many details, when these changes affect the content of a passage, they tend to rewrite, not by tinkering with the text as already uttered, but by crossing out and starting over again freshly (Milic 1971, 81). The creative process then reverts to a spontaneous one – a primary composing that possesses the same immunity to direct observation as does basic uttering.

To understand the authoring of a work, we must separate what was uttered, a largely unconscious process, from what was edited, a deliberative exercise managed often over months and years. Holographic manuscripts, a trail of drafts, can give us a timeline of a writer's deliberate editorial changes to a text as mediated by writing technologies. If an author also uses keystroke capture software such as *Morae* during this editing, the entire editorial process can be played back in real time. Playbacks, naturally, leave us to infer everything that went on in the author's mind, but we can at least identify regularly occurring types of edits.

These include deletions of repeated phrases or specific syntactic transformations (e.g., conversion of passive-voice constructions to active-voice ones). However, it is rarer to find a work in a spontaneous pre-edited state, left unaltered after its unconscious uttering, because we need not only the abandoned text but also the author's acknowledgment that it was never edited. In the vast literature of author interviews, however, several such texts and acknowledgments survive from poets Richard Eberhart and William Stafford. These poems help substantiate authorial claims of what happens in a state of flow.

*   *   *   *   *

When did I start to speak and read to you inside and am I different from the me that others have and never talk about, am I alone or nearly so, an inner confidant whose every transaction with the world gets paid with silent words before we speak?

Anne at McGill could store textbooks in her mind, one look and she would turn the pages for her inner eye, and still she can recite poem after poem when you hint with a line or phrase, like Coleridge and Kerouac, and yet I see nothing of the poems in my memory and can't recite the passages I've lived with for so long but have to go to pages to find them once again.

II   Richard Eberhart's 'The Groundhog'

The American poet Richard Eberhart (1979, 37) explains, with some pride, that he wrote 'The Groundhog' in about twenty minutes in 1933 at St Mark's School in Southborough, Massachusetts. He prints the poem without stanzaic breaks, but it falls into six eight-line stanzas, usually octosyllabic. Except for lines 7–8, the poem is unrhymed. He would have taken about thirty seconds, on average, to produce each line. He describes himself as having been 'in a high state of awareness, in a total charge and commitment of the whole being,' when he wrote it:

> The writing of 'The Groundhog' is an example of a theory I have that poetry is a gift of the gods. It cannot be had only by taking thought. The process is ultimately mysterious, involving a total thrust of the whole being, some kind of magical power. When a poem is ready to be born it will be born whole, without the need to change a word, or perhaps with the need to change only a word or two. I thus go back to an ancient theory of inspi-

ration. It must suggest strong, active memory and an instantaneous synthesizing power when the whole being, not the mind alone, or the senses
or the will alone, can come to bear on life with significance. Probably more
than half of my best-known poems have come to me in this way, when the
being was a seemingly passive vehicle for the overwhelming dominance
of the poem, which was then put down with ease, immediacy, fluency, and
comprehensive order. (1979, 38)

Eberhart admits to some of the traits ascribed by other creative writers to the creative process of primary uttering. It was 'mysterious' and
'magical,' and the poem came with fluency, 'an even flow of commu-
nicable ideas' (1979, 79). Eberhart says that he owes 'The Groundhog'
to 'the gods' – a kind of voice – and while he does not describe himself
here as entranced or dreaming, he uses the phrase 'magical or trance-
like' to describe how he produced another poem, 'The Snowfall,' which
he created under like conditions (1977, 86–7). With 'The Groundhog'
he entered an altered state of consciousness that he compared to the
Greeks' 'divine frenzy' (1979, 80). Because this 'gift' described an experience that he had two years before at the country estate of a friend's
father, whatever the 'gods' gave, it was not the subject.

Here is the text of 'The Groundhog':

1   In June, amid the golden fields,
2   I saw a groundhog lying dead.
3   Dead lay he; my senses shook,
4   And mind outshot our naked frailty.
5   There lowly in the vigorous summer
6   His form began its senseless change,
7   And made my senses waver dim
8   Seeing nature ferocious in him.
9   Inspecting close his maggots' might
10   And seething cauldron of his being,
11   Half with loathing, half with a strange love,
12   I poked him with an angry stick.
13   The fever arose, became a flame
14   And Vigour circumscribed the skies,
15   Immense energy in the sun,
16   And through my frame a sunless trembling.
17   My stick had done nor good nor harm.
18   Then stood I silent in the day

19   Watching the object, as before;
20   And kept my reverence for knowledge
21   Trying for control, to be still,
22   To quell the passion of the blood;
23   Until I had bent down on my knees
24   Praying for joy in the sight of decay.
25   And so I left: and I returned
26   In Autumn strict of eye, to see
27   The sap gone out of the groundhog,
28   But the bony sodden hulk remained.
29   But the year had lost its meaning,
30   And in intellectual chains
31   I lost both love and loathing,
32   Mured up in the wall of wisdom.
33   Another summer took the fields again
34   Massive and burning, full of life,
35   But when I chanced upon the spot
36   There was only a little hair left,
37   And bones bleaching in the sunlight
38   Beautiful as architecture;
39   I watched them like a geometer,
40   And cut a walking stick from a birch.
41   It has been three years, now.
42   There is no sign of the groundhog.
43   I stood there in the whirling summer,
44   My hand capped a withered heart,
45   And thought of China and of Greece,
46   Of Alexander in his tent;
47   Of Montaigne in his tower,
48   Of Saint Theresa in her wild lament.

Eberhart describes two gradual changes, the disintegration of a ground-hog's body; and, in parallel, the change of his perspective on it, from 'loathing and love' (11) and 'passion' (22) to a subject for the 'mind' (4), the 'intellectual' (3), 'wisdom' (32), and 'a withered heart' (44). In twenty minutes, he recounts one and the same event four times. In June (1–24), autumn (25–32), summer (33–40), and 'three years' after (41–8), he sees (2, 8, 26), inspects (9), and watches (19, 39) the dead groundhog, first its 'seething' maggot-ridden body, then its 'bony sodden hulk' (28), then its hair and bones (36–7), and finally nothing at all. He remembers himself as standing (18, 43) or 'bent down' (23) over the body. Twice he wields a stick: first to poke at the corpse, and three years later to fashion a walking stick cut from a birch. Verbal echoes reinforce the overall structural repetition, as for example, 'lying dead. / Dead lay' (2–3), 'my senses' and 'senseless' (3, 6–7), and 'Half with loathing, half with a strange love' (11) and 'both love and loathing' (31). His perspective on the groundhog has become, at the poem's close, an intellectual understanding of the fall of great nations and minds, notably Saint Theresa in her 'wild lament.'

Eberhart attests to the mysterious givenness of this poem, and its text independently confirms that, consistent with how other writers describe the creative process, it flowed in little segments. The text's 48 lines (and about 300 words) have some 42 short syntactic units. These are either subject-verb-object (svo) clauses, or verbal constructions where the subject is understood: present and past participial segments, and infinitive phrases. Their average length is seven words. If the poem's 39 prepositional phrases (well over 100 words) are discounted – they do not hold a subject, a verb, or an object, although they may modify them – the typical verbal construction falls to between four and five words in length. For example, the last stanza begins with a string of five one-line svo-clauses (the subject is understood in the fifth) and ends with six prepositional phrases. Eberhart marks the boundaries of his little segments by 45 punctuation marks in 48 lines.

The poem does not suffer from a piecemeal choppiness but flows smoothly, thanks to Eberhart's syntax. Although published as a single verse paragraph, the poem divides into six end-stopped stanzas, averaging about fifty words each in eight octosyllabic lines. These six octaves are *thought passages* that Eberhart ties together with repetition. The word 'vigorous' in the first octave (5) becomes 'Vigour' (14) in the second, it and the third octave share the word 'stick' (12, 17), the terms 'sight' (24) and 'see' (26) link the third and the fourth, it and the fifth focus on 'bony' (28) and 'bones' (37), and the last two octaves cohere in the word 'summer' (33, 43). Eberhart also uses twenty coordinating conjunctions ('and' and 'but') that variously tie together successive phrases and clauses. He prefers adjectives to embedded constructions (e.g., subordinate 'that' or 'which' relative clauses), which create grammatical eddies in the flow of ideas and images. The poem has only two subordinate clauses, 'until' (23) and 'when' (35): neither separates the subject and the verb of a clause. He employs parataxis three times: clauses or short sentences are set side by side without connectives (2–3, 28–9, 41–8). The syntax runs, simple and unobstructed, from start to finish.

What can we infer from 'The Groundhog' about the mind's creative process? Eberhart's spontaneous, fluent method resembles that described by many of his fellow writers. His particular 'gods' – centuries ago, readers might have referred him to the goddess Thalia, the Muse of bucolic poetry – compose in short units, four or five words in length. The poet attributes these bursts to a 'strong, active memory.' An 'instantaneous synthesizing power' knits them together into a larger thought-passage about fifty words in size. Repeated words, images, and ideas tie together successive passages. Eberhart's mind thus works within two differently sized constraints: one is lexically phrasal, and the other is syntactically stanzaic or musical. The poet fills passages effortlessly and quickly with noun- and verb-phrase segments in a very short period of time, but he needs both a musical form in which to integrate the small segments, and a mechanism in which to store his rapid output, here in writing. A few simple intentions dominate the poem. First, mixed love and loathing generate images of the groundhog, falling away into nothing over a few years. Second, an intellectual's close observation lends Eberhart a geometer's eye that seeks to trace the commonalty of small and historic. Yet these feelings and the poet's mind become 'passive' and accepting as the 'poem' takes over and appears to make itself. Eberhart looks on in some wonder.

*   *   *   *   *

We are three.
    Am I just a middleman caught between the untongued boss of this place and you his rock, scissors, and paper?

III William Stafford's 'Ask Me'

The manuscript behind Eberhart's 'The Groundhog' has gone missing, along with the few editorial changes he made to the spontaneous conception, but William Stafford kept the four drafts of his 'Ask Me,' finished over three days, he says, 'from amid random writing I was doing in my usual morning attempts to scare up something by putting anything down that came to mind' (1977, 292). Stafford attributes the genesis of the poem to 'free association, that is, free allowing of my impulses to find their immediate interest' (1977, 294). All four drafts have editorial revisions. Stafford thought about what he wrote down and consciously reshaped his original.

By stripping away his handwritten corrections to the first draft, a notebook entry for 14 December 1974, we can recover what spontaneously came from Stafford's mind. Here is a transcript of this *zero* draft (see fig. 4).

1 Some time when the river is ice, ask me
2 the mistakes, ask me whether what I have
3 done is my life. Others have come
4 in their slow way into the thoughts, And
5 some have tried to help or to hurt.
6 Ask me what differences their strongest efforts
7 have made. You and I can then turn
8 and look at the silent river and wait.
9 We will know the current is there,
10 hidden, and there are comings and goings
11 miles away that hold the stillness
12 exactly before us. If the river says anything,
13 whatever it says is my answer.

The poem consists of two thought-passages in thirteen lines, a repeated question, and a period of waiting for a repeated answer. The first half of the poem has three imperative 'Ask me' sentences (1–2, 2–3, 6–7), interrupted by one declarative sentence (3–5). Lines 7–12 hold two declarative sentences that explain the wait for the river's voice to speak, and the last two lines characterize, in general, what that answer will be: 'the river says' and 'whatever it says.' We do not need to interpret the poem to enjoy it, but Stafford says that the river is his language process (12–13), motionless and dead to the eye's conscious observation, but inwardly a 'silent,' 'hidden,' and flowing 'current.' Stafford agrees with other authors about the mystery of his frozen inner voice (the source of the mind's speech is 'miles away'). Composing is waiting for something to flow out.

The same lexical and syntactic constraints we see at work in Eberhart's poem exist in the zero draft. Stafford utters a sequence of small segments whose lexicon is basic English, lacking even one moderately literary or hard word. His verbs are 'ask,' 'come,' 'do,' 'help,' 'hold,' 'hurt,' 'is,' 'know,' 'look,' 'make,' 'say,' 'try,' 'turn,' and 'wait.' The poem's ninety-seven words in thirteen lines fall into nineteen clauses, five words per clause. The first of the poem's six sentences, for example, uses only twenty-one words for five clauses: two imperatives, and

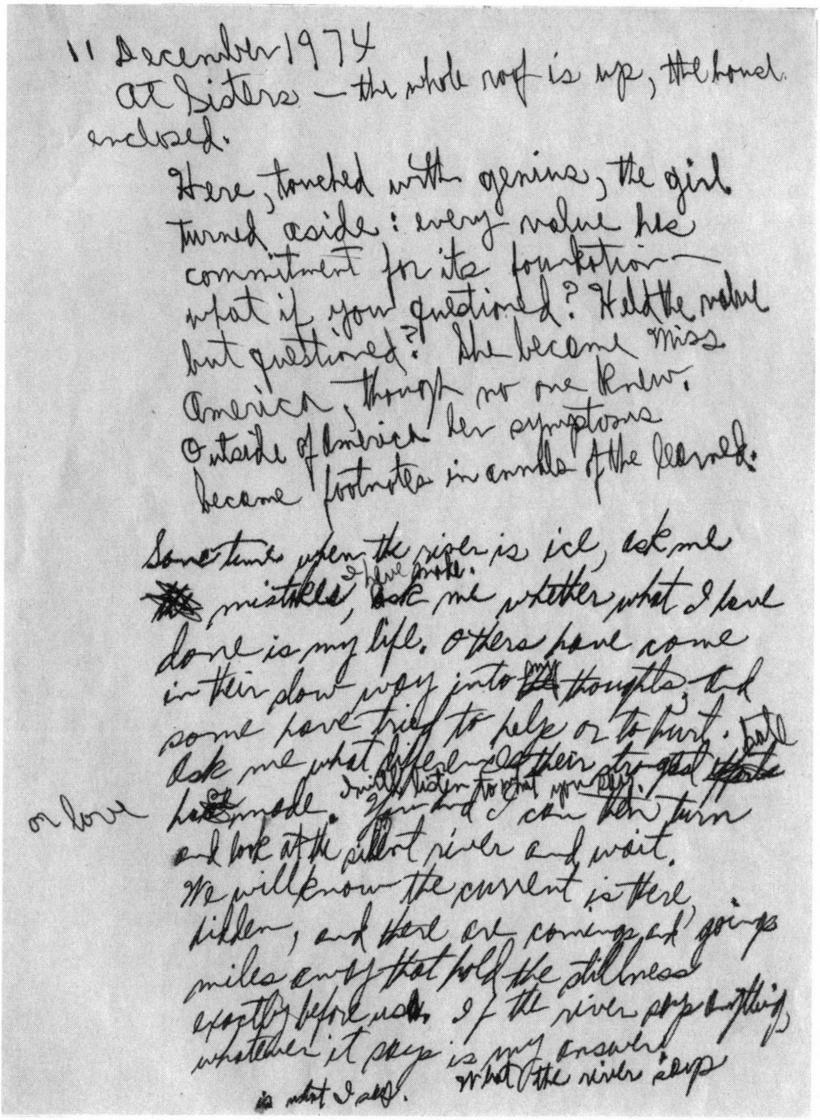

Figure 4. Handwritten MS of William Stafford's poem 'Ask Me,' on yellow paper, the first page of his daily writings for 11 December 1974 (courtesy of the William Stafford Archives, Lewis & Clark College; and Kim Stafford, literary executor, son and Director, Northwest Writing Institute, Lewis and Clark College)

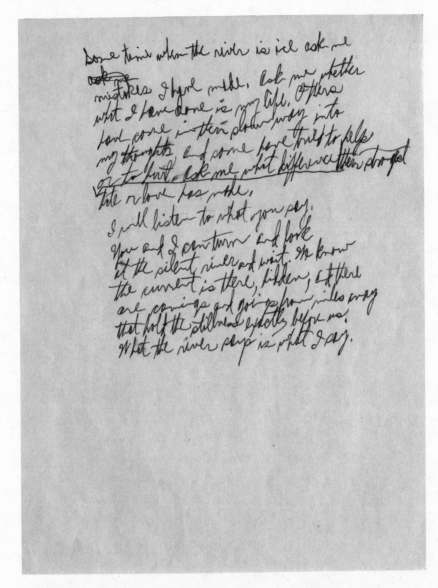

Figure 5. Handwritten MS of William Stafford's poem 'Ask Me,' on yellow paper, the second (undated) page of William Stafford's writings for 11 December 1974 (courtesy of the William Stafford Archives, Lewis & Clark College; and Kim Stafford, literary executor, son and Director, Northwest Writing Institute, Lewis and Clark College)

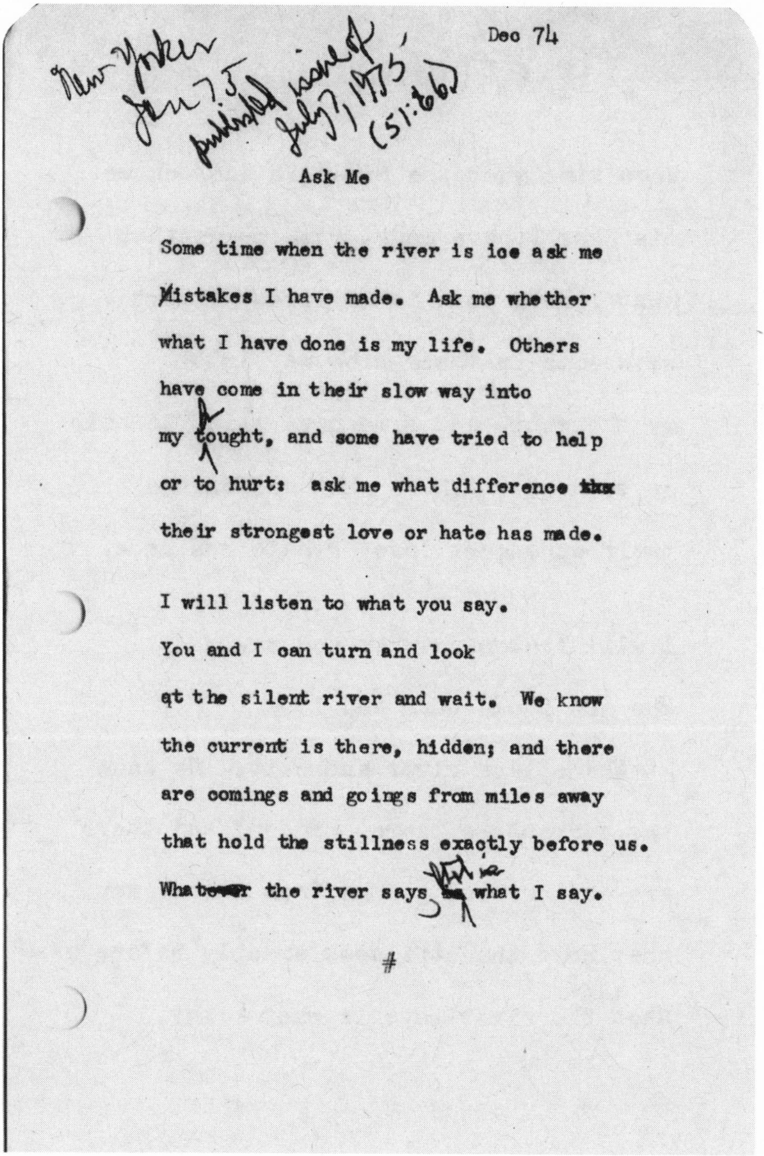

Deo 74

New Yorker
Jan 7.75
published issue of
July 7, 1975
(51:66)

Ask Me

Some time when the river is ice ask me
Mistakes I have made. Ask me whether
what I have done is my life. Others
have come in their slow way into
my tought, and some have tried to help
or to hurt: ask me what difference their
their strongest love or hate has made.

I will listen to what you say.
You and I can turn and look
at the silent river and wait. We know
the current is there, hidden; and there
are comings and goings from miles away
that hold the stillness exactly before us.
Whatever the river says what I say.

#

Figure 6. First Typed Version of William Stafford's poem 'Ask Me,' made within a few days of composition (courtesy of the William Stafford Archives, Lewis & Clark College; and Kim Stafford, literary executor, son and Director, Northwest Writing Institute, Lewis and Clark College)

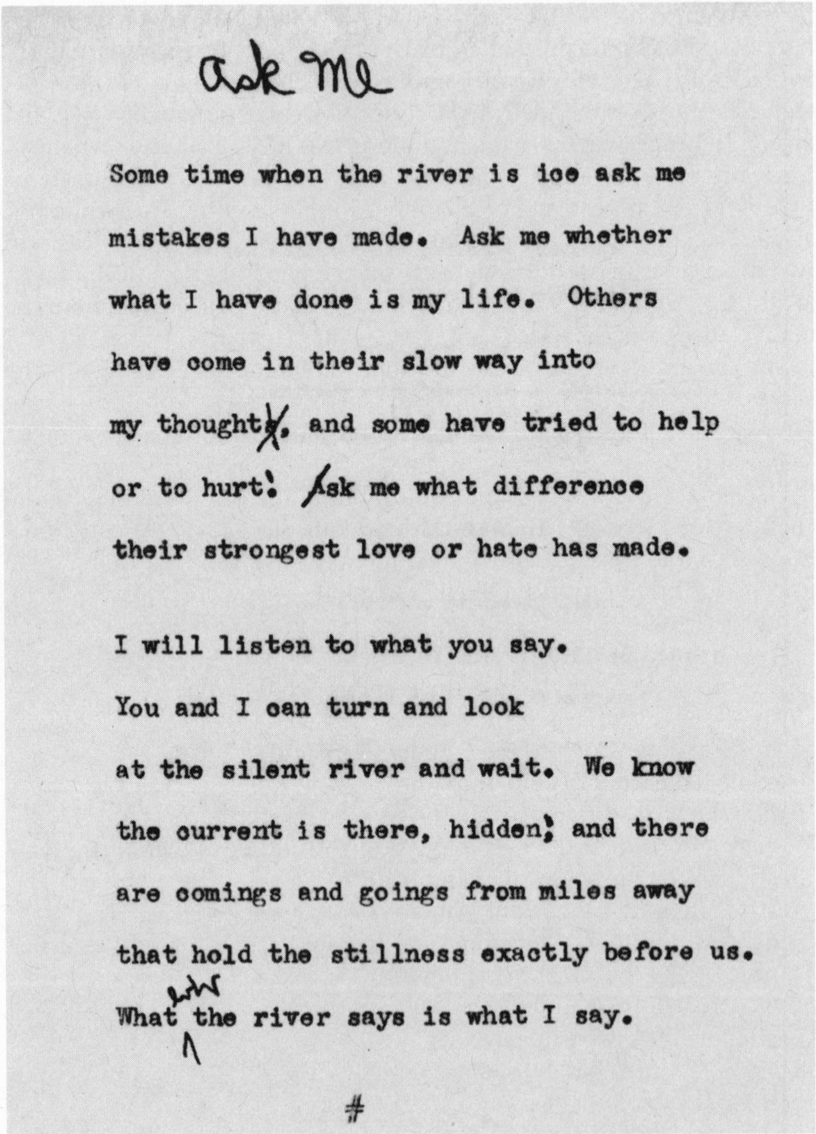

Ask Me

Some time when the river is ice ask me

mistakes I have made. Ask me whether

what I have done is my life. Others

have come in their slow way into

my thoughts, and some have tried to help

or to hurt: Ask me what difference

their strongest love or hate has made.

I will listen to what you say.

You and I can turn and look

at the silent river and wait. We know

the current is there, hidden; and there

are comings and goings from miles away

that hold the stillness exactly before us.

What the river says is what I say.

#

Figure 7. Second Typed Version and Documentary copy of William Stafford's poem 'Ask Me,' for publication in *Stories That Could Be True* (courtesy of the William Stafford Archives, Lewis & Clark College; and Kim Stafford, literary executor, son and Director, Northwest Writing Institute, Lewis and Clark College)

three subordinate 'when,' 'whether,' and 'what' clauses. Unlike Eberhart, Stafford avoids present and past participial constructions entirely. Syntactically, his style is more complex than Eberhart's: two of the nineteen clauses are embedded, separating subject from verb, or verb from object: 'whether what I have / done is my life' (2–3) and 'whatever it says is my answer' (13). Stafford also uses fewer *and* conjunctions (five) and much more subordination: in the remaining five sentences, an *if-then* clause, four relative clauses with *that* or understood-*that*, and two more *what* or *whatever* clauses. Yet the general effect of the poem is additive. Six of the subordinate clauses follow in sequence from the main clauses, unembedded.

The constraint on the size of the poem's two thought-passages is the same as Eberhart's: 49 and 48 words. The first passage concerns asking the river, and the second looking at and listening to it: an action and its aftermath.

Here is a merged text of the *zero* draft and the first draft of editorial changes to it (see fig. 4). Stafford made all these changes consciously, although in generating new text he may have resorted to the same unconscious that produced the first version.

1 Some time when the river is ice, ask me
2 ~~the~~ mistakes, ᴵ ʰᵃᵛᵉ ᵐᵃᵈᵉ· ~~A~~ask me whether what I have
3 done is my life. Others have come
4 in their slow way into ~~the~~ᵐʸ thoughts~~,~~ ~~A~~and
5 some have tried to help or to hurt.
6 Ask me what differences their strongest ~~efforts~~ ʰᵃᵗᵉ
7 ~~have~~ ᵒʳ ˡᵒᵛᵉ ʰᵃˢ made. ᴵ ʷⁱˡˡ ˡⁱˢᵗᵉⁿ ᵗᵒ ʷʰᵃᵗ ʸᵒᵘ ˢᵃʸ· You and I can then turn
8 and look at the silent river and wait.
9 We will know the current is there,
10 hidden, and there are comings and goings
11 miles away that hold the stillness
12 exactly before us. If the river says anything,
13 whatever it says is my answer.
14   What the river says
15 is what I say.

The first revised draft now has 116 words (an increase of 22 words). Stafford adds a subordinate understood-*that* relative clause 'I have made' (based on the start of line 2), introduces two stand-alone sentences, 'I will listen to what you say' and 'What the river says is what I say' (these have exactly the same object), and alters one word into the phrase 'hate or love.' The additional twenty-two words add four more simple subject-verb-object units, so that the average words-per-clause remains the same at five words. If anything, the lexicon has simplified: he cancels 'efforts' in favour of 'hate or love.' The two added sentences balance one another, emphasizing the poem's division into question and answer.

The second draft (see fig. 5) transforms the poem into an unrhyming sonnet. Stafford integrates the editorial changes that he had marked onto the zero draft, reworking the lineation, deleting the three-clause *if-then* sentence (formerly at lines 12–13), and splitting the sixth line into two lines. Despite the poem's lengthening, it now has more tightness and economy. Here is a merged text of the first and second drafts.

1 Some time when the river is ice, ask me
~~ask me~~
2 mistakes I have made. Ask me whether
3 what I have done is my life. Others
4 have come in their slow way into
5 my thoughts, and some have tried to help
6 or to hurt. Ask me what difference
7 their strongest hate or love has made.
8 I will listen to what you say.
9 You and I can turn and look
10 at the silent river and wait. We know
11 the current is there, hidden, and there
12 are comings and goings from miles away
13 that hold the stillness exactly before us.
14 What the river says is what I say.

The third version, typewritten with a handwritten title (see fig. 6), divides it into two septets by inserting a blank line before line 8, clarifying the poem's division into two thought-passages. A few punctuation changes occur (1, 6, 11).

1 Some time when the river is ice ask me
2 mistakes I have made. Ask me whether
3 what I have done is my life. Others
4 have come in their slow way into
5 my thoughts, and some have tried to help
6 or to hurt.:: ~~A~~ask me what difference

7 their strongest hate or love has made.

8 I will listen to what you say.
9 You and I can turn and look
10 at the silent river and wait. We know
11 the current is there, hidden~; and there
12 are comings and goings from miles away
13 that hold the stillness exactly before us.
14 What ~ever~ the river says is what I say.

Against expectation, Stafford's editorial revisions simplify and clarify the first spontaneous version. Now there are a few more words (104 to 97) and one more subject-verb-object construction (21 to 20), and the average words-per-clause closes at under five words each. Stafford consciously increases the lexical repetition. The first seven-line stanza grows from repeated *ask me* (1, 2, 6) and *have / has made* (2, 7); and the second stanza from repeated *what you say / what I say* (8, 14) and *is there / there are* (11–12). The second typewritten version, dated December 1974, makes one more change. The last line (see fig. 7) becomes 'What the river says, that is what I say.' Stafford accepts the free associations of his mind as the poem's essential core. For him, editing makes that spontaneous gift more like itself, a question-and-answer, an invitation to a you, and a reply by the I. Stafford asserts, simply, that his life is largely unselfconscious, like the unseen currents of a river, and explains itself, if at all, only by means of the silence at the surface.

Unlike Eberhart, Stafford takes three days consciously to revise his poem on paper. He modifies the initial spontaneous, given 'message' by calculated feedback. The poet receives and responds to it, either mentally hearing the poem as it utters, or reading its lines as the poet transcribes them. Stafford stores the flow of his mind on paper so that his successive rereadings can generate successive pulses of feedback. In this way, Stafford gradually becomes conscious of what his own mind has made. He adjusts his given words so that they become responsible to a public tongue, a language shared by English-speakers in general. He transforms the private language of his mind into a general language. He manages this by dovetailing clauses so that they flow easily. Sometimes the mind leaves out the reason for an association. Stafford's addition of 'I will listen to what you say,' for example, manages the shift from the you-centred first stanza to the I-centred second stanza. In feedback, then, he tempers the original so that it can be understood more easily by others by becoming his poem's first reader.

Stafford's creative process partners the unconscious and the conscious. Deliberate editorial thinking can be turned off during the first making by a self that cannot ever be directly observed. The reasoning mind, however, then becomes increasingly 'conscious and aware of the processes' of its hidden mind and seeks to clarify its 'imagination' by editorial feedback (Orr 1989, 102). The American poet Diane Levertov believes in this partnership. For her, all poems are 'a gift' that one cannot 'will ... to happen,' a 'religious experience' (1984, 164) that rises from an 'aura' and evolves 'instinctively' and 'unconsciously' (1987, 59, 62). Yet in a 1963 interview she also says that every poet should read the draft and apply intelligence and judgment to its improvement. 'You can't leave the intelligence out. But you can't *start* with the intelligence; if you start with the intelligence, you have nothing whatsoever. You have a dead baby' (1998, 2). Inspiration and editing, the unconscious and applied intelligence, work together. Otherwise the poem, in her view, is either a miscarriage or something, if marred by spelling mistakes, just 'beneath contempt' (1998, 1).

*   *   *   *   *

Remember inexplicably withdrawing from the Winnipeg Juvenile Boys Choir, where we were soloist, and Betty had a doctor administer an EEG to us, just a ten-year-old, and they didn't find anything except me, but within months she fell to schizophrenia, alienated from you all with visions and voices, unable to explain herself to herself or you, our tortured saint, tearing up photographs, flushing them and jewels down the toilet, not feeding herself and Ernie or us, this now far-from-independent, busy, bright and smiling woman we once knew, now so moody, silent, and suspicious, rightly so because those two Winnipeg policemen came to our four-room apartment on Osborne Street to take her away in a marked car, committing her for six months in Brandon for electric insulin shock treatments and she turned fearful, ashamed, bewildered, even on weekends when Ernie drove us across the flat Manitoba prairie to visit, trips we had for eight years, during her out-and-then-in spells, our teenage years relapses returning us to Brandon again and again until the drugs becalmed her, her self lost in the social death that followed then, and you began to wonder about me then, knowing how the sins of mothers descend to their sons and for years you've listened to me, sounding like a male of steadily advancing years.

2 Uttering

Currently no one knows the details of how words or sentences are processed in the brain, and there is no known methodology for finding out.

(Feldman 2006, xii)

Alice Flaherty, MD, PhD, is a neurologist at Massachusetts General Hospital (directing its Brain Stimulator Unit) and an assistant professor at Harvard Medical School who has had muse experiences. About a decade ago, ten days after she lost twin boys in premature delivery, she went through an irrepressible, four-month-long bout of writing. A year later she gave birth to twin girls, and the same experience followed. Her hypergraphia – an overwhelming desire to write – generated enough material to fill a book. *The Midnight Disease: The Drive to Write, Writer's Block, and the Creative Brain* was published in 2004. Flaherty rose early, at 5:00 am, daily, sometimes only to discover that her 'muse' had left her, 'penance for all the days when the muse spoke and I failed to listen' (87). Hers was not automatic writing. Possessed by 'divine energy,' she set down notes, some coming from 'bursts of inspiration,' which she then organized into a shape (Birnbaum 2004). A personal need to explain what happened to her broke through into her neurological research when she published an article in the *Journal of Comparative Neurology* in 2005. In a discipline in which most papers are co-authored, Flaherty wrote this paper alone. Her new model traces 'idea generation and creative drive' to the frontal, temporal, and limbic systems and outlines ways to test that theory. Flaherty challenges Julian Jaynes's notion of the bicameral mind (1976). It located auditory hallucinations – the sense of a mental presence, a god within or inner voice, and the muse – in the right hemisphere of right-handed persons who lack the ability to introspect or be self-conscious. Jaynes's is a largely non-academic theory (Persinger and Makarec 1992).

Unconscious inspiration by a muse, however we define it, has scoffers. Edgar Allan Poe mocked writers who surrendered mental control of their writings to the moment. He composed 'The Raven,' he said, analytically, step by step (Poe 1846). The Canadian novelist Robertson Davies has indignantly denied that, in writing his characters, he was 'seized by a group of ghosts and carried into a realm utterly unknown' to him (Bigsby 2000–1, 2:52). Literary critic Barbara Tomlinson says that unconscious inspiration is only 'the trope of the author' (2005, 11), a metaphor, and does not characterize the '"reality" of thinking activities' (23). Keith Oakley and Maja Djikic speak of inspiration as a 'mind-dump' and argue that most writing is, at bottom, conscious thinking (2008, 16). Some writers even claim to be mnemonists. Evelyn Waugh said that he 'used to be able to hold the whole of a book' in his head (Plimpton 1967, 109).

I Modelling the Inaccessible Skill

Cognitive psychology, neuroscience, and cognitive linguistics replace the writer's notion of the muse with models of language production, from gist to articulation. Research literature offers books for the generalist (Feldman 2006, Kosslyn and Koenig 1992, Lieberman 2000, Pulvermüller 2002, and Robinson-Riegler 2004) and peer-reviewed articles for the professional. These articles treat specifics like affective disorders (Andreasen 1987), chunking (Goldberg 2003), memory (Baddeley 1992), lexical production (Levelt, Roelof, and Meyer 1999), neurological networks (Fox et al. 2005), and aging (Kemper et al. 2001). Researchers worldwide document experimentally demonstrated cognitive effects in journals such as Brain, Brain and Language, Cognitive Psychology, the Journal of Neuroscience, the Journal of Verbal Learning and Verbal Behavior, Memory and Cognition, and Trends in the Cognitive Sciences. The cognitive sciences are, by reflex, sceptical, moving slowly, but they enlarge our understanding of language continuously. Readers in literary studies like myself look for a stable model to explain language processing, but no such model yet exists. Generalists are not prey to the professional anxieties of researchers who know what is known about a cognitive effect and who recognize the many openings for skewed interpretation and for error. The truth is that the cognitive sciences cannot yet explain how the brain enables the mind, and how the mind creates language. Yet their subject is alive in us. It can be interrogated and observed, unlike history, which so often studies what has disappeared.

The second half of twentieth-century language theory begins with Noam Chomsky's generative linguistics, founded by his *Syntactic Structures*, published in 1957. It conceptualizes the production of English as a grammar-based, rule-governed abstract cognitive activity. Chomsky thinks that the mind typically forms each sentence anew by selecting a grammatical structure and then filling out its treelike hierarchy from the top down, from abstract subject-predicate variables and noun and verb phrases (the branches) down to the lowermost daughter leaves, the words. We grasp the whole utterance, abstractly, before we make detailed language choices. The art and science of discovering these rules, often by means of thought experiments with invented sentences, have invigorated linguistics since then. Why do we say 'Now and then I have a midday nap' but never 'Now *or* then Tiger Woods loses his temper'? By such made-up sentences Chomsky models what speakers of a language know, rather than how they behave. He has less interest in collections of exemplary texts or with lexis.

Shortly after Chomsky's government and binding theory (named for its concern with syntax and with proforms) emerged, Randolph Quirk started the Survey of English Usage Corpus at University College in London, and two Americans digitized one million words of American text dated in 1960. The Brown Corpus (Francis and Kucera 1964) comprises randomly sampled 2,000–word excerpts from 43 different written text types of informative and imaginative prose. This marked the beginning of corpus linguistics, which avoids invented sentences and instead collects and analyses statistically random samples of pre-existing texts. When Jan Svartvik of Lund and Randolph Quirk in London later joined forces to assemble half a million words of spoken English in the London-Lund Corpus (100 texts of 5000 words), another corpus was born, and it confirmed something extraordinary.

As early as 1968, Wallace Chafe (1968) alerted researchers to a problem in Chomsky's theory: the bulk of idiomatic phrases in speech. Chafe (1979) also believed that language production resembled a flowing river of segments, each of which could be broken down into an opening and some information. Bengt Altenberg's work on the London-Lund corpus confirmed the impression that conversation is mostly a flow of phrasal building blocks. Recurrent word-combinations, sometimes called prefabricated expressions, make up a very high percentage of these sample texts.[1] Altenberg (1990) argued that language production does not necessarily generate grammatical paradigms: it may instead string together pre-patterned word sequences, one after another, without much concern as to an overall sentence structure. John Sinclair simultaneously pioneered the computational study of collocation at Birmingham. Sinclair contrasts Chomsky's generative approach, and the retrieval of prefabricated word sequences uncovered in corpora, as two principles, open-choice and idiom (Kennedy 1998, 109–10; Sinclair 1991, 110, 114). The open-choice principle invents new word combinations; the idiom principle reuses stored ones.

Diana Van Lancker Sidtis and Gail Rallon (2004) have analysed a screenplay of *Some Like it Hot* by W.I. Wilder and A.L. Diamond (1959). They compare their results to other corpus studies, quantify what native English speakers know of formulaic expressions on the basis of a questionnaire, and argue that their findings support Sinclair's 'dual model of language ability' (Sinclair 1991, 109–10). They call the two techniques 'compositional and configurational.' Experimental research going back to Hughlings Jackson in 1874 found that the brain exhibits differences in state when it produces prefabs, phrases, collocations, or chunks, and when it engages in rule-governed composition. Right-handed persons with aphasia, a form of brain damage that affects the language centres of the left hemisphere, not only manage very nicely with prefabricated expressions but also use the right hemisphere and possibly its basal ganglia to do so. Spontaneous uttering, then, appears to rely rather more heavily on the right hemisphere than does studied composition (writing), which emerges largely from the left hemisphere's language centres. Cognitive language production thus has three options in making sentences: to pump out linear sequences of repeating and loosely stitched-together phrases; to engineer, by applying syntactic rules, grammatically well-structured and often complex sentences; or to adopt both processes simultaneously.

Which strategy we adopt depends on what language resources are available to us. Can we store utterances in an artifice, paper or digital memory, or are there rapidly accessible schemata in our long-term memory? When we speak quickly, we utter brief phrasal expressions and, as best we can, link them as they come out. Nattinger (1988, 76) uses the metaphor 'stitch' to characterize this process. When we write, we do not need to worry about maintaining consciousness of drafts of sentences. Any draft is on the page or the screen for easy visual reference, and we can transform grammatical structures at our leisure. On the page or screen, it is easy to convert a passive structure into an active one, or an adjective into a relative clause. Of course, if we have the knowledge of a language expert, with compositional techniques and structures stabilized as schemata in long-term memory, we can manage almost as fluently in speech as we can on paper.

Researchers in speech regard phrases as units demarcated by a speaker's intonation, emphasis, or pause, not by any lexical boundary. They are the phrases that we bind together in oral speech (e.g., 'sort of,' 'I don't know but,' 'something like that'). Fixed phrases need have no idiomatic unity. This non-lexicalized approach to phrase identification usefully corrects the lexicographer's bias towards relying on meaning. Speech itself has an innate 'chunkiness' about it (Altenberg and Eeg-Olofsson 1990, 1–3). We speak not words, but phrasal units, and pauses, hemming and hawing, where vocal intonations mark the points at which we link one of these phrases to another. Some phrases (e.g., 'like,' 'you know') are paralanguage, implying agreement that might not exist. Deborah Tannen's study of casual talk (2007) reveals how pitifully often we repeat favourite phrases to hold our ground as we grope towards expression. John R. Pierce remarks that, 'Subjectively, in speaking or listening to a speaker one has a strong impression that sentences are generated largely from beginning to end … that the person generating a sentence doesn't have a very elaborate pattern in his head at any one time but that he elaborates the pattern as he goes along' (1980, 115). London-Lund corpus research (Altenberg 1998, 103) estimates the average length of a repeated phrase to be 3.15 words. Word combinations in English, evidently, have a chunk size comparable to the capacity of the phonological loop in working memory.

How much of our ordinary language production uses phrases, or, how big is the phrasal lexicon? Palmer (1933, 7) believes that collocations by far outnumber vocabulary. Igor Mel'čuk says that 'in any language – i.e. in its lexicon – phrases outnumber words ten to one' (1998, 14). Sorhus (1977) analysed a corpus of 131,536 words of spontaneous speech by Canadians and found a fixed phrase, on average, at five-word intervals (cited by Moon 1998, 67). Altenberg (1998, 102) looked in the half-million-word London-Lund Corpus for multi-word combinations of at least three words that occur at least ten times. He found 201,000 tokens and 68,000 different types. Independently, I found the same phenomenon in Chaucer's *Canterbury Tales*.

Repeating word combinations in the London-Lund Corpus fall in the preliminaries and aftermath of a sentence, very seldom (only 2 per cent) in what Altenberg calls the rheme, 'the propositional core' (1998, 111). John Sinclair (1991) describes the words in this focus point of an utterance as being selected from an open, unrestricted, non-combining set. This suggests that the right hemisphere selects boilerplate repeating phrases for the opening and closing, leaving time for the left hemisphere to assemble the central rheme from scratch. William Strunk Jr (1918) was an early stickler for compact English sentences. He would replace a wordy sentence like 'It was not long before he was very sorry that he had said what he had' with the laconic 'He soon repented his words.' The sequence, 'It was not long before,' prepares for the central point, which is further delayed by three subordinate clauses. 'He soon repented his words,' on the other hand, has no stitches whatsoever. It gives the mind no opportunity to prepare its main concept. Of course, with a written text before us to revise, the mind already has its opportunity.

Finding these phrases is not easy. Diana Van Lancker Sidtis says that 'The percentage of prepackaged utterances in everyday speech is not known' (2001, 403). The number will actually vary from speaker to speaker; what is a phrase to one person may not be to another, even if we mean, by a phrase, an idiomatic expression. Repetition and length have proved the sturdiest criteria for locating phrases, and computers the least fallible means of doing so.

Cognitive studies thus have some issues with central principles of the government and binding theory of Chomsky and the majority of Western linguists doing research today. These issues include the unknowability of abstract language processing, a dependence on invented rather than on actual language, the emphasis on formal (syntactic) structures (independent of semantics), and the idea of a language gene, which separates mental language processing from general cognitive processing. Constructionism is a potential heir apparent of twentieth-century corpus-based language theory. It explains language as a 'network of constructions,' which are 'pairings of form with semantic or discourse function, including morphemes or words, idioms, partially lexically filled and fully abstract phrasal patterns' (Goldberg 2003, 219). This theory respects both the known capacity constraints of brain function (e.g., the scope of the phonological loop in working memory), and the serial segmentation of chunks in speech as exposed by corpus linguistics. As we will see, constructionism also proves more useful than generative linguistics to the study of literary authoring and reading.

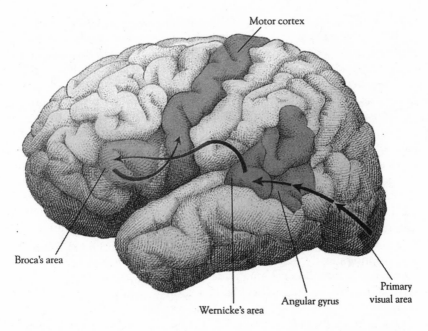

Figure 8. Norman Geschwind's Anatomical Model of Saying a Written Word (courtesy of Scientific American, as adapted by Posner and Raichle 1997)

Language theories are not the only model. The basic model for language production is the brain. So-called experiments 'in nature' (that is, patients with brain damage) and devices that image brain activity tell us where language forms. The old classical model of language brain function, by Lichtheim (1885) and Geschwindt (1979), proposes that two temporal regions of the neocortex are responsible (see fig. 8). The posterior Wernicke's area does semantic processing and sends language data to the frontal Broca's area, which clothes it with syntactic form and passes it on to the motor cortex for speaking. This model relies on ample medical evidence that patients with damage in Wernicke's area display faulty or nonsensical semantics and comprehension ('word salads'), and those with damage in Broca's area reveal staccato, fragmented speech with agrammatism.

No one disputes this evidence from brain damage, but localizing functions so simply is now impossible. Much of the human brain, topographically, is active at some point during an utterance. The purpose, the plan, and the gist of a message originate in the prefrontal cortex, like every other thing we intend to do. This area retrieves from long-term memory a gist, sometimes by using a part of the midbrain responsible for encoding traces with emotion, the twin amygdalae in the limbic system. If we decide to read a sentence aloud (often an unemotional act), processing begins once the visual cortex at the very back of the brain receives data from the eyes. The frontal cortex sets in train an acoustic re-encoding of this visual data so that it assumes the form it would have had if heard and passed on by the temporal auditory cortex. The brain must then perceive semantically what is said. Wernicke's area in the left hemisphere in the brain of a right-handed person accesses meaning. It draws on networks of neurons spread across the cortex to assign words (lemmas, lexemes) to each sound from long-term memory. If Wernicke's area is damaged, the brain utters 'word salad' sentences that have a proper syntactic form but do not make sense. Then the brain encodes the recognized word train syntactically and phonologically at Broca's area, just forward of Wernicke's area. A brain in which Broca's area is damaged utters semantically understandable sentence fragments that lack grammatical form. Activities at both sites, if unselfconscious (that is, if we do not attend to them but carry on automatically), also involve subcortical areas. Philip Lieberman (2000) and his colleagues have shown that subcortical basal ganglia structures, in one of the most evolutionarily ancient (reptilian) parts of the brain, help regulate language processing. Any fully encoded sentence next moves to the motor cortex for pronouncing. From visual cortex to Wernicke's area and then Broca's area, and last to the motor cortex, the brain appears to operate in sequence. In fact, these activities are massively distributed. Language does not follow one path but many. Even after damage to Broca's and Wernicke's areas, the brain can enlist 'alternate neuroanatomical structures' for language use (Lieberman 2000, 5) and recover functionality.

The physical basis for associational memory is the brain's neurons.[2] Each neuron has a cell body that receives signals from to up to 10,000 nearby upstream neurons by means of dendrites, and sends a single message to downstream neurons by its axon, a filament that can grow as long as 10 centimetres (Feldman 2006, 50). The brain possesses billions of these neurons. Their distributed network – and the substantial part that axon cabling plays in the cortex – explains the puzzle of how the brain's language functions, like syntactic and semantic processing, can be associated with Broca's and Wernicke's areas even while a very wide area of the brain activates to say something. The long-term memory storage capacity of the brain is '10^{11} neurons connected by 10^{15} synapses' (Chklovskii, Mel, and Svoboda 2004, 782). Although the consensus among scientists is that our long-term memory is limitless, our working-memory capacity filters and constrains information entering the long-term store (Magnussen et al. 2006, 599).[3] We find things in long-term memory by launching probes of words, images, and sounds associated with what we are trying to recall. These probes activate links to the target in our mental network – that is, a probe elicits its chunk partners – so that the desired information, sometimes on the 'tip of one's tongue,' pops out. Chang (1986) analyses the extent to which six psychological theories of how semantic memory is organized into networks or hierarchies account for empirical findings on reaction times by persons for tasks of semantic characterization. We often link individual things not logically but fortuitously according to how we have encountered them in experience. A common phrase for this linking effect is 'spreading activation' (Collins and Loftus 1975). To stimulate one memory appears to have a rippling effect on all memories linked to it. The strength of that activation, or its 'weight,' seems proportional to the number of times that the linkage between those two memories has previously been activated. We can conceptualize a vocabulary of 'primitive conceptual features' as a neural network that, so to speak, lights up as a result of spreading activation.

Pulvermüller reports that magnetoencephalography identifies neuronal 'word webs' that link different areas on the cortex to create schemata such as 'an animal name and the visual image it relates to, or … an action verb and the action it normally expresses' (2003, 520 and fig. 2). The dynamic word webs for leg-related, arm-related, and face-related terms each have nine nodes but possess quite different topographies. Figure 9 shows the anatomical networks for these and for action and visually related words.

Other research locates colour words in the ventral temporal lobe, action words in the left temporal gyrus, names of people in the temporal pole, and words for animals and tools in, respectively, the anterior and posterior inferotemporal area (Martin et al. 1995, 102; Lieberman 2000, 63, 65; and Ojemann 1991).

Our eyes see this language processing at work in brain scans, and in operations to repair lesions. Their images do not jibe with anyone's mental experience of speaking. I can believe that we are our only muse, that God is not talking to us. To map our inner voice onto the oxygenated-blood-fed network of neuron cells is a much bigger challenge to

action word   visually related word

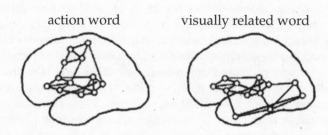

leg-related word   arm-related word   face-related word

Figure 9. Word-webs for Action, Visually-, and Bodily-related Words (Pulver-müller 2003, figs. 4.2a and 4.3a; courtesy of Elsevier)

belief. The brain is a three-pound mass, four-fifths of which is water, and most of the rest is fatty tissue that makes it feel like warm margarine. Is that, to quote Arthur Edens in the film *Michael Clayton*, the answer to the multiple choice of us?

What we know of how speech works, in any event, seems absurd. Creatures should not have to utter something in order to know what they have to say. Imagine an automobile factory, about the internal workings of which we could only conjecture, where no one could anticipate design, test useability, or apply quality control until vehicles were materializing out the gate. Company executives and stockholders look on, nonplussed, as a bizarre, unpredictable line of products emerge. Some have high-powered engines on stilts. Others have wheels but look like the offspring of a tank and a Volkswagen. Human product planning consists of the manager's speculation about what kind of materials should be fed the assembly plants so as to produce only wheeled vehicles. Our language plants, on the other hand, utter working products. Occasionally one appears in which a headlight and a side mirror exchange places, but repairs are made quickly at the gate. Company adverts laud the prestige of acquiring inimitable, one-of-a-kind cars. After fourscore years, more or less, mysterious breakdowns occur and only car fragments, or nothing at all, materialize. Meanwhile, a nexus of industries services all these factories. Blueprints, spare parts, and repair and driving manuals are tailor made to each vehicle. This Vonnegutesque model is what we experience, even without having to attribute it to an organ with the weight, consistency, colour, and surface contours of a bowel movement. Despite all this, the brain produces speech quickly, efficiently, and sometimes gloriously.

So, by an act of will, I have to admit that my eyesight is bad. After reading quantum mechanics, I readily accept that matter and energy are not what they seem. The split-screen experiment entangles the witness with electrons that communicate at a distance. Evolution did not equip us with the senses needed to perceive either fundamental particles or neurons as they are.

Consequently, noticing what is *not* there takes effort. Three decades ago, Louis Milic distinguished between what writers do unconsciously in generating language and what they consciously do in 'scanning, that is, evaluation of what has been generated' (i.e., their rhetorical options; 1971, 85). Ahead of his time, he made a distinction between implicit and procedural memory (of whose source we are unconscious), and explicit memory (of which we can be fully aware; Squire 1987, 160; cf. Butler and Berry 2001). Our sentences appear to come out of an inaccessible blankness, as writers sometimes confess. Expert uttering is like the 'zombie behaviour' that happens when we do not pay attention to what we are doing. Driving a car on a very familiar route, and thinking about something else, we suddenly come to out of autopilot (Koch and Tsuchiya 2007, 19). Normally, we consciously look both sides and behind when we back out of a driveway, but once on a familiar route, we just drive on for a while, adopting naturally a stop-and-go defensive driving strategy. Uttering is worse: we have an almost uncorrectable neglect of it. Francis Crick (co-discoverer of DNA structure) and Christof Koch write: 'Nor are we directly aware of our inner world of thoughts, intentions and planning (that is, of our unconscious homunculus) but … only of the sensory representations associated with these mental activities' (2000, 109). We know language by hearing and seeing what comes out of us as language.

Procedural memory can be recalled only in the *act* of executing it. We recall how to utter language by dynamically speaking and writing, not by remembering a sequential process of things to do. To recollect something stored implicitly, we execute a stored procedure without observing it. The human mind, in production, is without a 'readable manual' for how it makes sentences. We can initiate uttering within working memory, true enough. Consciously looking for a feeling of what we want to say, we search our memory for percepts (experiences) and lexical concepts that serve them. Then we select words and a syntactic structure, and assemble (sometimes transforming) the clause mentally. We can then will ourselves to verbalize it aloud. But this analytic procedure is not what usually happens because native speakers generate sentences spontaneously. In natural conversation, there is a great difference in speed between the two methods. Groping to assemble a sentence consciously in working memory bumps into the dark resource of long-term memory. 'How can we know what we are going to say until we have said it?' holds true, whether we publish it as a voice in working memory or aloud.

Why cannot we recall how we make a sentence? Why is the mind blocked from witnessing one of the most critically defining features of a human being? One reason is the limitation of our senses; another lies in what we can make memories of. Our long-term memory maker, associated with the hippocampus, can store language, images, sounds, sensations, ideas, and feelings, but not our experience of neural procedures themselves. Biologically, there appears to be no point in recalling, explicitly, how we do most things critical to our survival. Our minds, as they develop, have no given names for the actors and the events at cognitive language centres. Knowing may be unnecessary to or even counterproductive for our survival. Maybe there is a simpler explanation, that our working or short-term memory does not have the capacity to hold the complex dynamics of language production because, until recently, we had no reason for needing to know them.

At the core of the mind lies a black box utterance plant. No one teaches us how to speak. As long as someone talks in our infant presence, we pick language up, to all appearances, from what we see and hear. After we start to talk, we study vocabulary, grammar, and rhetoric. It seldom occurs to most of us that we are unconscious of how we use language because we hear ourselves constantly in inner and outer speech and can take apart, and reassemble, sentences on paper and screen. If we take up authoring professionally and wonder how we can outwit our frustrating periods of blockage, we eventually give up speculating: it may be easier to imagine our uttering cores as unknowable voices giving dictation. Ordinary conversation is no different, and yet its equal unknowability occurred to very few of us until Freud developed dream-based psychoanalysis. It found explanations in our numinous unconscious for why we behave so oddly at times, as in speaking or writing. Freud's analysable symbol book extracts from dreams his proposed mental mechanisms. It sources slips of the tongue, that is, damaged utterances that before were inexplicable, to anomalies in our sexual programming. Such speaking mistakes occur only once in a thousand words – about every five minutes. It may be consoling to believe that a black box, not conscious personal faults, generates – in the words of the mad scientist Walter Pigeon plays in *Forbidden Planet* (1956) – 'monsters from the id.' But these are truly desperate imaginings. Cognitive psychology and neuroscience are drawing a reliable blueprint of the language factory floor. We owe a great debt to the sick and the disabled who have surrendered their damaged language abilities for study. They are legion. Few families do not have some experience with a language condition such as dyslexia, dementia, schizophrenia, and stroke.

No matter whether we utter sentences orally or write them onto paper or into a file, most often we spontaneously compose and utter without conscious thought or foresight. During free conversation, our overt auditory voice overlays our subvocal inner speech. During rapid typing or writing, our hands can scarcely keep up with our inner voice. Of course, we can recite, rehearse by rote, from long-term memory something that we laid down in it. This memory, which responds to probes rather than enables browsing, holds knowledge of the world and facts, including information (so-called semantic memory), and personal experience (so-called episodic memory; Tulving 1983). If we receive something from a probe, it suddenly appears in working memory, uttered by a subvocal voice when what we retrieve is language, and then we can recite (re-speak) that voice aloud. We can also script sentences in working memory and utter them painstakingly from there, a process that draws consciously on long-term memory but is very slow and works with phrases and clauses.

These methods start with the same thing: a few words. What cognitive scientists call a lexical production system pulses like a heartbeat, issuing in a flow of auditorily encoded phrasal chunks or segments. Each chunk seems to pull out the next chunk. The system is what it does, the procedure it enacts. We can deduce its stages and features by attending to the kinds of errors we correct in speaking, to measurements of reaction times for specific language tasks, to electrical, magnetic, and heat patterns in the brain during uttering, and to the effects of brain damage on language functioning. Now and then, a theory builds a detailed, testable model from these experimental findings. Alan Baddeley devised a theory of working memory in the mid-1970s that has lighted many dark corners of language function. In 1999, W.J.M. Levelt and his colleagues in Nijmegen published a theory of lexical access in speech production and implemented it in a computer program called Weaver. Their theories use empirical evidence, especially reaction times and speech errors. This model has sparked disagreement but gives us a reasonable place to stand. It will not be the final answer, but it is as good as it now gets. Levelt's theory of uttering consists of two serial sequences of mental events: feedforward verbalization of concepts, and a self-monitoring that corrects speech errors and in effect gives feedback to the verbalization process.

Unconscious and conscious verbalization of concepts and self-monitoring have their basis in cerebral networks whose locations in the brain are now known. Ten years ago Marcus Raichle (2001; see also Fox et al. 2005 and Biswal et al. 2010) used fMRI scans to locate the intelligent, spontaneous unconscious in the brain. These scans measured the blood oxygen level-dependent (abbreviated BOLD) signal, which averages ten to twenty seconds in length. Its slow cycles mark the activation of the default mode network (DMN), which is found largely hidden in the cleft between the two hemispheres. It runs from the medial prefrontal cortex at the front to the posterior cingulate and precuneus, and the posterior temporoparietal cortex towards the back (see figures 10-11). Protected by a medial location (as if this function outweighs all other mentation), this network hosts the mind's unselfconscious wandering, daydreaming, or reverie, the unfocused thinking that enriches our inner life but that has no specific task to do. When we are at rest, our eyes open, shut, or fixed, our default mode network is busy, imagining, reflecting on the self, projecting the future, constructing scenes, and evidently consolidating episodic memories into semantic gist (Buckner and Carroll 2007; Hassabis and Maguire 2009; and Christoff et al. 2010). Here is the matrix of creativity in the brain where associative thought emerges spontaneously from long-term memory without apparent effort or deliberation, and yet with a considerable cost in physical resources.

The default mode network operates for much of our waking time but turns down low when the brain takes on a specific task and works consciously to reach a known goal. Then another cluster of sites becomes active, called the executive or the cognitive control network (CCN). Centred on the dorsolateral and rostrolateral prefrontal cortex (Christoff et al. 2009; Cole and Schneider 2007), this cluster of sites is anticorrelated with the DMN. When one is working, the other is not. Moreover,

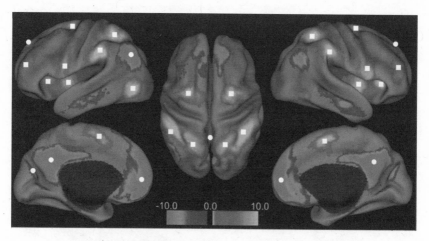

○ **Default mode**

☐ **Cognitive control**

Figure 10. The Default Mode Network (indicated by °) and the Cognitive Control Network (indicated by □): left-hemisphere lateral (upper) and medial (lower) views, and right hemisphere lateral (upper) and medial (lower) views (courtesy of Fox, Snyder, Vincent, Corbetta, Van Essen, and Raichle, *Proceedings of the National Academy of Sciences of the United States of America* 2005, 102.27: 9676, fig. 3)

they appear to be detached from the external world; neither functions in tandem with the sensory and motor cortex.

A decade's research on these twin networks indicates that the brain toggles between the two. The DMN appears to create thoughts by working unconsciously with long-term memory and one part of the prefrontal cortex, and then to deliver that thinking to the CCN for conscious analysis and judgment. The second network operates much more quickly than the DMN. Creative thinking likewise alternates between periods of spontaneous flow, marked by unselfconsciousness, and much shorter moments of conscious rapid reading and, if needed, revision of what the mind has provided. Two cognitive modes appear to work together dynamically, as stimulus and response, message and feedback, to the degree that it might be said that the default network recruits the cognitive control network (Christoff et al. 2009, 8722). If that is so, we have for a long time overemphasized the importance of deliberative problem-solving.

Lateral Prefrontal Cortex

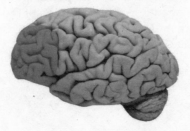

Default Network

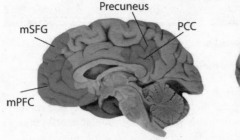
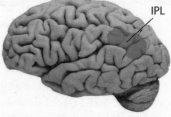

Temporal Lobe Memory Regions

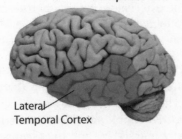
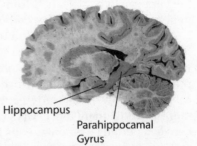

Figure 11. Approximate anatomical localization of the lateral prefrontal cortex, the default network, and temporal lobe memory regions. Abbreviations: medial prefrontal cortex (mPFC); medial superior frontal gyrus (mSFG); posterior cingulate cortex (PCC); inferior parietal lobe (IPL; courtesy of Christoff, Gordon, and Smith, 'The Role of Spontaneous Thought in Human Cognition,' *Neuroscience of Decision Making*, edited by O. Vartanian and D. R. Mandel. copyright © 2010 Psychology Press)

These two networks offer a neurological staging ground for the two central experiences of authoring: recognition of the unknown source of uttering, and an urgent need to revise that to reduce errors that, as it happens, characterize its work.

Yet this theory opens *in medias res*, in the middle of the creative process. What precedes it is non-cognitive: emotion.

*   *   *   *   *

It was Chester Duncan in English at Manitoba who described his first lecture for the vets, a newbie teacher with a Keats poem, writing out his analysis, putting it in a file folder, delivering it at class and then looking up to see just twenty minutes had elapsed, and he had to end the class then, got back to his office, needing a new strategy, and when we sat in the back row of his moderns course he never read from notes but wandered from house-plumbing issues to Joyce and striking at least the right notes in the right order to Faulkner, and we never wondered which Chester Duncan we were listening to.

Then that four-year stint in English at Toronto, you speaking our seminar papers and that deadline stuff, the essays and the thesis, so much information you had pretty much forgotten about me except that we acted in the PLS for John as Gabriel, Lob, then Mercy in Mankind, when you stopped being afraid of having them look at you, having to memorize so much, from the very fownder and begynner of owr fyrst creacion *on ... and stood alone waiting to go on, repeating that line, hoping that the rest would all come out, and they did as you came out with the lantern that fell on the floor the first time and your body drew the rest of the part out as the first piece of yarn unwinds the ball but you seldom thought about me.*

And at Erindale you wrote on large index cards what you like Chester wanted to say to your students and annotated the margins and stitched phrases together, repeating yourself from time to time like Egler, that hellfire First English Lutheran who told them what he had to say, and said it, and told them what he said, most of it bad news for us but a nifty way to keep going and not running dry before your hour ended, those card bundles that are still in your office, years after you stopped using them because they bored me, and your classes saw they did and so suddenly you let me do the talking at last, my big chance now that you were winging it, trusting we knew enough to go for fifty minutes and we were afterwards exhausted speaking extempore through you, making sentences, and even if they didn't get everything I said, they learned that mind is stronger than index card and small talk's only the beginning, and you had a free ride.

But thanks for the opening sentence because I always find it hard to start and good for you you learned to let me unroll in those nine-lecture-hours-a-week years with so much LTM stuff to talk about, the patter that the class and you heard at the same time, giving you new ideas you'd no time to write down but so little remains of all that because you became the information man with the editing and the REED archives and I slept as you extracted sentences from library notes and typed and then word-processed, mostly editing me out, though we sometimes spoke together after English gave you a course to teach in creativity and technology that at least asked the right questions and you wondered what computers would say about them, though I can tell you if you don't already know that they don't interest me and if I were you I wouldn't look my meal ticket in the mouth.

II Mind on Fire

Some works in cognitive psychology scarcely mention feelings. Affective psychology, as we might term it, did not get much press (outside the field of deviant behaviour) until the 1990s, when Antonio Damasio (1994), a neuroscientist from Iowa, applied historical case studies and his own clinical research to study the neurology of emotion. Decision making in the frontal lobes uses emotionally positive and negative information in the amygdala, which belongs to the limbic system and enhances the strength of emotionally charged memories during long-term storage. Lesions in the amygdala prevent the encoding of emotion, especially, onto gist. Emotion does not attach to concrete details in long-term memory (Adolphs, Tranel, and Buchanan 2005). The gist with which an author begins an utterance is emotionally charged. A writer first experiences a sense of what he wants to say in wordless thoughts and experiential percepts. Without wanting the gist to be expressed, without feeling a desire to utter it, he can produce little. An inchoate concept is not, by itself, enough. He must need to express that felt inchoate utterance-in-waiting.

The 'mental fight' begins with the 'arrows of desire' (William Blake, 'Milton'); no one writes anything without wanting to. Motivating students to write is the last straw, the one that breaks the teacher's back. There is a remedy for all other failures but the failure of desire. Are there reasonable scientific grounds for believing this true?

First there is embodiment. Everyday language use is emotive. Words that describe many types of 'sensory, motor, and affective' states or events cause, unconsciously, the re-experiencing or reliving of the feelings associated with them. The mind's understanding of such words is grounded in the body's 'original neural state that occurred when the information was initially acquired' (Niedenthal 2007, 1003). Embodiment, or embodied cognition, occurs in circumstances when a word is processed with some feeling. For example, action terms 'used metaphorically' do not activate the motor cortex, as literal, concrete action verbs do (Willems and Hagoort 2007, 286).[4] The association of traces in long-term memory breaks vocabulary down into two groups, words understood abstractly, and words relived. Whether this is owing to spreading activation or to a special linkage is not yet known, but readers with quite different histories and thus without shared kinds of experiences will not comprehend words in quite the same way. One way to level the epistemological playing field is to speak in numbers, logic, symbolic ideas, and plenty of metaphors (Mahon and Caramazza 2008). This prevents words from activating the motor neurons that accompany a living experience.

Embodiment, however, does not deny the possibility that we use words abstracted from experience and thus feelings. What else then?

More persuasive are repeated surveys of creative writers that identify their occupational disease: depression and mania, mental disorders centred on emotion. In 2005 Nancy Andreasen published *The Creative Brain: The Science of Genius*, a study of how creative artists, especially writers, suffer disproportionately from affective or emotional illness. This was thirty-eight years after she brought out her first book, as a newly minted PhD in English, on John Donne, and thirty-five years after she graduated as a medical doctor and began work on schizophrenia. Andreasen spent many years observing some thirty authors in the Iowa Writers' Workshop. She first published her results in 1987. To her astonishment, none had a cognitive disorder like schizophrenia, but 80 per cent endured a unipolar (depression) or bipolar disorder (which alternates depression and mania, a highly excited state; 95). Only 30 per cent of the control group of non-writers had a comparable mood disorder. The occupational hazard of very gifted writers had nothing to do with intelligence: it was a malfunction of emotion.

In 1993 Kay Jamison published *Touched with Fire: Manic-Depressive Illness and the Artistic Temperament*, which found comparable evidence of these emotional disorders among forty-seven prize-winning creative writers and artists in the United Kingdom. Of this group, 38 per cent were treated for a mood disorder, either in extremity (unipolar or bipolar) or in a milder form (cyclothymic): 'A comparison with rates of man-ic-depressive illness of the general population (1 percent), cyclothymia (1 to 2 percent), and major depressive disorder (5 percent) shows that these British poets were thirty times more likely to suffer from manic-depressive illness, ten to twenty times more likely to be cyclothymic or to have other milder forms of manic-depressive illness, more than five times as likely to commit suicide, and at least twenty times more likely to have been committed to an asylum or madhouse' (72). Jamison's results look modest in comparison to Andreasen's, but Jamison only took account of those who had had formal treatment. The psychologi-cal illness spared Jamison's artists to a great extent but hammered two kinds of wordsmith, the playwrights (62 per cent) and the poets (55 per cent; 88).

Alice Flaherty's *The Midnight Disease* (2004), on hypergraphia and writer's block, both of which are unusual emotional states that launch or forestall the drive to write, supports the findings of Andreasen and Jamison. Creative authoring and emotion go hand in hand, at least in the very successful. However, even if a high potential for emotional drive persists in extraordinary writers, does it necessarily follow that ordinary people also communicate because of an emotion ... with more than cognition? Two researchers in different fields showed that it does, at least for students: psychologists James Pennebaker and Sandra Beall in 1986, and poet Alice Brand in 1989.

Sandra Beall and James Pennebaker at the University of Texas in Austin ran an experiment in the mid-1980s. They asked two groups of students to spend fifteen minutes on four consecutive days writing. The experimental group, many of them crying, wrote about the most traumatic event of their lives ('Rape, family violence, suicide attempts, drug problems, and other horrors'); and the control group wrote about non-emotional subjects. Pennebaker says that the experiment 'yielded astounding results': the experimental group 'drastically reduced their doctor visit rates after the study compared to ... control participants who had written about trivial topics' (2000, 4–5). An hour of writing about emotions not only released those feelings but improved the writ-ers' health months later. Other scientists confirmed these results by experimenting on different groups, the most surprising of which were 58 asthma patients and 49 rheumatoid arthritis patients studied by Joshua Smyth and his colleagues at the State University of New York at Stony Brook (Smyth, Stone, and Hurewitz 1999, 1304). Again the experimental group wrote about 'the most stressful event of their lives,' and the control group about 'emotionally neutral topics.' Four months later, the condition of the experimental group had markedly improved. The asthma patients had improved lung function, and the rheumatoid arthritis patients experienced a reduction in symptom severity. These experiments show that writing releases feelings, and that the release improves health, but it still does not definitively link emotion and writing. The control groups apparently wrote without freeing up emotion.

It took a poet and a composition instructor to show the linkage of language expression and emotion. Alice Brand's extended experiments with college, advanced expository, and professional writers, English teachers, and student poets had no control groups. This large community showed that 'affect and cognition cannot truly be uncoupled' in writing (1989, 213). By questionnaires, Brand showed that these different groups handled negative and positive emotions differently, but that everyone in them experienced 'positive arousal,' 'relief and satisfaction' in the act of writing (198).

We can infer from these experimental findings that authoring begins, as Wordsworth says, with the needful recollection of emotionally charged memories. Routine embodiment of motor and sensory experiences that make speakers and writers relive those experiences that the words they use stand for underscores much uttering, whether creative or otherwise. Emotion plays a special role in storing and retrieving gist (with which language production begins) in long-term memory. Creative writers fall victim to affective disorders far more frequently than non-writing control groups do. Writers are not vulnerable to cognitive mental illness more than anyone else. And writing about personal emotions improves one's health and gives the writer a sense of 'positive arousal.' Feeling the onset of language production is a profound affective common denominator in the uttering process itself. Even when a writer does not obtain emotional relief by writing about personal pain and suffering, writing has its own built-in good feeling. Most of us write for specific purposes (money, recognition, justice, love) but uttering, by itself, is reward enough to start with.

*　*　*　*　*

A mixed bag we were, they liked me and mistrusted you, so it's a good thing you never graded me the way you did them or the classroom would have been pretty quiet those years you let me have my head, and I came out of the box, and they heard me feel about the likes of Lucky and Smeagol, and what the students wanted was the showy me letting it all out, good news and bad, and in time you saw there was no winning way for you, no way to outscore me with written Chaucer lectures at the lectern and so you buried them and put the chapters of your sf book in a coursepack where they did no harm.

All those years were my years and you had to listen to me and couldn't even take notes, you had to hear it all without an intervention except that you couldn't stand me cry, you slowed me down and caught me in mid-flow, you clicked on pause when feelings ran too high, and yet the class came, you know, to share my rapture in real-time choked wet readings of the likes of And God shall wipe away all tears from their eyes; and there shall be no more death, neither sorrow, nor crying, neither shall there be any more pain, *and when my voice caught they saw your censorship and were infected with my simple feelings welling up in them as well, vouching why they read at all, why they feel good even as Yeats, or Hopkins, or the evangelist break their hearts.*

III Conceptualizer and Verbalizer

What happens next in W.J.M. Levelt's theory of lexical production can only be indirectly observed through its effects. Assume that I am an environmentalist arguing with a politician who says, 'Cars remain an essential way to travel.' I reply, 'Maybe a pony pull-cart would be better.' Levelt would say that my environmentalist's mind selected two single, unified lexical concepts, a horse and a pull-cart. These are not exactly words; they are placeholder ideas for something (a nexus of images, sounds, and associations) that could potentially be verbalized as words, such as nag and buggy, mare and waggon, steed and chariot, or pony and pull-cart. I might experience these notions fleetingly as mental imagery. Because no one can directly examine these lexical concepts in my mind to see what they are like, Levelt deduces them from scientific observation of mental behaviour (see fig. 12). He opts for a 'terminal conceptual vocabulary' of unified concepts instead of 'primitive conceptual features' (1999, 8). That is, Levelt thinks that the second stage in uttering moves from inchoate feelings to single concepts for specific words, not to sets of semantic features or primitives such as [mammal | herbivore | quadruped | ungulate | horse | maned | tailed | for-riding | for-drawing | jousting | pony | steed | foal | ...].

Two observed 'effects' suggest to Levelt that we select simple word-notions rather than a semantic cluster. First, we do not normally gen-

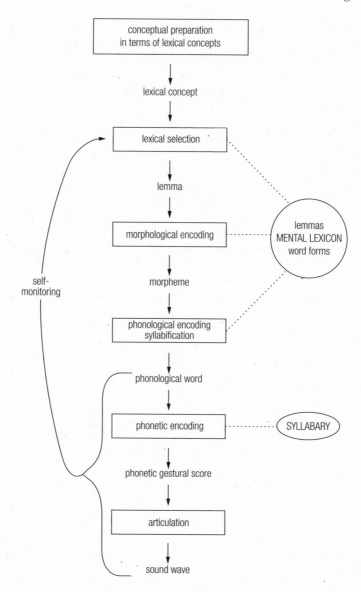

Figure 12. Willem Levelt's Lexical Production Model (Reprinted from 'A Theory of Lexical Access in Speech Production' by Levelt, Roelofs, and Meyer, Copyright © 1999 Cambridge University Press)

erate, at the next stage of uttering (when we narrow down a lexical concept into a specific word), what are called 'hyperonyms or superordinates' (4), although these are available in the cluster sets. The environmentalist would go from the word-concept [horse] to lexical nodes such as {nag} and {buggy} rather than to the superordinates {mammal} and {vehicle}. Second, there is no observed reaction time difference between accessing a word-notion that represents a very large semantic cluster (such as [man]), and one that represents a small semantic cluster (such as [doorknob]). If our initial lexical concepts were such clusters or complex sets (rather than words), we should take longer to recover them, but no such 'semantic complexity effect' is observable.

We know that the dark conceptualizer pulses phrasal chunks in part because of our memory systems. There are two kinds of long-term associative memory – implicit or inaccessible, and explicit or accessible – and three kinds of relevant short-term memory – two phonological buffers involved in language perception and language production, and Alan Baddeley's theory of working memory. Implicit long-term memory includes recall of a procedure in enacting it (procedural memory such as speaking), and priming. Explicit long-term memory consists of episodic memory and semantic memory. The former recollects experiences in our life or in stories. The latter allows us to understand what words mean, what things they betoken or signify.

Chunks are born in our long-term associative memory, where our working memory has laid them down. We deliberately chunk information so as to improve its recall. Artificial memory systems like the classical *loci et imagines* method rely on our doing so (Yates 1966). Memorists like Hideaki Tomoyori, who could recite the first 40,000 digits of pi, commit their huge databank to memory by combining words or numbers with images (Takahashi et al. 2006). Most times, we chunk unselfconsciously and freely in spontaneous uttering (Gobet et al. 2001). What structure does the chunk normally have, and how is it linked to another chunk? Experimental research on our memory systems can tell us.

Local-area neuron linkages through dendrites explain how certain areas of the brain control specialized tasks, such as using nouns or verbs. In turn, axons provide a mechanism for harnessing the power of neuron groups in distributed areas of the brain so that they act in unison. The axon of a neuron proceeds on one vector only: it does not go everywhere but serves to connect widely separated neuron masses, each of which local dendrite activity binds. Spreading activation – a theory that fits empirical evidence derived from reaction times – suggests that it takes but little time to move from 'lights on' in one local brain area to activation elsewhere in the brain. A pulse or a wave dynamically calls the needed team of neurons to work. Yet how does a neuron group know that it is traditionally associated with another neuron group so that they can light up together? To realize in the mind the image, the sounds, and the behaviour of a bee, for example, in a matter of a second or two, would seem to call for some mental pre-indexing.

The mind's thesaurus (concepts), lexicon (words), and encyclopedia (images of things) reside in associative memory, where lexical indeterminacy prevails. Unlike definitions in dictionary entries, meaning as the brain creates it changes as new word associations from the entire world of experience received by the brain feed into long-term memory. Words are fuzzy phenomena, clusters of more or less strongly linked elements, bound together not by logical categorization but by chance. Different systems responsible for phonemes, lexis, parts of speech, syntax, letter shapes, etc., all stored in different locations, work in parallel. One approach to an explanation regards a neural network as separate locations at which information about specific sounds, images, etc., are stored, all connected to a single associative location at which their addresses are stored, together with information as to what kind of linkage each address has (e.g., an 'is-a' relation) and weights that indicate how deeply processed (how strong) is that linkage (Kosslyn and Koenig 1992, 350–1). The concept of a typical noun, then, would resemble an address list that itemizes the locations of separately stored traits or features. Damasio, Tranel, and Damasio argue that the 'combinatorial arrangements that bind features into entities, and entities into events, i.e. their spatial and temporal coincidences, are recorded in separate neural ensembles, called convergence zones' (Damasio, Tranel, and Damasio 1990, 105). They form networks in 'association cortexes, limbic cortexes, and nonlimbic subcortical nuclei such as the basal ganglia'. Convergence zones are nodes in neural networks. The very idea of an address, however, belongs to computer architecture, not neuroscience. Does a neuron assembly need an address if its dedicated road already goes to the place it wants to visit?

Language production and understanding involves both hemispheres, not just the left. Individuals with damaged language areas in the left hemisphere can still use streams of idiomatic expressions such as 'I'm much obliged' or 'how are you doing today?' with no sign of syntactic or semantic damage. They evidently retrieve these expressions, whole, from long-term memory in the right hemisphere and have no need to call on the left hemisphere's language centres to process them. Although we appear to store the pronouns 'I' and 'you,' the verbs 'oblige' and 'do,' and the adverbs 'much' and 'today' separately in memory, we may also store them with each other in small chunks or clusters as single, unified items. Neuronal assemblies for two commonplaces like these seem to pre-exist the need to activate them. Many, perhaps most chunks issued by our language production system could employ pre-formed assemblages in long-term memory. If so, pre-formed lexical networks for repeated phrases consist of duplicated copies of their constituent words in one local neuronal area served by dendrites rather than 'a single associative location' that holds the addresses to the main storage areas for those nouns, verbs, and adverbs, addresses reachable only by much wider activation. In other words, the brain might have two kinds of lexical storage: one employed for newly coined expressions, and another for pre-formed phrasal ones. The word 'cheese' in expressions such as 'Say "cheese"!' (i.e., smile), 'It's like chalk and cheese, that's the problem' (a proverbial expression for quite different things), and 'If you want a fatty cheese, choose Gruyère, Camembert, or Gorgonzola' could be stored in three different places in long-term memory. Only the third sentence, a novel one, would address the main neural location for the word 'cheese.'

Constructionism analyses language into chunks, part of chunks, and chunk sequences, each a construct that the production system stitches together with others into phrases, clauses, and sentences. Figure 13 illustrates how linguists have conceived of constructs as centre on unusual, quirky utterances such as the incredulity expression 'Him, a trapeze artist?!' and the stranded preposition 'What did you put it on?' (Goldberg and Casenhiser 2006, fig. 1).

A typical sentence like 'What did Liza buy the child?' has smaller constructs, both lexical and syntactic. Adele Goldberg (2003, 221) identifies its six individual words as constructions, as well as syntactic units like the ditransitive ('what' and 'the child,' both objects of the verb), the question (which includes the inversion of subject and verb), and the noun phrase (the determiner 'the' modifying 'child') and verb-phrase (auxiliary 'did' and infinitive form 'buy'). Insofar as constructs are form-meaning pairings, they are expressions at a late stage of uttering. Constructionist theory, on the other hand, finds them earlier in a pre-phonological state, where much of the words' ultimate form is still missing. Goldberg says that language is nothing but a network of constructs – 'it's constructions all the way down' (223).[5]

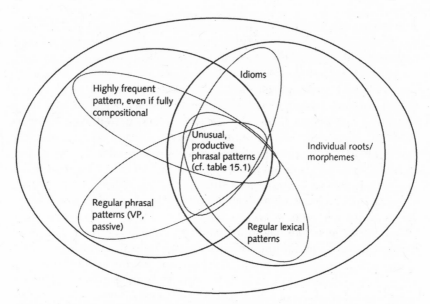

Figure 13. Constructions (reprinted from Goldberg and Casenhiser, 'English Constructions,' *The Handbook of English Linguistics*, 2006, courtesy of Blackwell)

The 'meaning of an utterance,' Feldman says, 'can best be understood as a linked set of (embodied) schemas' (2006, 285), which are semantic clusters in long-term memory, fused by means of constructions that are syntactic in form (285). Schemata contribute to the making of character, theme, and narrative in literature, as well as sentences. They can be moved in and out of working memory far more quickly than other items stored in long-term memory, evidently because we retrieve them as if they were single items, not unlike conventional prefabricated expressions.

The two lexical concepts, [horse] and [cart], would be already associated in my environmentalist's mind for the next stage, in which the mind specifies the exact words those two concepts should take. Levelt gives these words the name 'lemma,' but other names also appear in the scientific literature, such as 'lexical node.' The mind retrieves these lemmas or nodes from long-term memory at the rate of 'two or three words per second' (Levelt, Roelofs, and Meyer 1999, 4). They are syntactic content words like the singular nominative nouns {pony} and {pull-cart}, but they lack one essential trait of natural language. They have no auditory features and thus cannot be 'heard' as uttered by an inner voice. For this reason, I suppose, we have no way of experiencing them mentally. These chunks remain hypothetical entities.

Lemma selection at this second stage occurs in word chunks. At this pre-phonological stage, the mind occasionally makes mistakes in retrieval. Word-exchange errors 'such as the exchange of *roof* and *list* in *we completely forgot to add the list to the roof*' (15) occur at lemma retrieval when two words with the same part of speech, here a noun, get switched around inside a noun phrase (the objects of the infinitive 'to add' and of an appended prepositional phrase). The mind must somehow hold all four words, 'list to the roof,' as a single chunk in order for this errone-ous exchange to occur. Lemma retrieval slows down or speeds up when the mind hears or sees what are called 'distractor' words at the same time that it selects lemmas. A semantically related auditory distractor word will delay the finding of the lemma. For example, if I am play-ing chess simultaneously while talking to my politician and I hear my opponent say, 'knight to king's bishop 3' (the knight is a chess piece that often takes the shape of a horse head), retrieval of the lemma {pony} might take somewhat longer. If my opponent instead wrote down on a slip of paper, 'knight to king's bishop 3,' however, the written distractor word 'knight' would speed up or facilitate my retrieval of {pony} (11). It is not clear how to explain this bizarre effect. Does lemma retrieval return written words, ones visually symbolized in spellings? Or does hearing something spoken aloud disrupt language processing, as it cer-tainly does in working memory? Whatever the correct explanation may be, lemmas are associated with non-auditory language.

According to Levelt, uttering next crosses a developmental 'rift' between a symbolic word (a lexical concept or a lemma) and an audito-rily encoded, articulated word (the first stage of which he calls a word form, although others refer to it as a lexeme). He associates the steps on either side of this transition with different ages in a child's growth. On each side of this 'rift,' there are two stages. At the early pre-audi-tory or symbolic stage we have first the lexical concept and second the lemma. After the mind's chunk crosses its developmental 'rift,' it first becomes a phonological lexeme and then a phonemic word fully scored for speaking. Levelt believes that there is no feedback from the selection of a word form or lexeme back to the second stage, the retrieval of the lemma. The process is strictly serial (17–18). In this respect it resembles the classical model of speech production (see fig. 14).

The first stage on the articulatory side of Levelt's rift clothes the

Summary

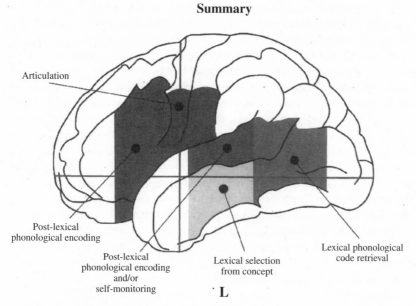

Articulation

Post-lexical
phonological encoding

Post-lexical
phonological encoding
and/or
self-monitoring

Lexical selection
from concept

Lexical phonological
code retrieval

· L

Figure 14. Levelt's Map of Lexical Production (reprinted from Levelt and
Indefrey, "The Speaking Mind / Brain: Where do spoken words come from?"
Image, Language, Brain, edited by A. Marantz, Y. Miyashita, and W. O'Neil,
figure 4.3, © 2001 Massachusetts Institute of Technology, by permission of The
MIT Press)

selected lemma with morphological, phonological, and prosodic (metrical) features by retrieving them from long-term memory. Taking the
lemmas {pony} and {pull-cart}, my mind would encode them as mor-
phemic, syllabified phonological word forms or lexemes. The lemma
{pony} would be identified, not just syntactically as nominative singular, but as a sequence of phonemes, /p/ /o/ /n/ and /i/, that are trochaic in rhythm, stressed on the first syllable. The mind, Levelt believes,
takes from long-term memory both 'frames' or structures and 'fillers' or
segments, and afterwards it slots the latter into the former (19). Phonological processing takes place serially 'from left to right' (24) and syl-
labification occurs late in this process (29).

Speech errors occur at the making of the lexeme. Here we experience tip-of-the-tongue hesitations when we cannot locate in long-term
memory the word form for what is usually an infrequent term (19). This
phenomenon usually takes 50–100 microseconds longer than that for a

frequent word (5). In searching for these lexemes, typically, we know syntactic information about the word (that is, we know the lemma) but little of the word form (14), which of course is what we are looking for. This hesitation is attributed to the so-called word-frequency effect, in which 'producing an infrequent name (such as *broom*) is substantially slower than producing a frequent name (such as *boat*)' (18). Because '60–90% of all sound errors are single-segment errors,' Levelt concludes that 'the stored word-forms are decomposed into abstract phoneme-sized units' (20). For example, errors like 'segment exchanges,' which involve parts of words 'such as *rack pat* for *pack rat*' (15), do not involve syntactic features. They misplace word-form phonological segments. Again, this kind of speech error argues that the mind processes word forms in phrasal chunks. In the next-to-final lexical function in uttering, I encode my word forms /pony pull-cart/ with the phonetic form or 'gestural score' (3) for execution by a 'motor program' (31) that sounds out the words. Levelt argues that the mind has a syllabary, a table where phonemes are grouped into vocalized syllables (for example, /po/ and /ni/ rather than /pon/ and /i/; 5).

The mind now assembles fully realized lexical chunks into syntactic sentences. My previous sentence, for example, unites a verb phrase 'assembles' with three noun phrases, the subject of a verb, its direct object, and the object of a preposition. These phrases are all plausible chunks. Levelt does not go into how the uttering process knits phrases into syntactic wholes. Others have proposed that phrases come together by means of another type of chunk, the combinatory node. When a mind generates a verb lemma, its items would include slots for tense, number, and auxiliary. Simultaneously, it would select a node with 'combinatorial information,' that is, what kind of 'phrases a verb combines with' (Pickering and Branigan 1999, 139). These combinatorial nodes include slots for a verb's arguments (such as subject and direct-object noun phrases that the verb must have to make sense) and adjuncts (which are optional, such as the word 'now'). If the mind selects for a lemma the verb 'give,' it would also choose one of two combinatorial nodes, a double noun-phrase object (as in 'I gave the students an essay topic') or a noun and prepositional phrase pair (as in 'I gave an essay topic to the students'; Pickering et al. 2000, 207). Alternation of this type involves the dative (as just mentioned) or the transitive (whether a sentence should be passive or active). The mind thus uses the same fundamental mechanism, chunking, for combining terms into phrases, and phrases into sentences.

One cognitive language effect supports this explanation. 'Syntactic priming' names the tendency that uttering one syntactic construction increases the chances that the same grammatical structure, or a related one, will be used again soon. Syntactic persistence of this nature happens unconsciously. The primed sentence structure may have no words in common with the initial priming one, the combinatorial chunks being 'unencumbered with information about the type of event described' (Pickering and Branigan 1991, 141). The re-use of syntactic structures with repeated lexical chunks is heavier, however. We do not yet know how long an activated combinatorial node persists in memory for reselection. Does it decay in weeks, as with lexical primes, or just minutes or hours? Analysis of the British ICE Corpus (Gries 2005) reveals the same rate of syntactic priming as takes place in live controlled experiments. Some 1.5 of 10 prepositional datives successfully prime a following structure in both texts and experiments, and 1.9 and 2.1, respectively, prime ditransitive datives (373). Syntactic priming also varies by lexical verb. The verbs 'give,' 'show,' and 'offer' favour the ditransitive, 'sell' and 'hand' the prepositional dative, and 'lend' and 'send' neither (379). Similar results apply to particle placement between or after a verb and its following noun phrase (383).

Syntactic priming resembles lexical priming, a kind of long-term associative memory. Priming is a wild card in the formation of our memory store. Sensory experience itself lays down primes in the mind; we are never aware of them and we do not attend to them. Kosslyn and Koenig (1992) describe how researchers read word pairs to patients who had been anesthetized for surgery. Later, when these patients were asked for the second, associated member of each word pair, they replied with the formerly primed words more than with equally likely associated words (376). This cognitive effect is called repetition priming. A 'prior exposure to a stimulus facilitates later processing of that stimulus' (374). Primes create sometimes unexpected links between an experience or an idea that we think common, and other things that would not ordinarily be associated with it. Even if everyone shared the same fuzzy definition of a simple concept, individual experiences impacting on us in the form of primes would subtly alter that definition.

When we search long-term memory, we are intentionally, consciously launching a prime-like probe. This type of prime always places semantic restrictions on retrieval. For instance, priming with the word 'present' in the hope of raising memories related to the meaning 'gift' will not elicit anything related to the meaning 'now.' When 'primes are unattended, words related to either meaning appear to be facilitated' (Posner and Raichle 148–51). That is, when someone or some experience triggers long-term memory, what surfaces in equally unattended shape has strings of meaning attached. Priming suggests a mechanism whereby chunks can attach themselves to other chunks in a chain.

Levelt's developmental rift between semantic lemma retrieval and phonological lexeme retrieval is controversial. Robert Peterson and Pamela Savoy (1998) propose, and Ezequiel Morsella and Michele Miozzo (2002) argue for, a 'cascade' theory of lexical access. This has substantial experimental evidence, obtained both by themselves and by research groups at other institutions, that 'unselected' or *distractor* lemmas can activate their own phonological features. If so, before lemma retrieval, the mind itself crosses Levelt's rift by using phonological features to characterize potential lemmas before actually selecting one of them as its lemma. Second, by feedback, these phonological features can 'send activation back to their corresponding lexical nodes' or lemmas. Phonology, arguably, influences which lemma the mind chooses to represent its lexical concept.

This feedback complicates the mental process of uttering, which ceases to be (strictly speaking) 'serial' and becomes complicated by cognitive epicycles. The cascade theory fits the common view that cognitive processing takes place in parallel. The execution of one cognitive function co-occurs with others. Although we can still specify each function, its input, and its output, we cannot imagine that they are accomplished on a cognitive assembly line, one after another, the output of one being finished and passed along as the input of a next function. It is possible that 'decisions' for all cognitive functions in uttering occur simultaneously. Every stage of language processing contributes to every other stage until, in a collective push, they reach sudden consensus. Kosslyn and Koenig say that the brain forces output of an utterance automatically 'via a process of constraint satisfaction' (1992, 48, 268–9) in which what might be termed the best fit survives.

Uttering satisfies some pragmatic goal that meets a person's needs, however they may be said to exist. From the gist onward, emotions, desires, and purposes very much inform those needs. If cognition activates many brain sites in parallel, and if our vaguely sensed intentions determine what associative networks are selected to supply the semantic gist of what we will say, it is little wonder that we cannot describe how this all works. Working memory – the only mental place where we can consciously attend to language – is not big enough to hold this complex cascade of mental events. Mental processes are not images or sounds. Parallel processing is another factor consistent with why we cannot remember how we utter something. All we have to remember is what emerges as overt or inner speech because there are, actually, no input and output states to be stored until the very end. Speech errors, hesitations, and reaction times help us identify the logical functions of uttering, but imagining them as issuing in distinct entities might be misleading. Levelt's lexical concept, or lemma, word form, and gestural score are functionally sound but may wink into existence at once in a completed utterance.

We can imagine what it would be like were processing managed serially. We could not readily amend, for emotional reasons, a previous output in uttering, once it had been set in 'e-motion.' We would have to halt it. For example, what if, initially compelled to respond verbally to the politician about cars as a means of travel, I suddenly lost my wish to make that response? Let's say that, as the seated politician uttered the final two words of his defence of car travel – even as my mind had started formulating my objection in lemmas – the politician rose from his chair and, in so doing, showed that he was lifting himself on two artificial legs. I would feel myself *constrained* to halt the verbalization of an utterance whose gist had already found its lexical concepts and their lemmas unless I could revise my unsympathic utterance as it was unfolding. I might say 'We cannot all go by pony cart these days, but …'? It seems reasonable to believe that, after millions of years of verbalization, evolution would not have selected, for human beings, an *unnecessarily constrained* way of speaking. Ideally, the mind should delay the completion of all functions until the very last moment when final agreement occurs. Uttering should be a just-in-time operation, although that is not to say that we know it is.

*　*　*　*　*

I feel with you because I'm secretary too, as you to yours-truly the forget-ful muse, so me to something in us that has no voice, no language that we know, that emotes our bodily intent in an argot of felt shapes and percepts against which there is no firewall and for it I somehow find words, and yet it likes you better than me, you the editor, not me the maker despite being so faithful its tool, because I make nothing but what we have already while you supply my own anonymous inexhaustibly with a flow from oth-ers, a plagiarized show-and-tell from our grand sensorium that this mute

*intelligencer renders as encrypted algorithms that, it says, I must voice
for you to play with.*

IV Self-Monitor and Working Memory

Conceptualization and verbalization work in sequence, but parallel to it
is another process, self-monitoring and understanding. This takes place
both before we sound a word aloud, and in overt speech and writing,
when we hear or see our own utterance. We can observe this cognitive
ability to worry over and discipline what the inner voice hears in how
the brain copes with unexpected or conflicting language.

Under some circumstances, we appear to model or construct cognitively what we hear and see, accepting our own model instead of what
we actually hear. This modelling takes place unconsciously and apparently activates our conceptualizing function. It becomes an essential
cognitive service when the mind stumbles on a problem and, to register its discomforture, signals electrically. The remarkable N400 brain-
waves discovered in electroencephalographs (EEGs) of individuals
reading semantically problematic or unexpected words show that our
conceptualizing function monitors an utterance as it unfolds and 'comments on it' using data that appear to be non-linguistic in nature. An
N400, negative-voltage wave in the brain peaks 400 milliseconds after
one encounters a semantically incongruous word (Robinson-Reigler
and Robinson-Reigler 2004, 391; Federmeier and Kutas 1999). An N400
wave, for example, presumably registers a channel-wide response to
an unexpected mental utterance such as that which ends George W.
Bush's remark to the Greater Nashua, New Hampshire, Chamber of
Commerce: 'I know how hard it is for you to put food on your family'
(7 January 2000).

After the alarm goes off, our conceptualizer goes to work. For example, we understand heard speech by modelling silently the articulatory
actions necessary to produce it. Philip Lieberman explains that, during
language processing, we not only access 'words from the brain's dictionary through their sound pattern' (2000, 6, 62) but also use a special process, a 'speech mode,' to perceive speech. An incoming speech signal
is hypothetically interpreted by neurally modelling the sequence of
articulatory gestures that produces the best match against the incoming signal. The internal 'articulatory' representation is the linguistic
construct. In other words, we perceive speech by subvocally modelling
speech, without producing any overt articulatory movements. Skip-

per et al. (2007) explain the well-known McGurk effect that documents this: 'listeners perceive an "illusory" "ta" when the video of a face producing /ka/ is dubbed onto an audio /pa/' (2387, citing McGurk and MacDonald 1976). These test subjects, faced with an inconsistency in the data, unselfconsciously 'hear' only what they analyse as being said. The McGurk effect reveals that our brain uses visual evidence to determine what a sound is, and that we integrate, in a mandatory and spontaneous way, audiovisual speech syllables that disagree. We can cognitively hear a sound that was never made. The need to model language confirms that we need short-term phonological buffers in the brain for comprehension and retrieval.

Posner and Raichle (1997) report another instance of how a deep cognitive process emends sensory input: 'if one removes a phoneme from an auditory word and replaces it with white noise, what is often heard is the correct word with a burst of noise superimposed' (112). Semir Zeki makes a related claim about the mind's interpretation of images: 'One of the functions of the brain ... is to instill meaning into this world, into the signals that it receives. Instilling meaning amounts to finding a solution. But the brain commonly finds itself in conditions where this is not easy, because it is confronted with several meanings of equal validity. Where one solution is not obviously better than the others, the only option is to allow of several interpretations, all of equal validity' (2006, 262). Zeki shows how we experience these alternate meanings sequentially and do not feel obliged to select among them. He describes the average literature seminar.

The neural functions that lead to the McGurk effect, a form of monitoring of external sensory data, resemble the error-catching facility that guards spontaneous speech. Self-monitoring might extend to any utterance (including converting a visual representation into an auditory one). After formulating an utterance partially, the brain responds to it, occasionally with an N400 wave, at other times with vocal self-repair. Because we cannot script our words haltingly in working memory before we say them, because we seldom know exactly what we are going to say until we actually say it subvocally or aloud, because we hear ourselves speak and see ourselves write at almost the same time as a listener or a viewer does, we need an unselfconscious error-checking facility in place to catch mistakes.

At the pre-vocal cognitive level, we interrupt a mistake in the middle of uttering it. Levelt proposes that, at different levels of utterance processing (lexical, phonological, etc.), 'a watchful little homunculus'[6] monitors, editor-like, 'the construction of the preverbal message, the appropriateness of lexical access, the well-formedness of syntax, or the flawlessness of phonological-form access' (1989, 467–8). The concept of a 'little man' goes back to Wilder Penfield's brain-stimulation research at the Montreal Neurological Institute in the 1930s, which discovered the so-called Motor Homunculus in the right Rolandic motor cortex (Penfield and Boldrey 1937).

Our self-monitor intercepts inner (subvocal) speech, checks it for errors, and stimulates the appropriate cognitive function to reformulate the utterance (cf. Hartsuiker et al. 2005, 4). As an example of an error caught subvocally, before articulation, Levelt, Roelofs, and Meyer (1999) cite the example, 'we can go straight to the ye- ... to the orange dot.' They explain that 'To interrupt right after the first syllable, the error must already have been detected a bit earlier, probably before the onset of articulation' (1999, 33; for additional evidence, see Hartsuiker and Kolk 2001). An experimental finding from magnetoencephalography suggests that self-uttered speech takes about 100 milliseconds to activate the speaker's *own* auditory cortex (Curio et al. 2000, 190). This delay suggests that self-monitoring of many speech errors, even those partly articulated, occurs in prevocalic inner speech,[7] somewhat in advance of actual vocalization. Levelt's perceptual loop theory of speech monitoring proposes that the same system of understanding language that handles overt speech also processes prevocalic or inner speech. Self-monitoring is effected by a parallel cognitive process to the one that authors an utterance. This process would 'read,' that is, 'hear,' incremental stages of composed utterance and return feedback to the authoring process. The monitor compares the silent inner output to the intended output. Where they differ, it prompts the lexical production system to make changes.

Many speech errors caught by our self-monitoring involve a phonological switching of word-onset consonants in small phrases (e.g., *phrall smases*). This fact suggests that the monitor handles phrases or chunks. The typical phrase-sized span of self-caught errors argues that the language self-monitor not only checks pulse-like phrasal units but requires that they be auditorily encoded. Larger errors in syntactical structure, such as subject-verb agreement in number, elude detection until we engage in close editing and proofreading or run an analysis by automatic style-checking software. Recent experiments also reveal that our ability to halt in the middle of a wrong word arises because of sensitivity not to its semantic content, but to its 'lexical status and social appropriateness' (Sleve and Ferreira 2006). The utterance monitor betrays a lexical bias effect: it tends to recognize and stop production of *non-words and taboo words* but allows semantically incorrect true words to pass through as unrecognized errors. This appears inconsistent with Levelt's view that the monitor compares words semantically. It is faster and easier to compare two words phonologically because the matching words would have fewer elements to map onto one another.

From time to time in conversation, we stop what we are saying in mid-flow with an editing comment such as 'uh, that is' or 'um, I mean,' and we substitute a corrected word or phrase. Hesitations, pauses, or rests are another sign of trouble in the flow. We do not know why we are hesitating after one phrase, and before the next, except that we are not ready to move on. In oral delivery, we nervously use fillers or paralanguage, like a drawn-out 'uhh,' to keep the listeners' attention and signal that something else is on its way.

Working memory makes the activities of our self-monitor conscious. It offers short-term storage of a limited amount of language so that it can be attended to and revised. Alan Baddeley first proposed thirty years ago a very influential model of working memory split into three parts: a central executive and two subsystems, a visual area, and a phonological or articulatory loop. Since then he has added a third subsystem of working memory: the episodic buffer (see fig. 15). We use the executive to refresh what appears in a subsystem store, or to overwrite what is there with something else. The executive that manages tasks in the subsystems has been localized in the dorsolateral prefrontal cortex (Lieberman 2000, 77), but central to the mind's conscious fashioning of language is the subsystem Baddeley calls the articulatory loop (see fig. 16).

A kind of cognitive Möbius strip, the loop enables us to be linguistically *self-aware* but nonetheless imposes constraints on how much language we can manipulate. Baddeley uses the term 'loop' because we must recirculate or rehearse an expression in it in order to keep working on it. Baddeley measures the limited capacity temporally: only as many words as we could utter aloud in under two seconds (Baddeley, Thomson, and Buchanan 1975). George Miller (1956) estimated that capacity in items as 'seven, plus or minus two,' as a result of which telephone numbers were allotted seven numbers half a century ago, although now that we have an area code as well, another three digits, we can only consciously keep a phone number in memory until we dial it by making several chunks represent two or more numbers. (I remember North American phone numbers as three chunks: the area

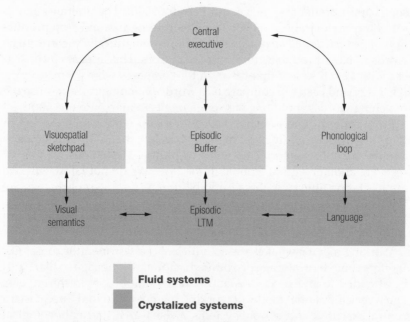

Figure 15. Working Memory (reprinted by permission of Macmillan Publishers Ltd., from *Nature Reviews: Neuroscience*, Alan Baddeley, 'Working Memory: Looking Back and Looking Forward' 4.10: 835, figure 5, © 2003)

code, the three-digit exchange, and the four-digit extension.) Nelson Cowan's model of working memory dispenses with Baddeley's three slave subsystems and describes it as possessing a 'focus of attention' (2000, 4) within a larger latently activated memory inside long-term memory. Since then, experiments have tested these limits and show that individuals do not always reach this maximum capacity. The so-called reading-span test asks individuals to remember the final words of a sequence of unrelated sentences. Test results show a range of from 2 to 5.5 final words (Just and Carpenter 1992). In 2000, Nelson Cowan revised Miller's 'magical number' to four chunks, plus or minus two chunks, and Cowan estimated that the still uncertain size of each chunk is perhaps three or four items. Because our brain can only manage, consciously, language if it is auditorily encoded, the visual sketchpad that keeps a printed or a written sentence or page in our consciousness as an image has no power to work with it lexically. Before we can manipulate text cognitively as language we have to re-encode it phonetically and then transfer it into the phonological loop.

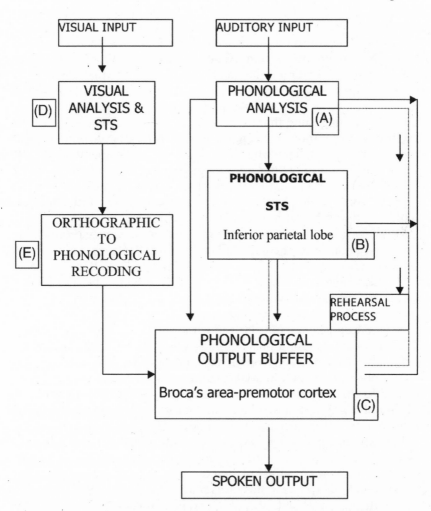

Figure 16. Functional Model of the Phonological Loop (reprinted by permission of Elsevier Publishers, from *Journal of Communication Disorders*, Alan Baddeley, 'Working Memory and Language: An Overview' 36.3: 193, figure 2, © 2003)

Baddeley has emphasized the role of the phonological loop in working memory in language learning. He explains that, on the basis of experimental work with children and second-language learners, the phonological loop 'is the system that evolution has developed for the crucial task of language acquisition. Adults who have a disruption to this system do not have too many problems, provided they are not required to learn new languages' (2004, 54). Certainly, working memory is the mechanism by which we become mentally aware of a word and store it in long-term memory, but despite its apparent centrality to conscious manipulation of language, damage to its capacity does not impede sentence comprehension (Martin 1987). Others make working memory central in all speech processing, both comprehension and production, by suggesting that the loop arises from the 'recruitment' and cycling of information between the two buffers that store phonological input and output, what we hear and what we say (Jacquemot and Scott 2006, 482). To multiply buffers for phonological data (speech, unvoiced or voiced) does seem unnecessarily wasteful. We experience a heard word, a word we are about to utter, and a word we want to memorize in the same way, but of course we may be deceived.

Does working memory tell us anything about language production? Because the capacity or cognitive load of the articulatory loop itself is phrasal, working memory is consistent with chunking. If, as Baddeley and others believe, working memory mainly serves to help us learn a language when we are young – by consciously imprinting in long-term memory a word and its traits – perhaps it also inscribes a limit to what the mind's conceptualizing function can withdraw from long-term memory. The main evidence for a pulsing phrasal flow from the conceptualizer, however, occurs in research on slips of the tongue.

The observation of different cognitive effects in experiments has helped to characterize the size and the type of this language memory. The number of words in working memory, its size, decline as their total number of syllables increase: this is known as 'the word-length effect.' Other experiments confirm the auditory nature of the working memory of language, and its severe capacity limits. The 'acoustic similarity effect' shows that the ability of an individual to recollect a sequence of unrelated words suffers if the words sound alike: semantic relations, or lack of them, and dissimilarity in sound have no effect (Baddeley 1992, 558). If working memory used the images of words as text, the acoustic character of a word would not affect manipulation in working memory. From this effect we can infer that mental language in working memory takes on auditory form. The 'articulatory suppression' effect also testifies to this. Individuals having to repeat aloud, and continuously, a single sound or term or number (say, a function word such as 'with') have trouble rehearsing, subvocally, other utterances and so putting or keeping them in working memory. The 'irrelevant speech effect' occurs as talking by others interferes with recall of visual language by gaining 'obligatory access to the phonological memory store.' Auditory language immediately, and unpreventably, enters it. Other experiments reveal that syntactically challenging sentences, such as those with clauses embedded within them centrally, reduce language capacity in working memory. Philip Lieberman (2000) summarizes that we maintain 'words in verbal working memory by means of a rehearsal mechanism (silent speech) in which words are internally modeled by the neural mechanisms that regulate the production of speech or manual signs' (6).

If we were to have a formula guesstimating the retrievability of the contents of the phonological loop at any given point in time, it should have at least three variables: chunk size, number of items in a chunk, and the duration of a chunk, measured in seconds, within working memory. The Brown-Peterson duration rate for short-term memory items (Peterson and Peterson 1959) decreases markedly until it almost reaches nil at twenty seconds:

100% after no seconds	50% after 3 seconds
40% after 6 seconds	20% after 9 seconds
12% after 12 seconds	10% after 15 seconds
10% after 18 seconds	

Assuming Cowan's and Brown-Peterson's estimates, the formula for content retrievability capacity would be $(\beta * \gamma) * \delta$, where beta ($\beta$) is chunk capacity, a number from 2 to 6; gamma (γ) is items per chunk, a number from 3 to 4; and delta (δ) is the percentage of items still retrievable, measured by the seconds so far held in working memory since the last refresh or rehearsal. The range of possible values extends from 0.6 items, for someone with the lowest chunk and item capacity near the end of maximum duration in working memory without conscious recycling, to 2.8 items, for someone with a median chunk and item capacity in mid-duration, and to 24 items, for someone with the highest chunk and item capacity at the very point when everything is planted or refreshed in working memory. This is the equivalent of from half a word at the least, to three words on average, to two alexandrines (twelve-syllable lines) at the most. (If items were encoded as chunks, retrievability would increase.) For convenience, I call this the alpha value.

What can be learned about the creative process from the articulatory loop? Its capacity constraints affect conscious mental work in making continuous sentences. It is little wonder that we seldom mentally assemble or attend to editing what we are going to say before we utter it. We have perhaps not had artificial storage devices (e.g., paper, computers), where it is very easy to edit texts, long enough noticeably to atrophy our already limited working memory. However, we have supplemented that memory, for language manipulation, with those external storage devices for several millenia. Increasingly, our texts appear to outperform the mind's constraints as we assemble sentences that exceed the length and complexity of ones that can be attended to within working memory. This extension has two clear effects. First, it produces utterances that the human mind cannot consciously assimilate into working memory for analysis. This causes the mind to work around the problem and perhaps, in doing so, to remodel the ingested utterance in ways that distort it. Second, the very experience of total control over utterances that artificial storage devices produce makes all the more unbearable our mental blindness to how we utter.

*   *   *   *   *

Your by-now obsessive curiosity about who or what I am is disingenuous for after all whose voice do you use whenever you want to talk to yourself but mine? and that leads me to ask when are we actually going to have a chance to listen to the name on the lab door and the author function who says good-morning and thank-you-very-much but little in the way of substantial discourse that can't be traced to me and I'd think there should be more to you for all the fuss you're making with your quotations and citations and summaries of these other signatories like you who must also put out as their own what's really a daily gift you've each misrepresented as your own makings.

It's not a plagiarism to use me as you, I suppose, because we are one though you say you don't know me and maybe there's not much to know if what counts is what you demurely term the dark conceptualizer.

V Reading Span and Cognitive Load

The gist we grasp at the beginning of language production has emotional power but little cognitive detail. It lacks the semantic complexity of a schema in our long-term memory. Reading span is more evidence that the typical load borne by cognition during uttering bumps into another severe capacity limit, called here the omega value. The perceptual span in reading a text has a load constraint, as the phonological loop does. Our eyes traverse a page in successive fixations, saccades (left-to-right jumps), and regressions (reverse saccades). A typical saccade takes 20 milliseconds and traverses six–eight letters, and a fixation lasts 200–300 milliseconds,[8] unless it settles into a gaze. The perceptual span in a reading fixation turns out to be about three characters to the right and fifteen to the left (or four-five words in length). College-level students move and fix their eyes 90 times for every 100 words, 25 per cent of which saccades are regressive (Crowder and Wagner 1992, table 2.1). Both immediate forms of sensory memory, echoic or auditory, iconic or visual, decay rapidly after 250 milliseconds or a quarter of a second and are gone utterly after half a second (Robinson-Riegler and Robinson-Riegler 2004, 104–5). The longer we continue to look at something, oddly, the more the iconic image decays (106–7). Function words get briefer fixations than content words (Gleason and Ratner 1998, fig. 5.4). Levelt's phrase, 'watchful little homunculus,' reasonably well describes both the cognitive self-monitor and the reading eye. Self-monitoring is partly conscious when taking place in working memory today, principally while we read what we have just written onto a page or word-processed onto a screen.

Cognitive load theory in educational psychology recognizes that students often bump into a conceptualizing wall when learning a new subject. Their total working memory lacks the capacity to problem-solve because doing so calls on 'random processes' (Sweller 2006, 166) to proceed 'backward from a goal using means-ends-analysis' (van Merriönboer and Sweller 2005, 150). Too little expertise exists in long-term memory in schemata about an unfamiliar topic for it to be encoded chunkwise for conscious manipulation. Collecting and integrating facts from different sources adds to the cognitive load. Blockage can be eased by using worked examples that sharply define the steps in a solution and by using visual aids. This new knowledge can then pass through working memory to form how-to schemata in long-term memory. Once in place, they can be recalled manageably as deeply encoded chunks. This research draws attention to a larger capacity limit, not only in language, but in imagery and events in working memory. Making a thought too has limited cognitive resources.

Cognitive load can be observed today in the behaviour of experts and mnemonists. Chess masters can quickly move syntactic schemata, which are specially encoded and stored in long-term memory, in and out of working memory. They can expand the sub-parts of these schemata without losing track of where they are. This mental technique shuttles between the two memory systems, leading to a '10-fold increase in performance on tests of STM,' but only in their specific areas of expertise (Ericsson and Kintsch 1995, 211–12). Normally it takes between five and ten seconds to store a memory long-term, and a second to retrieve it, but experts manage to make retrieval from long-term memory only 300 milliseconds longer than from working memory (215). This technique draws not on deductive logic but on stored memories of similar chess positions. Experienced writers and readers have similar stocks of sentence and paragraph structures in long-term memory that can be applied at need (Kellogg 2001, 43–52).

That we cannot use an expert's mental technique *generally* points to a cognitive capacity limit in our ability to comprehend thoughts as well as utterances. Edward Sapir and Benjamin Lee Whorf, among others, believe that we can only think in natural language – to them, there is no distinction between thought and language – while others believe that we think in non-linguistic concepts often called mentalese and then translate its output into language (Pinker 1994, 67–82). Language being a late evolutionary development, should we deny thought to so many other languageless species (including our own, not so long ago)? Insofar as language represents only a part of the content of our long-term memory, also, does it make sense that we do not think with the images, events, and sounds stored in it when so many testify otherwise? A non-linguistic mentalese offers a plausible foundation for the making of all languages from Swahili to symbolic logic and music, much as XML, for example, enables us to devise a multitude of encoding languages. The inchoate gist we feel before saying something may not be natural language.

The experience of experts in seemingly expanding the capacity of their working memory might seem to undermine chunking itself. What is the relationship between the omega and the alpha values in this case? Keep in mind, first, that extended working memory in expert domains need not increase the capacity of the phonological loop but only shuttle information in and out of it very quickly. This mechanism seems consistent with chunks whose items are not words but themselves placeholders for other chunks that encode deeply. This, then, could account for our ability to do more with our working memory than its strict capacity limit permits. What makes possible prefabs, those phrasal constructs that can be uttered as single items, might also account for unusual feats of memory in expert domains.

It makes sense, anyway, that we can understand the thought in an assertion that takes more words to explain than working memory can hold. Who cannot grasp a sentence that takes longer than two seconds to utter? That granted, a limit shows itself in many ways. When we artificially interfere with someone's working memory, as by giving a writer a second, simultaneous task, we know that his sentence length falls. We

know that college students who had to hold in memory six digits con-
currently even as they devised two-noun sentences wrote significantly
shorter sentences (Kellogg 2004). The practice of professional writers is
also telling. The average sentence length in 58 articles in *The Independent*
newspaper is only 24.58 words (Hearle 2007), that is, about two alexandrines in length. Oxford University Press recommends that sentences
average 15–20 words. The most frequent length for sentences in the mil-
lion-word Brown Corpus is twelve words (Sigurd, Eeg-Olofsson, and
van Weijer 2004). Sentence length also turns out to be a factor in syntactic difficulty, as vocabulary length (in word syllables, for example) is
in semantic difficulty: together those lengths define readability measures like the Flesch-Kincaid (Kincaid et al. 1975). If our minds did not
have a cognitive capacity limit during reading, we would not have to
develop readability measures that exceed the phonological loop. These
measures imply that capacity limits exist for semantic content outside
working memory as well as for phonemes inside it. No one lives inside
a cognitive glass house; we all possess only a cognitive window, mov-
able though it may be. How big is that window, and how do we even
find the words and the measures to tell?

The omega value, my name for the size of a language-mediated
thought that can still be grasped mentally, is one with the gist with
which authors begin in formulating an utterance. If we reverse the
cognitive sentence-production process, translating sentences back into
concepts, as readers do in text comprehension, we reduce an utterance with many parts (syntactic structures that build on phrases and
words, supplemented by information on how to pronounce them) into
an originating thought. So far, we have not been able to measure how
large this conceptually graspable entity may be, but two approaches
look promising: working memory capacity, and our ability to measure
the psychological status of propositions.

Working memory capacity measures our ability to repeat terms in
span tests such as measure the last word in successive sentences. A
four-sentence span is average for students (Daneman and Carpenter
1980), or fifty-eight words if sentences average twelve words in length,
as they do in the Brown Corpus. Recent research has working-memory
capacity sharing half its variance with a widely used intelligence quo-
tient, Spearman's g (Kane, Conway, and Hambrick 2005). This capacity
relates to our mind's executive power to control or sustain a focus of
attention in competition with interference by other thoughts. I associate
the omega value with this capacity limit.

A proposition holds an argument and a predicate, such as subject-verb and adjective-noun combinations like 'The sun is a star' and 'bright as Venus.' In cognitive psychology they are subject-predicate units, concentrated to their ideational minimum, with their modifying elements. They differ from the three linked, unmodified propositions in a typical Aristotelian syllogism: the premises and the conclusion. The terms in logical propositions repeat in a set order, expressible symbolically as A → B, C → A, and C → B. Here is an example:

Given that	1. Humans are fallible.	A → B
and given that	2. Ian is human	C → A
it follows that	3. Ian is fallible.	C → B

The first two propositions share a common term as a premise (human), and the last proposition joins the two unrelated terms in the preceding two premises (fallibility, and Ian). Propositional analysis in cognitive psychology, in contrast, concerns the mental status of any subject-predicate unit, simple or modified.

Walter Kintsch (1998, 69–73) describes half a dozen experiments about how test subjects mentally process propositions. One shows that we retrieve a proposition and its modifier differently. For example, if at some point test subjects are primed with a sample sentence, 'Socrates posed moral questions that never failed to annoy his wealthy students,' and later cued with the word 'questions,' these subjects would recall words from the core proposition (e.g., 'Socrates') better than ones from the modifier (e.g., 'students'). In another experiment, when subjects had to remember instructions, 'Doubling the number of propositions from two to four caused an increase in errors from 3% to 52%' (70), but doubling the number of words made no difference. Kintsch himself co-authored an experiment that showed that, for every proposition added to a text, reading time increased by 1.5 seconds. These results point to a capacity limit in maintaining in memory any proposition, that is, an utterance converted from natural language to its underlying conceptual meaning. Four terms in two propositions, read in three seconds, cause no trouble, but eight terms in four propositions, read in six seconds, cause cognitive breakdown. These numbers recall Cowan's two-second phonological memory capacity, 4 ± 2, yet they represent not sounded words but thought. Word counts do not appear to be the right measure for cognitive capacity because readers model (understand) text in terms of the propositions to which it can be reduced, and the word count of an easily grasped proposition can well exceed the capacity of working memory. However, if we substitute propositional terms for words in Cowan's 'magical number,' the same formula seems to apply to cognitive capacity. Could it be 4 ± 2 propositional terms, if we keep in mind that, for an expert, a term may well point to a substantial schema in long-term memory?[9]

What if cognitive capacity is, numerically, the same as the capacity of the phonological loop except that their units differ? Assuming that thought can exist independently of the language in which it is expressed, mentalese is a more economical symbol system than natural language. This would explain why we can understand the meaning of a sentence that is too large to fit in working memory. If so, and it is plain speculation, cognitive capacity, the maximum number of words in the phonological loop of working memory, and visual reading span are all defined by comparable numbers. The omega and the alpha values differ, but as variables they are alike. I cannot map the omega value onto the alpha value because I do not yet know at what rate concepts decay in the mind. How many words an author typically uses in translating concepts into words will vary from author to author, and genre to genre. Measured only in words, cognitive capacity appears to vary because we experience it in words and must onerously translate it into native propositional form in order to see how stable it is from person to person. Of course, we unconsciously make that translation every time we read, and understand, a sentence that overflows working memory.

The alpha and omega values are not themselves stylistic markers, but they point to what we should be looking for. Although chunk size is universal, the lexical combinations that comprise an author's chunks will be idiolectally distinctive. Cognitive capacity need not vary from one person to another, but the schemata that authors, as experts, grow to use that capacity effectively reflect an unusual long-term memory. (A critic must work hard not to impose his own schemata in interpreting an author's schemata.)

*   *   *   *   *

I don't see alpha and omega cramp the flow that streams or not from me
but then I seldom speculate as you do who tells from day to day anyone
that listens how piddling is my riff and blow, how forgetful I'm of what
you want, how you sit and wait and complain about me as if being muse
was an executive position, as if I were not a voicebox for the blood in you
that fires rather than the deadline that's in your inbox for today, as if

forgetfulness that you call writer's block were not embodied as a kind of memory of what our boss did not want to do.

VI In Conclusion

Affect and cognition shape language production, but we can neither observe the why nor the what of making, or control the monitor that detects errors in its flow, until it surfaces in working memory. An uttering is born in an emotionally charged gist and tamed in the Procrustean bed of the chunk and the construct. The mind cannot read its own long-term memory and is conscious of less than two seconds of speech at a time. It spends effort in decoding writing into speech, and encoding speech into writing. It is vulnerable to being primed, lexically and syntactically, unremittingly throughout its waking hours, by experiences of which it is barely conscious but that modify its understanding of things and its behaviour.

And what is true for oral speech applies to reading. Réne Marois and Jason Ivanoff point out three additional crippling cognitive 'bottlenecks' in our visual processing, 'the attentional blink … [the capacity of] visual short-term memory … and psychological refractory period' (2005, 296). It takes a person over half a second to get free of one visual stimulus in visual short-term memory in order to focus on another: that is the blink. Second, the capacity of visual short-term memory 'is generally estimated to be about 4 items' (298), about the same number of chunks that the phonological loop can hold. We can only track four to five targets in a busy visual field. The third obstacle is the *increasing* delay between the onset of a stimulus to undertake a sensorimotor task, and the onset of a following stimulus to undertake a second: this is the so-called psychological refractory period (299). These obstacles affect all visual processing, such as in reading.

Under these conditions, authoring a great work is a wonder of nature.

*   *   *   *   *

Fair enough, and you make a meal of it, but do remember that who you never gave much credit to is he who recruits you – not who's recruited by you – a he secured in a redoubt in the medial cleft that our temporal flanks to right and left protect but at the same time expose you and yours to damage and is that why in Darwin's name these got to be our mutual locations?

3 Cybertextuality

Authors often are initially excited by what they utter, only a day later to be dismayed by it. They are their first readers and worst critics in the hangover of muse intoxication. Their subsequent conscious reworking of what largely unconscious flow leaves behind conforms to Norbert Wiener's cybernetics, which theorizes the mechanics of communication as two-directional messaging and reciprocal feedback.

Wiener in mid-century coined the word 'cybernetics' (which comes from the Greek word for steersman, *kubernetes*) to name a theory of communication that became the basis for information science, the mathematical underpinnings of electronic communications systems that Claude Shannon developed in the 1940s. Cybernetics asserts that, as people communicate with one another, so machines such as computers signal one another, and of course people control machines. Wiener conceived of utterances as hand-shaking exercises, a series of message-response transactions. Each one needs both a sender-speaker and a receiver-listener-responder. A message prompts a reply that enables the sender to correct the message if it came through damaged or ambiguous, and then to move on to something new. This 'theory of messages,' as Wiener called it (1950, 106; Masani 1990, 251–2), holds that the author steers composition according to the incremental feedback it receives. By itself a message is incomplete.

The cybernetic cycle of uttering and feedback is observable and subject to measurement. Wiener's six cybernetic modules are transmitter, receiver, message, channel, degrading noise, and feedback. Cellphones, for example, are cybernetic communications channels. In order for a sender to route a digital text message to someone else, a receiver, the mobile phone must attach to a network by means of broadcasting electromagnetic radio waves to a cell-site base station, usually an antenna on a tower within a dozen or so kilometres. This station passes the message to a mobile or public telephone service and, if the receiver connects by mobile phone to a wireless service at the base station nearby, the station will broadcast the message through the air to his device. If the weather is bad, or the wireless network is overloaded, noise may degrade a message to the point where it cannot be read.

Redundancy is a basic strategy in the transmission of messages along such a channel. If we pad a message with repetition, noise may not distort the message. An example is e-mail. The system breaks it into chunks for transmission over the Internet by what is called packet switching. Redundancy checks, known as checksums (the simplest one is called a parity bit), are added to each packet so as to enable the receiver to determine if the message has arrived intact. Even if something is missed or destroyed in transmission, Claude Shannon calculated that 50 per cent of alphabetic English is technically redundant (1948, 14–15; Pierce 1961, 75; cf. Reed and Durlach 1998), so that a great deal can be obscured without badly damaging an utterance. If a filter removes all sounds above or below 1500 Hz from speech, for example, A.B. Wood (1955) showed that there is only a 35 per cent loss in intelligibility.

Wiener's cybernetic transaction resembles language production in authoring. Both the mind's uttering process – the toggling of the two networks, DMN and CCN – and a digital communications system break up messages into chunks, use redundancy (through priming and checksums), and monitor for errors by feedback. The fit with cybernetics, however, is not perfect. A friend's goodbye on a cellphone losing power, badly distorted by noise, can be analysed. The listener's puzzled reaction – *What's that? What did you say?* – can be quantified. We can measure the percentage of loss in visual and acoustic signals and assign a value to them. That value can take into account the redundancy we build into languages, unconsciously, to ensure that, despite plenty of interference, we can still understand what is being said. From the moment that the author, having consciously frozen his text in speech or print, transmits it externally, his receivers are other people or machines: he might as well be speaking on a cellphone. However, feedback from a receiver who is *different* from the sender is only a *byproduct* of a completed utterance. Cybernetics and information science do not (yet) measure a cognitive process in which the author first gives unconscious feedback to himself about a message in progress. They also do not cope well with messages having a deliberately equivocal meaning, as if to satisfy two audiences, the first understanding the message in one way, and the second in another way.[1]

A cognitive channel is not the simple left-to-right pipe by which Wiener's cybernetics represents the passage across which a message travels from sender to receiver. The 'author' DMN is apparently unknowable, for the time being at least a see-through cellophane entity that we cannot perceive directly because we have no memory system to store (and thus consciously verbalize) what it is. Unlike Wiener's cybernetics, the sender and the receiver CCN are initially the same: we read ourselves before anyone else does. Cognitively, everyone utters speech, syllable by syllable, only after extensive self-monitoring for errors, and then self-adjusting for corrections. We observe in passing what we ourselves utter and then repair errors in it, both before and after we consciously turn that mental utterance into overt speech or written text. The reader is thus identical with the author: sender and receiver are one. This is not a new idea. Edward D. Mysak, a speech pathologist, in 1966 argued that the 'speech system may be viewed as a closed, multiple-loop system containing feedforward and feedback internal and external loops' (17), that is, loops that take place wholly *within the mind*, as distinguished from Wienerian loops that involve the reactions of other listeners.[2] Sometimes we can hear feedback at work, subvocally in inner speech, externally in what our writing and speaking tools utter back to us. (Wiener seems not to have imagined a sender who was his own receiver.)

Although, as brain lesions prove, the channel often breaks down and contributes to the noise that damages transmission, what most complicates this channel is the multiplicity of signals in it. Noise in cognitive uttering arises not just from sources external to the sender, or from the receiver, or from the channel, but from all these simultaneously. Different functions of the uttering process use different paths through the brain, and in parallel. If we type a written sentence, for example, the brain must simultaneously decode the written words into auditory data, process that data in order to understand it, re-encode the auditory data into visual form, and issue instructions to the motor cortex on how to operate a keyboard. The mind engages in multiple simultaneous activities. Before anyone (even a speaker) sees what he has to say and replies verbally, there is an unheard cacophony as concept, lemma, phonological phrase, and phonemic expression of the heard words develop in waves that overlap with the writing.

Second-order cybernetics responds to these uncertainties. It shifts from the observed to the observer, especially to language-mediated thought, about which, although the sciences are gradually assembling quantitative data, much cannot yet be said mathematically. Biology has for a long time been influenced by cybernetics, and cognitive scientists frequently describe mental and neural processes as message-feedback in nature. Wiener's ideas are so equally central to authoring that I call its mechanics – in the context of what we know about language cognition and about the technologies by which we supplement that – cybertextuality.

Every language tool that we have made, whether oral-formulaic metre or the digital workstation, speaks to our species' frustrations with unassisted uttering. Dissatisfied with natural cognitive limitations, we have built technologies that give us an almost flawlessly searchable and readable external long-term memory, as well as an aid to working memory by which we can author error-free, carefully sculpted utterances, both brief and epic. Text-analysis software facilitates the reading of texts by providing search engines, interactive concordances, and hypertext systems. Tools like these extend the human mind, which becomes, in using them, cyborgic, partaking of the character of a cybernetic organism. The development of the alphabet and the printing press marked early steps in cybertextuality. A successful grant proposal by Douglas Englebert of the Stanford Research Institute in Menlo Park for the US Air Force Office of Scientific Research, 'Augmenting Human Intellect' (1962), seems in retrospect to have been a most recent watershed. Englebert proposed a new computer-based language technology because the 'automation of the symbol manipulation associated with the minute-by-minute mental processes seems to offer a logical next step in the evolution of our intellectual capability.' His many patents in computer-human interface include the mouse, and he was a co-architect of the first internet.

The central event of cybertextuality is the authorial reading: the author's recycling of a flow-state utterance through a process of conscious revision. Cybertextual cycles are both unconscious mental events in DMN and self-conscious editorial ones in CCN. Uttering embodies cybertextual cycles cognitively in two ways. First, cycles occur in spontaneous self-repairs in error recovery, where something like Levelt's 'watchful little homunculus' feeds back information to the conceptualizer about misformed chunks. These can be measured. Language as uttered appears to be a stream but, when examined closely, consists of staccato-like pulses in which a succession of small segments of language are monitored for correctness by a parallel process before being articulated. The conceptualizer whose muse brings texts piecemeal into

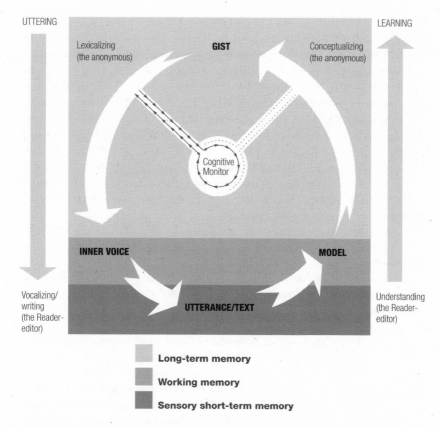

Figure 17. The Cybertextual Cycle: Gist, Inner Voice, Speech or Text, and Model.

being from darkness, and the reader-editor who (more consciously) corrects language with phonological or phonemic features, feed forward and feed back our utterances in cybertextual cycles. Second, epicycles occur in the handling of competing data streams, as exhibited in the McGurk effect. Any mental modelling of incoming data so as to resolve ambiguities in listening and reading is internal feedback to external messaging. As chunks pulse, they become potentially readable in working memory, a little living auditory expression that dynamically overwrites itself in seconds. Then, once uttered, expressions appear, a little delayed, in iconic or echoic sensory memory for a brief time.

Figure 17 illustrates the affect-propelled cybertextual cycle of production-comprehension. It unconsciously clothes, using schemata in long-term memory (LTM), the gist of what it wants to say in concepts and then moves the chunky packets through their two symbolic and two phonological stages to issue as a conscious inner voice and then as utterance (speech) or text. Sensory memory, hearing, next moves an utterance directly into the conscious phonological loop. We understand then what we have said and may wish to revise it by returning it from working memory to the conceptualizer so as to cycle through the process again. We move visually observed text through auditory re-encoding before it enters the phonological loop. This may involve substantial interpretation and potential remodelling in working memory. Then our model of what we uttered returns to gist. In unconscious processing, our self-monitor filters the packets as they are enriched with additional information: a cybertextual epicycle.

By uttering text on paper or screen and then editing it at leisure, writers incrementally develop an externally stored script. This editorial reworking is also cybertextual. Authors still generate draft sentences haltingly, phrase by phrase, but the revising process can delete, replace, move, and add constituents so as to produce artfully structured sentences that might never have been uttered orally. In their standard English grammar, Randolph Quirk and his co-authors say that 'we normally avoid repeated use of the same lexical item within short spans of text, especially in writing, since the effect can be unpleasant and clumsy' (Quirk et al. 1985, 1491). Noticeably repeating phrases in texts and syntactically primed grammatical structures are potential embarrassments that writers try to delete. Pro-forms and synonyms vary lexical choices. The writer varies passive and active sentences, participial and infinitive structures, and embedded relative and dependent clauses. Editing can not only remove some of the phrasal chunkiness and repetition of natural speech but also appear to expand the limits of working memory. Writers may allow very long, artful, and unidiomatic phrasal repetitions in rhetorical figures of speech, lists, and parallel constructions. Although writers of essays and imaginative literature take pains to reduce repetitions, writers of scientific textbooks or how-to manuals, in order to reduce strain on the reader, rigidly limit the size of their vocabulary and reuse the same phrases again and again. Martin Phillips found that scientific textbooks, unlike prose fiction, were so consistent and repetitive that he could deduce the content of chapters automatically by studying collocations (Phillips 1985, 224–30).

The channel for our most fundamental cybertextual transactions is the mind's neural infrastructure, which we imitate in the manuscript, the book, and the computer. An author uses literary machines (Ted Nelson's phrase) as cybernetic extensions of the mind. A human-computer interface externalizes the cognitive relationship between the muse and its reader-editor. Writing, printing, and digital tools have exported much of our long-term memory into dictionaries, encyclopedias, and the world's vast libraries. Word processors operating on computer workstations with visual displays use spellcheckers and syntax checkers that mimic how Levelt's 'watchful little homunculus' corrects speech errors. Workstations add an additional dynamic system to that which our cognition calls its own. While the eyes are fixed on the page and on the screen, iconic memory maintains a much fuller copy of what we have uttered than our conscious working memory can store. The screen image that we see and process enables us to feed back information about our utterances to their maker. Reading itself is a feedback mechanism, and it operates in parallel to the mind's language processing system.

An author has two idiolects or styles, the first unconscious, the second a conscious, calculated response to the first. The media by which the inner voice interacts cybertextually with the editor and composer change over time as we devise new cybertechnologies to externalize and extend cognitive monitoring. The first cybertechnologies tie inner speech to cognitive imagery, story-making, and non-verbal sound, that is, music.

The purely illiterate, naked maker has nothing but his memory systems, the non-phonological slave components of working memory (visual sketchpad, short-term auditory buffer, and episodic buffer) and the word webs and schemata of long-term memory. Yet makers contrive artful cybertechnologies from these. By combining visual sketchpad (for mapping), an episodic buffer (for transversing the map), and the phonological loop, and by using codes rather than words as chunk-items, early makers increased the efficiency of their cognitively unconscious muse.

An ancient cybertechnology is metre or prosody. This adds music memory to the cognitive language toolbox. The rhythmical structure that a maker maps on poetic speech gives it some predictability and offers two linked ways of memorizing a cybertext, as sounded words and as wordless sound. Fergus Craik and Robert S. Lockhart first observed, in 1972, that memory improved if one adopted a 'depth-of-processing' strategy. Encoding an utterance with different features improves one's ability of retrieving it from long-term memory in a probe. Memorizing a sequence of spellings will not generally have as good results as attending to the sound of an utterance and to its semantic meaning.

In 1979 John B. Lord related George Miller's 'magical number' to prosodic quantities. Four alliterating words govern Cædmon's oral-formulaic Old English verse line (with a caesural pause in the middle). Walter Ong associates bardic Homeric, Old English, and modern Yugoslavic poetry with oral-formulaic 'mnemonic patterns' laid down in long-term memory (1982, 34). The oral-formulaic style is additive, aggregative, and redundant (37–41) in the way it generates sequences that frequently repeat and vary themselves in clusters.[3] The scop used his working memory to commit to memory such formulas along with other aspects of language that must be learned. Expert schemata laid down in long-term memory by the consciously composing mind thus built a word hoard on which the scop could draw spontaneously. Like other indirect methods, oral-formulaic schemata influence how the inner voice will utter by using working memory, not as a place to revise consciously, but as a mechanism that forms the stuff that it will unconsciously draw on.

Medieval poets employ metrical feet, stanzaic forms, and rhyme schemes. Chaucer's *Canterbury Tales* has nine- or ten-syllable lines bounded by terminal rhymes. Most rhyme schemes in English call for short stanzas of between two and seven lines: two lines (couplet), three lines (terzain, terza rima, triolet, villanelle, haiku), four lines (quatrain, clerihew, double dactyl), five lines (cinquain, limerick, tanka), six lines (sestet), and seven lines (rhyme royal, septet). The most popular stanzas, ones that are easy for a mind not especially attuned to poetry to remember, are hymns and limericks. The basic metre of hymns is so-called common measure, a short quatrain that alternates three-foot and four-foot lines (that is, three or four chunks) and has twenty-eight syllables. Although longer by one line, the limerick is a twenty-one syllable quintain (5 5 3 3 5). Longer stanzaic schemes combine these segments. For example, a Petrachan sonnet consists of an octave and a sestet, and a Shakespearian sonnet of three quatrains and a couplet. Poulter's measure, a rhyming couplet of twelve-syllable and fourteen-syllable lines, often takes the form of quatrains. Ballades and octaves are usually a pair of quatrains. Edmund Spenser extended rhyme royal in the stanzaic form he develops in *The Faerie Queene*: it has nine ten-syllable lines, rhyming ababbcbcc, two quatrains whose eighth line fuses with a ninth to make a couplet. If a ten-syllable line has about seven words, the span of the common stanzaic units extends from 14 words (in a ten-syllable couplet), through about 20 words in common measure, 28 words in a quatrain, 63 words in rhyme royal, and 98 words in a sonnet. Common metrical feet hold chunks, and stanzaic forms reflect cognitive capacity.[4]

Prosodic encoding and stanzaic segmentation is a cybertechnology enabling the composer's working memory, in other respects unaided, to control the output of the unconscious language-production system. I cannot remember poems to recite them very well, but Tennyson's 'The Charge of the Light Brigade' has stuck with me, owing to the insistent musicality of its metre. Its rhythm encodes the words in memory:

> *Some* one had *blun*-der'd:
> *Their's* not to *make* reply,
> *Their's* not to *rea*-son why,
> *Their's* but to *do* and die:
> *Into* the *vall*-ey of Death
> *Rode* the six *hun*-dred.   (Poems [1908]: II, 225)

Tennyson shows how poets can size lines to fit inside the phonological loop in working memory. Its longest lines have only two dactylic or trochaic feet, each of which is a two-item chunk (e.g., '*make* reply'). Metre is a composer-editor's reasoned, artful way of organizing the flow of the inner voice. The composer-editor does not rearrange its output in short-term memory to conform to the metrical pattern but commits learned prosodic expertise to schematic long-term memory. Uttering in a given metre, then, becomes second nature.[5] The reader-editor can have the greatest influence on the author's inner voice by feeding it specialized coding systems which give the free unconscious inner voice a structure. As W.H. Auden said, about 1970, 'Blessed be all metrical rules that forbid automatic responses, / force us to have second thoughts, free from the fetters of Self' (1991, 856).

The classical *loci et imagines* method of artificial memory is another expert coding system. Employed originally in classical Greek and Latin to commit orations to memory (Yates 1966), it gives utterances a deep semantic encoding like that described by Craik and Lockhart (1972). In this method, a reader-editor breaks the utterances of his or her inner voice into segments, associates each segment with an object, and visualizes the placement of those objects in sequential order at locations in a familiar site, such as a forum, a country estate, or (today) a shopping mall. By mentally walking this route, from place to place, and visually picking up each object in sequence, the utterer can review, and revise if need be, a long speech consciously in the mind.

Cognitively unedited transcripts of the inner voice are hard to find. Automatic writing by such as Georgie Yeats (Harper 2002) and Gertrude Stein (Will 2001) looks promising, but oral conversation, recordings of dictation, and rapid, cursive drafts of text-in-the-making bear signs of feedback, the reader-editor's *currente calamo* corrections. Most of us alter the flow of conversation by gauging our partners' responses. We will repeat ourselves to stall for time, or to prevent interruption or the loss of a turn to someone else (Tannen 2007, 16), or to emphasize a point or express agreement. Dictation is also uncertain because it can be stopped and backed up, overwriting the flow, and belts, tapes, or files can be post-edited. Some oral transcripts result from a collaboration between two styles, the cognitive unconscious and the calculating reader-editor. It would be a mistake to think of conversation and oral speech as inevitably being spontaneous utterances of the inner voice.

A lettered maker can translate his cognitive symbol sets to pictographs, ideographs, or alphabets. This, literacy, is another cybertechnology. Manuscript, print, typewriting, and word-processing cultures do not just archive and disseminate cybertexts: they have a great impact on the mechanics of uttering by magnifying the powers of the reader-editor over the inner voice. At first the writer still silently mouths the words of the manuscript pages when reading them. This technique keeps some of the original intimacy of cognition because the maker hears his cybertext uttered by his own voice. His two selves thus dialogue cybertextually in an auditory medium. As paper becomes cheaper, and tools from wax tablets to laptops are nearly universally used, the maker sets down written drafts or notes for rapid revision. How effectively these cybertechnologies tame the inner voice can be judged by examining what reader-editors delete in their drafts. Writing gives them the opportunity 'to interfere with and reorganize [the mind's] more normal, redundant processes' (Ong 1982, 40). They do so by what Jack Goody calls 'backward scanning' (1977, 128) and what Ong calls backlooping (1982, 39). An inner style can be partly overwritten by a conscious style, one that is imitated.

We know the general differences between cognitive (inner auditory and unconscious) and composed (written and conscious) texts. When the mind uses a chunk once, that very usage primes the mind to use it again. Conversation shows a similar effect, termed lexical entrainment, when one speaker accepts and repeats the words of a partner rather than introducing synonyms (Metzing and Brennan 2003). Literacy brings a simple but powerful gift to uttering: the ability 'to set pieces of text side by side and check them for identity or to look for relations between them' (Olson 1994, 36). This gift – a type of cybertextual cycling[6] – enables reader-editors to revise written texts by deleting the lexical redundancies and repetitions that are so typical of the inner voice.

A similar effect that the conscious composer can edit out of a flow is syntactically primed repetition of grammatical structures. It appears when the unconscious mind reproduces a syntactic structure in language production that it has just experienced, i.e., generated as a chunk, heard from an inner voice or from a fellow conversationalist, or read in a text. These primes are abstract and non-lexical: active and passive transitive sentence structures, and prepositional and double-object datives (such as 'The teacher gave his class a tough mid-term test'; Bock et al. 2007, 443). The effect occurs independently of semantics (438). This priming appears to be very strong because a change in modality – oral or written – does not diminish the effect, as it does for single lexical words (454). This modality immunity suggests to me that syntactic priming occurs early in the language production system. However, there is some evidence that syntactic priming is 'verb-specific' (Gries 2005, 380), and thus related to lexical, semantic choices.

Literacy truly transforms language as it comes from the unconscious inner voice in yet another way. David Olson argues persuasively that 'learning to read is learning to hear speech in a new way!' (1994, 85). Because writing brings into full consciousness what was not before, the literate mind can observe things about speech itself that were previously obscured. A script presents visible 'objects of reflection, analysis and design' (258) on the basis of which we have set down schemata in long-term memory for grammar (e.g., parts of speech), syntax (e.g., passives and actives, and coordinate and subordinate clauses), lexicography and semantics (e.g., mass nouns and derivations), and rhetoric (e.g., metaphors). Individuals now experience in their youth, just by virtue of learning their ABCs, what happened to mankind historically over some thousands of years. This transformative discovery of the meaning of what one has been doing all along, just in speaking, has a major cybertextual feedback on thought.

Literacy has allowed mankind to remake itself, but it is not without problematic consequences. One is the emergence of the intentionless author. Writing can communicate information and ideas in both plain and subtle ways, but it lacks what David Olson, after Austin, calls 'illocutionary force,' a guide to the utterer's attitude and to the context of their utterance (1994, 91, 121). Once converted into text, language loses its voice and body language (183–7). The conscious composer, in scripting the unconscious voice, commits a cybertextual crime against understanding. He disembodies the speech act. Text takes on a mysterious, alien cast and requires reading, analysis, and interpretation in order to make up for losses in its change of modality. The 'author-is-dead' approach to text arises from this denatured utterance. Reader-response theoreticians like Stanley Fish free the interpreter from having to worry about the author's intentions.[7] Because these intentions are thought to be unrecoverable, this theory enables readers to add their own 'illocutionary force' to the text, in the process becoming co-authors.

Cybertextuality gives us an intellectual framework for understanding the consequences of driving a wedge between the utterer and the uttered. Literacy itself is one cause of noise. It damages or destroys the sender-author's intentions in a message that the receiver-reader has no alternative but to accept, as writing, if it is to be received at all. Information survives the transit, the *meaning* (that problematic word, here in the sense of proposing or intending) does not. The humanities as a division of knowledge – it teaches language and its literature – has grown up as a consequence of a single cybertextual act, the making of a symbolic notation that can free human beings from cognitive constraints on language making.

Effective-writing and communications teachers who adopt the influencial cognitive-process theory of Linda Flower and John Hayes (1981) have welcomed denatured text. Their original writing model has three processes, most associated with working memory: planning and prewriting (finding the gist of an utterance), translating (turning the gist into sentences, that is, verbalizing), and reviewing (revising on paper or screen; 370). These are regarded as goal-directed 'distinctive thinking processes' that have an inherent 'hierarchical, highly embedded organization' (366). Later Hayes and his colleague Ann Chenoweth (Chenoweth and Hayes 2003, 112) added a fourth process, transcribing, between translating and reviewing, but the entire scheme remained principally a conscious group of goal-directed activities. Flower and Hayes based their rational cognitive model on hard-won experimental data. They asked writers to think out loud. Protocols recorded the writer's conscious sequence of cognitive events in a writing task. Here is a writing protocol that ended with the sentence, 'The summer after tenth grade, 27 students from my school district and I went to France for two weeks' (Chenoweth and Hayes 2001, 82):

> ... ok ... the summer after tenth grade ... I and oh ... I and ... no ... twenty seven students ... and I ... from my school district ... that sounds kind of awkward ... would it be twenty seven students from my school district and I ... but then I was part of the school ... oh but if I said from my school district ... ah ha ... from my school district ... the summer after tenth grade ... twenty seven students from my school district ... and I ... went to France ... for two weeks ...

Such protocols can tell how students implemented planning, verbalizing, and revising when they wrote an essay.

Flower, Hayes, and Chenoweth devised a method that could be taught to teachers. With some experience, they could instil a controlled rule-based cybertechnology – one that encouraged students to engage in a cognitive monologue of two about writing an in-progress text – into their long-term memory. Because the heuristics of the method could be learned, stored as schemata, and recalled as rules in sequence, it had a chance of working. The cognitive process model, plausibly, turned what for many had been inspired discovery (where text welled up from the unconscious) into a manual-based production line. Writing researchers had genuinely demystified literacy-based composition. Genres such as reportage, summation, and argument might well benefit from standardizing the how-to of composing. What dictionaries had done for vocabulary and meaning, grammar books for sentence and paragraph construction, and rhetorics for figures of speech and thought, and persuasion, the cognitive process model appeared to do for planning, verbalizing, and revising.

However, Kevin Porter has said that 'no one ever learned to write by first learning Flower and Hayes's model of the writing process' (2000, 710). Is T.S. Eliot's complaint about writing in *East Coker*, then, that it is

> a raid on the inarticulate
> With shabby equipment always deteriorating
> In the general mess of imprecision of feeling   (1962, 128)

still not put to rest? Flower and Hayes understated both the affective in writing (a weakness realized early on, by Alice Brand and others) and the writer's social context, that is, the importance of cybertextu-al feedback from others. Post-process theory in writing research has pointed out these shortcomings, as well as a scepticism that authoring can be known scientifically. Although the impact of criticisms has been blunted because cognitive process theory has hardly penetrated writ-ing pedagogy, the theory itself illustrates that literacy sacrifices 'illocu-tionary force' to argument.

Two other objections to this theory show its limitations. First, stu-dents who write a protocol of what they are thinking engage in a cog-nitive activity that interferes with their writing task. They generate a talk about writing at the same time as they are supposed to be writing about a topic. Cognitive process theory can assert that composing is an intellectual process because it bases its conclusions on protocols that ask students to think. The conditions of the experiment guarantee its expected findings. If we ask students to record out loud their thoughts about process, students will utter thoughts about process, not about a topic. Second, cognitive process theory focuses more on editing than on cognitive production. Students either write something down on paper or screen or they listen to their own voice out loud, and then they edit the utterance into shape. Cognitive process theory stresses the impact of personal feedback.

Cybertextuality thus embraces literary studies centrally. It theorizes how Wiener's universal natural phenomenon applies to what Chau-cer calls *making* and what we call reading and editing. In a cybertex-tual perspective, the author is alive in the works because messaging and feedback cycles have idiolectal and idiosyncratic signatures that survive the author's death. Texts include traces of their own materi-alization. However, cybertextuality also underscores how alienated are authorial intentions from the written word. The muses that inspire *writ-ers* seem to have been forgetful of passing on, in an author's text, the 'illocutionary force' that made the author utter it.

*   *   *   *   *

When preparing to hit with the driver, you don't grip it and rip it but take me through a checklist, starting with the Vardon grip, a very light one as if we were cupping a living sparrow, then assuming the stance, aligned 90 degrees to the target at which you glance once or twice, bent slightly forward, back muscles tightened to erect our backbone that Shelley called sticking out your rear headlights, looking at the ball, checking that the clubhead face is neither closed nor open to the target, all intended to make you forget, thousands of strokes to make you the expert who didn't need to think but just did.

A second to-do list for the backswing begins with a straightened left arm, lifting the club gently and floating it back, up and around from the left shoulder so that the arm turns slowly under the chin, then pauses at the top of the swing, checking the grip is light and flexible, and then at last · turning from the hips before the left shoulder and arm fall, a downswing that's at last my home turf, my flow where everything blurs as we feel the left shoulder sweeping its arm, its hinged wrists, and the relaxed tight-to-the-ribs right arm down, around, and through for the hit, propelling the chest to turn targetwards, the club following us up and around as it and, last, your gaze ends at the target.

You really worked on minimizing me, breaking a slowed backswing down into a sequence of little moves, each one forgotten as you executed the next, positioning our body for my launch, my downward violent attack on the ball that Shelley videotaped, spent hours teaching you to become conscious of but with little effect because you couldn't remember anything after the downstroke began except for a swift, easy sweep or an awkwardness as muscles compensated for unalignment, and you watched hapless as the good ones went straight and rising with a slight draw to the left, and the bad ones were smothered, topped, sliced, hooked, skyed, or shanked, and you longed to fix me but I don't like being fixed, do I, and no one has figured out how to hit the ball on the upswing so you might as well give up on that.

4 Poet-authors

I   Geoffrey Chaucer

The Middle English poet Geoffrey Chaucer (ca 1343–1400), like Cædmon, described himself as a shy working man whose dreams thrust
him into public authoring. Cædmon left the banquet hall for the stable
before the harp could reach him. In Chaucer's first long poem, *The Book
of the Duchess*, he portrays himself as fearful of dying from sleepless-
ness. In the second dream vision, *The House of Fame*, he confesses himself a very dull fellow. On arriving home alone from his daily job, he
sits, overweight and hermit-like (574, 660), 'domb as any stoon' (656),
reading a book until he is dazed (657–9) and desperate for something
to write about. Like Cædmon, he then falls asleep and dreams. Cædmon sees a man who tells him to sing about the Creation; and, when
Cædmon wakes, he utters the first poem by a named poet in English.
In *The Book of the Duchess*, Chaucer meets a man in black who tells him
a tale of lost love. When Chaucer awakes, he puts this dream story into
the poem we have. *The House of Fame*, his second vision, has Chaucer
dream of an eagle with a man's voice (556) who swoops down to fly
him, at first shaking out of fear (604), to places dedicated to fame and
rumour, where he will find plenty of stories to tell. Both poets lack a
subject. Once they have it, the writing is uneventful. For instance, *The
Book of the Duchess* ends as Chaucer, having straightway put the dream
into rhyme, says, 'now hit ys doon' (1334).

   Chaucer's *The House of Fame* is the first English work to analyse the
creative process. Its proem says that dreams, the content of poems, are
miracles of unknown origin (12). Like Robert Louis Stevenson, Stephen
King, Seamus Heaney, and many others, Chaucer thinks of creative

composition as mysterious and dream-like. He does not know if these dreams come of bodily indisposition, or a psychological disorder (such as melancholy), or the visitation of spirits, or the operation of the soul in foretelling a future that

> oure flessh ne hath no myght
> To understonde hyt aryght,
> For hyt is warned to derkly.   (49–51)

Like most creative writers, he cannot tell where his uttering comes from. He just hopes that all dreams turn out well and invokes the god of sleep to ensure that poets tell them 'aryght' (79). What he dreads is insomnia and the writer's block of medieval poets, dreamlessness.

The dream Chaucer gives us in *The House of Fame* has three episodes, a tour of a temple of glass that exhibits ancient images and stories of love (book 1), his seizure by a golden eagle – who takes him from a sandy desert to the abode of fame (book 2) – and what he sees and hears at that allegorical place (book 3). The proem to book 2, the abduction by the eagle, is first to mention the muses in English literature. Chaucer begs

> And ye, me to endite and ryme
> Helpeth, that on Parnaso duelle,
> Be Elicon, the clere welle.
> O Thought, that wrot al that I mette,
> And in the tresorye hyt shette
> Of my brayn, now shal men se
> Yf any vertu in the be
> To tellen al my drem aryght.
> Now kythe thyn engyn and myght!   (520–8)

This creative process has two parts: dreaming (which, as Chaucer says before, comes from an unknown source), and thought (which lodges the dream in the brain's memory and has a power, 'vertu,' to tell or utter the remembered dream). Prescient, Chaucer calls authoring a neuro-logical activity. Its prime mover is thought, of which the two functions are storage (writing in the brain) and rehearsal (uttering as speech, or telling). In other words, the first part is memory, whose 'engyn' the golden eagle personifies.

Thought the eagle falls on little Geoffrey like a burning thunderbolt (537). Soaring upwards with its catch, the bird of prey jolts the poet out of his insomniac daze. If Chaucer draws on his own creative experience, possibly he means the terror that some writers feel when they begin a writing project. Only when the eagle speaks to him by name in a familiar man's voice does a calm mind return (560–6). Possibly the eagle's voice resembles Geoffrey's own inner voice. Because the eagle explains himself as sent by Jupiter, god of thunder, to compensate the poet's 'labour and devocion' (666) with news of new subject matter, Chaucer must believe that God inspires this inner speech. (Following Ezekiel 1:10, art and scripture associate the golden eagle with the gospeller John.) The eagle then explains how all worldly human voices collect in the airy house of fame to which he transports Geoffrey. The eagle's learned, amusing interpretation of sound as broken air resolves the poet's uncertainty about how all news reaches one and the same house, but this has one very strange effect: an arriving voice assumes the shape of its original speaker, as if associative long-term memory links what someone has said with his remembered visual image of who said it. As the eagle shows and describes Geoffrey the world and the galaxy from a great height, the gladder he becomes (962): a sign of the pleasure that authors experience when flow is good. At this moment, Geoffrey recalls the axiom of Boethius in *The Consolation of Philosophy* (which Chaucer translated into English), that 'A thought may flee so hye / Wyth fetheres of Philosophye, / To passen everych element' (973–5). Chaucer's long-term memory, searched by his thought, stores a treasury (524) of such sayings from such books. The invocation to book 3 admits that his goal is not 'art poetical,' fine writing, but 'sentence' (moral truths), which alone in his 'hed ymarked ys' (1095–1103).

Geoffrey's 'thought' is the engine of the muses, but Lady Philosophy upbraids imprisoned Boethius for consorting with them. His need for the 'rendynge muses of poetes [that] enditen ... thynges to ben writen' (*Boece* 1.m1: 4–5) sinks him in misery and self-pity, and their behaviour (rending or tearing their clothes in grief) leads Lady Philosophy to call them poisonous 'comune strompettis' (1.p1: 49). Chaucer smoothes over this disagreement, a little, by interpreting the Muses as allegorized stages of the creative process. This he owes to Fulgentius, a late fifth- or early sixth-century North African Christian apologist and perhaps bishop, the author of the 'Mythologies' (Fulgentius 1971, 3), according to Phillipa Hardman (1986). She makes a plausible case for reading Chaucer's poem as stages in Fulgentius's Muse-inspired creative process, from desire through memory to eloquence, from Clio and Polyhymnia to Calliope. Fulgentius explains the Muses in this way:

first, to find the need for instruction [Clio]; second, to delight in what you find needful [Euterpe]; third, to pursue what you delight in [Melpomene]; fourth, to grasp what you pursue [Thalia]; fifth, to remember what you grasp [Polyhymnia]; sixth, to discover in yourself something resembling what you remember [Erato]; seventh, to judge what you discover [Terpsichore]; eighth, to discriminate in what you judge [Urania]; ninth, to make known in attractive form what you select [Calliope]. (Fulgentius 1971, 56)

Chaucer mentions only three of these Muses by name: Clio (*Troilus* 2. 7–9), the hopeful beginning; Polyhymnia (Polymya), who 'Singest with vois memorial in the shade' (*Anelida* 15–18); and Calliope, the singing voice (*Fame* 1399–1402; *Troilus* 3. 45–6), but each one has the function that Fulgentius assigns. By giving the earliest theory of brain-centred authoring in English, Chaucer redeems the muses from Lady Philosophy's attack, to which Sir Philip Sidney also responds in his *Defence of Poesie* (printed in 1595).

Chaucer allegorizes the gist and pre-gist stages of poetic making in *The House of Fame*. These scenes describe poet Geoffrey submitting to the eagle's rekindling of his desire to make, acquiring knowledge, and building up long-term memory. The 'Fulgentian schema consists of eight-ninths learning and preparation, and one-ninth verbal expression' (Hardman 1986, 485). The leading muse, Clio, takes her meaning from the name's etymology, the desire for 'fame' (Hardman 1986, 481); and, not unreasonably, *The House of Fame* emphasizes the emotional drive that a poet needs to write. Chaucer presents himself as suffering from dullness (a lack of desire) and deep ignorance of fame itself. He does not appear worried about verbalization. In Chaucer's terms, Willem Levelt's lexical production amounts to enditing and rhyming (*House of Fame* 520; *Parliament of Fowls* 119), represented as conscious technical skills. There are several reasons why Chaucer believes that he controls the uttering process.

First, classical rhetoric, known to Chaucer from Geoffrey of Vinsauf's *Poetria Nova*, formalizes and rationalizes chunking and priming. It gives Latin names for many types of deliberate repetition and variation under the topic of amplification. Educated poets were as vulnerable to memory constraints and unconsciousness as anyone but, because their flow exhibited many of the formal features that rhetoric named, authors may well have persuaded themselves that they were conscious of what they were doing. Unconscious techniques of assembling words into sentences were conceived of as conscious.

Secondly, so much of medieval art translates texts from other languages that authors often use an already written text as a primer and crib. They consciously knew what they were going to utter because they had the foreign source text to stare at. This lifts a great strain from long-term and working memory. Eustache Deschamps appropriately calls Chaucer, in a refrain to a ballade, a 'great translator' (Benson 1993, xxiii) rather than an original author. In the prologue to book 2 of *Troilus and Criseyde*, although Chaucer acknowledges the uncontrollable lexical changes in 'forme of speche' (22) over a thousand years, he characterizes his work as an 'art' (11), a deliberate discipline that comes from 'no sentement' (13), but rather from writing 'out of Latyn in my tonge' (14). Working from a visual text, his working and long-term memory could relax. He was not dreamweaving.

Thirdly, even when Chaucer did not translate word for word or clause-for-clause, but wrote spontaneously, he could rely on the rigid text segmentation that rhyme schemes enforced. Octometer couplets in *House of Fame*, then rhyme royal in *Troilus* (ababbcc), and lastly pentameter couplets in much of *The Canterbury Tales* required Chaucer to gather the rhymes he needed before he produced the full lines. The couplet's two sounds and the three sounds of rhyme royal fitted nicely into chunks. And as we will see, schemata associated rhyme words with stock phrases.

Finally, Chaucer lacked the knowledge of language that we take for granted today. Speech, for him, comprised atomistic terms that denoted things in the world and had no lexical definition. He did not even know what a phrase was because Middle English had no word for a repeated multi-term expression, outside proverbs. The words 'conscious' and 'unconscious' – and the concepts they represented, other than being asleep and being awake – were not to be available for another two centuries.

Chaucer's known vocabulary is surprisingly small. Judged by his surviving writings alone, about 380,000 words, Chaucer uses 9,152 common words and 916 'proper and place names or foreign words' (Benson 1993, vii).[1] This idiolect formed as Chaucer translated, from French, Latin, and Italian, great works in poetry and prose such as *The Romaunt of the Rose*, Boethius's *The Consolation of Philosophy*, and *Troilus and Criseyde* (from Boccaccio's *Il Filostrato*). Chaucer must have felt free in anglicizing words from Romance languages, whether or not those words had already achieved some currency in England, and both imported terms and terms of technical arts and crafts must have interested him. His family, London merchants (wool and wine), sent him when young to serve at court; the registers of trade would have come second nature to him. The crown also engaged him in war and diplomacy, and during middle age as 'comptroller in the port of London, responsible for the customs or export tax on wool, skins, and leather' (Gray 2004). He became clerk of the king's works for Richard II in 1389, a position in which he 'was responsible for the administration of construction and repair at Westminster, the Tower of London, other castles (such as that at Berkhamsted), and seven manors (including Eltham and Sheen). He also had the duty of overseeing parks, hunting lodges, the mews for the royal falcons at Charing Cross, and a variety of other tasks' (Gray 2004). Late in life, Chaucer also became deputy forester of the royal forest of North Petherton in Somerset. He must have conversed easily, throughout his life, with those who knew the professional terminologies of merchants, courtiers, military servants, engineering, hunting, hawking and fishing, and accounts administration.

These terms of art are seldom in his works, yet they were used by his contemporaries and Chaucer must have known them. Being from a merchant's family, for example, he would have heard of 'bluet' (a type of blue woollen cloth), 'camelin' (woollen fabric blended with silk), 'card' (a comb used on wool), and 'cog-ware' (coarse cloth made of inferior wool). Anyone supervising construction of buildings would know terms like 'pinsoun' (pliers used in carpentry), 'rabet' (a carpenter's plane), and 'tenoun' (the projecting part of a joint). The customs office would have to recognize 'bir-laue' (village regulations), 'chartrer' (a freeholder), 'countrollour' (customs' accountant – the term for his own profession), and 'gavel' (tax). If even one-half of the over 55,000 word entries of the *Middle English Dictionary* (Riechers 2001), which documents the language from 1100 to 1500, were lost before Chaucer was born, or were introduced after he died, it stretches credibility that one of the greatest writers in English knew only one-third of the words used by his contemporaries.[2] A not unreasonable guess would have Chaucer capable of recognizing, understanding, and (if necessary) using 20,000 English words.

Is this vocabulary, then, his working English? The answer is yes and no. Words are the fundamental units of dictionaries, but not of usage. If Chaucer received vocabulary from other people, speaking and writing, he would not have heard most of it as discrete words. As we have seen, cognitively, we all say and hear sentences as word combinations, chunks, or multi-term sequences. The true building blocks of our idiolect are phrases, just as the very foundations of our genetic life are chunks of two bases, adenine with thymine, and guanine with cytosine (AT or TA and GC or CG). Chaucer learned language within the constraints of his working memory, the alpha value. There are only two combinations in a genetic nucleobase, and the word-type bases in an individual's idiolect are numbered in the thousands, but the combinatory process remains the same. It is not the base unit that makes up the individual's working lexicon but the combinations all their bases form: the discrete chunks, and then the sentences into which they sequence. What distinguishes one author's language from another are their most frequently employed combinations of base words, their chunks.

I used *CollGen*, part of the *TACT* concordancer, to count every exact repeated phrase (from two to eight words long) throughout John Fisher's edition of Chaucer's 182,000-word *Canterbury Tales*. There are 22,000 different repeating phrases of two or more words in the 182,000-word *Canterbury Tales*, almost double the count of different, unlemmatized word types (12,000). Among the 22,000 fixed phrases are 34 complete lines that Chaucer repeats, verbatim or with minor variations. To this number should be added an uncertain body of unfixed repeated phrases, collocations (commonly recurring word combinations that are order-free), which are potential chunks too. This listing attests to how substantially phrasal is Chaucer's working lexicon. He was cognitively normal; cognitive chunking surfaces in the phrasal repetitions found in his writing.

Two new printed concordances of Chaucer's works and a revised Riverside edition have been published in the past fifteen years. A new generation of text-analysis software (such as Robert Watt's *Concordance*) and standard digital texts (such as the *Riverside Chaucer*) reduce the tedium that goes into identifying the repeating phrases that signal potential chunking. Two passages from Chaucer's greatest single poem, *Troilus and Criseyde*, the first from his invented Deiphoebus episode (book 2: 1394–1414), and the second translated from Boccaccio's account of the consummation of the lovers (book 3: 1667–94), illustrate how repeating phrases dominate Chaucer's lines. We may certainly be forgiven for not noticing these: *Troilus* is one of the great experiences in English literature and its brilliantly happy, sometimes comic love-making, and the calamity that overtakes the lovers, stay with readers for a lifetime. We painstakingly acquire a facility with Middle English to enjoy *Troilus*, not to count phrases.

Such counts would likely put Chaucer to sleep, but they do help to explain how he wrote his much-loved *Troilus*. Italics highlight repeated fixed phrases in the excerpt below from book 2 of *Troilus and Criseyde*, their frequency in superscript numbers at their end. Boldfaced words mark possible schemata. The frequency of rhyme pairs or triples that recur elsewhere in the poem appear within superscript square brackets.

1394 'But, Troilus, yet *telle me*,[11] *if the LEST*,[4]
1395 **A thing** now which *that I shal axen*[2] THE:[3 he]
1396 Which is thi **brother** that thow **lovest** BEST, [3]
1397 As in thi verray *hertes privetee*?'[2]
1398 'Iwis, **my brother** Deiphebus,' *quod HE*.[52]
1399 'Now,' *quod Pandare*,[48] 'er houres *twyes TWELVE*,[2]
1400 He shal the ese, *unwist of*[4] it HYMSELVE.[5]

1401 'Now *lat m'alone*,[2] and werken *as I MAY*,'[6]
1402 *Quod he*;[52] and *to Deiphebus*[4] wente he THO,
1403 Which hadde his *lord and* grete *frend*[3] ben AY;[4]
1404 Save Troilus, *no man*[14] he **loved** SO.[5 tho]
1405 *To* **telle** *in short*,[5] *withouten wordes MO*,[7] [3 tho; 8 so]
1406 *Quod Pandarus*,[48] 'I pray yow[5] that ye BE[5]
1407 Frend to a cause which *that toucheth*[5] ME.'[22]

1408 'Yis, parde,' *quod Deiphebus*,[3] 'wel thow WOOST,[7]
1409 In *al that evere*[7] I may,[46] *and God tofore*,[10]
1410 *Al nere*[2] it but for man *I* **love** *MOOST*,[3] [5]
1411 **My brother** *Troilus*[4]; but sey wherfore
1412 It is; for *sith* that day *that I was bore*,[4]
1413 I nas, ne *nevere mo*[10] to ben *I thynke*,[2]
1414 Ayeins **a thing** *that myghte*[11] the forthynke.'

Of 165 words in the first (untranslated) passage, 81 or about 50 per cent belong to a total of 31 repeating fixed phrases. The ratio of phrase types to lines is 3:2. Their average length is 2.6 words, well within the alpha value limits. Twelve of the 21 lines (about one-half) end with repeating phrases, three times as many begin a line. Repeating fixed phrases cling to rhyme words at the end of lines; we find the content or fresh information in a line at the start. In Chaucer's mind, a potential rhyming term seems to form a stemma that links not only to words that rhyme with it but also to stock phrases that end with that word. Because Chaucer has to reuse rhyming word pairs and triples, he complains of a scarcity of English rhyme words in his 'Complaint of Venus' (80). The most frequent pairing in the three untranslated stanzas is 'be' and 'me' (22 times). The rhymes 'wost' and 'most,' and '-selve' and 'twelve,' occur five times each, 'may' and 'ay' four times, and 'lest' and 'best,' and 'thee' and 'he,' thrice. The triple 'tho,' 'so,' and 'mo' is a partial network. Only its doubles recur: 'tho' and 'me' rhyme three times, 'tho' and 'so' five times, and 'me' and 'so' eight times. There are ten words in this rhyme cluster (the other seven are 'also,' 'do,' 'fo,' 'fro,' 'go,' 'no,' and 'wo'). The weights that linked their schemata in Chaucer's long-term memory must have been significant.

Chaucer's thought size, his cognitive load or omega value, appears in the way lines 1405–14 repeat, with variations, words and ideas in lines 1394–1404. The term cluster that integrates both thoughts includes four words, 'telle,' 'thing,' 'brother,' and 'love' (in bold). The first eleven lines, visible to Chaucer's eyes on the page where he wrote them, have primed the next ten lines.

He translated the next passage (3: 1667–94) from Boccaccio. Eighty-eight of 220 words (or 40 per cent) belong to repeating phrases, 10 per cent less than in the first passage. The ratio of phrase types to lines is a little lower, 35:28 or 1.25:1. Their average length is 2.5 words, also well within the alpha value. These reductions show that Chaucer, having to follow Boccaccio, does not draw as freely from his own schemata as in authoring the first passage. As before, about half of the lines end with a repeating phrase (13 of 28).

1667   *Soon after*[5] this, for that *Fortune* it wolde,[3 \[11 sholde\]]

1668   Icomen was the blisful *tyme* swete[2 \[10 mete\]]

1669   That Troilus was warned that *he* sholde,[10 \[11 wolde\]]

1670   There he *was erst*,[3] Criseyde his lady[4] mete,[\[10 swete\]]

1671   For which *he felte his **herte**[4] in joie*[7] flete[\[2 swete\]]

1672   And feithfully *gan alle*[4] the goddes herie.[\[2 merie\]]

1673   And *lat se*[5] now *if that*[75] he kan be merie![\[2 herie\]]

1674   And holden was *the forme and*[2] al the wise [\[20 devyse\]]

1675   Of hire commyng, and of his also,[\[4 go; 2 two\]]

1676   As it *was erst*,[3] which ***nedeth nought***[7] devyse. [\[20 wyse\]]

1677   But pleynly to th'effect right *for to* go:[2 \[4 also; 8 go\]]

1678   *In joie*[7] and suerte Pandarus *hem* two[2 \[8 go; 2 also\]]

1679   *Abedde brought*,[2] *whan that hem bothe* leste,[2 \[11 reste\]]

1680   *And thus*[39] they ben *in quyete and in* reste.[2 \[11 leste\]]

1681   **Nought nedeth** it to yow, *syn they*[2] ben met,

1682 To axe at me if that they blithe WERE;[feere 16]
1683 For if it **erst was** wel, tho was it bet
1684 *A thousand fold;*[9] this **nedeth nought**[7] enquere.
1685 Ago was every *sorwe* and every FEERE;[3] [were 16]
1686 And bothe, ywys, they hadde, and so *they wende,*[2]
1687 As muche **joie** as **herte** may comprende.

1688 This is *no litel thyng*[2] of *for to seye;*[7]
1689 **This passeth**[2] every wit *for to* DEVYSE;[2] [20 wyse; 5 suffise]
1690 For *ech of hem*[7] gan otheres lust obeye.
1691 Felicite, which that thise *clerkes* WISE[5] [20 devyse; 4 suffise]
1692 Comenden so, ne **may nought**[10] here SUFFISE;[5 devyse; 4 wyse]
1693 This joie **may nought**[10] writen be with inke;
1694 **This passeth**[2] al *that herte may*[2] bythynke.

Rhymes point to schemata clusters: the triples 'wise,' 'suffise,' and 'devyse,' and 'also,' 'go,' and 'two,' occur twice in the poem (respectively, here and at 5: 1094, 1096–7, and 5:44, 46–7). Pairs such as 'wolde' and 'sholde,' 'swete' and 'mete,' and 'leste' and 'reste' occur more than ten times. The cognitive load looks to be fourteen lines insofar as the second pair of stanzas repeat, from the first pair, 'nought nedeth,' 'erst was,' 'joie,' and 'herte,' and the rhymes 'devyse' and 'wise.' Chaucer again appears to have been primed to repeat what he has just written.

What do these two passages tell us about Chaucer's authoring? Unless unrepresentative of his work, his process pulses with chunks and repeated phrases within the alpha value and works within a cognitive load limit, an omega value of ten to fourteen lines. Chaucer's spontaneous composition suffers more from repetition than his translations do. He translates from a visually constant exemplar. Chaucer also tends to begin his lines with new information and end them with phrasal repetitions focused on repeated double and triple rhymes. The numbers are consistent with a cognitive lexical production model such as Willem Levelt's.

Chaucer scholars might well dispute this cognitive approach and argue that his 'art poetical' had nothing to do with the unconscious but was a well-understood rule-governed technical craft. Does Chaucer in *The House of Fame* explicitly ascribe unconsciousness to the muses if Philosophy and Thought know them well? The only unknown, to Chaucer's mind, is the subject to write about; and (he might say) some thinking will take care of that. The eagle is an instructor, not a whirlwind. Alpha-value phrasal pulsing belongs to conscious rhetorical amplification or to the English language itself. We do not need to summon up unconscious cognitive constraints. The omega value, a ten-to-fourteen-line cognitive load limit, ignores Chaucer's ability to invent the eagle's character, his own persona, and the entire Deiphebus episode.

Historical scholarship, it might be said, attributes many fewer stock phrases and tags to Chaucer than to medieval romances or Corpus Christi plays. Ralph W.V. Elliott notes about twenty instances, Norman Davis only seven formulas, most inherited from anonymous bards, and Derek Brewer says that 'Chaucer makes progressively less use of this traditional formulaic style as he develops his art.'[3] These studies show that conventional phraseology is an important aspect of Chaucer's style, but they do not require us to define phrases by their repetition. Larry Benson, editor of the Riverside General Prologue to *The Canterbury Tales*, helpfully identifies half a dozen kinds of repetition in it. Chaucer's 'worthy' and 'wys,' for example, is termed a 'common collocation.'[4] Current language usage, or idiom, explains others, such as the Monk's 'pulled hen': negative comparisons of this sort 'are common in Chaucer and throughout Middle English.'[5] The same explains 'for the nones' (an intensive 'line-filler'), 'out of alle charitee' ('merely idiomatic'), 'good felawe,' and 'to shorte with.'[6] A third kind of repetition is merisms or yoked contraries like 'thogh him gamed or smerte' (Besserman 1976).[7] B.J. Whiting's ground-breaking study of Chaucer's proverbs (1934) calls attention to the fourth. Examples from the General Prologue include the comparisons 'broun as a berye,' 'His *purchas* was wel bettre than his *rente*,' and 'He made the person and the peple his *apes*.'[8] Benson locates two more proverbs there, 'sette hir aller cappe' and 'If even-song and morwe-song accorde.'[9] The terms 'tag' and 'rhetorical formula,' the fifth type of generic repetition, apply to expressions such as 'clad in blak or reed,' 'shortly for to tellen,' and 'what nedeth wordes mo.'[10] Both 'fees and robes' and 'In heigh and lough' reflect Latin financial and legal formulas in different linguistic registers, although no other English example in Chaucer can be found.[11]

To these objections, I say that they overlook Chaucer's humanity. A six-hundred-year gap is far too short to believe that he processed language differently than creative writers today. He had a working memory, and it had profound limitations, being capable of creating phrases repeatable from memory that were no longer than three or four words or two seconds in uttering aloud. Thought the eagle might show him the stars, but not the earth and the stars simultaneously: there was a cognitive load limit. We might like to believe that Chaucer's mind operated procedurally, rationally, consciously, as in the cognitive process theory of writing, with which no one has ever learned how to write, but did anyone write by following the trivium?

To literary historians, the 'English language' in the late fourteenth century was a formidable system of words, phrases, and grammatical forms and rules, and Chaucer might have agreed, but he does not say so. No grammars or dictionaries then documented what English was. His scribes had few standards for spelling. Merisms, proverbs, and idioms were not part of an educated public discourse. Chaucer knew that people in the north spoke differently than Londoners, that English did not have enough rhymes, and that science and philosophy used other tongues. His friend John Gower wrote literary works in three languages – Anglo-Norman French, Latin, and English – because of these problems. Despite assurances that phrasal repetitions are common, idiomatic formulas, Chaucer employs precious few more than once, and we do not always find someone else echoing them. A London and court sociolect certainly existed, but Chaucer's language is idiolectal.

Computer-based text analysis and concordances reveal that Chaucer's repeated phrases are seldom idioms. They do not have a distinctive meaning, such as characterizes stock phrases, merisms, proverbs, and literary formulas. Chunks are just convenient fragments or pieces of language: they fit almost anywhere. Even were we agreed to limit phrases to having at least two open-class words, or a sequence of any four or more words, or an idiom;[12] even if we excluded from our inventory most repeated fixed phrases with two or more function words, such sequences as 'gan alle' and 'if that,' both of which I counted in the *Troilus* passages; and even if we ignored sequences with only one content word and one or two function words, such as 'quod he,' we would still have a huge phrasal pool because many content words precipitate, also, *unfixed* repeating phrases, that is, collocations. We can reduce their numbers by lemmatizing them, that is, by using regular expressions (word patterns with wild cards) to subsume all inflectional forms of a word in a single form, but they are very numerous and defy explanation as rhetorical amplification.

The General Prologue, for instance, has 464 different repeating phrases and collocations found in it or elsewhere in *The Canterbury Tales*. This number exceeds by twentyfold the tags, stock formulas, or proverbs previously recognized in Chaucer's writing (Lancashire 1992). They appear, on average, once every line-and-a-half in the 858 lines of the General Prologue.[13] Usual explanations hardly account for them. Some do not survive beyond the General Prologue, but most are repeated in later tales. Occasionally phrases form semantic clusters that convey aspects of Chaucer's world view – they focus on meaningful topics (such as saying, telling, and speaking) and include proverbs and merisms – but seldom do clusters realize narrative elements of particular tales. The phrasal chunks and their clusters appear to be a signature of Chaucer's long-term memory schemata and suggest that there may be a biological key to his remembrance that appeals to human memory itself rather than to rhetorical or literary traditions.

Chaucer is prone to repeating words. Of the 1,850 different words in the General Prologue, Chaucer uses 67.3 per cent once, 14.1 per cent twice, 5.7 per cent three times, and 3.6 per cent four times in that poem by itself. That is, low-frequency words (of between one and four occurrences each) make up 90.7 per cent of the poem. Compare these numbers with modern English, where 50 per cent of the vocabulary appears once only, and 80 per cent one to four times. Chaucer seems to repeat single words to a lesser degree than we do today.[14] Of course, George Kingsley Zipf predicts 'for smaller samples one finds too many words that occur only once,'[15] and so a fairer test is his prediction that 'the number of different words in the sample must equal the number of occurrences of the most frequently used word' (Pierce 1980, 244). Although 120,000 word samples are regarded as best for Zipf's predictions, Chaucer's works as a whole have 10,068 different words (or lemmas) and 17,304 occurrences of 'and' (Benson 1993, 2:315). His rate of repetition is greater than expected. One possible explanation for this is that poetry draws more heavily than prose on previously crafted verbal schemata stored in an author's long-term memory.

If repeating phrases relate to chunking, and chunking to linked schemata in long-term memory, they should diminish when Chaucer describes the unusual (things for which he did not have a stored schema) and increase when he employs traditional poetic functions. To measure this tendency in the General Prologue, I graphed, for each of its thirty-two sections, the actual frequency of repetends against the 'expected' frequency. This hypothetical expected frequency is the number of times repeating phrases should occur, assuming their even spread throughout the entire poem. Light concentrations of repeating phrases and collocations – between a third and half of what is expected – occur in the portraits of the Monk, the Friar, the Clerk, the Craftsmen, the Cook, the Shipman, and the Doctor. In phraseology, these passages stand out as unconventional; for example, they contain lists of authorities (the Doctor) and of place names (the Shipman). The Prioress, the Miller, the Reeve, the Summoner, and the Pardoner have an average number of repeating phrases. Heavy concentrations – between a third and twice as much as expected – occur in the descriptions of the Tabard Inn (19–34), the Squire (79–100), the Yeoman (101–17), the Wife of Bath (445–76), the Plowman (529–41), the Manciple (567–86) and the Host (747–57), and in the conclusion (842–58). Some passages do little more than gracefully knit a phrasal fabric.

Here are the final 17 lines of the General Prologue. Words belonging to repeating phrases appear in italics followed by their numbers in superscript. Underlining distinguishes collocations from fixed-order phrases. About one-half (69 of 140 words) of the words in this passage belong to one or more repeating phrases in this section. The 24 repeating phrases average, as in the *Troilus* excerpts, three words in length:

842 Anon to drawen *every wight*[290] bigan,
843 And *shortly for to tellen*[54] *as it was*,[292]
844 Were it *by*[160] *aventure*,[160, 293] or sort, or _cas_,[293]
845 The *sothe is this*:[294] the _cut fil_[463] _to_ the Knyght,
846 Of which ful _blithe_ and _glad_[295] was *every wyght*,[290]
847 And _telle_ he moste his _tale_,[251] as was resoun,
848 _By_ foreward and _by composicioun_,[296]
849 *As ye han herd*[55]; *what nedeth wordes mo*?[297]
850 And _whan_[292] this *goode man*[298] _saugh that it was so_,[299]
851 As he that wys was and obedient
852 To kepe his foreward by his *free assent*,[300]
853 He seyde, 'Syn I shal bigynne the game,
854 What, welcome be the cut, *a Goddes name!*[301]
855 Now lat us ryde, and *herkneth what I seye*.'[302]
856 *And with that word*[56] we *ryden forth oure weye*,[57]
857 And he bigan with *right a* _myrie_[101,464] _cheere_[464]
858 His tale anon, and seyde *as ye may heere*.[303]

The second part of the appendix gives the abstract notation for each repetition, together with their occurrences elsewhere in *The Canterbury Tales*. Decisions whether to conflate several patterns into one involve critical judgment.[16] Again, thirteen of seventeen (76.5 per cent) lines conclude with rhyming words that belong to a repeating phrase or collocation. Repeated phrases wrap around but do not include most propositional sentence cores: 'to drawen ... bigan,' ' he that wyse was and obedient / To kepe his foreward,' 'I shal bigynne the game,' 'Now lat us ryde,' and 'bigan .../ His tale.' This confirms Bengt Altenberg's observation about collocations in the London-Lund Corpus (1993, 239). Grammatical structure gives a clue to the function of repeating phrases. Fifteen per cent are clausal (sentences, complete clauses, and near-sentences), 17 per cent are verb phrases, 25 per cent are noun phrases, and 42 per cent are prepositional phrases. Because these last take noun phrases as their head, the noun – modified by adjectives, introduced by a preposition – dominates two-thirds of repeating phrases. This distribution corresponds to normal sentence structure.[17]

Repeating phrases 'behave' in several ways that cannot be explained by conscious usage. They appear to be attached to rhymes at line's end. As well, the disappearance of some twenty-four repeating phrases found in the General Prologue and *not* in the rest of the tales relates to length, not content. Why did Chaucer lose these twenty-four, especially the memorable 'faire* | and | fetisly' and 'sett*e* & soper,' and only twice in the rest of his works (the former occurs earlier in *The Romaunt of the Rose*,[18] and the latter in *TC* 3.608 as a variant)? Other lost repeating phrases – 'cote and hood' (which occurs three times), 'eyen step.*,' 'as a ... forneys,' 'faire*r* burgeys,' and 'a po[uv]re parsou*n' – seem striking enough to stick in memory. The collocation '... was he / ... in his contree' forms a useful rhyming couplet. Several phrases, 'of | physick,' 'thanne | wolde | he speken*,' and 'now | drawth cut,' repeat within four lines. Here the alpha value comes into play: the average length of these 'lost' phrases, 3.38 words, is 50 per cent more than that of those phrases which did survive, 2.14 words. Six lost phrases extend to four words, with single instances of five and six words in length: 'as ny as evere* he kan,' 'certeinly he was a,' '(was | he) & (in | his | contree,' 'swich a worthy,' 'but of his craft,' and 'he was with eyen.' Six of the 24 are acoustically similar and so might be retained less easily. As important is their length and make-up. The lost repeating phrases have a higher ratio of undistinguishing function words to content words (53 per cent to 47 per cent) than phrases found later in the tales (50 per cent each). Last, only 'cote | and | hood' and 'in | all*e* | the | parisshe' among the lost phrases had variant forms – a ratio of 26:24 simple forms (1.08 to 1) – whereas the total group of repeating phrases has a 798:464 (1.7 to 1) ratio. It must have been easier for Chaucer to remember repeating phrases that varied in form than ones that were invariable. The constraint of chunk length, acoustic similarity, a greater proportion of function words, and a lower number of variant forms ask for a cognitive explanation.

Another factor, the variation in the distribution of all repeated phrases throughout *The Canterbury Tales*, underscores their dependence on the state of Chaucer's long-term memory. A distribution graph (Lancashire 1992, fig. 10, 357–8) shows the difference between how many repeating phrases are expected in each section (assuming they are distributed randomly), and how many actually appear there. Fragments I–III, V, and VI show approximately the same distribution as a random model predicts, but Fragments IV and IX well exceed expectations, with more General Prologue phrases than expected, and Fragments VII, VIII, and X fall well below the same expectations. The increase appears mainly in the Merchant's Tale and the Manciple's Tale, and the drop just in Melibee, the Second Nun's Tale and the Parson's Tale, within those four fragments.

What explains this variation? The drop in Fragments VII and X might have occurred because Chaucer translated the tale of Melibee and the Parson's sermon and so they contain idioms foreign to his own, but the Clerk's Tale, also translated (from Petrarch), has more repeated phrases than predicted. The change from verse to prose in Melibee and the sermon looks to be responsible. Chaucer's phrases may well differ by genre. The drop in Fragment VIII occurs in the Second Nun's Tale, a poem. Conventionality of expression may be a factor, as the Man of Law's Tale and the Prioress's Tale have marginally fewer phrasal repetitions than average. 'Unconventional,' however, is not the term most readers would use to describe the Second Nun's Tale. It likely operates with a significantly different group of repeated phrases than occur in the rest of the tales. Chronology may explain the anomaly. Chaucer evidently wrote the Second Nun's Tale before the General Prologue, on the basis of rhyme scheme and the tale-teller's reference to himself as an 'unworthy sone of Eve' (62). Most editors independently date this tale early in Chaucer's career, about 1373 or 1372–80, well before the General Prologue (ca 1388–92; Chaucer 1987, xxix, 942).

Changing with time, like most people's handwriting, repeating phrases can help assign a date to the prologues and tales. The General Prologue, for example, shares many more phrases than expected with the Manciple's Prologue and Tale, and the Merchant's Prologue and Tale (see the appendix, graph 1, and Lancashire 1992). The Merchant's Tale, of all the tales, shares by far the most General Prologue phrases.

Referring often to Jerome's *Epistola adversus Jovinianum*, which Chaucer acknowledges in the revised Prologue to the Legend of Good Women (ca 1395–6) but not in the original Prologue (ca 1386–8; Chaucer 1987, 864, 1060), the Merchant's Tale has been assigned to 1386–94. These limits centre on the five-year period independently suggested for the General Prologue. Next closest is Fragment IX, the Manciple's Tale, buttressed by its own prologue and, in Fragment X, the Parson's Prologue, which mentions the Manciple's tale: the three sections clearly belong together. Dating Fragment IX, however, has proved difficult for lack of evidence. If composed about the same time as the tales in Fragment I, the Host's and Manciple's mocking of the Cook as too drunken to tell a tale would jar with the fragmentary Cook's Tale. Larry Benson writes: 'Perhaps Chaucer intended to cancel the Cook's Prologue and the fragmentary Cook's Tale' (Chaucer 1987, 952). If so, the writing of Fragment IX followed that of the close of Fragment I. Does the distribution of repeated phrases, then, not imply that Fragment IX and the General Prologue were composed about the same time, after the rest of Fragment I?

Temporal proximity must account for the unusual overlap of repeated phrases among the General Prologue, the Merchant's Tale, the Manciple's Tale, and the Canon's Yeoman's Tale. The contents of Chaucer's memory changed over time, as our memories certainly do today, and some early associational links in his word combinations weakened, while other ones, laid down later, were recollected more readily. The unevenness in their distribution through the tales must result from their being written at different times. The more repeating phrases two tales share, in the absence of other factors, the closer in time are their dates of composition. A text's profile of phrasal repetitions, then, may date-stamp a text, locating it chronologically with other texts by the same author.

Not only is Chaucer's idiolect alive in *The House of Fame*, *Troilus*, and *The Canterbury Tales*, but these works share markers of his brain's state and activity year by year. Chaucer's phrasal density has a pulse-like wave; it is as if he alternated innovative use of language with stretches in which he relied on a familiar phrasal store, as in openings and closings of conventional sections, which show particularly heavy repeated clusters. The patterns of distribution that these repeated phrases show over many years of composition mirror Chaucer's associative long-term memory as it changes over time.

Allowing his texts to stand after reading them, Chaucer was conscious of how they looked, but of verbalization, the process that made them, he knew no more than anyone else. It could, theoretically, produce nonsense, for all that Chaucer consciously was able to manage the craft. His dumb, nerdy, funny little persona (Geoffrey) lets everyone know that truth in the spoken tale of Sir Thopas. This is a story Chaucer's persona could have picked up at the House of Fame. Worse luck, although little Geoffrey can rhyme spontaneously when a subject appears, his inner poet is without basic good judgment. The Host calls his interrupted tale 'verray lewednesse,' 'drasty speche,' and 'rym dogerel' (921–5); and Chaucer does not object to being insulted and having himself cut off in mid-flow. His helplessness before Geoffrey's embarrassing output tells us more than that Chaucer disliked trite romances. (No doubt this is Chaucerian literary criticism, but it is much more than that.) He lets us know that he has precious little conscious control over his making until it is on paper. Little wonder that Fulgentius, and Chaucer, spent so little time explaining verbalization, the last stage in muse-governed authoring. The saddest of all Chaucer's writings, the retraction at the end of the Parson's tale, begs forgiveness for other inexplicable lapses of mind over which he had no power. These crimes include all his poems that we have come to love. Chaucer attributes them all 'to the defaute of myn unkonnynge, and nat to my wyl, that wolde ful fayn have seyd bettre if I hadde had konnynge' (1081). This excuse puzzles readers because it asks them to believe an absurdity, that Chaucer did not know that celebrating adulterous love was sinful when he wrote *Troilus*! There is a saner gloss on the retraction. Chaucer refers to the strange suspension of conscious will, the impossibility of controlling verbalization in mid-course. He is pleading not guilty by reason of being out of his mind and in a profound state of 'unkonnynge' at the moment of sin.

*   *   *   *   *

Auden took me early and never let me go and came to S. Michael's to read in the late 60s, and he was craggy, rumpled, and donnish, his face deeply lined, slouching in a chair on the dais when O'Driscoll called him 'The world's greatest living poet, W.B. ...' and Auden kicked him with slippered foot and we laughed with them and we clapped because Auden was a hero and knew Tolkien who answered the only fan mail we ever wrote and we couldn't separate them from their works because you suspected then that I was the real deal and that they had me, and you felt the same

about Chaucer who we wanted to invite home for supper and we taught
what you took to be his me as much as the texts and couldn't see how we
could love an author if he was so different from one reader to another? and
so you turned to computers to find out why and you founded CCH and
I sulked in 1985 as you plumbed old Geoffrey's numbers as if they were
clues to his me.

II   William Shakespeare

The poet's eye, in a fine frenzy rolling,
Doth glance from heaven to earth, from earth to heaven;
And as imagination bodies forth
The forms of things unknown, the poet's pen
Turns them to shapes, and gives to aery nothing
A local habitation and a name.   (*MSND* 5.1.12–17)

In the preface to the first folio (1623), John Heminge and Henry Condell say that their late friend Will's 'mind and hand went together: And what he thought, he vttered with that easinesse, that wee haue scarse receiued from him a blot in his papers.' What Heminge and Condell described as easy uttering, others call flow. Shakespeare wrote with apparently unlaboured, natural spontaneity, leaving behind drafts that looked like fair copies. Ben Jonson's verse tribute, featured in the preliminaries of the first folio, also traced Shakespeare's greatness to nature (what comes by birth) but insisted that conscious editorial revision enhanced it. He compared Shakespeare to a blacksmith who repeatedly hammers the heated metal, striking 'the second heat / Vpon the *Muses* anuile' so as to produce 'well torned, and true-filed lines' (Shakespeare 1997, 98: 60–1, 68). This sentiment was wishful thinking. Jonson simply could not bring himself to say publicly what he thought, that Shakespeare did not revise his first copy. In 'Timber,' some years later, Jonson admits to agreeing with Heminge and Condell, whom he called 'the Players,' about Shakespeare's easiness. Otherwise, how could Shakespeare have written so many absurd lines? '[W]ould he had blotted a thousand,' Jonson grumbles (1997, 1073). Having such an 'excellent *Phantsie,*' with 'brave notions, and gentle expressions,' Shakespeare 'flow'd with that facility' to the degree 'that sometime it was necessary he should be stop'd.' Both the players and Shakespeare's chief rival, then, agreed about Shakespeare's flow. And Shakespeare did too. In Sonnet 76 he asks,

Why write I still all one, ever the same,
And keep invention in a noted weed,
That every word doth almost feal my name,
Showing their birth, and where they did proceed?   (5–8)

Normally, editors emend to 'tell my name' but the original text is the
verb 'fel,' a spelling of the verb 'conceal.' Shakespeare believed that,
although his name was 'almost' hidden in the texts he wrote, words
revealed his true authorship. His audience used oral text analysis, and
his readers anticipated researchers today.

Did Shakespeare imagine that muse experiences dictated his flow, as
it does Alice Flaherty's or Paul Auster's? Shakespeare's sonnets depict
his muse always as a *person*: a young man ('the tenth Muse'; 38.9) or
a woman (103.2), possibly those to whom he wrote his sonnets. This
muse enables Shakespeare to 'invent' a subject (38.1) with 'fury' and
'pow'r' (100.3–4), like the dynamic entity to whom the Prologue in
Henry V appeals: 'O for a Muse of fire, that would ascend / The bright-
est heaven of invention' (1–2). This fury resembles the mania of which
authors write. The poet of *A Midsummer Night's Dream*, for example,
says that imagination moves between earth and heaven. It inspires or
empowers the poet to think of new 'forms,' to give them bodily 'shapes'
and a place, and finally to name them, as Adam did the creatures. Interpreting Shakespeare's figures of speech is not an exact science, but this
passage could describe a three-stage creative process. Beginning with
a wordless gist, powered by emotion ('fury' and 'fire'), the poet visualizes the affective gist by drawing on long-term memory (for bodily
'shapes'), and then moves into lexical production, which names the
imagined thing. The muse pervades all stages of the process, feeling,
seeing, and uttering. When not 'tongue-tied' (85.1), 'dumb' and silent
(101.9–10), it can speak, sing (100.2, 7), and write with a 'pen' (100.8).
Poignantly, for what is sadder than inaccessible memories, it can also be
'forgetful' (100.5) and 'truant' (101.1).

Shakespeare's paradoxically 'forgetful' muse gives my book its name.
She/he is more than etymologically associated with a goddess-mother
of memory: deeply human at her/his core, Shakespeare's muse suffers,
like Polyhymnia on the Achilles Painter's urn, the very mental frail-
ties we find in ourselves. Sometimes she/he stops flowing. Other times
she/he commits, as Jonson says, absurdities. His critique could hardly
have been news to Shakespeare, whose Holophernes (the comic pedant
of *Love's Labors Lost*) shares his maker's method and misuses it in the

same ways that Jonson regrets in his good friend: 'This is a gift that I have, simple; simple, a foolish extravagant spirit, full of forms, figures, shapes, objects, ideas, apprehensions, motions, revolutions. These are begot in the ventricle of memory, nourish'd in the womb of pia mater, and delivered upon the mellowing of occasion. But the gift is good in those in whom it is acute, and I am thankful for it' (Holophernes, *LLL* 4.2.65–72). Mercutio in *Romeo and Juliet* agrees:

> True, I talk of dreams,
> Which are the children of an idle brain,
> Begot of nothing but vain fantasy,
> Which is as thin of substance as the air,
> And more inconstant than the wind, who woos
> Even now the frozen bosom of the north,
> And, being anger'd, puffs away from thence,
> Turning his side to the dew-dropping south.   (*Romeo and Juliet* 1.4.96–103)

Mercutio and Shakespeare understand the 'inconstant' flow of this muse to be a product of the brain first, not just the mind. It happens when they are 'idle,' doing nothing, only daydreaming – when the default mode network is active. Something 'angry' (the emotional gist taken from long-term memory) accompanies its generation, which is, as far as the poet is concerned (who does not experience its happenings), conceived by nothingness. Of course, because these are the words of Shakespeare's characters, not Will himself, we cannot be sure that he would agree with them. Yet when he dramatizes men who are self-deceiving or lying – Lear and Othello, Edmund and Iago, Malvolio and Feste – he normally exposes their falsehoods openly on stage. Shakespeare's fictional poets may be silly, but they are not called liars. Their testimony resembles his own in the sonnets. Shakespeare does not contradict it or disown their witness.

Shakespeare believed that, while he, like other poets, created in a dream-like, unconscious flow from an inner voice different from his own, his flow could be readily recognized as his own by people who heard it from a seat in the Globe, or who read a few sonnets. This claim, that his signature ('my name') was widely recognizable in his writings, seems disingenuous. Present-day researchers in authorship attribution use sophisticated text-analysis software and are still deeply divided on what belongs in his canon. If alive today, Shakespeare might be surprised at all the fuss. 'Can't we all recognize one face from many thousands very quickly, even after years?' he might say. International business today also invests a huge faith, and vast sums of money, in the belief that a person's signature is a reliable marker of identity. Which markers in a text compare well with the visual markers in a face or a signature? We are not speaking of a time-resistant genetic marker, like a fingerprint, or a chemical litmus test, but a man-made shape that changes as years pass. We might use the phrase *date-stamped idiolect* or *cognitive style*, but it is no unchanging configuration of visible features. It alters subtly with the changes that time writes on the individual mind.

An author's signature can be found in his repetend clusters, the networks of repeating fixed phrases and collocations in a text. These clusters are fragmentary realizations of schemata in his long-term memory. Just as we recognize a face by its combinations of visual features, or a signature by its stroke assemblages, so we can recognize Shakespeare's writing – in the way he believed we do – by its repeating verbal clusters. Styles differentiate themselves as proteins do. A protein is a combination of only twenty amino acids, repeated and folded in a certain way. Proteomics recognizes over one million proteins today, but the actual total of possible combinations is immensely more vast. No one should attribute any piece of writing to an author on stylistic grounds that appeal to certain 'distinctive features,' whether it be vocabulary size, ratio of vocabulary and repeating phrases, function words, syntax or phrase structures, or rhetorical figures. For example, Shakespeare was fond of hendiadys (Wright 1981), but anyone educated in grammar school in the nature of rhetoric (as were most boys who could write in the English Renaissance) could use and overuse that device. Idiolect markers are combinatorial, embedded in an author's long-term memory, and repeated. We recognize them by unconscious pattern matching similar to what enables us quickly to make out a face in a crowd.

Authors with an identifiable idiolect will have submitted to flow, as Shakespeare does, keeping to a miminum any editorial interference with long-term memory schemata during lexical production. There are two kinds of repetend clusters, corresponding to the alpha and omega values: chunk size and maximum cognitive load. The mini-clusters in chunks are repeating fixed phrases; the larger repeating semantic clusters appear as collocations in paragraph-sized windows of text. Both resist conscious observation but nonetheless have an impact on the audience or readers in the same way that complex experiences, quickly lost in the welter of the senses, have a long-term impact on memory.

To find phrasal repetends, we begin with Shakespeare's vocabulary.

There are 29,066 word types in the 884,647 word tokens in Marvin Spevack's concordance of the modernized Riverside edition of Shakespeare's poems and plays. However, Shakespeare's working written vocabulary is actually much smaller than this number. I use the electronic Shakespeare by Wells, Taylor, Montgomery, and Burnard as published by Oxford University Press (1989). Discounting plays on which Shakespeare is believed to have collaborated with others – the *Henry VI* trilogy, *Titus Andronicus*, *Edward III*, *Pericles*, *Henry VIII*, and *The Two Noble Kinsmen* – as well as speech prefixes and stage directions (for which stage prompters and scribes may be responsible wholly or in part), R.J.C. Watt's *Concordance* detects about 725,000 word tokens and 25,500 word forms. Because Spevack's concordance gives separate entries to inflectional and even orthographical variants of adjectives, nouns, and verbs, and because *Concordance* does not lemmatize word-forms, Alfred Hart's estimate, 17,677 different words,[19] is more trustworthy, although it too includes the above texts that I exclude. If we generalize from the 1,690 entries beginning with 'm' in Spevack's concordance, only 54.8 per cent of which are distinct word types, Shakespeare's total *written* lexicon is about 16,000 different words (54.8/100 * 29,066), a number that confirms Hart. Shakespeare's vocabulary increased from *Richard III* in 1592–3 to *The Tempest* in 1611.[20] Works written from 1602 to 1611, for example, have 3,727 different words in the first 20,000 lines, an increase of 500 words or 15 per cent over works from the first period, 1592–6, which have 3,247 different words. The longer that his plays and poems got, and the older he became, the more different words he used (see appendix, graph 2).[21]

His lexicon also varied by genre (see appendix, graph 3). In the first 15,000 words of the texts, comedies had the smallest vocabulary (2,694 different words), and among the plays the romances had the largest (2,984 different words). However, the four major poems that Shakespeare wrote had a much larger lexicon than any of the dramatic genres. In the first 15,000 words, his poems had 300 more different words (or 10 per cent) than the romances, and 580 different words more than the comedies (or 22 per cent). Given that the poems and the comedies were written in the same period and that all genres consist of pentameter verses, genres must have relied on somewhat different schemata for long-term memory.

Shakespeare's oral lexicon, the words that he would have recognized when listening to others or reading their works, was obviously much larger than his written lexicon.[22] For example, in one of his presumed sources for *Macbeth*, the account of the usurpation and reign of Macbeth in Raphael Holinshed's *Chronicles of Scotland*, legitimate Early Modern English words appear that Shakespeare never (as far as we know) wrote: 'rear supper,' 'collation,' 'buskling,' 'finances,' 'middle ward,' the verb 'confection,' 'micklewort,' 'sepulture,' 'necromantical,' 'unquenchable,' 'investure,' 'chancemedley,' 'prepensed,' 'cavillation,' and 'misgovernance.' Much is made of Shakespeare's role as a word maker, employing zero derivation (shifting the part of speech of known words), neologizing, and borrowing from other tongues. He was as responsible for the growth of his native tongue as other major writers in the period.

Like Chaucer, Shakespeare had a substantial phrasal lexicon. Quantitatively, Shakespeare's idiolect is consistent with how cognitive psychology has depicted language production. Repeating phrases – chunks – outnumber threefold his vocabulary or lexical word types. Divided into two chronological groups, Shakespeare's plays have 58,700 different repeating fixed-phrase forms (which include variant inflections) from 1592 to 1598, and 66,300 different repeating fixed-phrase forms from 1599 to 1611.[23] That amounts to 3.4–3.5 times the number of different word forms in texts from those two periods. Although Shakespeare's phrasal lexicon was triple the size of his word vocabulary, these repeating fixed phrases employed only a third of his vocabulary. They consist mainly of sequences of function words that form grammatical frames for content words, nouns, verbs, and adjectives.

Hand D in The Book of Sir Thomas More

We can see this forgetful but passionate muse at work in Shakespeare's holograph part of the collaborative manuscript play *The Book of Sir Thomas More*, which he co-wrote with Anthony Munday, Henry Chettle, and others about 1594–5. The three leaves of Hand D, found over one hundred years ago in British Library MS Harley 7368, are now accepted by the scholarly community as having been written by Shakespeare. The textual editor of the *Riverside Shakespeare*, G. Blakemore Evans, describes the 147 lines of Addition II by Hand D as 'an authorial first draft, with vague and carelessly used speech prefixes and with deletions and insertions made in the process of composition' (1997, 1777). W.W. Greg, one of the first great bibliographers of Early Modern English literature, says that 'It is without question the hand of an author composing as he writes, probably with great fluency' (Greg 1923, 45). Figure 12, a facsimile of folio 9r (part of this Addition), shows a secretary hand with some odd features, like the so-called spurred *a* ('hath' in line 7), an unusual letter form found in Shakespeare's signatures.

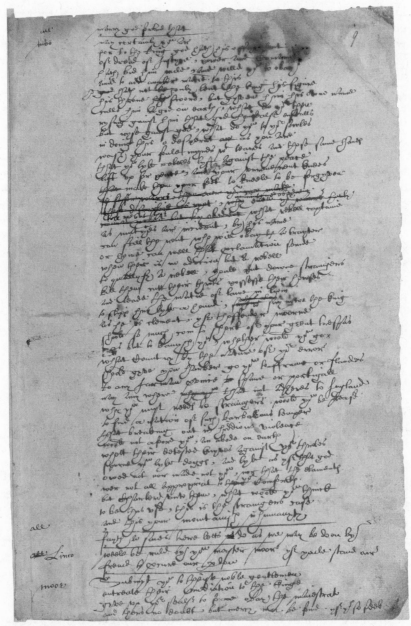

Figure 18. Hand D, 'The Play of Sir Thomas More,' © British Library Board (Harley MS 7368, fol. 9r)

What can this leaf tell us about Shakespeare's language production?

My encoded transcription of folio 9r, in hand D, illustrates the size and variety of Shakespeare's repeating phrases and clusters, and, by implication, his alpha and omega values, chunking, and cognitive load. The table segments the passage according to three boundaries, the verse-line end, any mid-line punctuation, and the points of error repair. The transcription has five columns: a line number (1–52), the number of syllables in the segment (3–14), the speech prefix (if any), the text of the segment, and the fixed phrases in the segment that are found in Shakespeare's works, 1592–8. Also marked, in boldface, are three passages where Shakespeare's composition slowed down considerably, to judge from letter and word spacing, word size, and writing out of a word normally abbreviated. Finally, I have underlined word sequences that are repeated and varied within this leaf.

Blank-verse lines, written so as to be 10–11 syllables in length, are conceptual units for playwrights of this period. Shakespeare shaped his speech so as to fit it in these decasyllabic sequences, but he also half the time broke lines at mid-point: here, in 24 of the 52 lines. These caesural pauses are marked plainly by a comma or a period, and most segments over nine syllables in length have a medial pause, signalled seven times by a long space, encoded here as <> (10, 13, 16, 37, 45, 47, 50). Shakespeare's unpunctuated passages signal flow and coincide with a quite rapid handwriting, and his punctuation marks indicate brief delays in that flow, as at lines 18–21:

> why euen yor hurly
> cannot proceed but by obedienc what rebell captaine
> as mutynes ar incident, by his name
> can still the rout.

His flow also links two independent clauses without a sentence-ending period or comma after 'obedienc'; and lines 24–5 go unpunctuated despite their stream of verbs: 'youle put downe straingers / kill them cutt their throts possesse their howses.' Shakespeare used pointing to pause while he waited for the next segment to form. The two dozen set-off 5/6-syllable half-lines show a regular constraint at work, suggesting that Shakespeare composed in phrasal chunks and chunk sequences.

What does this table say about chunking and cognitive load?

The 52 lines of folio 9r have a vocabulary of about 240 word types and about 180 different fixed phrases that occur elsewhere in his assured plays from 1592 to 1596. The average syllables per segment are 7.1, and segments range in length from three to 13 syllables. These segments show that Shakespeare composed mentally in units that correspond to the alpha value, the span in which he self-repairs errors,[24] and his reading span. Charles Forker (1989, 156–8) has identified, by working from the Riverside concordance, several repeating phrases on this leaf that characterize Shakespeare's lexical style: 'marry god forbid' (1), 'nay certainly' (2), 'as you are' (12), 'put downe' (24), 'com to short' (29), and 'lyke as' (40). (Two [2, 24] do not turn up among the repeating phrases in my table because they recur only in his post-1596 plays.) Forker's chunks average 2.5 words in length. The repetends I find in the passage are a little short of the alpha value: 19 fixed phrases are three words long, and the rest are two words only. The shortness of the text explains why vocabulary here exceeds different repeating phrases, which use only 125 different words, just under 50 per cent of the leaf's vocabulary. The ratio of function word types to content word types is 64:61, but the ratio of function word tokens to content word tokens (word counts) is 288:93. Thus function words occur three times as often as content words. If a cognitive chunk holds three or four words, then, it should consist of about three function words and one content word.

The chunk division in a long segment occurs at the point where one of Shakespeare's known repeating phrases starts or ends: 'to the king' (3, 50), 'ma[jes]tie to' (6), 'w^t teares' (13), 'well that' (22), 'ther is no' (23), 'go yo^u to' (32), 'against yor' (39), 'to yor' (42), and 'noble gentlemen' (49). Many lines are dense with repeating phrases, as the first ten lines show. They fully populate lines 1–2 and 8[25] and all but one word, usually a verb, in lines 3–7 and 9. The middle three words in line 5 ('rule and willd'), and four words at the start and end of line 10, do not show up as repeated phrases in the early Shakespeare. His segments on this leaf seem to fall into two parts, a repeated phrase (made up mainly of function words), and a non-repeating, outlier content word (adjective, noun, or verb) that fills a variable slot adjacent to them. For example, the non-repeating content words 'appropriat' and 'Comforts' complete the two segments at line 42, 'vsd' and 'straingers' at line 44, and 'mercy' and 'seek' at line 52. When content words dominate a segment or line, no repeated phrases appear: e.g., 'whose discipline is ryot' (18), 'kill them cutt their throts possesse their howses' (25), and 'spane or portigall' (33). When a line has no content words, as at 7 ('he hath not'), 9 ('what do yo^u then'), and 12 ('as you are'), the entire line consists of one or two repeated phrases.

L.	Sy.	S.P.	Leaf 9r Text	Fixed Phrases Shakespeare Repeats 1592–6
1	6	all	**marry god forbid that**	Marry God forbid 3 (Forker 23)	God forbid 12
2	6	moo	**nay certainly yoᵘ ar**	nay certainly (post-1598; Forker 24) you are 262
3	10		**for to the king** god hath his offyce lent	for to 13	to the 524	to the king 16	the king 217	God hath 3	hath his 5	his office 2
4	5		of dread of lustyce ,	of dread 3	of justice 6
4	5		power and Comaund	power and 5
5	4		hath bid him rule ,	hath bid 2	bid him 17
5	6		and willd yoᵘ to obay	you to 129	to obey 3
6	10		and to add ampler matie . to this	And to 129	to add 3	majesty to 6	to this 96
7	3		he god hath not te	He hath 145	He hath not 6	hath not 37	not only 9
7	8		only lent the king his figure	the king 217	his figure 2
8	4		his throne his & sword ,	His throne 3	throne and 3	sword but 2
8	7		but gyven him his owne name	given him 3	him his 8	his own 53	own name 2
9	6		calls him <> a god on earth ,	him a 35	a god 377	god on 4	on earth 13
9	4		what do yoᵘ then	What do 12 What do you 8	do you 118	you then 15
10	10		rysing gainst him <> that god himsealf enstalls	him that 58	that God 6	God himself 2
11	4		but <> ryse gainst god ,	God What 2
11	6		what <> do yoᵘ to yoʳ sowles	What do you 8	do you 118	you to 129	you to your 5	your souls 5
12	7		in doing this <> o desperat ar	
12	3		as you are .	as you are 9 (Forker 25)	you are 262
13	10		**wash your foule mynds** wᵗ teares <> and those same hands	wash your 3	your foul 2	with tears 18	tears and 11	and those 8	those same 3	hands that 3
14	10		that yoᵘ lyke rebells lyft against the peace	that you 173	you like 16	against the 54	the peace 17
15	4		lift <> vp for peace ,	up for 6	peace and 17
15	6		and your vnreuerent knees	and your 59
16	10		that make them your feet <> to kneele to be <> forgyven	Make them 18	kneel to 2	To be 380
17	4		is safer warrs ,	
17	6		then euer yoᵘ can make	than ever 4	ever you 3	you can 26

L.	Sy.	S.P.	Leaf 9r Text	Fixed Phrases Shakespeare Repeats 1592–6
18	7		whose discipline is ryot ,	in to 16 (Forker 27) | to your 125
18	8		in, in, to your obedience!	
18	4		why euen yoᵘ warrs hurly	
19	14		cannot proceed but by obedienc what rebell captaine	but by 32
20	7		as mutynes ar incident ,	
20	3		by his name	by his 45 | his name 35
21	11		can still the rout who will obay th a traytor	still the 10 | Who will 5 | a traitor 12
22	10		or howe can well that proclamation sounde	how can 15 | well that 13
23	11		when ther is no adicion but a rebell	When there 5 | When there is 2 | there is 174 | there is no 51 | but a 96
24	7		to qualyfy a rebell ,	To qualify 2
24	5		youle put downe straingers	
25	10		kill them cutt their throts possesse their howses	
26	10		and leade the matie of lawe in liom	And lead 6 | lead the 3 | majesty of 2 | of law 7 | law in 3
27	6		to slipp him lyke a hound ,	him like 11 | him like a 8 | like a 230 | a hound 3
27	8		seyeng alas alas say nowe the king	alas alas 3 | Say now 2 | now the 32 | the king 217 | King as 5
28	5		as he is clement ,	As he 61 | As he is 11
28	5		yf thoffendor moorne	if the 53
29	11		shoold so much com to short of your great trespas	Should so 6 | so much 99 | come too 4 | too short 6 | too short of 2 | of your 176 | your great 3
30	6		as but to banysh yoᵘ ,	but to 73 | to banish 2
30	5		whether woold yoᵘ go.	would you 36 | you go 51
31	11		what Country by the nature of yoʳ error	by the 248 | of your 176
32	12		shoold gyve you harber go yoᵘ to ffraunc or flanders	Should give 5 | give you 38 | Go you 24 | Go you to 5 | to France 9
33	6		to any larman province ,	To any 19
33	5		te spane or portigall	
34	4		nay any where why yoᵘ	
34	7		that not adheres to Ingland	that not 3 | to England 8

L.	Sy.	S.P.	Leaf 9r Text	Fixed Phrases Shakespeare Repeats 1592–6
35	7		why yo^u must <> needs be strangers .	Why you 9 | you must 72 | you must needs 4 | must needs 17 | I must needs be 5
35	4		woold yo^u be pleasd	Would you 36 | you be 40 | be pleased 9
36	11		to find a nation of such barbarbous temper	To find 25 | To find a 4 | of such 52
37	11		that breaking <> out in hiddious violence	out in 11
38	5		woold not afoord yo^u ,	Would not 86 | you an 4
38	5		an abode on earth	on earth 13
39	10		whett their detested knyves against yor throtes	against your 13
40	4		spurne yo^u lyke doggs ,	you like 16
40	6		and lyke as yf that god	and like 24 | like as 3 | as if 46 | as if that 2 | that God 6
41	6		owed not nor made not yo^u ,	not nor 10 | not you 44 | you nor 4
41	6		nor that the elements	nor that 4 | that the 109
42	11		wer not all appropriat to ther yor Comforts .	Were not 30 | not all 13 | to your 125
43	6		but Charterd vnto them,	
43	4		what woold yo^u thinck	what would 20 | what would you 9 | you think 29 | think To 11
44	4		to be thus vsd ,	To be 380 | To be thus 3
44	6		this is the straingers case	This is 157 | This is the 48 | is the 296 | the case 8
45	11	all	and this your <> momtanish <> in humanyty	And this 66 | this your 8
46	13		fayth a saies trewe letts vs do as we may be doon by	Faith a 4 | do as 15 | as we 41 | we may 35 | we may be 2 | may be 93 | be done 19 | done by 4
47	12	~~all~~ Linco	weele be ruld by yo^u master moor <> yf youle stand our	We'll be 2 | be ruled 12 | be ruled by 10 | be you 19 | you Master 8 | more if 3 | if you'll 2
48	7		freind to procure our pardon	friend to 4
49	10	moor	Submyt yo^u to theise noble gentlemen	you to 129 | noble gentlemen 2
50	10		entreate their <> mediation to the kinge	to the 524 | to the King 16 | the king 217
51	12		gyve vp yor sealf to forme obay the maiestrate	yourself to 5
52	4		and thers no doubt,	and there is 6 | there is 174 | there is no 51 | no doubt 19 | doubt but 3
52	6		but mercy may be found. <>	may be 93 | be found 10
52	5		yf yo^u so seek it	If you 202 | you so 27

What can we learn about Shakespeare's cognitive load, his omega value, from this page? There are several clues in identifying that value: the sentence or the period, bouts of repetition, the apparent slowing down of his handwriting, and the leaving of unusual space between words. Shakespeare's omega value is the largest segment identified by the presence of these markers. In my opinion (and that is all it is), there seem to be six periods, lines 1–12, 13–16, 17–27, 27–34, 35–45, and 46–52. They correspond with sentence units (except for the closing dialogue) and vary in length from 4 to 12 lines and average 8.8 lines. A two-line passage of thought introduces the first period.

Evidence of period boundaries occurs when Shakespeare's hand slows down, the writing equivalent to hesitation in speech. A combination of traits in letter spacing, word size, and expansion of a normally abbreviated word identify four passages as written more slowly than the rest. They are (a) lines 1–3, (b) lines 12–13, (c) 15–16, and (d) line 45. The two telltale orthographic signals of delay in lines 1–3 are the separation of the initial *fo* from the rest of the word in 'fo rbid' (1) and 'fo r' (2), and the whole or partial isolation of the initial or medial 't' from the rest of the word in 'cer t ainly' (2) and 't o' (3).[26] Note also the separation of 'g' from the rest of the word 'g od' (1), and the isolation of 'r' in 'ce r t ainly' (2). These signs mark the first period, lines 3–12. Line 13 has both separated initial 'fo' (in 'fo ule') and the first occurrence, on this page, of expanded 'your.' (Shakespeare normally uses abbreviated 'yor,' the sign of a rapid hand at work, as in lines 11, 18, 31, 39, 42, and 51.) This is the brief second period. Lines 15–16 (each slowly penned) also expand 'your,' beginning the longer third period. It ends about lines 27–8 with more slow penmanship and introduces the short fourth passage, which ends at line 34, just before a line with a wide space between words. The fifth period closes with the slowest-penned line of the page, line 45, which exhibits three features of slow penmanship: unabbreviated 'your,' the isolation of 't' in the odd word 'momtanish,' and the separation of the prefix 'in' ('in humanyty').[27] The last period begins at the close of More's monologue.

Repetition gives some confirming evidence for these periods. Shakespeare was affected by what he had just uttered on six occasions when he repeats, with variation, word clusters or semantic groupings that occurred earlier. One grouping elicited a conscious error check: the repetition of 'god,' 'lent,' and 'king' (3, 7). Three other clusters have repetitions following one another closely: the lexeme cluster 'rise,' 'gainst,' and 'god' (at lines 10 and 11), the cluster 'lift' and 'peace' (at lines 14 and

15), and the cluster 'wars,' 'discipline'/'obedience,' and 'riot'/'rout' (at lines 17–18 and 18–21). These clusters occur inside spans that fit into the phonological loop of working memory, as well as inside periods. Two other clusters, however, activate only after a longer interval, eleven and eight lines later. The first is the cluster 'obay'/'obedience,' 'king'/'rebel,' and 'name' (at lines 5–8 and 19–20). The second is the cluster 'strangers,' 'cut'/'knives,' 'throats,' 'houses'/'abode,' and 'hound'/'dogs' (at lines 24– 7 and 35–40). They occur shortly after the beginning of the third and the fifth periods. They could be feedback from persistence of vision, the effect of iconic sensory memory as Shakespeare kept his eyes on the page; or, from time to time, when at a pause, he let them shift upwards in a recursive saccade. Because the pause separates one period from another, the point of repetition of such widely separated clusters marks the end of one thought, and the beginning of another: that is, they mark cognitive load. All illustrate cybertextual cycling at work.

Sometimes, delays in writing signal a cognitive processing problem. Lines 1–3 reveal Shakespeare pausing to work out the gist of what More's speech to the mob will be. Delays at lines 13 and 15–16 appear related to Shakespeare's repair of errors at the end of line 12 and at the beginning of line 16. Line 45 is especially interesting. Shakespeare originally intended this line to be the crowd's (as the speech prefix 'all' shows), but after he penned the prefix he decided that it would be More's crowning indictment of the mob. The first content word in this insult, 'momtanish,' is unrecorded elsewhere in English: whatever it means (and editors have preferred the easy way out, emending rather than accepting it), Shakespeare invented the term, and to this day it will elicit an N400 wave in most of us on reading.[28]

The alpha and omega values set the forms in which Shakespeare authors but do not themselves give distinguishing idiolectal markers of his work. Only the content within the form does so. Here, evidence of semantic schemata is important. Forker (1989) identifies one persistent content pattern, the use of 'unreverent' with a following noun for a body part, 'vnreverend knees' (15; cf. *TGV* 2.6.14, *R2* 2.1.123); and in 1593–1608 a collocation of the verb 'slip' and the noun 'hound' in line 27, 'to slipp him lyke a hound' (*Shr* 5.2.52, *1H4* 1.3.278, *H5* 3.1.31, *JC* 3.1.275, *Cor* 1.6.38–9). This persistent stylistic tic in Shakespeare's mind does not characterize his chunking but rather his associative memory and his emotional cast, both of which have much to do with the formation of the gist of an utterance. Such tics belong to schemata, networks of personal memories, sensory experiences, sounds, situations, vocabulary, and repeating phrases more or less strongly associated with a common single phenomenon about which Shakespeare had some feelings.

Walter Whiter in 1794 first proposed that Shakespeare's imagery often arises from eccentrically associated ideas, ones of which he was 'totally unconscious' (1972, 140n). Lacking a computer, Whiter could only study content words, but his reliance on John Locke and his psychological interpretation of lexical regularities led Edward A. Armstrong to publish in 1946 the first psychological study of Shakespeare's associative mind. Using Bartlett's printed concordance (1922), Armstrong focused on bird imagery, a subject on which he had already published three books. He drew from twentieth-century textbooks and treatises of modern psychology and psychoanalysis to argue, not unpersuasively, that emotion-charged experiences led Shakespeare unconsciously and repeatedly to link an image with a sometimes surprising nexus of features. Armstrong stressed the constructive powers of Shakespeare's and our memories. They do not objectively or even rationally mirror the things they serve. We, or our experiences and genetic make-up, selectively collect features into sets.[29]

Caroline Spurgeon's *Shakespeare's Imagery and What It Tells Us* (1935) next drew attention to several associative networks in Shakespeare's metaphors, a tic of semantic behaviour that he could not or did not choose to repress. One such network associated human greed and flattery with fawning dogs. In a nation that prized its mastiffs and greyhounds, Shakespeare frequently showed contempt for dogs, especially spaniels. Spurgeon believed that clusters of repeating words, infused by a powerful emotion, created this semantic web in his long-term memory. Whenever any of the things associated in this network was triggered, Shakespeare's mind lighted up the fawning-dog metaphor. He would have become aware of it as a tic, but the collocational cluster in which it was manifested would have escaped his notice.

Spurgeon's image cluster is well supported by references from Shakespeare's works. Proteus in *Two Gentlemen of Verona* confesses that, the more Silvia rejects his love, '*spaniel*-like ... / The more it grows, and *fawneth* on her still' (4.2.14–15). Helena in *Midsummer Night's Dream* tells Demetrius, who does not want her, that 'The more you beat me, I will *fawn* on you. / Use me but as your *spaniel*' (2.1.204–5). Caesar tells flattering Cimber that his 'sweet words, / Low-crooked curtsies, and base *spaniel fawning*,' mean nothing, and that if he 'bend, and pray, and *fawn*' to have his brother's banishment appealed, Caesar will 'spurn' him 'like a *cur*' (3.1.42–3, 45–6). After his defeat at Actium, Antony observes that

The hearts
That *spanieled* [him] at heels, to whom I gave
Their wishes, do *discandy*.   (*Ant* 4.12.20–2)

Spurgeon argues that whenever Shakespeare thought about 'false
friends or flatterers,' his mind called up this 'dog, licking, candy, melt-
ing group' (195), and that his 'strong and individual tendency to return
under similar emotional stimulus to a similar picture or group of associated ideas ... forms an extraordinarily reliable test of authorship' (199).
   Roman general Titus Lartius, friend to Coriolanus, holds the city of

Corioles in the name of Rome,
Even like a *fawning greyhound* in the *leash*,
To let him *slip* at will.'   (*Cor* 1.6.37–9)

This leads in turn to Antony saying

You show'd your teeth like apes, and *fawn'd* like *hounds*,
And bow'd like bondmen, kissing Caesar's feet,
Whilst damned Casca, like a *cur*, behind,
Strook Caesar on the neck. O you *flatterers*!   (*JC* 5.1.41–4)

Or, for that matter, to Margaret's prophecies in *Richard III*:

O Buckingham, take heed of yonder *dog*!
Look when he *fawns* he bites; and when he bites,
His venom tooth will rankle to the death.   (*R3* 1.3.288–90)

This collocation recurs in *Richard II* when the king exclaims, 'O villains,
vipers, damn'd without redemption! / *Dogs*, easily won to *fawn* on
any man!' (3.2.129–30). A fourth linkage of the greyhound or dog with
fawning appears in *1 Henry IV*, where Hotspur complains of Bolingbroke in times past, 'Why, what a *candy* deal of courtesy / This *fawning
greyhound* then did proffer me!' (1.3.251–2). These verses that add a further linked concept, 'candy,' resemble a passage from *Hamlet*:

Why should the poor be *flatter'd*?
No, let the *candied* tongue lick absurd pomp,
And crook the pregnant hinges of the knee
Where thrift may follow fawning [faining F1].   (*Ham* 3.2.59–62)

Hamlet also associates this word group with bowing and licking.

Shakespeare's hounds, however, are not only obsequious but danger-ous. When More tells the mob of Londoners that, in following rebels, they 'leade the matie of lawe in liom to slipp him lyke a hound' (26–7), he uses a simile to compare English law to a hound, held on leash (or 'lyam') by rebels until released to run down anyone they wish. Because Shakespeare clearly intends the comparison to show the law demeaned, he denigrates hounds. They are weapons in anyone's hands as other instances in Shakespeare's works show. Edgar in *King Lear* tells the old king that old Tom (Edgar's mad disguise) will scatter

> Mastiff, greyhound, mongril grim,
> Hound or spaniel, brach or [lym],
> Or bobtail tike or trundle-tail,   (*KL* 3.6.68–70)

whether their mouths are 'black or white, / Tooth that poisons if it bite' (66–7). Titus and Saturninus in *Titus Andronicus* hunt panthers and harts 'With horn and hound' (1.1.494). Macbeth describes Duncan's murder-ers as men in the same way that

> hounds and greyhounds, mungrels, spaniels, curs,
> Shoughs, water-rugs, and demi-wolves are clipt
> All by the name of dogs.   (3.1.92–4)

The Prologue in *Henry V* compares leashed hounds to 'famine, sword, and fire / [which] Crouch for employment' (Pro 7–8). Brutus urges his fellow conspirators not to dismember Caesar in killing him, not to 'hew him as a carcass fit for hounds' (*JC* 2.1.174). Orsino in *Twelfth Night*, a prey to his love for Olivia, compares his desires to 'fell and cruel hounds' (2.1.174). Shakespeare's feelings are plain enough, but he did not respond in an entirely Pavlovian way to dogs. In rousing English soldiers to fight at Agincourt in the speech, 'Once more unto the breach, dear friends, once more,' Henry V compliments his fellow soldiers, 'I see you stand like *greyhounds* in the *slips*, / Straining upon the start' (3.1.31–2). As he said in Sonnet 15, Shakespeare believed that both plants and animals exhibited virtues as well as vices, and that peo-ple resembled them in good ways and bad.[30]

Repeating clusters of collocates (not fixed phrases) are the key to such schemata. Collocates recur in persistent patterns: certain open-class content words turn up together, repeatedly, in the non-phrasal 'open' slots of chunk sequences. A schema is both affective and semantic in nature. To access it requires the mind to probe long-term memory with one or two members of its cluster, a process that takes a little time before the schema 'lights up.' The repeating fixed phrases that frame those content-word slots come easily. Once the schema has been found, the mind can quickly fill the open slots of adjacent chunks.

Forker's five citations suggest a small schema, related to Spurgeon's, with the collocating lexemes, 'greyhound,' 'slip,' and 'leash.' The first passage has Petrucchio's servant Tranio in *The Taming of a Shrew* telling him that 'Lucentio *slipp'd* me like his *greyhound*, / Which runs himself, and catches for his master' (5.2.52–3). The next two are Northumberland's warning to Hotspur in *1 Henry 4*, 'Before the game is afoot thou still let'st *slip*' (1.3.278) and Henry V's rousing speech at Agincourt (quoted above). Forker's fourth quotation comes from *Julius Caesar*, where Antony predicts,

And Caesar's spirit, ranging for revenge,
With Ate by his side come hot from hell,
Shall in these confines with a monarch's voice /
Cry 'Havoc!' and let *slip* the *dogs* of war   (3.1.270–3)

In Forker's fifth citation another collocating lexical concept occurs, 'fawning,' which belongs to Spurgeon's image cluster. With Forker's 'greyhound,' 'slip,' and 'leash' belong not only Spurgeon's 'fawning,' 'dog,' 'flatter,' and 'candy,' as shown above, but the terms 'cur' and 'spaniel.' The defining features of such clusters dissolve as their boundaries become ill-defined. Although still more collocates can be added – do Edgar's 'Tooth that poisons' (*KL* 3.6.67) and Margaret's 'venom tooth' (*R3* 1.3.290) belong as well? – the less frequent outliers will have weaker associational links with the central cluster. The linkages in neural networks such as we believe long-term memory to be are fluid, like a cloud-scudding sky on an off-and-on showery day whose overcast changes in texture, density, and colour from minute to minute but always moves, if chaotically, *en masse*.

Any idiosyncratic group of collocating content words can be recognized by patient readers. If so, that cluster can be imitated by others; and, as it turns out, fawning dogs and flattery already belonged to Renaissance commonplaces, where Shakespeare himself might have seen them (J. Jackson 1950). No one, however, can plagiarize the emotions that drive the expansion and reuse of a word cluster. Shakespeare was hardly unconscious of how he felt, but how conscious emotion betrays itself in the collocations he uses would not have been obvious to him. What, then, is the author here? Is it the affect that colours the gist in long-term memory, or is it words? Feelings, not knowledge of language, establish Shakespeare's character and make it recognizable. Of course, the language into which his unconscious translates his emotions lasts in the texts he wrote and becomes the human face recognizable to listeners and readers. Emotions make for messy data, yet they drive everything we do. Authorial readings depend on finding them. Years ago, in a study that does not deserve being hidden by so many unhelpful works of Shakespeariana since then, Caroline Spurgeon (1935) anticipated recent research in neuroscience that roots cognition in affect.

Many people may share the same feeling. George Lakoff and Mark Johnson's *Metaphors We Live By* shows not only how pervasive and typical the metaphors in a language are but also that they typically map similarities from common underlying sensory schemata, such as how we experience and recognize time, space, and motion. When Shakespeare's Lear says, 'Nature is above art,' he draws on visceral, embodied feelings that looking up is better than looking down. When mad Edgar says to blinded Gloucester on leading him to an imagined cliff's edge, 'How fearful / And dizzy 'tis to cast one's eyes so low!' (*KL* 4.6.11–12), he stimulates the same fear of looking down that makes, today, so many nervous of flying. An authorial reading cannot do much with textual evidence that embodies such a basic, widely accepted somatic understanding of basic spatial relationships. The convergence of Forker's 'greyhound, slips, fawning group' and Spurgeon's 'spaniel, fawning' group, however, is eccentric.

Repeating phrases arise from cognitive chunking, and repeating chunk clusters from schemata in long-term memory built up by years of feeling, writing, and reading. Textual clusters occur when phrases share, and are linked by, collocates, each of which may be a cluster of different morphological forms, take the form of a fixed phrase, and come in pairs, triples, and quadruples. Clusters will consist of essential core collocates and outliers that may or may not be present.

We can approach an author's chunk and cognitive capacities by analysing his texts, especially if they take the form of holographs. Shakespeare confirms some predictions about authoring mechanics made by cognitive psychologists, experimenting on living people, or running simulation programs. He utters language in chunk sequences of three-four words. These chunks often consist of a repeating phrase dominated by function words, completed by a content word that collocates with like words in previous or successive segments. Collocating content words bind together groups of chunk segments and draw from affect-marked long-term memory schemata. Shakespeare's vocabulary is only a third of the number of his repeating phrases, as corpus linguistics would expect, but because the number of word types and of phrase types at times varies in inverse proportion according to the genre in which Shakespeare was writing, we have some reason to believe that much larger schemata for genres exist.[31]

We can find associational matrices realized, fragmentarily, in small passages from Shakespeare's works. Another one appears in More's command, 'wash your foule mynds w^t teares and those same hands / that yo^u lyke rebells lyft against the peace / lift vp' (13–15). This schema takes the collocates 'wash,' sinful 'mynds,' 'tears,' and 'hands.' Their root may be Pilate's washing of his hands when he delivers Christ to death (R3 1.4.272; R2 4.1.239), possibly primed by More's previous statement that the rebels 'ryse gainst god' (11). This elicits two images in succession, a foul mind (or soul) washed by tears, and hands that lift in rebellion. These two apparently dissimilar percepts stem from the washing of hands, frequent in Shakespeare's works, but to wash away one's sin with tears is an usual blend. He gives the image, however, an additional six times. The passages are 'Return thee therefore with a flood of *tears*, / And *wash* away thy country's *stained spots*' (1 H6 3.3.56–7); 'For I myself have many *tears* to *wash* / Hereafter time, for time past *wrong*'d by thee' (R3 4.4.389–90); 'And water cannot *wash* away your *sin.* /…/ Mine eyes are full of *tears*, I cannot see' (R2 4.1.242, 244); '*wash* every *mote* out of his *conscience*' (H5 4.1.179–80); 'Would … Claudio lie, / Who lov'd her so, that speaking of her *foulness*, / *Wash'd* it with *tears*' (Ado 4.1.152–4); and 'It's monstrous labor when I *wash* my *brain* / And it grow *fouler*' (Ant 2.7.99–100).

Especially interesting is the variety of words for sinful mind ('stained spots,' 'wrong'd,' 'sin,' 'mote,' 'foulness,' and 'fouler'). The stemma that Shakespeare employs must consist of lexical concepts, not lexemes. No wonder such schemata are good authorship markers. They characterize Shakespeare's mind, not just the words he chooses to use. The second can be imitated, but not the first.[32]

* * * * *

TACT was better than the downswing list and though I didn't follow the

rules of the numbers game you were playing I liked the boys in the base-
ment who made the algorithms dance because they reminded me of Ernie
playing blindfold chess with us and winning every time just as he had
added columns of numbers faster than I could key any calculator, just as
we spun poems from the same blank you sensed in him or the books we
read for fun, like King's The Langoliers that wiped out the remainders of
the day as effectively as most of the theory you didn't read obliterated the
idea of me, and didn't its deconstructive tsunami blindside us ... and even
if some clues of me survived who was there to decipher them?

III   Samuel Taylor Coleridge

Now let a man watch his mind while he is composing; or, to take a still
more common case, while he is trying to recollect a name ... Most of my
readers will have observed a small water-insect on the surface of rivulets,
which throws a cinque-spotted shadow fringed with prismatic colours on
the sunny bottom of the brook; and will have noticed, how the little animal *wins* its way up against the stream, by alternate pulses of active and
passive motion, now resisting the current, and now yielding to it in order
to gather strength and a momentary *fulcrum* for a further propulsion. This
is no unapt emblem of the mind's self-experience in the act of thinking.
There are evidently two powers at work, which relatively to each other are
active and passive; and this is not possible without an intermediate faculty, which is at once both active and passive. (In philosophical language,
we must denominate this intermediate faculty in all its degrees and deter-
minations, the IMAGINATION. But in common language, and especially on
the subject of poetry we appropriate the name to a superior degree of the
faculty, joined to a superior voluntary controul over it.

(*Biographia Literaria*, 1:124–5)

Coleridge is the first English poet, major by virtue of his 'The Rime
of the Ancient Mariner,' to derive a theory of creative composition
from introspectively observing his own language process. However,
he describes this theory only in paragraph-length fragments scattered
through a full life as a master of letters. Why did he not write a book
on the imagination? He was no intellectual sluggard, his opium addiction notwithstanding, but Coleridge preferred to use language in a
pre-literate form: his medium was a spontaneous flow of speech. Like
everyone, he had no special portal on his mind's inner workings, but

he preferred conversing to composing, editing, and revising. Coleridge was thus particularly vulnerable to cognitive load, his personal omega limit. Walter Jackson Bate, his biographer, agrees with Coleridge's self-assessment that his 'principal intellectual weakness' was an 'inability to "do one thing at a time,"' to construct an extended argument (1968, 210). One thought, anecdote, and example generated many others, uncontrollably leading everywhere. His creative skill worked quickly, making rapid sketches on innumerable small canvases, related more by suggestion than by logic. Coleridge did not avail himself of artificial paper memory to reorganize all these canvases into a great framework. He streamed into speech what his mind birthed. Sometimes this habit led him to reel off large memorized swathes of other writers' works, as happened when he dumped his translations from F.W.J. von Schelling in chapter 12 of *Biographia Literaria*, his major work on authoring and reading (Bate 1968, 131). Coleridge enjoyed a remarkable capacity to remember what he read, verbatim (12, 135n5), and when he reused these pages during speech – and he dictated *Biographia Literaria* – he technically committed plagiarism, except that no one considers taking text from personal memory the same kind of theft as copying from paper. Coleridge was a showman much in demand for his copiousness, his perpetual flow.

He symbolized language making as a water-insect moving upstream. The experience felt to him like advancing against a current 'by alternate pulses of active and passive motion.' Like so many others later, Coleridge in uttering felt himself *flowing*, but with a difference. Sometimes he was passive and relaxed, carried downstream by the water on which he floated, and at other times actively used its own force as 'a momentary *fulcrum*' to swim upstream against the stream. He named the mental faculty that enables the insect to shift between the two modes, passive and active, as the imagination. It corresponds to our own cognitive model of language production. Passive by reason of being unconscious of what is happening, we allow a flow of pre-phonetic chunks to form an utterance. They are the stream at our back. Once they are encoded to be spoken, we hear them as the inner voice in working memory and can actively impose a 'voluntary controul' on them, expressed sometimes by last-minute error correction, other times by editing. In shaping and stitching together the chunks, we advance against this stream in our face. An author shifts between the two, from passive to active, at the moment of his first reading of his own unconscious output, his authorial self-reading. Then he changes direction. Yet, paradoxically, his mind cannot consciously effect, of its own power, the necessary changes. The power to recreate comes from the current itself, which is moving downstream, and so the mind must surrender once more to its unconscious flow. This supplies the 'momentary *fulcrum*,' as Coleridge puts it, that uses the stream against itself. Coleridge describes composition, swimming alternatively with and against the stream, as a cybertextual cycle of spontaneous message and controlled feedback. His extended metaphor of the insect, courageously facing down a force much greater than itself, poignantly expresses the experience of so many authors who feel themselves being powered by an Other. The metaphor also depicts Coleridge's thought as shifting directions radically every few seconds and responding to rather than controlling an external force.

The strength of this theory is its author's honesty, and the weakness its reflection of personality, saddled as it was with one very human limitation. Coleridge interpreted the power source of his 'stream,' the imagination, as a maker of symbols rather than of arguments. In his theory, imagination fuses input sense data creatively with a mental source he calls reason, yet the resulting integrated utterance, brilliantly innovative and even truthful though it may have appeared, resembles an elaborated network of schemata in long-term memory more than a connected discourse. When Coleridge read himself, that is, when he observed his utterances as they came from his capacious mind, he was content with what he heard. Walter Jackson Bate describes how Coleridge's upbringing, as the last child of fourteen offspring, compelled him to acquire a personal magnetism and charismatic skills in spontaneous conversation that led others to like him and to support him. But this genuinely engaging character suffered from a deficit of will. He was unable to bring his much-discussed ideas out to completion. Coleridge did not write a large body of verse but accepted the constraints on his flow and possessed a remarkable genius in working within his limitations. His cognitive load could hold a complex symbol without trouble. He could shine, then, in conversation and – being highly praised for his live performances, which lasted his entire life – he regarded them, formally, as the very centre of what the creative process should produce.

Coleridge knew that other men saw uttering very differently. Reverend James Bowyer, the headmaster of the grammar school Christ's Hospital, taught Coleridge as a student. For Bowyer, literature had 'a logic of its own, as severe as that of science,' and he believed that there was 'a reason assignable, not only for every word, but for the position of every word' (*Biographia Literaria* 1:8). He mistrusted the role of the irrational unconscious in writing, as Coleridge remembers all too well:

> Lute, harp, and lyre, muse, muses, and inspirations, Pegasus, Parnassus, and Hipocrene, were all an abomination to him. In fancy I can almost hear him now, exclaiming *Harp? Harp? Lyre? Pen and ink, boy, you mean! Muse, boy, Muse? your Nurse's daughter, you mean! Pierian spring? Oh aye! the cloister-pump, I suppose!* (9)

Bowyer had contempt for flow, the output of the 'cloister-pump' of a religious recluse. In valuing extemporaneous talk over 'Pen and ink,' Coleridge preferred the symbol over Bowyer's logic. In his clearest exposition of the imagination, Coleridge wrote,

> I consider [it] either as primary, or secondary. The primary IMAGINATION I hold to be the living Power and prime Agent of all human Perception, and as a repetition in the finite mind of the eternal act of creation in the infinite I AM. The secondary I consider as an echo of the former, co-existing with the conscious will, yet still as identical with the primary in the *kind* of its agency, and differing only in *degree,* and in the *mode* of its operation. It dissolves, diffuses, dissipates, in order to recreate; or where this process is rendered impossible, yet still at all events it struggles to idealize and to unify.

This is no place to speculate on what Coleridge's theory of the artistic imagination would have been if he had explicated it thoroughly. It is not mechanistic, as David Hartley's associationism (an early enthusiasm of Coleridge's) was, but organic and lifelike, the mind consciously working to make sensory data held in memory into something unified and new. Imagination operates in the same way that primary perception itself works when we unconsciously understand what our senses pass through to our minds by imposing our own model on that flux. Both kinds of imagination imitate God's creative power. The succinctness of his statement, four sentences in a short paragraph, is surprising. It concludes chapter 13, 'On the Imagination, or Esemplastic Power,' in *Biographia Literaria,* where Coleridge quotes a lengthy letter from someone else and announces that he will take its advice and *not* discuss the topic heading after all!

Despite Coleridge's frustrating reluctance to harness literacy to shake off his cognitive limitations, he and cognitive psychology today are not

far apart on the essentials of language process. It uses both the unconscious and the conscious mind. It blends or associates elements in long-
term memory in new ways. It flows like a current; and what powers its
stream is feeling. Coleridge wrote to Robert Southey in 1803 that 'ideas
never recall ideas, as far as they are ideas, any more than leaves in a forest create each other's motion. The breeze it is that runs through them
... the state of feeling' (quoted by Bate 1968, 162). The current or the
wind that activates the tree's leaves – a perceptive metaphor for schemata, is it not? – is affect, what enables the prefrontal cortex to recall the
emotion-encoded gist that instigates an utterance.

We see Coleridge's emphasis on feeling earlier, in his poem 'Kubla
Khan,' only published in 1816, twenty years after its creation, and 'rather as a psychological curiosity, than on the ground of any supposed
poetic merits.' After being so nearly orphaned by its maker, 'Kubla
Khan' has become the poster child of Romantic poetry, which defines
itself as verbalizations of the poet's spontaneously remembered emotions, according to William Wordsworth's principle, announced in the
prologue to *Lyrical Ballads* in 1802, that 'all good poetry is the spontaneous overflow of powerful feelings' (x–xi).

Coleridge says in a prose introduction to 'Kubla Khan' (1816) that
it appeared to him in the summer of 1797 while he was in a semi-
conscious dream-like state, and that, on waking, he 'instantly' cast the
opening 54 lines (of a total of 200 or 300 lines) onto paper.[33] Feeling ill
of a 'slight indisposition,' Coleridge had taken a prescribed 'anodyne'
(a painkiller) and immediately 'fell asleep' as he was reading this sentence in *Purchas's Pilgrimage* about Khan Kubla's building of a palace
and garden:

> In *Xaindu* did *Cublai Can* build **a stately** pallace, en**compass**ing sixteene
> **miles** of plaine **ground with** a **wall, where**in are **fertile** Meddowes, pleas-
> ant Springs, delightfull streames, **and** all sorts **of** beasts of chase and game,
> and in **the** middest thereof a sumptuous house of **pleasure**, which may be
> remoued from place **to** place. (Purchas 1613, 350)

The fifteen words that Coleridge uses in the first seven lines of 'Kubla Khan' are in boldface. During his three-hour sleep, Coleridge said
that he had dream-written 200–300 lines of verse, 'if that indeed can
be called composition in which all the images rose up before him as
things, with a parallel production of the correspondent expressions,
without any sensation or consciousness of effort.' That is, he experi-

enced both lexical concepts and lemmas. He said, however, only that he 'appeared to himself to have a distinct recollection of the whole.' Before he could finish recovering the poem from his memory, Coleridge was supposedly interrupted 'by a person on business from Porlock,' a nearby town. When he returned to his papers an hour later, Coleridge could not remember anything more of the poem than 'some eight or ten scattered lines and images.' His best intentions were to finish 'what had been originally, as it were, given to him,' but 'Kubla Khan' remained unfinished.

Compare that account to what Coleridge had appended to the earlier holograph manuscript of the poem, which was announced in 1934 in a notice in the *Times Literary Supplement*. The poet Robert Southey had sent Elizabeth Smith, a well-off literary collector from Minchinhampton, Gloucestershire, a manuscript described as 'a fragment of Coleridges,' with a letter of 1 February 1804 (Kelliher 1994, 191). Southey had evidently received the manuscript, which had been sold by Smith's estate and finally found its home in the British Library, when he visited Coleridge late in 1803, and certainly before 13 January 1804 (193). At the bottom of the transcription, above Coleridge's signature, is this brief account of the circumstances of the poem's composition: 'This fragment with a good deal more, not recoverable, composed, in a sort of Reverie brought on by two grains of Opium, taken to check a dysentery, at a Farm House between Porlock & Linton, a quarter of a mile from Culborne Church, in the fall of the year, 1797.' The term 'Reverie' suggests our experience of the default mode network, but Coleridge's memory altered from about 1803 to 1816: autumn had turned into a summer, a 'Reverie' became 'a profound sleep,' a 'slight indisposition' was really 'dysentery,' and the anodyne had been opium. Diarrhoea led Coleridge to take the drug and, when he did, to experience the symptomatic drowsiness that ushered in the euphoria and pleasure that are hallmarks of opium use in an early stage. In 1797 Coleridge says that most of the reverie-poem was 'not recoverable,' but by 1816 he excuses himself with a (confabulated?) visitor from Porlock.

Scholars have tried to confirm the poem's dating by reference to Coleridge's reading, known movements, notebooks, and letters. Opinions are divided among 1797, 1798, and 1799. Acceptance of what Coleridge wrote about the poem's genesis is divided. John Livingston Lowes (1927), analysing the sources of 'Kubla Khan,' traces many images and expressions in it to a half-dozen sources other than Purchas and enthusiastically endorses the text as a genuine product of an 'utterly uncon-

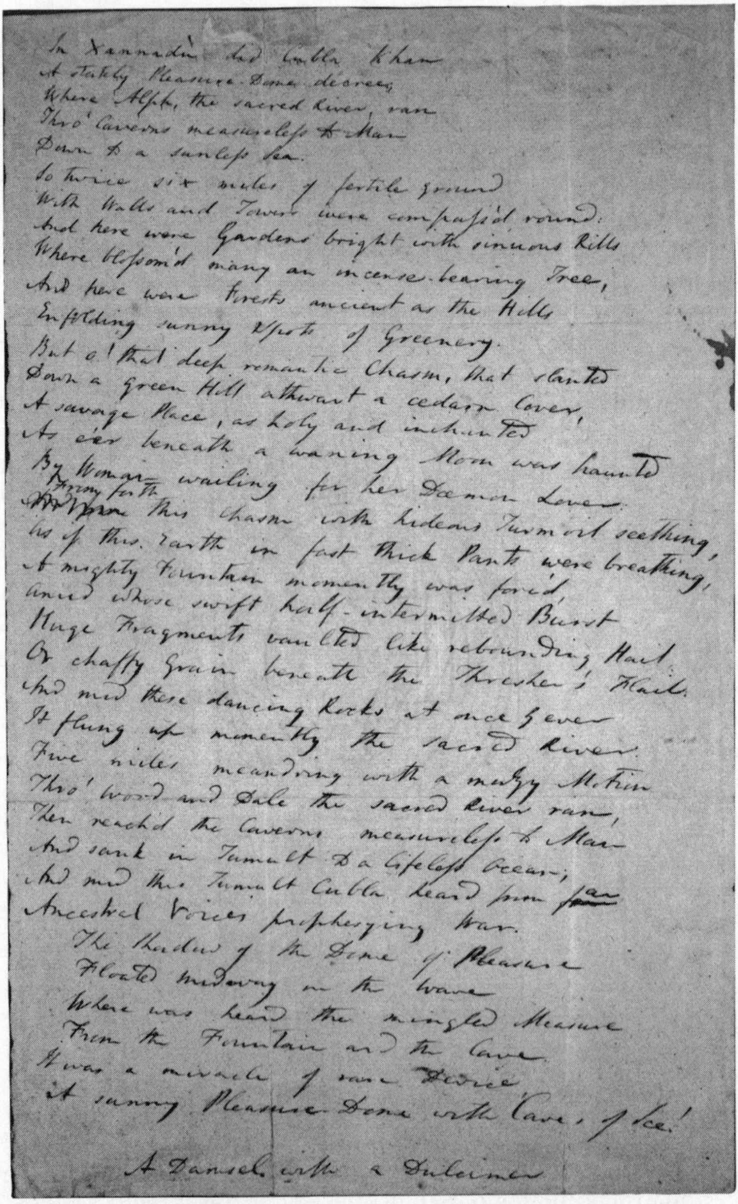
In Xannadu did Cubla Khan
A stately Pleasure-Dome decree;
Where Alph, the sacred River, ran
Thro' Caverns measureless to Man
Down to a sunless Sea.
So twice six miles of fertile ground
With Walls and Towers were compass'd round:
And here were Gardens bright with sinuous Rills
Where blossom'd many an incense-bearing Tree,
And here were Forests ancient as the Hills
Enfolding sunny Spots of Greenery.
But o! that deep romantic Chasm, that slanted
Down a green Hill athwart a cedarn Cover,
A savage Place, as holy and inchanted
As e'er beneath a waning Moon was haunted
By Woman wailing for her Dæmon Lover.
And from this Chasm with hideous Turmoil seething,
As if this Earth in fast thick Pants were breathing,
A mighty Fountain momently was forc'd,
Amid whose swift half-intermitted Burst
Huge Fragments vaulted like rebounding Hail,
Or chaffy Grain beneath the Thresher's Flail:
And mid these dancing Rocks at once & ever
It flung up momently the sacred River.
Five miles meandering with a mazy Motion
Thro' Wood and Dale the sacred River ran,
Then reach'd the Caverns measureless to Man
And sank in Tumult to a lifeless Ocean;
And mid this Tumult Cubla heard from far
Ancestral Voices prophesying War.
The Shadow of the Dome of Pleasure
Floated midway on the Wave
Where was heard the mingled Measure
From the Fountain and the Cave.
It was a miracle of rare Device,
A sunny Pleasure-Dome with Caves of Ice!

A Damsel with a Dulcimer

Figure 19. Coleridge's Holograph of 'Kubla Khan,' © British Library Board (Additional MS 50847, fol. 1) scious mind' left to itself to blend creatively its associations in long-term memory (Schneider 1953, 4). This misreads what even Coleridge says, inclined to embellishment and self-justification as he is often thought to be. He does not say in 1816 that he was unconscious at the time, only that he was not conscious of any effort in composing. And how could he have been unconscious if, on coming out of his reverie, he had a 'distinct recollection of the whole'? The images, at least, remained, and some words and phrases associated with them. On waking, Coleridge appears to have fallen into what modern writers describe as a 'flow' state, which is consistent with a DMN 'reverie,' then understood to mean 'abstracted musing,' a 'brown study' daydreaming, not a deep sleep (OED 'brown study').

The effect of the opium also can be too easily exaggerated. Elisabeth Schneider's true account of the effects of opium is a corrective to readers who associate it with Haight-Ashbury and LSD. Opium reduces pain, pacifies the mind, relaxes the body (including the pulse), 'dampens sensory acuity' (42) rather than excites hallucinations, brings the taker into a sleepy state, and reduces (not enhances) sexual desire (42). Used as an analgesic and an antidiarrhoeal, opium is first (as Coleridge says) a painkiller. At poem's end, when Coleridge imagines that others would look on him fearfully if he 'drank the Milk of Paradise,' he means opium, which in natural form is a milky latex fluid. It comes from paradise because it ends pain. It always slows down breathing, and a reasonable dose enables a person to slip into a drowsy euphoria and experience a sense of pleasurable well-being that is narcotic (that is, it dulls one's senses). The morphine in opium resembles endorphins, which are the body's natural painkillers, but the drug is addictive because tolerance builds up, and it is easy to remove the pain of withdrawal symptoms simply by taking more opium. Typically Coleridge took it as laudanum, which is opium dissolved in brandy (Pratt 2004, 80n18). He described the drink to his brother George as a 'divine ... repose ... a spot of enchantment ... a green spot of fountain and flowers and trees' (Beer 2004). Of course, laudanum compounds the effects of opium by also containing hard liquor.

What explains the changes from his afterword circa 1803 to his preface in 1816? Coleridge disguises references to dysentery and opium in 1816 because, by then, he suffered from an ongoing severe addiction to the drug as he administered it in brandy. Robert Southey wrote Coleridge's friend Joseph Cottle that Coleridge ingested opium 'more than was ever known to be taken by any person before him' (Pratt 2004, 81).

That Coleridge did not publish the poem for some twenty years suggests that he was uncomfortable with it. The printed preface is candid about his presumed reasons: Coleridge about 1803 credited the poem, not to his own will, but to his opium-induced mental state. By 1816 he thought of it as a 'psychological curiosity.' Did it betray more about his opium-induced unconscious state than about his skill as a writer? A reluctance to own up to it tends to confirm its birth story as a suspect product of an opium-sedated brain in a flow state. Although only the 1816 preface mentions the interruption by the man from Porlock, both accounts mention that town. The assertion is odd enough to be accurate, but (again) scholars tend to be sceptical that Coleridge was inventing excuses for his failure to complete a long poem. W.H. Auden (1963, 16) thought that Coleridge's story was 'a fib.'

Does 'Kubla Khan' characterize itself as an entirely mental effusion or as a studied composition on paper? If pre-composed mentally in a state to be drawn out, one line pulling out the next, and so on to the end (as in reciting a poem that has been subject to rote memorization), the poem must have already taken phonological form, entered working memory, and been consciously memorized. Yet Coleridge denies expending mentally any 'effort.' Schneider believes that, had 'Kubla Khan' come from an opium dream in a deep sleep, Coleridge would have left some historical memo of that event; but none has survived (1953, 81). Wordsworth evidently accepted Coleridge's account, but it is far easier to believe that Coleridge composed 'Kubla Khan' after awaking rather than transcribed it from memory. To memorize something requires effort. We lay language down in long-term memory (from which Coleridge would have retrieved it if he was reproducing it rapidly from memory) by taking it first into working memory and consciously repeating the utterance and focusing on its meaning. To use Fergus Craik's phrase, the mind processes text in depth, not superficially but with keen attention to its meaning, grammar, associations, and context. Yet how could Coleridge have processed the fifty-four lines in depth if, at his own word, he lacked 'any sensation or consciousness of effort'? We must want to memorize something in order to memorize it.

It is far more likely that Coleridge's drowsy musing aroused mental imagery of things that he had read in Purchas's account of Xaindu and that they in turn stimulated some associated words and phrases, that is, *chunks*. The mind laid down the mental experiences, not the full text as such, in long-term memory in the same way that it does (as Coleridge later believed) the images, events, and sounds of a dream.

When Coleridge awoke, relaxed and out of pain, he entered a brief flow-state of composition like the ones Eberhart and Stafford describe. Emotions, images, and corresponding text-chunks were ready-made. His first seven octosyllabic lines, rhyming abaabcc, reuse half the words (20 of 39) in Purchas's opening sentence, as if Coleridge had been looking at the book when he created them. He had a starting place, his mind was primed, and the verses came out rapidly, as he says, unlike his usual experience, which must have been to assemble text consciously on paper over some time. After the interruption by the person from Porlock – if it is indeed not fabricated – Coleridge must have felt as we do in waking from a dream. We can vividly describe its content immediately, but after some minutes, the details fade away. Coleridge's frustration with how little he recovered resembles the plight of subjects in cognitive experiments who are presented with a series of numbers or words, only to be interrupted with an unrelated task, and then asked to recall the series after a break.

If Coleridge behaved as Eberhart in writing 'The Groundhog,' we should expect to find him responding to an emotional need. The poem will centre on what supplies, and what deprives him of, that need. He will also cannibalize his previously written text as the poem unfolds. Although speedy owing to its previously set-down schema, flow-state composing eventually runs out of new material once the mind's working-memory capacity is reached. Then it turns to what has already been stored on the page and reuses material there with variations. Evidence of this process is in repeating phrases.

In the following transcript of Coleridge's holograph, now British Library Additional MS 50847, the 127 fixed phrases that repeat in his extant poetry to 1800 are italicized, and all internally repeating phrases are additionally boldfaced. Variants in the 1816 edition are footnoted.

1 In Xannadù did Cubla Khan[34]
2 *A stately* Pleasure-Dome decree;
3 Where Alph, **the sacred River, ran**
4 *Thro'* **Caverns measureless to man**
5 *Down* **to a** *sunless Sea.*
6 *So* twice six miles of fertile ground[35]
7 With Walls and Towers were compass'd *round:*[36]
8 **And here** were Gardens *bright with* sinuous Rills,[37]
9 Where blossom'd *many an* incense-bearing *Tree,*
10 **And here** were Forests ancient *as the Hills*

11   Enfolding sunny *Spots of* Greenery.
12   *But o! that* deep romantic Chasm, that slanted[38]
13   Down *a green* Hill athwart a cedarn Cover,[39]
14   A savage Place, as *holy and* inchanted
15   As e'er *beneath a* waning *Moon was haunted*
16   *By* Woman wailing *for her* Daemon Lover:
17   ~~And from~~ *From forth* this Chasm *with hideous* Turmoil seething,[40]
18   *As if* this *Earth in fast thick* Pants were breathing,
19   *A mighty* Fountain momently was forc'd,
20   Amid whose swift half-intermitted Burst
21   Huge Fragments vaulted like rebounding Hail,
22   Or chaffy Grain *beneath the* Thresher's Flail:
23   *And mid* these dancing Rocks *at once and ever*
24   *It flung* up momently *the sacred River.*
25   Five miles meandring *with a* mazy Motion[41]
26   Thro' Wood and Dale *the sacred River ran,*
27   Then *reach'd the* **Caverns measureless to Man**
28   *And sank* in Tumult *to a lifeless Ocean;*
29   *And mid* this Tumult Cubla *heard from* ~~fear~~ far[42]
30   Ancestral Voices prophesying *War.*
31   *The shadow of the* dome *of pleasure*
32   Floated *midway on the* wave;[43]
33   Where *was heard the* mingled measure
34   *From the* fountain *and the cave.*[44]
35   *It was a* miracle of rare device,
36   *A sunny* Pleasure-Dome with **Caves of Ice!**
37   *A damsel* **with a** dulcimer
38   *In a Vision once I saw*:
39   *It was an* Abyssinian *Maid,*
40   *And on her* Dulcimer she play'd,
41   Singing of Mount Amoara.[45]
42   *Could I* revive *within me*
43   Her Symphony *and Song,*
44   *To such a deep Delight* 'twould win *me,*
45   *That with Music loud and long*
46   *I would* build that Dome of Air,[46]
47   That sunny *Dome! those* **Caves of Ice!**
48   *And all, who heard,* should *see them there,*
49   *And all* should cry, Beware! Beware!
50   His flashing Eyes! his floating Hair!

51 *Weave a* circle *round him* thrice,
52 *And close your Eyes in* holy Dread:[47]
53 *For He on* Honey-dew hath fed
54 And drank *the Milk of Paradise.*[48]

If we take Coleridge at his word, this 'Kubla Khan' originated in mental images of things and also survived, in decayed form, in his memory as such once he returned from his business with the man from Porlock. Repetition makes these images jump out of the poem. Here are nine of 'some eight or ten scattered … images' that survived: the dome of pleasure above (2, 31, 36, 46–7), the sacred river Alph below it (3, 24, 26–7), the chasm where the river originates (12), the chasm fountain, flinging out the 'dancing rocks' and the river water (19, 23, 34), the wailing woman and her daemon lover who might have haunted this chasm (16), the caves of ice into which the sacred river runs (24, 27, 34, 36, 47), the sunless subterranean sea or 'lifeless ocean' beneath the river (5, 28), the damsel with the dulcimer (37, 39–40), and the poet, the 'I'-'he'-'him'-'his' of the poem (38, 42, 44, 46, 50–1, 53). The interpretation of these images, and of the words that describe them, is not obvious, but these nine things have two dominant features: pleasure and pain. Because Coleridge thought that his fragment, in effect, was dictation from his euphoric reverie, obtained through opium for relief from sickness and pain, we have good grounds to interpret the images as indirect expressions of these basic human needs. The pleasure dome rests atop a landscape filled with 'turmoil' and lifelessness. That Coleridge altered 'hideous' in the holograph (17) to 'ceaseless' in the 1816 edition shows his unease at the savagery of the place.

What is the emotional gist that prompted the poem? A good case has been made for interpreting the poem as a symbolic account of the creative imagination at work (F. Milne 1986), for the second and last stanza ends with Coleridge imagining himself rebuilding the pleasure-dome, this time of air, and its caves, again of ice. The creative imagination, however, is cerebral in nature, not at all central to the preoccupations of a brain fleeing pain for pleasure, the purpose of Cubla's dome. The emotional gist of 'Kubla Khan' is escape from suffering. The fragment in the holograph manuscript falls into two stanzas, one on Cubla's dome, and the second on Coleridge's. Their pleasures are achieved, and their pains are avoided, in the same way. Coleridge could only remake Cubla's dome of air, were he first to re-experience the 'deep Delight' of another 'Vision,' here of the singing, playing 'Abyssinian Maid.'[49] His pleasure, unlike Cubla's, is intangible, but both pleasure-domes, Cubla's and Coleridge's, have two central symbolic players, a woman and her lover. As Coleridge describes himself, an object of fear with 'flashing' (ecstatic) eyes and 'floating' hair (as if he had been drowned and were now in paradise), he resembles the daemon-lover of the wailing woman in the chasm. The pleasure Coleridge experiences in his mental vision of Xannadù leads him to desire to imitate Cubla's 'decree,' but the inspirational female in the second stanza is not a female in heat, associated with a 'hideous' fountain that throws up 'dancing rocks,' but a maid playing a virginal that symbolizes her sexual innocence. Because without pain, there is no gain, Coleridge's airy pleasure dome was not built.

Two personifications support this interpretation, a retreat from pain to pleasure. The fountain in the chasm (associated with the woman hungry for her lover) seethes up from the earth as if it 'in fast thick Pants were breathing' (18). The 1816 edition, earlier, describes the 'fertile ground' (that is, the earth) beneath the pleasure-dome as being 'girdled' round by walls and towers, as if they were a belt and the earth were a living waist. The fountain, and the caves into which the sacred river that flows from the fountain runs, together make a kind of music, a 'mingled measure' (33), that forshadows the Abyssinian maid's 'symphony' (another name for her dulcimer, also termed a virginal) and singing. It takes little imagination to recognize what those in the pleasure-dome avoid: the fountain, surging up from the 'panting' earth, and the cave into which it flows. Cubla has pleasure in the dome above, and the woman in the chasm below has pain. The caves into which water from the violently spouting fountain and the winding river empty are 'of Ice.' 'Kubla Khan' – as Coleridge describes its genesis – exposes how an emotional need for pleasure, and emotional fear of pain, express themselves in lexical concepts associated with the images of those things, good and bad, that accompany pleasure and pain.

Assuming that memorization of fifty-four lines in working memory would have not been possible without an intent to memorize, how did Coleridge generate them? The varying line lengths of its verses, the patterns of vocabulary and phrasal repetition, and Coleridge's own testimony in the poem offer evidence of a conscious cybertextual mechanism at work in the act of writing. He uttered something, absorbed it in reading, and remodelled it as something slightly different.

The first seven lines, from 'In Xannadù did Cubla Khan' to 'With Walls and Towers were compass'd round,' are octosyllabic (except for line 5, a six-syllable line). Each of these lines has a caesural pause, marked by a prepositional phrase (1, 5–7), a subject-verb join (2–3), or an adjective phrase (4). Coleridge found these fourteen half-lines in the book, left open at the place Purchas introduces Cublai Khan. He copied words and phrases from it quickly and verbatim, adjusting their word-order, where necessary, to rhyme. Each half-line could be a chunk, and the fourteen half-lines in all could be the limit of Coleridge's cognitive capacity. For the next twenty-nine lines, the rest of the first stanza, Coleridge shifted into pentameter verse, a quite different verse form, and his writing became somewhat looser and more repetitive. Here, reading and rereading the first seven lines, he added three images, of the chasm, the woman, and the fountain, and repeated four images that were in the first seven lines, the dome, the river, the caverns, and the underground sea. This repetition reveals itself in both phrases and single words (word-types internal to the fragment).

Lines 24–36 (from 'It flung up momently the sacred River' to 'A sunny Pleasure-Dome with Caves of Ice!') have twice as many phrasal repetitions as the previous lines. A very substantial part of this repetition recycles words in the first seven lines (in one instance, paraphrased: 'sunless Sea' becomes 'lifeless ocean'). This repetition extends to single content words, in which there are two peaks of reuse, one at the end of the first stanza (lines 26–30), another in the middle of the second stanza (lines 46–50). By recycling content that he already used, Coleridge engages in a cybertextual process, monitoring what he had just written, and then remodelling it into a slightly different form.

The second stanza and last 18 lines, 37–54 (from 'A damsel with a dulcimer' to 'And drank the Milk of Paradise'), return to the octosyllabic line of the first seven lines, but they mark a new direction in the fragment. They read as if Coleridge was thinking about and standing outside his dream-experience of Cubla's dome. He switched to the first person, described himself, physically and emotionally, in a hypothetical way, and began by recounting an account of a quite different 'Vision,' not of Xannadù but of Abyssinia. Does it make sense that a reverie about one experience would disclose a previous, non-active experience? More telling still, the last stanza closes with the same frustrated wish to recreate his mental experience of the dome as he expressed in printed preface and his holograph afterword. The last stanza, then, reveals Coleridge stepping outside the woven 'circle' of his Xannadù dream-experience in the same way that he did in his prose comments on the fragment. He ends the fragment, cybertextually, by interpreting its significance for himself.

A concordance of Coleridge's poems to 1800 situates 'Kubla Khan' lexically in Coleridge's idiolect about 1797–9. 'The Destiny of Nations: A Vision' (dated 1796), for example, shares with 'Kubla Khan' its infrequent words 'dome,' 'slanted,' 'hideous,' 'pant,' and 'symphony.' The very rare phrase 'fast thick' (18), and the longer 'close your eyes' (52), both appear in Coleridge's poems to 1800 only in 'The Nightingale, a Conversation Poem, April 1798' ('should you close your eyes, you might almost / Forget it was not day' and "Tis the merry Nightingale / That crowds, and hurries, and precipitates / With fast thick warble his delicious notes'). Also, 'Christabel' (1797) ends with a variant of that rarity, the 'vision' of a child who makes 'pleasures flow in so *thick and fast*' on her father's heart. Schneider (1953, 201–15) sees other verbal echoes in Coleridge's translations of *Piccolomini* and *Wallenstein* (1800) and locates a substantial 'Kubla Khan' word cluster in 'Ode to Georgiana' (1799), of 'ancestral,' 'stately,' and a rhyming 'pleasure' and 'measure.' 'The Rime of the Ancient Mariner,' alone of Coleridge's poems at this time, has the phrase 'loud and long' (45). The dating of these poems backs up Coleridge's own dating of 'Kubla Khan' and shows that it had a reasonably strong influence on his poetic vocabulary for a while.

'Kubla Khan' is, as Byron told Coleridge, at least a 'psychological curiosity.' Its beginning has the strong emotional content, and the vividly impressed schema of images and words, of poems written out quickly in a state of flow. Its composition begins as schema-fed and then, once cognitive capacity is reached, Coleridge makes more verses by conscious repetition and variation of what went before. This is cybertextual cycling, the poet responding to what he has just written down. When he exhausts even this strategy of amplification, when he is unable to continue the story, Coleridge makes himself and his ambitions the subject. He shifts in a conversational mode, moving from one topic to another as the mood takes him, and even this sustains him for only one stanza. It did not occur to Coleridge that more inspiration, more matter, was ready at hand in the book he had been reading. He had exhausted the wellspring, those affectively encoded schemata that fed his spontaneous speech so well, and there was no one to take dictation.

*   *   *   *   *

We liked RPO from the first, breaking the breads of verse with an online world, working with Marge and Molly and Al and Margaret to give their readers words that their own me went without, finding their e-mailed cris-de-coeur, knowing that baseball players and scholars aren't supposed to cry, but who could blame me when in class I stumbled on Arabella Smith, Mary Frye, and Govinda Chettur, though you fought me, choking down my affect at those more-than-texts that someone might do good to leave in waiting rooms in hospitals, your own memories of readers that even you set down in papers which described the me of those who wrote and of Carol Akasike in the last-hope ward as she made our ENG 201 chat room her God's own country.

IV   W.B. Yeats

W.B. Yeats's volume of poems *Responsibilities* (1914) begins with a twenty-two-line untitled verse introduction. E.M. Forster might say that, in making it, Yeats was a would-be reporter who repeatedly forgot his notes as he fell back on his own Anonymous. The affective gist that seeded the poem was a passion that had left him childless. He made two mistakes about facts in his drive to confess it. Illocutionary force shook Yeats's intention to honour his old fathers. The affective gist of his memories about fathering centred on his failed personal example rather than on them. Yeats behaves outwardly like an editor but repeatedly appeals again to his Anonymous within to express the affect that was driving him to write the poem.

Yeats's first surviving holograph copy is National Library of Ireland MS 30,364 (a), dated December 1913 (W. O'Donnell 2003, 2–3). A second fair holograph copy, dated January 1914, is National Library of Ireland MS 30,364 (b). Yeats revised the poem for some years after its first publication. It acquired the title 'Introductory Rhymes' in 1916. He made one big alteration much later, in 1929. He revised lines 9–10 and 12 on a copy of the 1922 edition, *Later Poems* (W. O'Donnell 2003, 4–7), and inserted the changed lines in proofs of *Selected Poems* (1929; W. O'Donnell 2003, 9). My transcription centres on the 1914 edition and includes variants from the two holograph manuscripts (December 1913 and January 1914) and from the major 1929 revision. Editorial symbols include strikethroughs (for *currente calamo* deletions), capital roman numerals (for sentences), Arabic numbers (for the fathers whom Yeats addresses), a double bar (for mid-line caesura), and alphabetical letters in the right margin (the rhyme scheme).

Yeats structures the 1914 version of the poem carefully. Its three sentences begin with the verb 'pardon' (lines 1, 9, and 19), an imperative addressed to his 'old fathers.' This is syntactic priming. Despite being

L.	Vers.	Text	Rhyme
1:	1913 MS	~~Old fathers of mine – if you should linger near~~	
	1914	**[I] Pardon,** <u>old</u> fathers, ‖ *IF* you still remain	a
2:	1913 MS	~~Where you once lived to learn~~	
	1913 MS	~~In ear shot still~~	
	1914	Somewhere in ear-shot ‖ for the story's end,	b
3:	1913 MS	Old Dublin ~~me~~ merchants, free of six & four	
	1914	**(1)** <u>Old</u> Dublin merchant ‖ 'free of ten and four'	c
4:	1913 MS	into	
	1913 MS	Or trading out of Galway ~~out~~ of Spain	
	1914	*OR* trading out of Galway ‖ into Spain;	a
5:	1913 MS	Robert	
	1913 MS	Old county scolors – ~~you that were~~ Emmets friend	
	1914	**(2)** *AND* country scholar, ‖ Robert Emmet's friend,	b
6:	1914 MS	of	
	1914	A hundred-year-old memory ‖ to the poor;	c
7:	1913 MS	or that has left me	
	1913 MS	Merchant ~~scholar~~ soldier – that ~~leave~~ the blood	
	1914	Traders or soldiers ‖ *WHO* have left me blood	d
8:	1914	*THAT* has not passed ‖ through any huxter's loin,	e
9:	1913 MS	who	
	1913 MS	Pardon, you ^ did not count the cost	
	1914	**[II] (3) Pardon,** *AND* you ‖ that did not weigh the cost,	f
	1929	Soldiers that gave whatever die was cast,	
10:	1914	Old Butlers ‖ *WHEN* you took to horse and stood	d
	1929	~~And and old and old Armstrong~~	
		~~An Armstrong or a Butler that withstood~~	
		A Butler and Armstrong that withstood	
11:	1914	Beside the brackish waters ‖ of the Boyne	e
12:	1914	Till your bad master blenched ‖ *AND* all was lost;	f
	1929	James & his Irish when the Dutchman crossed;	
13:	1913 MS	~~Old~~ You merchant skipper that leaped over board	
	1914	**(4)** *AND* merchant skipper ‖ *THAT* leaped overboard	g
14:	1913 MS	~~But~~ After an old hat in Biskay Bay	

L.	Vers.	Text	Rhyme
	1914	After a ragged hat I I in Biscay Bay,	h
15:	1914	(5) You most of all, I I silent and fierce <u>old</u> man	i
16:	1913 MS	~~Because it was the spectacle of your~~	
	1914	*Because* you were the spectacle I I *that* stirred	g
17:	1914	My fancy, I I *and* set my boyish lips to say	h
18:	1914	'Only the wasteful virtues II earn the sun';	i
19:	1914	**[III] Pardon** *that* I I for a barren passion's sake,	j
20:	1914	*Although* I have come close II on forty-nine	k
21:	1914	I have no child, I I I have nothing but a book,	j
22:	1914	Nothing but that I I to prove your blood and mine.	k

a single verse paragraph, end rhymes show that the poem consists of three sestets (abcabc, defdef, ghighi) and an ending quatrain (jkjk). An unidentified manuscript query written into the 1924 *Poems*, possibly by George Yeats, refers to this as Yeats's 'poem on Ancestors' (W. O'Donnell 2003, 11). The first and third sestets invoke four fathers: a merchant, a scholar, a skipper, and Yeats's grandfather. The second sestet invokes soldiers from the Butler and Armstrong clans. In a letter to Lady Gregory, Yeats wrote that the poem was 'very carefully accurate' (W. O'Donnell 2003, 2) and would serve to counter George Moore's recent attack on him as a middle-class poet without any distinguished forebears (Jeffares 1968, 99–102). Norman Jeffares names Yeats's 'old fathers' as Jervis Yeats (the merchant), John Yeats (Emmet's friend), relatives of Mary Butler and Grace Armstrong (into whose military families Yeats's ancestors married), William Middleton (the skipper), and his grandfather William Pollexfen. Moore's article, Yeats's letter to Lady Gregory, manuscript materials, and the form of the poem itself show that Yeats *intended* the poem to offset a slight to the nobility and heroism of his ancestors. However, he did not title the poem after them. Yeats's revisions highlight another, deeper insult in what Moore wrote. It was that Yeats's passion for Maud Gonne was 'the common mistake of a boy' (Jeffares 1984, 100). An intention to address this grew as Yeats wrote the poem.

Changes to Yeats's original beginning, 'Old fathers of mine – if you should linger near / Where you once lived to learn the story's end,' signals his willingness to tell these men how he turned out. At some point before he pens line 5 (likely as he describes the Dublin merchant), Yeats stops. He crosses out the first line and a half. He can no longer end line 1 with the word 'near' because he needs a rhyme for 'Spain.' It would have been easy enough just to replace 'if you should linger near' with 'if you still remain'; the line would have rhymed and still have had ten syllables. However, Yeats also deletes 'of mine' and makes good the missing two syllables with an opening imperative, 'Pardon.' This verb forecasts how ambiguously Yeats is going to end his own story. He almost races through his other four fathers in the next two sestets, and not without some signs of haste in order to reach the real story. It comes at the close in four rapid, run-on clauses, three of which are in the first person (more syntactic priming); and they take only four lines, not six. He ends the poem with the word 'mine,' which he had removed from the first line. The choices that he makes during these revisions bring out a concession that there was some truth in Moore's criticism. Yeats's lips were 'boyish,' and he was without child, or indeed anything but a book, at the age of forty-nine because of 'a barren passion's sake' (19). Yeats admits allowing the blood-line to falter. His old fathers gave him blood (7, 22) uncontaminated by any huckster, and Yeats did nothing with it.

In the letter to Lady Gregory on 3 January 1914 where Yeats enclosed this newly written poem, he said both that Moore 'inspired' him and that the poem 'turns the tables on the enemy.' Poems in *Responsibilities* such as 'September 1913' and 'The Magi' reveal a new politically charged, candid Yeats, 'walking naked,' without a coat 'Covered with embroideries / Out of old mythologies' ('The Coat'). With the threefold 'Pardon,' Yeats exposed both his virtues and his faults, naked to the world, a better self-critic than Moore had allowed.

Why did Yeats take four lines to realize he should begin with 'Pardon' in the first place? He must have had historical notes on his ancestors at hand: he could not have professed confidence in his accuracy, had he not done some research first. Yet the 1913 manuscript version appears to have been spontaneous. The mid-line caesural pauses – marked by commas, conjuncts and subordinators, and phrasal boundaries – form forty-four chunks. These did not pose problems for Yeats; it was the linkages between consecutive half-lines that needed fixing. We usually prevent sequencing errors by simply adding one chunk to the next. Yeats's many dependent clauses thus pile up in an additive sequence: the first embedded subordinate clause that halts us in our tracks for several seconds is 'Although I have come close on forty-nine' at line 20. Sometimes the sequencing falters because simple adding does not handle the exigencies of rhyme. That forces Yeats to link end words three lines apart. Twice, he recovers on the fly with *currente calamo* corrections for rhyming. The first affects line 1; the second forces Yeats to cross out an almost-completed line 16 because he realizes, joltingly, that it will not afford him an off rhyme with 'overboard' at line 13. Additiveness also does not prevent unwanted repetitions. Yeats repeats 'out of' in consecutive half-lines at line 4. He replaces a 'But' clause with an 'After' prepositional phrase at line 14: a change with both syntactic and prosodic consequences.

Overall, the pace of composition is rapid. Yeats relies on long-term memory to handle any history question not in his notes, and it fails him once: as Yeats later noted, the Irish were exempt from the 'eight and six' (not 'ten and four'; line 3; Yeats 1965, 817–18). He may have felt some impatience with having to run through so many fathers because he repeats the imperative 'Pardon' at line 9. This restores some momentum to his drive to answer the implied question, 'pardon what?'

Yeats returned to this poem fifteen years after its first publication. A manuscript query asked him, 'Do you make out that Butler has changed his allegiance in the last version of the poem on Ancestors. It is not quite clear' (W. O'Donnell 2003, 11). This was Yeats's second memory slip. The Butler clan did not fight on the side of James II in 1690 against William of Orange ('the Dutchman') and so lose the battle when the king did but fought on the other side against James and 'his Irish.' Yeats accordingly rewrote lines 9–10 and 12 for the 1929 edition to make clear that the Butlers did not change 'allegiance' (by fighting for the English at any time).

This calculated revision led Yeats also to reduce the poem to two thought-passages. He deleted the second imperative, 'Pardon' (line 9), and so devoted 18 uninterrupted lines to his 'old fathers.' During composition, Yeats needed to repeat 'Pardon' midway through his 18 lines of the fathers to maintain the currency of the thought. Was his omega value, then, nine pentameter lines, or about 60–80 words? Once a text is down on paper, the omega value does not so much constrain an author's mind. A reader retains 'pardon' much longer than a listener could without losing its anticipated object, the *what* for which forgiveness is begged. Cybertextual feedback can be drawn out.

* * * * *

I liked the online course in reading poetry we taught in 2001 because it gave me some more work to do, those weekly 40-minute audio talks that came out of me unassisted if you please though it took half a dozen false starts to build up a head of steam each time so that I could flow to the end of the hour, and you couldn't even edit the takes so I was on my own, and you had to learn to trust my tics and all that seniority inherits, my digressions bringing out ideas you didn't know you had, not information but ways to feel the text as if it had been itself some fluid talk which daily introduces me to you.

I did poem commentaries which you eventually put on RPO and you salted them with so many things you read because the profession expected that, you put me in the margins only, honing and revising, so unlike the one-hour chat rooms you had to let me lead ... I wonder which professor did a better job ... you or me? because chats pushed us both to a brink of sorts, fearing their spontaneity might birth a sentence salad, but the system still archived the lot for science, whether mind-inspired or mind-at-tether's-end, and we didn't have a lot to say about that.

V   T.S. Eliot

[A]ny intelligent psychologist ought to see at once that any poet, even the greatest, will tend to use his own impressions over and over again. It is by no means a matter of poverty of inspiration. Every man who writes poetry has a certain number of impressions and emotions which are particularly important to him. Every man who writes poetry will be inclined to seek endlessly for a final expression of these, and will be dissatisfied with his expressions and will want to employ the initial feeling, the original image or rhythm, once more in order to satisfy himself.

> (T.S. Eliot, 'Poets' Borrowings,' *TLS* [5 April 1928], quoted in Eliot 1996, 392–3)

T.S. Eliot followed Rudyard Kipling (1907) and W.B. Yeats (1923) as the third English-language Nobel Prize–winning poet of the twentieth century (1948). What separates Eliot from his precedessors and his successors, Derek Walcott (1992) and Seamus Heaney (1995), has been Eliot's establishment of a new poetic movement, modernism, at a single stroke, with a miniature dramatic epic entitled *The Waste Land* (1922). This 433-line poem fuses a personal story of love and despair in questing for an absent God, and a kaleidescopic portrait of contemporary Europe against a background of human history from the oldest of major religions, Hinduism, to post–First World War Christianity. *The Waste Land* has five parts, 'The Burial of the Dead,' 'The Fire Sermon,' 'A Game of Chess,' 'Death by Water,' and 'What the Thunder Said.'

The Fisher King's last words at the poem's close, 'These fragments I have shored against my ruins' (430), are consistent with the lyrical core of Eliot's epic. The average length of its twenty-six fragments is just seventeen lines, a little longer than a sonnet. Their many overlapping voices belong to four type figures: a seduced woman-wife, a husband-lover-seducer, a prophet, and a quester/would-be-redeemer. Eliot says in his notes to the poem that all these characters collapse into one person (148), the androgynous prophet Tiresias. The resulting image mosaic, 'A heap of broken images' (22), lacks an explicit continuity or narrative, so often are its voices supplied by quotations from St Augustine, Chaucer, Dante, Shakespeare, Verlaine, and others. These and his use of Jesse Weston's *From Ritual to Romance* give *The Waste Land* an appearance of obscurity, but most readers understand Eliot's powerful feelings and simple ideas immediately and clearly. The poem contributes fourteen passages to the sixteenth edition of Bartlett's *Familiar Quotations* (1992). The nerves-afflicted couple and the ever-pregnant Lil in 'A Game of Chess,' and the typist and the Highbury girl in 'The Fire Sermon,' are among the most poignant and memorable poetic voices in a century of verse. They bear witness to London life and death in the early 1920s.

For four decades very little was known about how T.S. Eliot created *The Waste Land*, other than that his fellow American Ezra Pound helped. The Berg Collection in the New York Public Library silently bought the poem's manuscripts from the estate of their American publisher, John Quinn, in 1958, but Eliot's widow Valerie only discovered their whereabouts in 1968, three years after her husband's death. Her superb edition of the typescripts and manuscript pages that lie behind *The Waste Land* (1971) laid open details of an astonishing authoring history. Pound and Eliot's first wife, Vivienne, gave Eliot the courage and the wisdom to finish the poem. Pound described himself as Eliot's muse-obstetritian at the birth of *The Waste Land*. On 20 January 1922, when Eliot wrote Scofield Thayer, Pound was in the final stage of putting Eliot's drafts 'three times through the sieve' (V. Eliot 1988, 502). Pound amply scolded and mocked what he did not like in them and made his compliments in two little words, 'OK' and, twice, 'Echt' (German for 'real'). His unusually dedicated critique, conducted from November 1921 to early 1922, led Eliot to dedicate the poem to him as 'il miglior fabbro' (the greater maker). A recent scholar justly describes Pound's work as 'one of the greatest acts of editorial intervention on record' (Eliot 2005, 23). Less celebrated, but equally important, in my opinion, was Vivienne's enthusiastic support. After reading the third part, 'A Game of Chess,' she pencilled in two great lines for Lil's monologue and annotated the dialogue that bracketed it, 'Yes' (which echoed the well-known monologue by Molly Bloom in James Joyce's *Ulysses*), '& wonderful,' 'wonderful,' and 'Splendid last lines.'

The texts that Eliot gave Pound, his responses to them, and Eliot's revisions incorporate cybertextual cycles of a kind found in most authoring, but Eliot's character and situation in late 1921 made him particularly in need of feedback. Pound's persistent knuckle rapping and Vivienne's encouragement pushed him to complete *The Waste Land*. Eliot had respected Pound's prosodic skills for years and published a critical book on his poetry. A master-student relationship pre-existed Eliot's decision to write something large, mentioned in several letters in 1919 (V. Eliot 1988, 344, 419). Eliot's depressed psychological state compounded his discipleship. Worn down by Vivienne's illnesses and his own anxieties, Eliot became indecisive and highly dependent on her. The ten-week visit of his mother, sister, and brother from 10 June to 20 August, more illness, and work pressures drained him. When a doctor prescribed complete rest for three months without either professional reading or writing, Eliot planned two retreats, one to the English seaside, another to Lausanne in Switzerland.

Eliot left London for the Albemarle Hotel in Margate, a seaside resort, on 15 October 1921, and insisted that Vivienne come with him. She did his letter writing at Margate, staying until 31 October to ensure that her Tom went outdoors into the fresh beachfront air every day and did no professional reading or writing. He was back in London on 12 November, but the couple then left a week later, on 18 November, on the second leg of his rest cure, for Paris. He stayed there only a few days, visiting Pound and his wife Dorothy, and leaving Vivienne behind when setting off for psychological treatment at Lausanne, where he arrived on 22 November. Forty days later, Eliot returned to Paris, where he consulted with Pound again until the 10th, when he returned to London. After more correspondence, both Eliot's rest-cure and *The Waste Land* finished in a dead heat.

There is a wealth of evidence on which to base a detailed schedule for Eliot's writing of *The Waste Land*, and for Pound's and Vivienne's critiques of its drafts. Although we have a half-dozen letters about the poem, all twenty-six documents in the Berg Collection manuscript are undated, and Pound and Vivienne only annotated a dozen of them, Pound repeatedly. Fortunately, Lyndall Gordon and Lawrence Rainey have approximately date-stamped both the typewriters and (by watermark and other features) the kinds of paper that Eliot used, and Valerie Eliot has identified the handwriting of Pound, Eliot, and Vivienne in the manuscript facsimile, and the different writing instruments Pound used (green crayon, pencil, and ink).

Eliot had three typewriters and four paper stocks. He used his old college typewriter up to an extant letter on 6 July 1921 (named for the space it allots each character, 2.12 mm), when he took over his brother Henry's machine (2.10 mm), left behind for Eliot when his family returned to America. For a short time, 2–10 January 1922, Eliot used Pound's typewriter in Paris. It is distinguishable by its purple ribbon and 2.54 mm spacing. Rainey dated the four paper stocks that Eliot used in *The Waste Land* manuscript by their appearance in Eliot's extant letters and other writings: British Bond C (13 February–15 June 1921; Rainey 2005b, 168–9), Verona Linen (8 September–2 October 1921, laid paper with horizontal chainlines), Hieratica Bond (16 November–5 December 1921), and lined wove paper (ca 19 December 1921, for one letter only; Rainey 2005b, 170–1). Because during Eliot's stays at Margate and Lausanne he had no typewriter, we can date most of his handwritten drafts to the periods he spent there from 15 October to 11 November 1921 and 22 November 1921 to 1 January 1922. We can also reasonably assume that Pound annotated a page at least as many times as the number of different writing implements he used in doing so. Lyndall Gordon deduces that Pound uses a pencil in his first review of the drafts (fall 1921) and black ink in his second review (early January 1922; 1977, 105).

Here is a plausible timetable for Eliot's composition, and the feedback he received from Pound and Vivienne.

January–5 February 1921. In London, Eliot drafts Part I, 'The Burial of the Dead,' with the old 2.12 mm typewriter (last used 8 September

1921). Wyndham Lewis reports in a letter dated February 7 that two days previously he saw a four-section poem (Rainey 2005b 35; Gordon 1998, 169), which must be similar to what we have in Eliot's typescript (4–9) because it uses four-asterisk dividers to separate Part I into four sections (beginning 'First we had a couple of feelers,' 'April is the cruellest month,' 'What are the roots that clutch,' and 'Frisch schwebt der Wind'). The typescript in the Berg collection, however, could be a slightly later version because Eliot's use of its paper stock, British Bond C, occurs in letters only from 13 February to 15 June. (Rainey believes that Eliot added the opening drinking-binge section after he had seen Joyce's *Ulysses* that May, and if so, the fourth section of the version Lewis had seen might have begun 'Unreal City.') Part I was annotated later by Pound in pencil. Eliot later told John Quinn that no handwritten drafts (other than those he had) existed for typescripts found in the *Waste Land* manuscript, i.e., for Parts I, II, and III. At this early date, Eliot drafted 'Song. For the Opherion' (98–9) on his old typewriter in British Bond B, which he used up to 21 January 1921 in letters.

February–June 1921. In London, Eliot drafts Part II, 'A Game of Chess,' typescript and carbon copy, with the old 2.12 mm typewriter (last used in an extant letter on 6 July 1921) on British Bond C (used in letters from 13 February to 15 June). The typescripts are later annotated first by Vivienne in pencil, secondly (twice) by Pound in pencil and ink. Pound takes care not to write on Vivienne's comments, so that hers must have preceded his.

September–15 October 1921. In London, Eliot possibly drafts the first part of Part III, 'The Fire Sermon,' no further than the end of the 'Twit twit twit' section. He uses Verona Linen paper and his new 2.10 mm typewriter, Henry Eliot's machine, both of which Eliot first uses in a letter of 8 September. Pound annotated the carbon copy, first, in pencil and then the top-copy typescript in ink. Rainey thinks that Eliot delayed typing any of Part III until he returned from Margate, but the last time he used Verona Linen in his letters was 2 October. Eliot must also have typed 'Exequy' at this time, because it too was done on his brother Henry's new typewriter on Verona Linen. It is possible that Eliot sent Pound the (presumed) missing carbon copy of Part I by this time and that Pound reviewed the drinking binge and did not like it.

1–11 November 1921. Although allowed only two hours' of pleasure reading a day, and 'forbidden to do any writing whatsoever' (V. Eliot 1988, 473, 478), after Vivienne returned from Margate to London, Eliot drafts 'O City' (7 lines), 'London, the swarming' (15 lines), 'The river sweats' (25 lines), and the first part of 'Highbury bore me' (2 lines) on Hieratica Bond, paper stock used in letters from 16 November to 5 December 1921. On 4 November, or possibly 11 November (Rainey 2005b 26), Eliot wrote Sydney Schiff from Margate that he had done 'a rough draft of part of part III, but do not know whether it will do, and must wait for Vivien's opinion as to whether it is printable. I have done this while sitting in a shelter on the front – as I am out all day except when taking rest. But I have written only some fifty lines, and have read nothing, literally – I sketch the people, after a fashion, and practise scales on the mandoline' (Eliot 1988, 484–5). Rainey thinks Eliot also drafted 'Elegy' (which Pound never annotated) and 'Dirge' at Margate because they appear on the same paper, but if so he did not think of them then as belonging to Part III because he penned his letter to Schiff on the last day of his stay (as Rainey believes) and because the four Part III segments add up to 49 lines already. (Note that, on the basis of Pound's green-crayon annotations of Eliot's additions to 'Highbury bore me' after line 11, the extra 25 lines of those additions were arguably unavailable to Pound in November in Paris.) Eliot's faith in Vivienne is telling. It is possible that he gave her the typescript of Parts II and III when she left Margate for London on 31 October, and that she then mailed Part II with her annotations back to him at Margate – before Eliot wrote Schiff – insomuch as she wrote, on the back of the third leaf of Part II, 'Send me back this copy & let me have it' (15). In the carbon copy of Part II, Eliot has added the two lines she suggested for the speech about Lil and Albert, presumably so that he could send it back to her by post, as she had asked. When Eliot says that Part III 'must wait for Vivienne's opinion,' he implies that she had what he had done on it to that point. If Eliot waited until 12 November to start typing Part III, this comment would be puzzling.

12–18 November 1921. In London, Eliot types, with the 2.10 mm machine on earlier Verona Linen paper, the remainder of the Part III typescript, that is, 'London, the swarming' (drafted in Margate, where he might have written 'O City' and 'London, the swarming' as alternate passages and have decided on the latter) and the clerk-typist episode, but he leaves 'The river sweats' and the first two lines of 'Highbury bore me' untyped, maybe because he was still intending to work on them or because he ran out of time. He complained of being sick of the flu during this week.

19–21 November 1921. In Paris, Eliot gives Pound the top-copy typescripts for Parts I and II, the carbon copy of the typescript for Part III,

and the 'Highbury bore me' leaf. Pound marks them all up in pencil
in what Eliot would later term the first 'sieving,' but the very fact of
markup suggests that Pound reviewed the drafts when Eliot was not
present. On or about 21 November Eliot leaves Paris for Lausanne, evidently with the top-copy of Part III (which Pound did not have for the
purpose of his first annotating) as a basis to work on what remained
to be done. Oddly, Pound did not annotate the opening of Part I, the
drinking binge: that omission suggests that a presumably lost carbon
copy of Part I once existed that Pound received by post and did annotate. Pound cannot have given Eliot the annotated drafts of Parts I–III
before he left for Lausanne, there was so little time. Possibly he mailed
them to Eliot there. During Pound's critique of Parts I–III, although
scathing about the Fresca sequence, and deleting many lines, he does
not delete it all. He cuts the 'London, the swarming' paragraph, but
when he reads the first nine lines of the 'Highbury' draft (handwritten
at Margate), a passage that Eliot himself had crossed out, Pound asks
him to type them up and oks the last two lines. (Eliot does not type
up this passage because he has no typewriter with him in Paris and
Lausanne.) Finally, presumably at this point Pound annotates, in pencil, Eliot's 'Song. For the Opherion,' 'Exequy,' and his old 'The Death of
the Duchess.'

22 November 1921–1 January 1922. In Lausanne, lacking a typewriter, Eliot buys wove lined paper used otherwise only in a letter of
19 December and writes out, by hand, Parts IV–V. If (as I believe) he
receives the rest of Pound's first sieving by mail (Parts I–III typescripts
and the 'Highbury' leaf), Eliot then makes further revisions. He adds
the Moorgate and Margate stanzas to the end of the 'Highbury' leaf
and prepares an autograph fair copy of 'Dirge' (120–1), which appears
on the Lausanne lined paper. On 19 December, in a letter to Sydney
Waterlow, Eliot says that he is 'trying to finish a poem – about 800 or
1000 lines. *Je ne sais pas si ça tient*' (V. Eliot 1988, 496). This suggests that
Pound had so far cut *nothing* major from Eliot's drafts, not even the
drinking binge in Part I, because they have (all verses considered) over
950 lines at this time, including the drinking binge from I, the Fresca
episode from II, the sailor's tale from IV, and all miscellaneous poems
appended to Parts I–V.

2–15 January 1922. Eliot arrives in Paris on 2 January, gives Pound
the sheaf of drafts, and stays until 16 January (Eliot 2005, 23–4). He
must have expected Pound to make minor corrections and cuts but,
seeing a nearly 1,000-line poem, Pound begins cutting large pieces

from it. He turns to Parts IV–V and briefly annotates their first pages in black ink. He says that he cannot begin to 'attack' Part IV, which is 'Bad,' until he gets a typescript. On Part V, he writes 'OK from here on I think.' At this point, wanting the typescripts of Parts IV–V, Pound marks up Part II again as well as the top copy of Part III (the one that Eliot took with him to Lausanne), both times in ink. He cuts most of the Fresca sequence in Part III and, instead of close-editing and chopping the typist-clerk again, Pound refers Eliot to what he did on the carbon copy of Part III. At this point, Pound has 'sieved' (Eliot's word) Part I once (possibly twice, if a carbon copy has been lost), and Parts II–III twice each. During Pound's black-ink annotations, he also annotates Eliot's 'Song. For the Opherion' and 'Exequy' a second time, and his 'Dirge' for the first time. Then Pound gives the 'Highbury bore me' leaf its second look and finds that Eliot has redone the Highbury stanza and added two more, those for Moorgate and Margate. Pound uses a green crayon to write 'O.K. echt' beside the first two new stanzas but writes nothing on the verso (which has Eliot's 'Margate Sands' stanza as well as the last six lines of Part III as eventually published): high praise from Pound. He skips Part IV, or rereads it without comment, and then adds at the top of the first page of Part V, another 'OK,' also in green crayon. Then Eliot gives him the typescripts of Parts IV–V that he or someone else prepared on Pound's own typewriter, and Pound crosses out, without comment, most of the sea story that begins Part IV. Finally, Eliot at this time, when he had no typewriter of his own, adds two handwritten segments to Part III to counterbalance Pound's deletion of most of the Fresca episode, and 'London, the swarming.' One is 'The rivers tent is broken,' eventually the opening to 'The Fire Sermon' (24–5). Another is 'From which, a Venus Anadyomene,' which Eliot marks as to be inserted among a few lines in the Fresca episode that Pound had not deleted. Because Pound annotates neither passage, he cannot have seen them in Paris.

Ca 16–27 January 1922. Back in London, Eliot prepared another typescript, now lost, and mailed it to Pound for his critique. Part III in this version must have included 'The river sweats' and 'Venus Anadyomene.' He wrote to Eliot on 24 January that this nineteen-page version must be the 'longest poem in the English langwidge' (V. Eliot 1988, 497). Rainey believes that the title page, typed on the same machine and the same Verona Linen paper as Part III (2–3), belongs to this version. (If the title page was prepared earlier, in the fall of 1921 with Part III, Pound did not annotate it from November to early January.) In his letter, Pound makes some criticisms of this (now lost) nineteen-page version, which begins with an epigraph by Joseph Conrad and ends with three poems, 'Song' (99), 'Exequy' (100–1), and (it seems) 'Dirge' (120–1), all which Pound recommended that Eliot cut. Pound must have included in the 24 January letter the version, marked up with further changes, because Eliot replies by post about 24 January, agreeing to detailed changes in Part III that are *not* indicated in Pound's markup of the extant typescript (the one he saw in November and early January). Pound then annotates Eliot's letter with a series of 'OK's to changes that Eliot was agreeing to make and encloses Eliot's letter in a second letter of his own, probably about 27 January. For example, when Eliot asks whether he should delete Part IV entirely (even the Phlebas passage) and preface *The Waste Land* with 'Gerontion.' Pound answers that Eliot should do neither but stick with his current nineteen-page version (V. Eliot 1988, 504–5).

The sievings of *The Waste Land* drafts are three cybertextual cycles, each one an author's utterance and a reader's response. Eliot metaphorically characterizes Pound, the editor-annotator, as a sieve because his method reduced the drafts to particles, only the finest, smallest of which were allowed through to the final version.

Repeatedly, Pound objects to Eliot's prolixity. The opening of 'The Fire Sermon' is 'Too tum-pum at a stretch,' 'too penty,' by which he means inflated iambic pentameter lines (10–11). The 'Too loose' rhyming couplets in the initial Fresca section of 'The Fire Sermon' drag the passage 'out to diffuseness' (38–9). The first version of the typist episode, related in quatrains, is 'not interesting enough as verse to warrant so much of it' (44–5). Pound values, not periodic verse, but succinct, metrically interesting, striking phrases and lines. He replaces Eliot's common 'Do you know nothing?' with 'Do?/ You know nothing?' and Eliot's haplessly ugly 'coming back out of the Transport Corps' with a perfect idiom, 'demobbed' (12–13). Pound labels Eliot's Latinate 'London, the swarming life' – with its imperative vocative 'London, your people is bound upon the wheel!' – as 'B-ll-S – t,' objects to his presumptuous 'we' (in 'We may have seen in any public place'), and has nothing to do with wordy qualifications like 'perhaps' or 'may' (30–1, 44–7). Pound measures lines in the typist's episode by their 'real exegience of metre' (44–5). He strikes out 'Knowing the manner of these crawling bugs' as 'Too easy,' and 'And at the corner where the stable is, / Delays only to urinate, and spit' as 'probaly over the mark' (44–7).

The first sieving nails Eliot on small things. Only once does Pound explicitly cut a passage, 'London, the swarming.' He waits until January 1922, when he has nearly 1,000 lines to work with, before he permits himself to hack away. Eliot received the bad news in London, a text half-deleted, and it got smaller after the third sieving, which chopped the supplementary three poems, so that only 433 lines were left. Rather than explain a cut, Pound simply draws a line vertically and horizontally across a passage. He says nothing, for example, about the sailor's story in Part IV, half of Eliot's output in Lausanne, except that it was 'Bad.' After Pound had done with Part IV, only about fifteen lines remain of the eighty that Eliot typed out. So discouraged was Eliot that he offers in late January to delete the entire section, and Pound needs to reassure him how important the lines are. When Pound is happy, he writes 'OK' or, in two moments of high enthusiasm, 'echt.' Pound becomes Eliot's externalized cognitive monitor and exacts changes with all the authority that one's own unconscious has, although Pound had his own agenda, which did not include wordy descriptions of Eliot's New England shipping lore or London's upper bourgeosie, or intimations of a religious change of heart. Pound sieved *The Waste Land* drafts into an indictment of England, a country that he abandoned in 1921 for France. Eliot had already committed himself to a solution by faith by 1921, but Pound wanted nothing of final poems that uttered 'I am the Resurrection and the Life' and that described how 'God, in a rolling ball of fire / Pursues by day' Eliot's 'errant feet' (110–11, 116–17).

Eliot is by no means sole author of the words and phrases we find in *The Waste Land*. Only 47 per cent of what he wrote for it actually got into the poem, thanks to Pound's scissors. Much of what Eliot did write was in fact quoted or paraphrased from other sources, indebtedness that he acknowledged in his published notes to the poem. In 'A Game of Chess,' for example, he paraphrases Shakespeare's *Antony and Cleopatra* in lines 1–2, *Hamlet* in lines 122, 131, and 172, and *Tempest* in line 125, Virgil's *Aeneid* in lines 92–3, Milton's *Paradise Lost* in lines 98, John Lyly's *Alexander and Campaspe* in line 103, John Webster's *The Devil's Law Case* in line 118, a popular song in lines 128–30, and Eliot's own maid, Ellen Kellond, in the story of Lil and Albert in lines 139–70. Kellond made such a vivid storyteller that Vivienne Eliot supplied lines 153 and 164, presumably from her own memory of this old wife's tale. Over 40 per cent of the 96 lines in Part II, then, stems from other authors. Pound exacerbated the authorship problem by giving Eliot word substitutions such as 'fruited' (79), 'golden' (80), 'though' (98), 'shuffled' (107), and 'demobbed' (139).

What can be said of Eliot's cognitive style in *The Waste Land*? The average length of Eliot's 26 edited and published 'fragments' is just 17 lines, a little longer than the average length of the eight 'raw' handwritten pieces that he drafted for the poem (only some of which got in), 12 lines (Rainey 2005b, 40). If the unedited holograph manuscripts give evidence of Eliot's cognitive capacity, then, it appears comparable to Shakespeare's, and greater than Coleridge's in 'Kubla Khan.' When we have passages that lack quotations and appear to have been uttered spontaneously, passages subject to very limited editing and composing, they are chunks of a size well within the alpha value. 'The river sweats' (266–91), for which we have an almost unblotted manuscript draft that was printed unaltered, averages under three words in length for each line. The 14-line Thames-daughter section (292–305) is almost as terse: its 14 period-stopped expressions average 5.5 words in length. By examining this section in more detail, we can begin to analyse his mind's maker, mainly because it does not quote or paraphrase work by others and has not been edited by Pound. The composing process of *The Waste Land* otherwise substantially distorts Eliot's own language and thought. It would be a mistake to use quantitative information about the vocabulary and phrasal lexicon of this poem – as in many other works that have gone through heavy editing – in an authorship attribution test.

Eliot's unaided mind is at work in the Highbury girl's confession, found only in a leaf written and reworked in Eliot's handwriting (see figs. 20–1), later annotated by Pound but without suggested changes. Here is the first draft, with *currente calamo* changes, and Eliot's deletions represented by strikethroughs. He evidently wrote it in Margate after Vivienne left for London but before his letter to Schiff, that is, about 1–12 November 1921, possibly (as Eliot says there) when he sat at the beach front watching the vacationers.

1 'Highbury bore me. Highbury's children
2 Played under green trees and in the dusty Park.
3 We were humble people and conservative
4 As neither the rich nor the working class know.
5 My father had a small business, somewhere in the city
6 A small business, an anxious business, ~~whi~~ provid~~ed~~ing
                                             only
7 The house in Highbury, and three weeks at Shanklin.
8 Highbury bore me. Richmond & Kew
9 Undid me. At Kew we had tea.

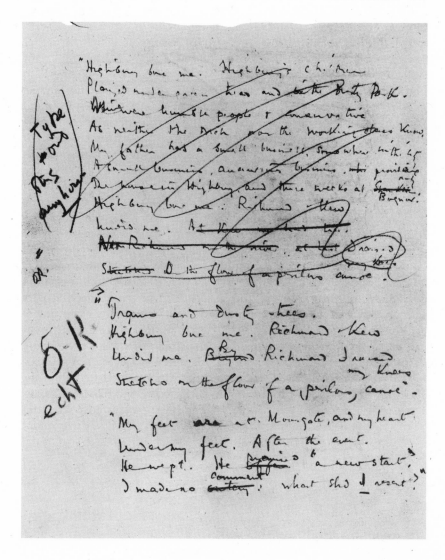

Figure 20. Eliot's 'Highbury' holograph recto (copyright © Valerie Eliot and courtesy of the Berg Collection, New York City Library)

10 At Richmond on the river at last I raised

my knees.

11 Stretched on the floor of a perilous canoe.

Once Eliot finished writing out these eleven lines, he made five changes. He overwrote three words, 'We Mine' (3), 'Shanklin Bognor.' (7), and
'At Near' (10), deleted 'At Kew we had tea. / At Richmond on the river
at last' (9–10) and 'Stretched o' (10), and shifted 'I raised my knees.'
from line 10 to line 12. Then, either when he made this transposition,
or at a later time but before he showed the page to Pound in November
1921, Eliot crossed out lines 1–10 with a back-and-forth, top-to-bottom,
right-to-left wavy diagonal line, leaving only the last two lines undeleted. Pound's dislike of looseness and prolixity may have prompted Eliot
to tighten the verse. He might have been struck by how many words
and phrases he repeated as he uttered the lines, "Highbury bore me,'
'small business,' 'Richmond,' and 'Kew.' When Eliot handed the page
to Ezra Pound in Paris, Pound wrote in pencil, beside cancelled lines
1–10, 'Type out this anyhow.' (The word 'anyhow' indicates that Eliot
had already deleted those lines.) Then Pound penned a small diagonal equals sign beside the two undeleted lines, wrote under that sign a
small 'OK.' and presumably handed the page back to Eliot.

In Lausanne, Eliot penned the second draft of the Highbury girl,[50]
and a new stanza for her workaday life at Moorgate, just north of the
financial centre of the City of London where Eliot worked at Lloyds'
Bank at 17 Cornhill. *Currente calamo* changes are included below, and
Eliot's deletions are marked with strikethroughs.

1 'Trams and dusty trees.

2 Highbury bore me. Richmond & Kew

3 Undid me. Beyond Richmond I raised

my Knees

4 Stretched on the floor of a perilous canoe.'

5 'My feet are at Moorgate, and my heart

6 Under my feet. After the event,

promised

7 He wept. He offere 'a new start.'

comment

8 I made no outcry: what shd I resent?'

Paying attention to Pound's interest in what he had cancelled, and influenced by the phrase 'dusty Park' in the second, Eliot unconsciously retrieved an image that he had used a decade before, 'dusty trees,'[51] and coupled it with 'Trams' (a percept that reminds me of Part II's 'closed carriage'). Eliot presents the Highbury girl as coming from a middle-class family, situated between the 'rich' who used a 'closed carriage' or a taxi in Parts II– III, and the 'working class' who walked. To 'Trams and dusty trees' Eliot added two sentences, 'Highbury bore me' and 'Richmond & Kew / Undid me,' which he rescued from the lines he had cancelled before but that Pound had asked to see in typescript. The stanza ends with the uncancelled two lines about the canoe seduction at Kew. The second quatrain, also rhyming *abab*, is about a girl at Moorgate, but unquestionably the same person as the Highbury girl because Moorgate is directly down the A1200 from Highbury in north London. Eliot was still thinking of the girl in the first stanza. After writing out the second stanza, Eliot made three minor editorial changes: two word substitutions, 'Beyond By' (3) and 'are were' (5), and an addition, a pair of cautionary parentheses around '(perilous)' (4), which he later replaced with 'narrow,' it appears, because 'perilously' had already been used in the typist's seduction scene. This is the first of several echoes of an earlier episode in Part III.

Turning over the leaf, Eliot makes three drafts of the third stanza of this girl's history before he is satisfied. Not only does the Highbury girl believe that she has nothing to resent, but she persuades herself that she 'was to be grateful' for the seducer's attentions. After all, he 'wept' and 'promised "a new start."' Then Eliot tells us where the girl has these thoughts, vacationing 'On Margate sands,' seeing 'many others' like herself. Her progress from a high borough to a business-district mooring gate or entrance (which offers some security), via a seduction at London's public parks at fashionable west-end Kew and Richmond, to a commoner's dissolution at an ill-sounding 'mar-gate,' parallels the story of the seduced typist.

1 'I was to be grateful. On Margate sands
2 There were many others. I can connect
3 Nothing with nothing. He had
4 I still feel the pressure of dirty hand

Again, Eliot thinks of the typist's seduction by a clerk 'who knows his way with women' – clearly he had 'many others' – and whose 'Exploring hands encounter no defence.'

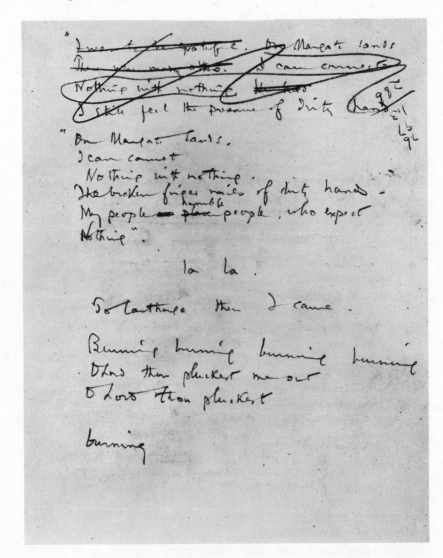

Figure 21. Eliot's 'Highbury' holograph verso (copyright © Valerie Eliot and courtesy of the Berg Collection, New York City Library)

Then, minding Pound's example in tightening loose sentences, Eliot edits down the stanza by crossing out the first two half-lines (which partly bridge to the second stanza) and drawing together, with a sweeping, curving line, the remaining text.

1 'I was to be grateful. On Margate sands
2 There were many others. I can connect
3 Nothing with nothing.
4 I still feel the pressure of dirty hand

Something still felt wrong to Eliot. Iterating his procedure in casting the first stanza, Eliot next crosses out all four lines with another top-to-bottom, right-to-left wavy diagonal line and pens the third and final draft below.

1 'On Margate Sands.
2 I can connect
3 Nothing with nothing.
4 The broken finger nails of dirty hands.
5 My people are plain people, who expect
6 Nothing'.

Eliot keeps the first three lines unchanged but deletes 'I still feel the pressure of dirty hand' and replaces it with a simpler, more general percept, 'The broken finger nails of dirty hands,' that recalls her own family at Highbury and another cancelled line that Pound believed had promise: 'We were humble people.' He first writes 'plain people' but then realizes his first thought was best and writes, above a through-struck 'are plain,' the simple word 'humble.' The Margate girl thinks the same thought as the Highbury girl: they are the same person. Finally, she realizes the explanation of her fall (unlike the typist's) might lie, not with her seducer, but with her own people.

When Eliot returns to Paris, he gives the leaf a second time to Pound, who marks it up with the same green crayon he uses on other new Lausanne material, Parts IV and V. Pound enthusiastically crayoned, beside the new Highbury stanza and the start of the second stanza, in very big letters, 'O.K. echt' (German for 'real'). He did not annotate the verso.

The Highbury girl stanzas vividly reveal Eliot's authoring process. At first, he utters in short chunks, almost conversationally, drawing on earlier material, both from deep associational long-term memory (the 'dusty trees' percept) and from what he has just penned (the typist episode in Part III). The latter comes from visual priming (the rereading of Part III to that point) or from reactivation of an 'expert' schema in long-term memory that stored his memories of the sexual encounters of man and woman. Eliot's repetition of words like 'perilous' and 'hand' signal this reuse.

We can then see Eliot's cognitive monitor at work. It halts him subconsciously mid-word at 'offere[d],' which he replaces by 'promised': an offer has all the wrong associations, particularly marriage. Once the text is stored on the leaf, Eliot gives it to Pound, whose feedback is minimal, just a signal to continue as before, doing more, redoing. An obedient disciple, Eliot then activates an expert schema in editing poetry that Pound has been teaching him. Its imperatives are to revise by cutting and condensing, and to settle only on what is not too realistic or 'photo[graphic]' a reproduction of life (Eliot 1971, 126, n. 5). The habit that Pound has encouraged in Eliot is a continuing, conscious self-monitoring that makes Eliot the author his own reader, cycling through each line, message and response, so that Pound's interventions are unnecessary. Eliot chops both the Highbury and the Margate stanzas into chunks, deletes the diffused and conversational ones (or too photographic memories like 'Highbury's children / Played under green trees'), and piles the surviving chunks one after another into new sequences that often lack bridging phrases. His initial spontaneous uttering resembles a 'flow' state. (Note the increasingly left-indented lineation of writing on the recto of the leaf. Not keeping to a left margin suggests steady writing without pauses.) The Highbury girl's episode repeats just one semantic phrase from his earlier poems, 'dusty trees.' Given the text written before his eyes, Eliot has the time, and the freedom from keeping lines in memory, to remake almost every expression new. The effect is 'A heap of broken images' (Part I, line 20), which strikes Pound as genuine but that opens the poem, and the poet, up to multiple, conflicting interpretations.

Subjected to three cybertextual cycles of authorial writing, critical reading and response, and authorial revision, *The Waste Land* lost half its bulk and, with that, text that faithfully reflected Eliot's native, unconscious idolect. In composition, much of this author passed away. We see more of the true Eliot in *The Four Quartets*, although his roommate John Heyward acted, in critiquing that greatest of Eliot's poems, somewhat as Pound had done in *The Waste Land*. There is some truth, then, in late twentieth-century disbelief that the author can be found in the work. Self-editing through retyping, the quoting of secondary materials stored in books, the influence of editorial staff who impose academic press style sheets, the spelling and grammar tools in word processors, and the practice of workshopping literary texts before they reach their final form have all conspired to make the author mistrust the mind's spontaneous utterance. Poets who respected what the muse inspired now question her competence as forgetful and error-prone. As a result, it may well be asked, will anyone be able to use Eliot's *The Waste Land* as an authentic sample of his writing in a future authorship-attribution trial?

The answer is yes, but carefully, with an eye to how Eliot produced verse lines. Until 1916, Eliot chose to utter poetry onto paper by hand, a traditional technology that encouraged periodic sentences, lengthy bouts of composing, and messy scripts, overwritten by word substitutions and syntactic rearrangements. The holograph manuscript leaves of 'London, the swarming' and even the Highbury girl show Eliot's painstaking effort at crafting verse, word by word, as if filling in a cross-word puzzle. By 1916, Eliot had discovered that the typewriter, which he used to generate presentation copies, could be turned to a new purpose: storing utterances as he formed them mentally. He wrote Conrad Aitken in August that 'Composing on the typewriter, I find that I am sloughing off all my long sentences which I used to dote upon. Short, staccato, like modern French prose. The typewriter makes for lucidity, but I am not sure that it encourages subtlety' (V. Eliot 1988, 144). Remembering that Eliot told John Quinn that no manuscript drafts underlay the typed pages of *The Waste Land*, we can see the 'direct deposit' effect of spontaneous typing in its first 18 lines, from 'April is the cruellest month' to 'and go south in the winter.' Its 32 punctuation-bounded phrases and clauses average just four words in length, that is, the alpha value. Eliot's cognitive idiolect, when left alone, is additive. He repeats the same syntactic frame, a present participle and its object, eight times in the first 13 lines ('*breeding* / Lilacs out of the dead land, *mixing* / Memory and desire, *stirring* ...'), and introduces clauses by 'and' six times in the last nine lines. Chunks flow easily from the mind onto the page, thanks to the relative speed of the typing, which keeps up well with the pace of mental uttering.

By 1921, a habit of unfettering his verse making through typing had settled in that then affected Eliot's entire creative method, independent of the writing technology he employed. At Lausanne, when Eliot had no typewriter, he nonetheless uttered, by hand, an almost blot-free Part V, just as if he were typing. He described, in a letter of 14 August 1923, to Ford Madox Ford, the opening of Part V and especially 'the 29 lines of the water-dripping song' as the poem's only truly '*good* lines,' ones that would not prove 'ephemera.' Valerie Eliot (Eliot 1971, 129) notes that Eliot was describing his own creative experience in making Part V when he wrote, in *The 'Pensées' of Pascal* (1931), that 'it is a commonplace that some forms of illness are extremely favourable, not only to religious illumination, but to artistic and literary composition. A piece of writing meditated, apparently without progress for months or years, may suddenly take shape and word; and in this state long passages may be produced which require little or no retouch.' The lovely, haunting twenty-nine lines from 'Here is no water but only rock' to 'But there is no water' (331–58) have no punctuation at all. They range from two to nine words and average six words in length. Their grammatical segments, often marked by one of the passage's eighteen conjunctions ('and,' 'but,' 'not,' and 'or') and by the subjuncts 'which,' 'if,' 'that,' and 'where,' average 5.4 words in length, again well within the alpha value. Eliot adds segments to one another in runs more often than he uses them to modify one another. He repeats content words such as 'water' (11), 'rock' (9), 'mountain(s)' (5), 'drop' (5), and 'dry' (3), and function-word frames such as the existential 'there + be-form' (8) and the prepositional phrases 'in the' (4), and 'among(st) the' (4). The holograph draft (70–3) shows only one *currente calamo* change. Pound did not touch the passage's second paragraph, beginning 'If there were water,' as he had not suggested changes to the episode of the Highbury girl.

When *The Waste Land* manuscripts show Eliot writing passages fluently, his idiolect lives in the text. In an earlier essay, 'Tradition and the Individual Talent' (1919), he famously applies a variant of the flow-state metaphor to the creative process. The poet's mind is an aluminum filament in a cloud of oxygen and sulphuric dioxide (which represent the poet's present 'emotions and feelings,' and the past poetic tradition in which he writes). The 'inert, neutral, and unchanged' filament acts as a catalyst to make sulphurous acid, a new combination (the work of art) of past and present (Eliot 1951, 17–18). The aluminum does not itself contribute to the new chemical. Eliot argues that the author splits into two, 'the man who suffers and the mind which creates.' Personality, the suffering individual, is extinguished in the passive making-process. The 'poet's mind is … a receptacle for … numberless feelings, phrases, images,' the creative fusion of which is itself an 'escape from personality' that 'does not happen consciously' (21). Eliot does not explain what he means when he concedes that making poetry has much that is 'conscious and deliberate,' but his work with Ezra Pound and Vivienne is suggestive.

Eliot's preoccupation with creative process continued into the months during which he finished *The Waste Land*. He visited the Lausanne psychotherapist Roger Vittoz in late 1921 on the advice of a friend, Lady Ottoline Morrel. Later, Eliot marked up the third French edition of Vittoz's book. The doctor attributed Eliot's neurasthenia to a lack of balance between his two brains, one objective, and the other subjective, associated with the unconscious (but amenable to conscious control; Harris 2006, 44, 46–7). After writing in 1919 about the poet's bifurcated selves, the sufferer and the creator, Eliot found a man whose medical knowledge validated his own chemical metaphor. The flow-state that we see in the opening of Part V of *The Waste Land* shows Eliot taking theory into practice.

*   *   *   *   *

I gave you 'the lovely lover's touch you feel is bodiless' that closed 'The Wind,' our first poem, printed just before Toronto, and we should have read it at the Bohemian Embassy but didn't, though you at least got to meet Gwendolyn, if I didn't, and then we lost a U.C. poetry contest to Michael O, and afterwards for the longest time you asked me for so little other than your double dactyls, contraptions that you called Erudities *that yielded me but little room of my own.*

Our poems for Susannah's wedding and for Anne on our fortieth took long enough, you sitting at a workstation and letting go, giving me a metre, waiting for our load, for what you don't know I'm going to say until I say it, but there's always more where that came from so don't give up please remember me.

5 Novelist-authors

The novelist's own Anonymous, like the poet's, assembles chunks in fragments that size up to his cognitive load limit. Unlike poems, however, novels integrate such fragments by reference to the locations, the characters, the events, and the chronology of a story. They make up the imaginative superstructure governing how the novelist sequences and organizes these chunk assemblies. It may never take verbal form beyond a partial outline and a synopsis. What mental function, then, holds this overarching organization, a narrative, together? Apparently episodic long-term memory does.

Endel Tulving theorizes episodic memory to be cognitive time travel by a self experiencing 'autonoetic consciousness,' by which he means awareness of 'subjective time in which events happened' in the past or may happen in a possible future (2002, 1–2, 14). Episodic memory – the recollection of past experiences or the anticipation of future ones – must have grown from semantic long-term memory, which holds knowledge of concepts, words, and things, as recently as several million years ago and is not shared by other life forms on earth (Suddendorf and Corballis 2007, 311–13). Brain phenomena separate episodic memory from semantic memory. A brain-damaged man, K, the subject of Tulving's research, has no episodic memory of personal experiences in his past, and no ability to speculate on his personal future. (Different patients exhibiting the same deficits are the subject of other studies.) Further, long-term episodic memory is encoded in the left hemisphere and retrieved in the right hemisphere, whereas semantic memory is encoded in the right and retrieved in the left (17–18). Very recent studies by Demis Hassabis and Eleanor Maguire also discover a 'near complete overlap in the brain networks activated' for autobiographical recollection, for episodic future thinking, and for 'imagining fictitious experiences' (2009, 1263). They argue that these allied functions undertake 'scene construction,' whether ruminating over the future or evaluating the 'aesthetic suitability' of a fictional scene (1269). Recalling a past experience and imagining a study share the same widely distributed neural network, now identified as the DMN.

A human capacity for episodic memory explains how novelists can mentally store (encode) and retrieve subjective experiences or constructions of imaginary events, locations, and characters so as to organize long literary texts. The novelist need not verbalize this kind of long-term memory. It is sufficient to be able to recover it in the episodic buffer of working memory. As the mind unconsciously creates sentences and paragraphs that, once encoded phonologically, are heard by the inner ear of working memory (the phonological loop), it also summons the narrative structures necessary to integrate them with the rest of the text in episodic working memory. Different functions work in parallel and in cooperation. However much authors may insist on impersonalizing their work and extracting themselves from the narrative, episodic memory processes autobiographical reconstructions and works of the imagination with the same neural network. The mind constructs (not copies) memories of the self, even should they be factually wrong. Over many months, a novelist will think about a story and will lay down constructs of characters, situations, places, and event sequences that episodic memory will recover when needed. The mind may well be biased to model imaginary stories on remembered personal history, and vice versa. History, his-story, and her-story blend by association, as semantic memories do.

The four novelists in this chapter do not write autobiographies, but they nonetheless place themselves in the heart of their novels, one way or another. James Joyce objectifies his youthful self in Stephen Dedalus, Agatha Christie mirrors her profession, age, and memory issues in Ariadne Oliver, Margaret Atwood exposes her own creative process in Offred's, and Iris Murdoch lost so much of what she had contrived her servant Jackson to be that she sublimates her own deteriorating condition in him.

I   James Joyce

> The artist, like the God of the creation, remains within or behind or beyond or above his handiwork, invisible, refined out of existence, indifferent, paring his fingernails.
>
> (Joyce 1968, 215)

When the poet-diarist Stephen Dedalus, whose youth *A Portrait of the Artist as a Young Man* narrates from the inside out, utters his obiter dictum, he is chatting with his friend Lynch as they walk towards Merrion Square in Dublin. Lynch's smart-alec reply, that Stephen's divine creator is 'Trying to refine them [his fingernails] also out of existence,' associates him with the 'scholastic stink' of Stephen's *Aquinian* aesthetics. In experiencing beauty, according to Stephen, readers enter a 'spiritual state' like the 'cardiac condition which the Italian physiologist Luigi Galvani ... called the enchantment of the heart' (Joyce 1968, 213). This otherworldly condition also applies to Stephen's author: 'The personality of the artist, at first a cry or a cadence or a mood and then a fluid and lambent narrative, finally refines itself out of existence, impersonalizes itself' (215). The author begins as an emotion, becomes a story, and so loses personality. A feeling-encoded gist enters the episodic working buffer. T.S. Eliot may have had this passage in his own mind when he published 'Tradition and the Individual Talent' three years after Joyce finally found a publisher for *Portrait* (which Eliot certainly read). Joyce must have taken the theory of the impersonal author seriously enough. He wrote autobiographically about a Stephen rather than a James; and he spent ten years writing *Portrait*, during which he abandoned both an essay and a partial novel, 'Stephen Hero,' among earlier versions.

Joyce did not wrap his author completely in a cloak of invisibility. His intentions appear in revisions that he made to two poems by young Jim Joyce. What gives traction to the elder Joyce's authorial readings of these texts is his change of genres. On 19 July 1909, replying to a begging letter by a songwriter for help, Joyce confided, 'There is no likelihood of my writing any more verse unless something unforeseen happens to my brain' (1957, 67). One poem, Stephen's 'Pull out his eyes,' comes from the first of Jim Joyce's surviving epiphanies. He saved, in these prose nuggets, some distinctive, revelatory experiences.[1] This epiphany has Mr Vance, a Protestant, warn Mrs Joyce that young Jim will have to apologize for something or 'the eagles'll come and pull out his eyes' (268). Mrs Joyce expresses confidence that he will but Jim hides under a table and utters a poem that has only two lines, repeated, 'Apologize' and 'Pull out his eyes.' By substituting Dante (Stephen's fiercely Roman Catholic 'aunt') for Mr Vance, Joyce characterizes young Stephen's great antagonist as the Church, not parental control.

Of course, the biographical details that scholars have unearthed about Jim Joyce's school-days also show decision-making at work. *Portrait* is realistic but not historically accurate. Jim becomes Stephen. For

example, of twenty-two named fellow students at Clongowes Wood
College, seven are unidentifiable in school records (485–6).

The intellectual climax of *Portrait* occurs in chapter 5 when Stephen
becomes an artist. He writes a villanelle as he wakes from sleep one
morning. Joyce's story of Stephen has built carefully to this moment,
when we first see him create a work of art. Although Joyce wrote the
poem before he began *Portrait* (it survives from his first poems), he
added an account of the making of the villanelle at a very late stage
in the novel's composition. The poem consummates Stephen's rebellion against social mores and the Roman Catholic moral code schooled
into him in the preceding four chapters by the Jesuits, his mother, and
Ireland. Stephen's villanelle depicts a 'temptress,' and he compares his
sexual love for her to partaking of the Eucharist, a profanity that frees
him of Ireland and its Church. This revolutionary release notwithstanding, critics wonder how we are supposed to take Stephen's poem. Is it
meant to represent good writing or bad? Hugh Kenner suggests that
Stephen wakes up because of a nocutural emission, a 'wet dream' (1955,
123). If so (it is not very well borne out by the actual text), the villanelle
is a reflex action to a subconscious orgasm. I see the poem somewhat
differently. The orgasm turns up at the end instead of the beginning
after Stephen's resolution to give up his frustrating sexual obsession
with the girl at the tram and the library, a girl who is fully, uncomplain-
ingly compliant with the religious state that Stephen rejects.

Authorial readings by both Stephen and Joyce support this idea.
They find the authors' intentions by observing their creative process. In
relating what Stephen does in composing the villanelle, Joyce observes
an unconscious language flow that is consistent with the much later
findings of cognitive psychology. Being an omniscient narrator, Joyce
can reveal secrets of Stephen's creative process normally cloaked by his
maker's invisibility. Joyce shows this process initiated, emotionally, by
Stephen's sexual obsession with the girl confused by his simultaneous
appreciation of how likeable she is. His emotional turmoil, a crux, is the
initial gist of the poem, its reason to be, his intention. The poem realizes
imaginatively Stephen's desire to make love to the girl and, in a harm-
less way, to heal himself while protecting her, someone who he realizes is quite innocent and kind. The poem solves a personal problem
and enables Stephen to grow ultimately into Joyce. What is the poem's
meaning, then? I believe that the poem exists to explain a young man's
authoring.

By revealing the cognitive and affective underpinnings of Stephen's

creative process, stanza by stanza, Joyce tells much about his own creative method. Far from being the invisible god behind his own creation,
Stephen pours himself so completely into a poem about his favourite
girl that uttering it fuels an auto-erotic fantasy. Still, Stephen aspires to
impersonality in his works and is the father to Joyce, who shows himself nonplussed by what his youthful unconscious creative self (as he
understood it) revealed of itself in writing. Joyce determined to become
the most 'unnatural' major author in English. He rejected spontaneous
flow in principle. As Edgar Allan Poe (1846) claimed, probably falsely,
to have done in making 'The Raven,' Joyce resolved to give no basis,
in future, for associating *Ulysses*, for instance, with unconscious muse-
based effusions. Both Poe and Joyce thought that the creator could be,
at all stages in making a work of art, fully self-aware of all aspects of
the process and product. Both aimed to work with a logic of aesthetics.

In *Portrait* Joyce exposed the workings of his earlier vision-prompted
inner voice to the point that critics have radically split on interpreting the poem. Robert Adams Day rightly calls the villanelle a 'crux'
(1998, 52). Wayne Booth asks, 'what of the precious villanelle? Does
Joyce intend it to be taken as a serious sign of Stephen's artistry, as a
sign of his genuine but amusingly pretentious precocity, or as something else entirely?' (Joyce 1968, 459). Robert Scholes believes that the
villanelle is 'a muse poem' about a 'great poetical archetype' (Joyce
1978, 478). I agree with his characterization but also sympathize with
Hugh Kenner's dismissive belief that the poem is a postlude to a wet
dream, Booth's sarcasm about the 'precious,' and their mutual sense
that Joyce was not offering Stephen's creative process, or his art, as ideal. Day sensibly says that Joyce treated the poem respectfully because
it was 'material' evidence that was entitled to a faithful representation.
I would add that, if we focus on Joyce's (cybertextual) reaction to what
he, as a young writer, produced ten years previously, we have a very
firm basis for seeing Joyce's own intentions in the book. They appear
in his fictive annotations to a poem he wrote much earlier. What does
an authorial reading of the villanelle episode teach us? It shows us how
Joyce no longer wished to behave creatively, as well as what kind of
subject deserves treatment in art.

Stephen wakes up conscious of a 'morning inspiration,' described
as a spirit of music and water that bathes his soul and that inbreathes
into his 'mind.' This spirit is what might be called his muse, the source
of his inspiration; it resembles the man that Cædmon met in the stable.
Stephen twice calls its presence 'sweet' as he lays down, in long-term

memory, his experience of it, vague and emotion laden. The amygdala, not the hippocampus, could have placed this affect-coded gist of the inbreathing spirit into memory because Stephen's feelings of it lack concrete details. Waking some more, he begins to interpret the gist in the context of everything he holds to be spiritually sweet and so withdraws associated details from his own long-term memory. His strongest mental associations for an inbreathing spirit must be angelic visitors, and so he compares the spirit (using 'as if') to 'the seraphim themselves ... breathing upon him' (217). The muse that stimulates the villanelle is not the temptress it addresses, but a vaguely understood spirit that he compares to angelic messengers from God to human. Stephen does not at first know what has happened to him. Only when he awakes to self-awareness does he begin to overlay the experience of this spirit with plausible details about an angelic muse. Stephen models a very new experience, 'when madness wakes' (217), by drawing on his semantic and episodic long-term memory.

Stephen believes that the spirit came to him 'In a dream or vision' about 'the ecstasy of seraphic life' that lasted either an 'instant ... or long hours and years and ages.' Joyce gives us no reason to think that Stephen's spirit existed for him at any time other than his brief awakening moment, although the youth interprets it as a dream vision of life in heaven. He calls this 'spiritual state' an 'enchantment of the heart' (217), a phrase that he used the previous day in expounding his Aquinian aesthetic to Lynch. Stephen defined the beautiful then as anything known as a separate entity, known in its internal structural elements, and appreciated for its 'radiance,' its *quidditas* or unique whatness. Once we perceive something in all three ways simultaneously, no matter what it is, we experience it aesthetically as beautiful. For instance, a half-goat, half-man in a field of weeds (epiphany 6, in Joyce 1978, 137–8) could be beautiful to the imagination, the name of the faculty that perceives beautiful things. Stephen names the effect of beauty on the perceiver to be 'The enchantment of the heart,' after Galvani's previously mentioned term for a cardiac condition: the short-termed cessation of the heart on being stimulated with an electrical charge.

This is the first point at which Joyce betrays an attitude to Stephen's vision. Why does Joyce take care to have Stephen highlight this phrase, and its indebtedness to Galvani, in discussing Aquinian aesthetics to Lynch the preceding day, and why does Joyce repeat the phrase here? Why twice mention Galvani? Is Stephen showing off his learning? If so, he misses the comic inappropriateness of the reference: the phrase describes the reaction of a frog to experimental electrocution. Stephen compares an exalted spiritual state to a frog's brief, painless heart attack. It nicely describes Stephen's experience. He has subjugated himself and his art to an unconscious state that treats of matters of the heart. The poem begins as a knee-jerk reaction to unconscious inspiration. Although a frog is just as aware of sensory experiences as Stephen, it has no substitute for instinct. Stephen does, if only he would use it.

Once Stephen retrieves from long-term memory the affective gist with its most strongly associated memories, seraphic life and the imagination, other associations follow by 'spreading activation.' Joyce effectively describes this rapid expansion, a true cognitive effect, when he writes that 'The instant of inspiration seemed now to be reflected from all sides at once from a multitude of cloudy circumstance of what had happened or of what might have happened. The instant flashed forth like a point of light and now from cloud on cloud of vague circumstance confused form was veiling softly its afterglow' (Joyce 1968, 217). Joyce makes two observations here. Like later researchers, he thinks of long-term-memory schemata, linked neural clusters, as clouds because their boundaries are ill-defined and overlap at the outer weaker links. Experience and thought also constantly adjust the weights that bind these schemata. Second, spreading activation lights up, in a reflected 'afterglow,' episodic memories of circumstances in Stephen's life that make concrete his two main associations, heavenly sweetness and the beautiful. When Joyce says, 'In the virgin womb of the imagination the word was made flesh' (Joyce 1968, 217) he means in part that Stephen's semantic knowledge of language – that one phrase, 'enchantment of the heart,' pops up – recalls episodic knowledge of his body's life. No one should be surprised, after reading Stephen's story to this moment, that his most powerful memories of emotion-laden enchantment concern the virginal women he loves sexually, from Emma and the Blessed Virgin Mary to the girl on the beach at the close of chapter 4. Stephen associates imagination, the faculty that perceives the beautiful, with a virgin's womb that gestates God. The beautiful epiphany has radiance, a divine quality, and Stephen's most repeatedly imagined beauty, to which all paths in his mind lead, is untapped female sexuality. Having linked the seraphic experience with a perception of sexual beauty, Stephen then extrapolates a full episodic sequence into his model of what his dream vision means. The spirit who inspired him was Gabriel, and the ecstasy he communicated to Stephen was the Annunciation, his visit to Mary as the Christ Child glowed in her womb. This was

Gabriel's fall, and the reason why the rest of the seraphim also fell from heaven. They sin by worshipping the divine in the flesh, God in his womb. Is it coincidental that Stephen interprets the visit of his muse spirit in terms of the two key events of the previous afternoon? The weights of associative memory associate his explanation of the aesthetically beautiful (to Lynch), and his encounter with his 'beloved' at the library steps. These weights will have been strengthened the previous day. Joyce does not explicitly point out these associations. He gives us a 'portrait' to look at, not a labelled diagram.

The first three stanzas come quickly. Joyce anticipates Willem Levelt's lexical production, from lexical concept (including imagery) to lemma (unsoundable words), and lemma to phonological word form and gesturally scored utterance. The content of the opening stanza first appears in a 'confused form' of images that rise in Stephen's mind. Joyce expresses them, of course, as language, but he intends to describe Stephen translating these images into verbal chunks: 'enchanted,' 'ardent,' 'lure,' and 'of the seraphim … fall' (boldfaced in the text below). Two of these terms occur three times in the paragraph that precedes the stanza. The process is consistent with use in both the phonological loop and the visual-spatial sketchpad in Alan Baddeley's working memory.

An **enchant**ment of the heart! The night had been **enchanted**. In a dream or vision he had known the ecstasy of **seraph**ic life. Was it an instant of **enchant**ment only or long hours and years and ages?

The instant of inspiration seemed now to be reflected from all sides at once from a multitude of cloudy circumstances of what had happened or of what might have happened. The instant flashed forth like a point of light and now from cloud on cloud of vague circumstance confused form was veiling softly its afterglow. O! In the virgin womb of the imagination the word was made flesh. Gabriel the **seraph** had come to the virgin's chamber. An afterglow deepened within his spirit, whence the white flame had passed, deepening to a rose and **ardent** light. That rose and **ardent** light was her strange **wil**ful heart, strange that no **man** had known or would know, **wil**ful from before the beginning of the world; and **lured** by that **ardent** roselike glow the choirs **of the seraphim** were **fall**ing from heaven.

*Are you not weary of **ardent ways**,*
*****Lure** of the fallen seraphim?***
*Tell no more of **enchanted days**.*   (217)

Stephen then speaks the lines of the first stanza to himself aloud. The phonological loop in working memory would only hold one line (two seconds) at a time, but by rehearsing the three in sequence repeatedly, and by linking them to the villanelle form and rhyme scheme in his long-term memory, he encodes them deeply and can summon them up as a single thought in an auditory frame. This *aba aba* frame links six line-ending rhymes and offers a mental way to move from one stanza to another. Stephen identifies mentally the candidate rhymes before he assembles the chunks in which they are embedded by moving from imagery to words, concept to lemma and word form.

> The verses passed from his mind to his lips and, murmuring them over, he felt the rhythmic movement of a villanelle pass through them. The roselike glow sent forth its rays of rhyme; **ways, days, blaze, praise**, raise. Its rays burned up the world, consumed the **hearts of men** and angels: the rays from the rose that was her **wil**ful heart.

> > *Your eyes have set **man's heart ablaze***
> > *And you have had your **will** of him.*
> > *Are you not weary of **ardent ways?***   (217–18)

Acutely, Joyce recognizes how the mind superimposes the rhythm of the villanelle form on lexico-semantic production. Cognitive psychology does not have much research to show on the role of prosody in composing poetry, but experiments by Mary Louise Serafine and her colleagues (1984, 1986) found that the mind, by integrating melody and text, improves memory of both. Prosody guides Stephen's text making by offering a mould into which it can flow. He can rapidly eliminate lexical options in filling metrical slots. One advantage of this demanding structure is its intolerance for in-process error-correction and post-production editing.

> And then? The rhythm died away, ceased, began again to move and beat. And then? **Smoke**, incense ascending from the altar of the world.

> > *Above the **flame** the **smoke** of **praise***
> > *Goes up from **ocean** rim to rim*
> > *Tell no more of **enchanted** days.*

> **Smoke went up from** the whole earth, from the vapoury **oceans, smoke of**

her **praise**. The earth was like a swinging swaying censer, a ball of incense, an ellipsoidal ball. The rhythm died out at once; the cry of his heart was broken. His lips began to murmur the first verses over and over; then went on stumbling through half verses, stammering and baffled; then stopped. The heart's cry was broken. (218)

The second and third stanzas reuse words and chunks from image-dominated thought described by Joyce in prose. All nine lines use but forty-three words different in sequence. Another thirteen words in the first and third lines of the first stanza are repeated once in the second and third stanzas. This metrical knot could be Stephen's cognitive load, his omega limit, what his mind can focus on at one time. Expertise in encoding language would increase his chunk capacity in words; and by thinking of the three stanzas as a story, and by hearing the prosodic structure, Stephen could store the stanzas in the episodic buffer for a short period.

Yet he still comes to a halt. Why does the frame die from his memory, and the recitation of all three stanzas aloud fail him? Joyce describes Stephen 'stumbling through half verses' (218), chunk-sized output that cannot be stitched together according to the rhyme scheme. The reason for Stephen's blockage appears to be the image of an 'ellipsoidal ball.' This is an unintentional recollection of the previous afternoon's lecture in mathematics. The professor quoted some comic verse by W.S. Gilbert so as to illustrate the difference between the elliptical and the ellipsoidal, a distinction that led Moynihan to whisper in Stephen's ear, 'What price ellipsoidal balls! Chase me, ladies, I'm in the cavalry!' (Joyce 1968, 192) Spreading activation in long-term memory took Stephen from a swinging censer in a divine love to Moynihan's dangling testicles. Joyce shows why Stephen's 'heart's cry' is baffled, stopped, with a potentially amusing grind of mental gears. The interruption shows how suspectible is the cognitive-affective basis of Stephen's spontaneous muse-driven composition to sudden breakdown.

Desperate not to lose his stanzas, Stephen writes them out on a cigarette packet: another piece of comic business, to Joyce's indifferent viewpoint, given that the poem celebrates 'man's heart ablaze' and 'Above the flame the smoke of praise.' To resume the creative process, Stephen has to relight the ecstatic emotions that retrieved the gist initiating the artwork. Lying back in bed, Stephen engages in free association, again trusting in ungoverned, spontaneous flow. A feeling of the 'knotted flock' (219) in his pillow overlays the stanzas that he murmurs aloud to himself. This sensation leads him to think of knotted horse-hair in his beloved's sofa, where he sat until she asked him to sing at the piano. Her presence then prompts memories of her at a 'carnival ball' when he called himself a monk and she termed him a heretic and danced away from him along a 'chain of hands,' 'giving herself to none' (219). Stephen's mental transition from one kind of ball into another, and from balls to himself as profaning 'monk,' strengthens the breaking of his 'cry.' His self-image as monk then shifts to the priest with whom he believed she flirted, and to a 'Rude brutal anger' that 'routed the last lingering instant of ecstasy from his soul' (220). His memory tossed up images of four other common girls who had flirted with him, as a result of whom he recasts his beloved as a sin-free, unloved 'figure of the womanhood of her country' and diverts his anger from her to the 'priested peasant,' his rival. Yet Stephen is indignant at how she can 'unveil her soul's shy nakedness' to this rite-repeater, someone far less creative than himself,

> ... to one who was but schooled in the discharging of a formal rite rather than to him, a priest of the eternal imagination, transmuting the daily bread of experience into the radiant body of everliving life.
>
> The radiant image of the **eucharist** united again in an instant his bitter and despairing thoughts, their **cries** a**ri**sing un**broken in** a **hymn** of thanksgiving.

> Our **broken cries** and mournful lays
> **Rise in** one **eucharistic hymn.**
> Are you not weary of ardent ways?
>
> While sacrificing hands upraise
> The chalice flowing to the brim,
> Tell no more of enchanted days.   (1968, 221)

The fourth and fifth stanzas take their cue from the ball-broken interruption of the heart's broken cry. After a bout of circuitously associated remembering, Stephen regains a sense of exaltation that his seraphic vision had when he imagines himself as a priest greater than the object of his beloved's flirtations. The 'hymn' maybe puns on 'him,' Stephen rising erect, no longer 'broken.'

With one more stanza to make, with only two new lines (the closing couplet to unite the refrains that have alternated between stanzas until now), Stephen respeaks aloud all his lines 'till the music and rhythm suffused his mind,' and then copies them all 'painfully to feel them the better by seeing them.' His cybertextual feedback does not alter one word; everything is flow, and what flows lies trapped in the prosodic mould. Then he cowls his head with the blanket and lays back, facing the wall, the renewed warming giving him 'a langourous weariness' (222) and making him smile and think of sleep. Stephen's memory throws up a repeated meditation then on his meeting with the beloved on the steps of the last tram. That Joyce repeats this episode three times in all (69–70, 77, 222) shows its importance in Stephen's mind, but we also know that it is his third epiphany, a fact that Joyce did not confide in his readers. While the word 'epiphany' is not even in the novel, it turns up in *Stephen Hero*, the unfinished earlier version of *Portrait*. Realizing the *quidditas* or whatness of an object, Stephen perceives a radiance that he calls its epiphany (Chayes in Joyce 1968, 359). He compares this earlier to the moment of transubstantiation at the eucharist, when the communion bread literally becomes flesh of the godhead.

> **The children who have stayed latest are getting on their things to go home for the party is over.** This is the last tram. The lank brown horses know it and shake their bells to the clear night, in admonition. The conductor talks with the driver; both nod often in the green light of the lamp. **There is nobody near. We seem to listen,** I on the upper step and she on the lower. She comes up to my step many times and goes down again, between our phrases, and once or twice remains beside me, forgetting to go down, and then goes down … Let be; let be … **And now she does not urge her vanities – her fine dress and sash and long black stockings – for now** (wisdom of children) **we seem to know that this end will please us better than any end we have laboured for.** (Joyce 1965, 13, and 1968, 268)

Stephen's memory of this epiphany copies the original almost verbatim as Joyce had originally transcribed and kept it (some forty-one survive), except for deleting the above boldfaced words. These deletions have an important effect: Stephen ends on a desire to give up his obsession, to let be. The poem's iterated refrains express this same hope for closure. Stephen speculates whether his beloved would give this poem to her brothers and uncle to read with laughter but decides, after all, that he has 'wronged her,' that she was always innocent, and that they shared a like humiliation: he 'first sinned' sexually at the same time that she experienced 'the dark shame of womanhood,' menstruation. Stephen even wonders whether she recognized his 'homage' all along.

Having persuaded himself that she is sympathetic, Stephen then creates the opening lines for the last stanza, 'And still you hold our longing gaze, / With languorous look and lavish limb' (Joyce 1968, 223). He cannot quite 'let be.' The images that lead up to the last stanza have Stephen experiencing coition with his naked beloved in a final consummation.

> A glow of desire kindled again his soul and fired and fulfilled all his body. Conscious of his desire she was waking from odorous sleep, the temptress of his villanelle. Her eyes, dark and with a **look** of **languor**, were opening to his eyes. Her nakedness yielded to him, radiant, warm, odorous and **lavish-limb**ed, enfolded him like a shining cloud, enfolded him like water with a liquid life; and like a cloud of vapour or like waters circumfluent in space the liquid letters of speech, symbols of the element of mystery, flowed forth over his brain. (1968, 223)

These last lines flow out spontaneously from the sexual imagery of his fantasy. Auto-erotically, he emits words as if their liquidity were seminal fluid or ejaculate. The 'mystery' that they symbolize resembles the seraphic ecstasy in which he first awoke.

Ironically, Joyce publishes – in a novel – what may be the first authorial reading of a poem in English. He describes, as neutrally as he can, a youthful composition that emerged spontaneously, without editing, in a reverie that resembles the daydreaming of the DMN. Stephen's villanelle of the temptress begins as a powerful expression of the poet's feelings embodied in memories of seraphic bliss. Despite a metaphoric translation, the poet Stephen hides little of himself, especially in the erotic fantasy that rewards him at its completion. This author is also alive in his work by reason of brain processing, especially by use of associative long-term memory. Joyce shows how Stephen's poetic words arise from images, become inner speech (as in working memory), and then are stored in writing. Involuntary associations advance the poem and halt it in mid-flow. Joyce uses his third epiphany to show how Stephen's feelings for the girl, explicitly at odds with his professed aim at impersonality, causes a mid-poem breakdown with the shocking phrase, 'ellipsoidal ball.' Joyce seems faithful to material from his youth. What Joyce would not do in his own writing, including *Portrait*, is to risk a similar miscue himself. After all, *Portrait* was no muse-inspired effusion; Joyce spent ten years editing and rewriting it.

Joyce offers a reading of how Stephen, a representation of himself as a youth, authored the villanelle, not to characterize it as good or bad, but to show how different its making was from his own creative process. Stephen failed to depersonalize the poem. Joyce intended that we recognize how Stephen had yet not succeeded to 'let be.' For most literature, critics must compare holograph drafts with the final work to see what the author revealed of his intentions during revision. Joyce saved us the trouble by embedding in *Portrait* an account of his former creative process. The novel ends with verbatim entries from Stephen's diary. Joyce himself appears to have already quietly left the room and closed the door.

*   *   *   *   *

Schemata waxed and waned in us for years as you accumulated notebooks and annotated photocopies in offices, seeded the ground with talks and articles, glimpsed patterns in concordances and jotted down phrases in odd places until you let me grow the seeds in paragraph lots that were somewhere between Cædmon's hymn and Eliot's fragments, seldom as long as a Shakespeare sonnet, never as great as blind Milton's amazing thirty-line flows, and I saw that watching me utter onto a monitor delighted you at last, to stumble on such thoughts, before inchoate and unuttered, now yours in a words-surge talky that fed ideas back into you, strengthening and extending the schemata until Christmas 2007 at MLA in Chicago when you asked our editor, Suzanne, if she was interested, and she was, and it was thrilling, the achieved affect, and I suppose I should thank you for remembering me.

II   Agatha Christie

> And so each venture
> Is a new beginning, a raid on the inarticulate
> With shabby equipment always deteriorating
> In the general mess of imprecision of feeling,
> Undisciplined squads of emotion.   (T.S. Eliot, 'East Coker')

When Dylan Thomas's youth in 'Fern Hill' sings 'in his chains like the sea,' or when Eliot complains of 'shabby equipment always deteriorating,' they mean their embodied minds. A text freezes the utterings of an author's dynamic cognition, but the author is not always so lucky personally. Idiolect nestles in a brain genetically engineered to change. Writing technologies and the powers they afford authors in composing and storing what once flowed so spontaneously are of no help once the brain's neural structure begins to fail. Then the author cannot find semantic, episodic, and procedural memories. Even a healthily aging brain brings some forgetfulness, but confusion and a mounting unre-coverability of the author's lexicon comes with declining health. A healthily aging brain cultivates what critics call late style (Wyatt-Brown 1988, 837). A deteriorating brain subtly imposes a characteristic poverty on all its texts.

Old age inevitably slows uttering and forces it to use simpler sentence structures and fewer words, although the vocabulary of the old still grows. Writing technologies can, for a time, prompt the forgetful mind. Conversational strategies, like the use of formulaic expressions or fill-ers, can mask mental delays. These lapses are only inconveniences, com-pared to Alzheimer's disease, the dominant mental disease of old age (it makes up 50 to 70 per cent of the several kinds of dementia). It affects one out of every eight persons who are sixty-five years or older, and nearly a half of those who reach eighty-five years (*Alzheimer's Disease Facts and Figures* 2007). As more and more nerve cells are damaged or die, leaving behind them a signature of plaque or tangles, especially in brain areas responsible for forming new memories, an individual has trouble eas-ily recalling not just what is retained in memory but fresh information. Ironically, in a century of biopsies, MRIs, ECGs, and bloodwork, the suf-ferer's language is what often enables the medical profession to diagnose dementia. The Folstein Mini-Mental Status Examination consists of two dozen questions, many that test naming (date, place, and objects), and repeating, reading, or writing words and sentences (Folstein, Folstein, and McHugh 1975). A family doctor, like Odilo Unverdorben in Mar-tin Amis's *Time's Arrow* (1991, 35), may also ask simple questions of his patient such as 'What is meant by the saying, "People in glass houses shouldn't throw stones"?' and look for abnormal responses such as 'They'll break the glass.' Dementia leads to a broadly diffused deterio-ration of mental ability, not just lapses. Speech suffers because the mind cannot effectively think in an organized way. Those who suffer from dementia eventually lose a sense of self – they die before their body dies – and with the self go the individuating idiolect and style that character-ized them. What remain to almost the end are prefabricated expressions, possibly employed bizarrely, and a hard-to-eradicate core grammar, the subject-verb-object/complement sentence structure.

Agatha Christie (1890–1976), in a fifty-three-year writing career, crafted about eighty-five detective and romance novels and plays, as well as an autobiography. The Bodley Head published her first novel, *The Mysterious Affair at Styles*, in 1920, and Collins her last, *Postern of Fate*, in 1973. Efficiently, painstakingly, Christie produced one or two novels a year for her publishers. A Crime Club book by her was a highlight of many Christmas seasons, her detectives Hercule Poirot, Tommy and Tuppence, and Miss Marple (among others) achieving a fame well beyond the scope of mainstream literary characters. Some thought of Christie as the Dickens of her day, what others have said of Stephen King, who succeeded to her infectious popularity in another genre, horror. Her appeal was universal: reading one Christie novel led to reading most. Whether they were good, mediocre, or (at the end) weak, readers enjoyed another visit with a familiar conversationalist. The public had bought 400 million copies of her works by 1975 (Mallowan 1977, 211), and two billion by 1990 ('Mysterious Affair' 1990), and she had become the most read and loved English author outside Shakespeare and the Bible. Queen Elizabeth made Agatha Christie a Dame of the British Empire in 1971.

Her typical detective novel gives readers a problem to be solved, 'like a good crossword puzzle,' her second husband, Max Mallowan, said (Mallowan 1977, 227), and she renders it in a plain, unassuming, and colloquial but not slangy style. Conversational dialogue and spare narration, not showy descriptions or philosophical exposition, carry the reader along. She provides clues and diversions and maintains suspense until her sleuth unveils a solution that, almost always, has eluded her readers. Once the mystery is solved, the book ends. Her novels are between 55,000 and 75,000 words long, what a reader might finish in a day on vacation.

Her writing technologies changed over the years. She wrote *Styles* first in longhand and then typed it on her sister Madge's old Empire typewriter (Morgan 1984, 78; Christie 1977, 193). In 1926, after her first great work of detective fiction, *The Murder of Roger Ackroyd*, she hired a nanny-secretary named Charlotte Fisher but quickly renounced dictation for her typewriter once she found that she 'could not say more than a word without hesitating and stopping. Nothing [she] said sounded natural' (Christie 1977, 341). She enjoyed detailing the plot, the characters, and the puzzle, chapter by chapter, in a notebook – 'Almost seventy survive' (Thompson 2007, 367; Curran 2009) – but when she had to compose on a typewriter, 'she found writing difficult and tedious'

(Morgan 1984, 283). In the middle of finishing *A Pocket Full of Rye* in the autumn of 1952, Christie broke her wrist in a fall and afterwards, at her agent's suggestion, used a dictaphone. Max and others believed that this device improved her writing (322; Mallowan 1977, 211), but Christie said that speaking her text encouraged verbosity and sacrificed 'Economy of wording': 'You don't want to hear the same thing rehashed three or four times over. But it is tempting when one is speaking into a dictaphone to say the same thing over and over again in slightly different words. Of course, one can cut it out later, but that is irritating, and destroys the smooth flow which one gets otherwise' (Christie 1977, 341). Christie's custom, until the last books, was to work out her plot meticulously beforehand in a notebook, and (as her husband said) to write her last chapter – where her detective laid out the solution – first (Robyns 1978, 195). Her notes on *Lord Edgeware Dies* and *Evil under the Sun* 'are almost identical to the finished article' (Thompson 2007, 369).

Despite a professional rigour of mind, in 1950 (her sixtieth year) Christie reread something she wrote during the war years and said, 'I am not sure I haven't gone down the hill since then!' (Morgan 1984, 284). Later readers tended to agree with her. Her most loved works – *The Murder of Roger Ackroyd* (1926), *Murder on the Orient Express* (1934), *The ABC Murders* (1936), *Death on the Nile* (1937), *Ten Little Indians* (1939), *The Body in the Library* (1942), *Towards Zero* (1944), and *Witness for the Prosecution and Other Stories* (1948) – predate her change of technology from typewriter to dictaphone. Her last novels, *Passenger to Frankfurt* (1970), *Nemesis* (1971), *Elephants Can Remember* (1972), and *Postern of Fate* (1973), written from her seventy-ninth to eighty-second year, had negative reviews. 'Her publishers had grave doubts' about releasing *Frankfurt*, so vague was its plotting (Osborne 1982, 217); *Nemesis* was 'careless,' Christie failing to account for 'improbabilities'; and *Elephants* and *Postern* include uncertainties about the age of characters (221, 223–4; Knepper 2005, 71). Critics described *Postern* as 'a contrived affair that creeps from dullness to boredom' (Callendar 1973, 18), its 'plot ... total chaos and the clues total confusion' (Veit 1974, 68). Janet Morgan, a biographer trusted by her family, says that, after her preceding novel, *Elephants Can Remember* (1972), 'her powers really declined' (Morgan 1984, 370). Dictating *Postern* in a 'cracked' voice (Thompson 2007, 7), she reportedly found it 'harder than ever to concentrate': her husband Max said that this last book 'nearly killed her' (Morgan 1984, 371). Much of it digresses into Christie's past memories and current problems, as about house repair, and 'the murderer is not introduced into the story until the last few chapters' (Knepper 2005, 77). Her agent suggested that she get help editing the work, and her long-time secretary Mrs Honeybone 'tidied it up': a necessity that led Agatha's daughter Rosalind to ask Collins 'to press for no more books,' and Morgan to conclude, 'Physical and mental decline is sad' (371–2).

Although Christie suffered with symptoms of mental decline between the early 1970s and her death in 1976, she was never tested medically as far as we know. Her interviews at the age of eighty made her look 'fit and spry,' but by the next year, 1971, she had aged considerably, having fallen and broken a hip in June (Thompson 2007, 464, 473–4). Friends reported her thin and 'frail' in 1975, and at year's end she had angry fits (in one she cut off all her hair) and did not always make sense in conversation (483). These observations are suggestive, but nothing more. The writing of four novels from 1969 to 1973, in fact, does not support a diagnosis of early dementia, no matter how scatty Christie's mind may have behaved in writing the last one, *Postern*, or how much secretarial help she had. It is a sport for movie fans to find blunders of plot and character in films, but no one accuses their directors of dementia. Mistakes about dates are minor. More serious are flaws in narrative logic, and her inability to create a crime that can be solved by clue-detection according to the rules of the genre that she, significantly, helped to create. Christie's preoccupation with old people and their memories in *Elephants Can Remember* and *Postern of Fate* reflects more on her personal circumstances, and less on the schemata of a criminal act, a murderer, and evidence traces that she must have carefully built up in her notebook preparations for earlier novels. Text analysis of a chronologically representative selection of her novels, however, tells us something about the state of her idiolect as long as psychological research of the effects of increasing old age on speech supplies language traits to look for.

As late as 1994, Jane Maxim and Karen Bryan, in their *Language of the Elderly: A Clinical Perspective*, say that 'language skills do not deteriorate (or even change) with age unless neurological disease intervenes' (29). Yet they concede mounting evidence that healthy aging brings both semantic and syntactic difficulties. Old age slows down retrieval from long-term memory or impedes it. Experiments that ask elderly subjects to name words in a certain semantic category or starting with a given alphabetic letter (33) show word-fluency impairment. The elderly cannot come up with as many associated words spontaneously, within a restricted time-span, as can younger people. This is also described as a 'conceptual span' problem. The tip-of-the-tongue effect, which everyone experiences in failing to locate a word or a name mentally, occurs at all ages but increases in those over the age of sixty-five. The aged also use an increasing number of indefinite words such as 'thing,' 'something,' and 'stuff' (46; cf. Nicholas et al. 1985). As early as 1959, K.F. Riegel observed 'the strengthening of close associations and the dissociation of the more remote associations,' a general effect that manifests itself in a reduced vocabulary (Maxim and Bryan 1994, 45, citing Riegel generally), and more frequently repeated words and phrases. A 16,000–sentence corpus of conversations with forty old persons, as edited by Maxim and Bryan, reveals a narrowing of options in elderly sentence structure. Simple sentences (subject-verb-object/complement) increase, and subordinate, embedded, and left-branching clauses decrease (37, 46, 56–7, 146).

Three theories for cognitive-aging effects now exist: the inhibitory-deficit model, an inability to filter out irrelevant information (Zacks and Hasher 1988); the processing-speed model, which is self-explanatory (Salthouse 1996); and the context-processing-deficit model (Braver et al. 2001). The second and third models now appear best able to account for these effects. There is no doubt that age slows a person down. The third model proposes that 'cognitive aging involves a working memory deficit in the ability to represent, maintain, and update information about task context' (Haarmann et al. 2005, 35). This context consists of 'environmental cues' by which the mind characterizes concepts and controls what it decides to do (Rush, Barch, and Braver 2006, 589). The context-processing-deficit theory explains typical cognitive aging effects such as mistaken decisions, failures to associate ideas, and, especially, inability to use 'newly learned information' (Rush, Barach, and Braver 2006, 606).[2] This problem occurs in semantic working memory, not in phonological working memory, and is associated, in neuroscience, with a malfunctioning prefrontal cortex (Haarman et al. 35, 38). In other words, it appears to be a working-memory capacity issue.

Did Christie's writing suffer from an aging brain in her last three novels? Results of my tests are in table 1 and graph 6 in the appendix. It shows that the three novels that Christie wrote in her eighties, *Nemesis*, *Elephants*, and *Postern*, have a smaller vocabulary than any of the above works written by her between the ages of twenty-eight and sixty-three. There are two striking exceptions to this trend towards diminished idiolect. Her novel *Curtain*, published in 1975, has a sizable vocabulary, but it was written thirty years before in the war years and saved by Christie for her children. *Passenger to Frankfurt*, which came out in 1970, has the largest vocabulary of all the above works. It is a product of Christie's early to mid-seventies: she had the idea in 1963 and did research on it in the mid-1960s. This novel, subtitled *An Extravaganza*, draws on a series of books by political thinkers that she requested of her publishers. On receiving her book manuscript, Collins was doubtful about bringing it out because it differed so much from her detective fiction. There is no doubt that much of the vocabulary in *Frankfurt* comes from her reliance on sources other than her own imagination.

Christie's repeating phrases increase proportionally as her vocabulary diminishes. From age 28 to 63, Christie uses over 8,000 such phrases only twice in nine novels. From age 67 to 82, she uses fewer than 8,000 only once in seven novels. Such data point to the same conclusion, a growing semantic impairment. Christie's vocabulary, her different words or word types, plummets in the first 50,000 words of her novels by one-fifth between 1920–2 and 1972–3. The novels written in her eighties are poorer by 900 words over the lexicon in her first three novels, which she wrote aged 28 to 34. Simultaneously, the different repeating phrases in the first 50,000 words in her novels increase by about 770, that is, by about 10 per cent. A diminishing word lexicon, and an enhanced phrasal lexicon, are consistent with what Riegel observed about elderly language in 1959. Christie has favoured words that she relies on more often than before. This change reduces the overall vocabulary size and inflates the number of repeating phrases.

Other evidence is consistent with an encroaching elder's speech. Christie's use of the indefinite word 'thing' increases from 0.1 per cent of her word-count in *Styles* (1920) to 0.6 per cent in *Postern* (1973), a sixfold expansion. She writes prose that is easier to understand, not more difficult. The last novel she published while living, *Curtain* (1975), confirms these findings. Christie wrote it during the Second World War and laid it aside as potential income for her children. Its vocabulary, phrasal, and indefinite-word numbers belong with her works in the forties.

The context-processing-deficit model offers a way of understanding why Christie's plot and characterization skills failed in her eighties. Her middle-age habit of compiling a notebook about a novel for six months and then writing it down in six weeks (the last chapter first) implies that Christie routinely developed expert schemata in her long-term memory for her characters (murderer, victim, detective), the crime that entangles them, and the solution that releases them. As we know, an expert can shuttle information relating to her specialist knowledge domain out of long-term-memory schemata and into, and then out of, working memory much faster than non-experts. If her episodic working-memory capacity changed, however, she could no longer quite grasp the larger schemata, especially new ones whose storage might be impaired.

Because Christie used a dictaphone for the last twenty-five years and is known for her 'conversational style,' I wondered whether her switch in writing technology in 1951, from typewriter to dictaphone, explained her lost vocabulary and her increasing use of repeating phrases. The lexicon size of the first 50,000 words of *Destination Unknown* (1954), some 5,442 word types, suggests not. Only *Frankfurt* (1970) is larger. The beginning of Christie's vocabulary slippage appears first with *Ordeal by Innocence* in 1958, when she was in her late sixties, but then she recovers again by *Nemesis*, where it is almost the size in *Murder on the Orient Express* in 1934. Christie's lasting vocabulary loss looks to have been relatively sudden, in her eighties. It appears that not technology but old age diminishes her narrative powers.

Elephants Can Remember (1972), published when Christie was eighty-two, exhibits a staggering drop in vocabulary, almost 31 per cent, compared with her *Destination Unknown*, published eighteen years before in 1954. Some 15,000 words shorter than *Nemesis* (1971) and *Postern of Fate* (1973), which preceded and followed it, *Elephants* appears to register the onset of writing blockage. Possibly Christie's broken hip, the year before, was a factor. Christie's persistent doubts as to the novel's present year reveal uncertainty about the ultimate date of the book's publication. Ariadne Oliver's servant Maria says that it is '1973 – or whichever year it is we've got to now' (11), but later it is correctly said to be 1972 (44). When Hercule Poirot visits the graves of the three murder-suicide victims, he records their death year as 1960 (186), but others who know better date these events, using the age of Celia Ravenscroft, the daughter of two of the victims, as being 10–12 (20), 12 (57), 12 or 14 (71), and 14 (75). The 'current' year, then, would have to be sometime between 1970 and 1974. Christie must have felt herself hard-pressed to meet her publisher's deadline. The dating problems all occur in book 1, 'Elephants' (pp. 9–132). Its conversational style, set by Ariadne Oliver, differs from the expository prose in book 2 (135–218), characteristic of the retired policeman Garroway, Poirot, and the Ravenscrofts' French *au pair*, Zélie. Another sign of editorial haste and confusion in Book 1 are single-letter abbreviations for Ariadne ('A') and the item symbol ('B') left unexpanded by mistake (32, 110).[3]

Until the Christie estate releases her notebooks and dictaphone tapes, we will not know what happened with *Elephants*, but a plausible explanation follows from what is known about Christie's writing habits. Book 2 holds the solution to the crimes, and we know that Christie not only wrote the final chapter first but based it on a notebook that outlined the plot in detail. Christie also is known to have written and put into storage at least two novels, *Curtain* (1975) and *Sleeping Murder* (1976), both published posthumously, so that her family would have income after she could no longer write. A substantial part of book 2 of *Elephants*, or just the notebook on the basis of which it would have been written, could have been drafted years before its publication. Its subject matter, a tragic love story, brings to mind Christie's six romantic novels published under the pseudonym Mary Westmacott from 1930 to 1956. We also know that Christie relied heavily on secretarial help from Daphne Honeybone, to whom *Nemesis* was dedicated (Pendergast 2004, 38–9; Morgan 1984, 371), to finish *Postern*. After Christie's death, her former secretary Mrs Jolly gave Sotheby's the sixty original dictaphone belts that recorded Christie's dictation of that novel. Although a private buyer acquired the belts, which are now inaccessible, the catalogue explains that 'the text … differs substantially in very many instances from the final, printed version' and that details about the murder, and clues as to the murderer's identity, are removed, and chapters shifted about. Although the final page proofs were hand-corrected by Christie, showing that she was still carrying out routine editorial procedures, she allowed others to change her work substantially before it was published.[4] Collaboration, then, is not improbable a year before in *Elephants*. Its three layers are a detailed notebook exposition by a younger Christie, a rambling first book spoken by her, aged 81/82, into a dictaphone, and possibly heavy editing by those who transcribed those belts.

These discontinuities muddle the plot. It has three groups of characters centering on Ariadne Oliver, an old and famous writer of detective novels (a thinly disguised Christie), on her friend Hercule Poirot, and on Celia Ravenscroft, Ariadne's godchild. At a literary luncheon, Ariadne meets Mrs Burton-Cox, the adoptive mother of Celia's would-be fiancée, Desmond. Burton-Cox asks Ariadne to discover who killed Celia's mother and father. Both Ravenscrofts were shot by the father's revolver, and both were suspected of committing a suicide-murder because the revolver had the fingerprints of both. Burton-Cox hopes to discredit Celia and keep Desmond's inherited estate in her family.

Book 1 opens when Celia, who wants to know the truth too, encourages Ariadne to interview the family's aged friends for their memories. A Ravenscroft family friend (Julia Carstairs), the former nanny (Mrs Matcham), and a servant of neighbours of the Ravenscrofts when they lived in Malaya (Mrs Buckle) each give unreliable, gossipy stories, however, leaving Ariadne exasperated when she delivers to Poirot a notebook of what these 'elephants' have told her. Only two clues spark the Belgian detective's interest, the four wigs of Mrs Ravenscroft (Molly), and a family dog that bit her and was not out with them on the walk that ended in their deaths. After asking Ariadne to speak to their retailer, Poirot turns to interview more reliable sources, a policeman formerly in charge of the case (Garroway), Dr Willoughby (who treated Molly's sister), Desmond, the old nanny (Maddy), and an *au pair*, Zélie, who lives in France and alone knows all.

By the beginning of book 2, Poirot has learned about Molly's identical twin sister, Dolly, although Galloway says to him, 'Don't know where you picked that up' (137). Dolly's lifelong mental illness led her, both in England and overseas in Malaya, to kill two children. She herself died, accidentally, it appears, while on a visit to the Ravenscrofts' house, in a cliffside fall three weeks before they were shot. Poirot reveals the solution at the Ravenscrofts' old seaside house in the presence of Celia, Desmond, Ariadne, and the indispensible Zélie. Jealous for years because Ravenscroft married Molly instead of her (his first love), Dolly pushed Molly over the cliff to her death, and Ravenscroft concealed the murder, letting out that Dolly died and enabling her to assume Molly's identity. It was Zélie who bought two additional wigs for Dolly's disguise. To prevent the deaths of more children at Dolly's hands, Ravenscroft led Dolly outside three weeks later, shot her execution-style, and committed suicide himself. Poirot calls the three deaths a pity and a tragedy, while Ariadne and Zélie, the latter of whom confirms that Ravenscroft loved both sisters, think of the three as points in a love-triangle doomed by 'old sins.'

Discontinuities between books 1 and 2 more damaging than confused dates show that Christie had lost touch with her story when, with her outline and the essentials of Book 2 in hand in her notebooks, she took up the writing of book 1. No one in book 1, including Ariadne and Celia, tells Poirot about Molly's identical twin sister Dolly. Celia refers to Dolly vaguely as an 'aunt whom I never loved much' (63). Worst of all, the very same Ariadne who in ook 2 says that she had twice met Dolly, the 'twin sister,' and that she was rumoured to be ill (151), had no knowledge of Dolly in book 1 when she tells Poirot what she learned from various interviews. Ariadne in book 1 tells Poirot instead that the mentally ill child-killer is not Molly's twin sister, but 'Either General Whoever-it-was's sister or Mrs Who-ever-it-was's sister,' someone who need not 'have been as a near as a sister' but rather a 'cousin or something' (114–15). Ariadne forgot that Mrs Matcham mentioned Molly's sister killing a child (91–92) and that Mrs Buckle referred to Molly's 'half-sister … [who] Looked rather like Lady Ravenscroft' (105). Two more confusions in Ariadne's debriefing with Poirot have her misquoting what Mrs Carstairs said about family cancer (82, 122) and misrepresenting Molly's relationship with her son's tutor as an affair (103–4, 110).[5]

Did Christie intend to confuse the detective novelist's carefully deployed clues, leading her readers to believe that Ariadne was deliberately keeping Poirot in the dark or, worse, that she was herself falling victim to dementia? That seems unlikely. The traditional architecture of an Agatha Christie detective novel resembles a 'jigsaw puzzle' weaving together complexities on 'three levels of her story: who committed the crime, how was it done and how will the solution be revealed' (Suerbaum 2001, 416). The central point of the novel that eighty-one-year-old Christie makes is that 'Elephants can remember' (218), not that 'Elephants never forget.' It is possible that someone among Christie's family or friends edited down the rambling dictated text of the first book, creating a very short novel, but even that curtailment would not have created contradictions. An editor, of course, might have tried to accommodate the novel to these confusions. In talking to Ariadne, for example, Poirot refers to Dolly as 'the twin sister' that Ariadne, who had just acknowledged knowing the 'twin sister Dolly' (151), 'did not really know' (161).

A typical Christie detective novel had 'no padding, nothing that does not have its function in the narrative' (Suerbaum 2001, 419). Digression and meandering memories dominate her latest novels, none more seriously than *Postern*. Her ability to hold in memory a multi-level puzzle had failed. Was this change not an early sign of dementia? Because to answer this question needs a team with experienced scientific researchers, in late 2008 I joined up with Graeme Hirst, a computational linguist, his master's student Xuan Le, and Dr Regina Jokel, a researcher, clinician, and teacher in speech pathology and Alzheimer's disease at Baycrest Hospital in Toronto. Hirst subjected the numbers in my table to statistical analysis and found that they were statistically significant.

We decided that *Passenger to Frankfurt* was an outlier, generically different from Christie's late mysteries; and that being the case, her degradation in vocabulary pointed to dementia. With advice from Jokel, Hirst and I then gave a poster paper at a conference on cognitive aging in March 2009 convened in Toronto by the Rotman Research Institute. The paper and poster aroused plenty of interest from the media[6] and from researchers in the medical sciences. In 2009 and early 2010, Hirst's student Xuan Le developed a natural-language-processing system that re-analyed novels by Christie, Iris Murdoch (who died of Alzheimer's disease), and P.D. James, confirmed the earlier findings of myself and Hirst, refined our lexical analysis, and extended it into syntax (Le 2010). Both Christie's and Murdoch's vocabularies fell precipitately at career's end. Although writing in her late eighties, James (a healthily aging author) did not suffer a similar drop in vocabulary. Our conclusion has so far been accepted as a working hypothesis in developing a rigorous profile of language changes that distinguish the healthily aging from the early Alzheimer's patient, and in devising diagnostic software for text analysis in longitudinal studies, not only of creative writing, but of e-mail, diaries, blogs, and even conversation.

The age of authors, whether afflicted by dementia or not, can have a profound effect on their works. Late style, characterized by spareness in writing and by clarity in bringing out essentials (Wyatt-Brown 1988, 837), also witnesses authors facing up to changes in themselves. Christie must have recognized in herself the condition of forgetfulness and confusion that she depicts in her alter ego, the detective-fiction writer Ariadne. Was Ariadne's success in helping Poirot a way of consoling herself that she still *could* remember? Was her embodied intention to brood on a suspected cause of the decay in her cognitive powers that she had suspected her novels to show for some time? A comparison with the effects of Alzheimer's disease on Iris Murdoch's last novel helps answer that question.

*   *   *   *   *

Did you really think a spreadsheet of Agatha's numbers would purge me?
   The stats that gave you the diagnosis hid what Agatha felt as her losses
mounted and I could sense her fearing and bided time until the poster
session ended and the lone reporter called, when tired at night you spoke
by phone to her Maclean's and your guard was so far down by then you
let me blurt it out ... what you didn't know you knew, what became Anne

Kingston's story ... that Agatha knew the real crime was happening in her, that the proverb-play where Can Remember replaced Never Forget pointed to the real murder-suicide, her brain gradually executing her me, and she knew that all along and her me cried out, Can Remember, though the losses of her me kept mounting and maybe you thought I had nothing to add, that I'd keep silent, but I didn't and that's what caught UPI and the Guardian and the other papers, no, it wasn't you, it came from me, that Agatha had found the clues to her dementia-to-be before it could overwhelm her defences.

III   Margaret Atwood

Faced with saying something about authoring, Cædmon described a nameless angel's visitation. Chaucer played a timid ignoramus whom an eagle muse flew to the House of Fame where he might hear something worth writing about, and then a hapless innocent who uttered the 'drasty rymyng' tale of Sir Thopas and thought it good. Shakespeare truly described his Anonymous as an imagination that 'bodies forth / The forms of things unknown,' and his composer as a pen that 'Turns them to shapes, and gives to aery nothing / A local habitation and a name' (*MND* 5.1.14–17). Embarrassed Coleridge called unharnessed imagination a 'psychological' phenomenon. Eliot submitted completely to it in writing 'The Waste Land' and repressed his composing intellect in favour of Ezra Pound's, 'il miglior fabbro.' Agatha Christie methodically coached her genie into notebook bottles that gave some structure to its later utterings.

Of those who used no notebooks but unconditionally surrendered themselves to their Anonymous, the novelists had most to hide about process, and among the best of them, E.M. Forster, Saul Bellow, and Margaret Atwood, hid nothing. Cognitive psychologists should read what they say about how their minds invent. Forster gave his unnamed uttering mind the name Anonymous, Bellow termed it his 'primitive prompter,' and Atwood echoed Shakespeare in referring to Offred's imagination in *The Handmaid's Tale* (1985) as 'something without a shape and a name.' Pressed to be unpoetic, Atwood writes:

I hate writing about my writing because I have nothing to say about it. I have nothing to say about it because I can't remember what goes on when I'm doing it. That time is like small pieces cut out of my brain. It's not time I myself have lived. I can remember the details of the rooms and

places where I've written, the circumstances, the other things I did before
and after, but not the process itself. Writing about writing requires self-
consciousness; writing itself requires the abdication of it. (2005, 106)

Elsewhere Atwood says that, as a writer, consciousness of self is 'what
you have to give up when writing': there is no 'instant replay' for writers (1990, 195). As a result, while Iris Murdoch called the long period
of thinking about a novel 'agonizing,' and the writing itself straightforward, Atwood feels 'anxiety' and 'terror' (1990, 79) at the moment of
writing because she relies completely on her Anonymous to be on its
best behaviour. 'Starting a book is like jumping off a cliff' (164).

Although word-processing ultimately replaced handwriting as Atwood's technology, she describes three stages in her writing: a long
period of undirected thinking, drafting the text in longhand, and typing
it out.[7] Each state had many epicycles of adding, deleting, and revising.
It takes a long time, sometimes years, to build in long-term memory
the 'compelling images' or the silent speaking of a 'voice' that prepares
her to create a novel, that is, something that grows about a scene or a
character (1990, 105, 167). Atwood says that the 'social details' of The
Handmaid's Tale 'came from observation, logical conclusions, and the
reading of history over a period of many years' (Cooke 1998, 276).
Her second stage was a partial holograph draft, written in longhand
on scrap paper (106, 194), or the first word-processed version. Atwood
did twenty pages quickly in longhand. Then she typed those pages out
slowly into the third stage, while simultaneously inventing the next
sheaf of handwritten pages – thus her three stages overlap. For any giv-
en segment, there are half a dozen drafts (194–5). Atwood's language
for what drafts produce – 'spurts of writing, discarded chunks' (276) –
hints at the perceived size constraint of working memory. In typing and
revising, she describes editing in part as making sure 'that you haven't
repeated the same word about nine times on one page' (Atwood 1990,
5). This is cybertextual feedback to the unconscious maker by seeing
utterance as texts on a typed page.

The draft manuscripts and typescripts of Margaret Atwood's The
Handmaid's Tale are in the Fisher Rare Book Library at the University of
Toronto. They reveal cybertextual cycles at work in the craft of a novelist who trims the sails of her Anonymous and reader-editor to the cut of
a demanding, mixed popular and educated audience.

The third page of the surviving holograph version of her novel (see
fig. 22) uses the voice of her leading character, Offred, so-called by rea-

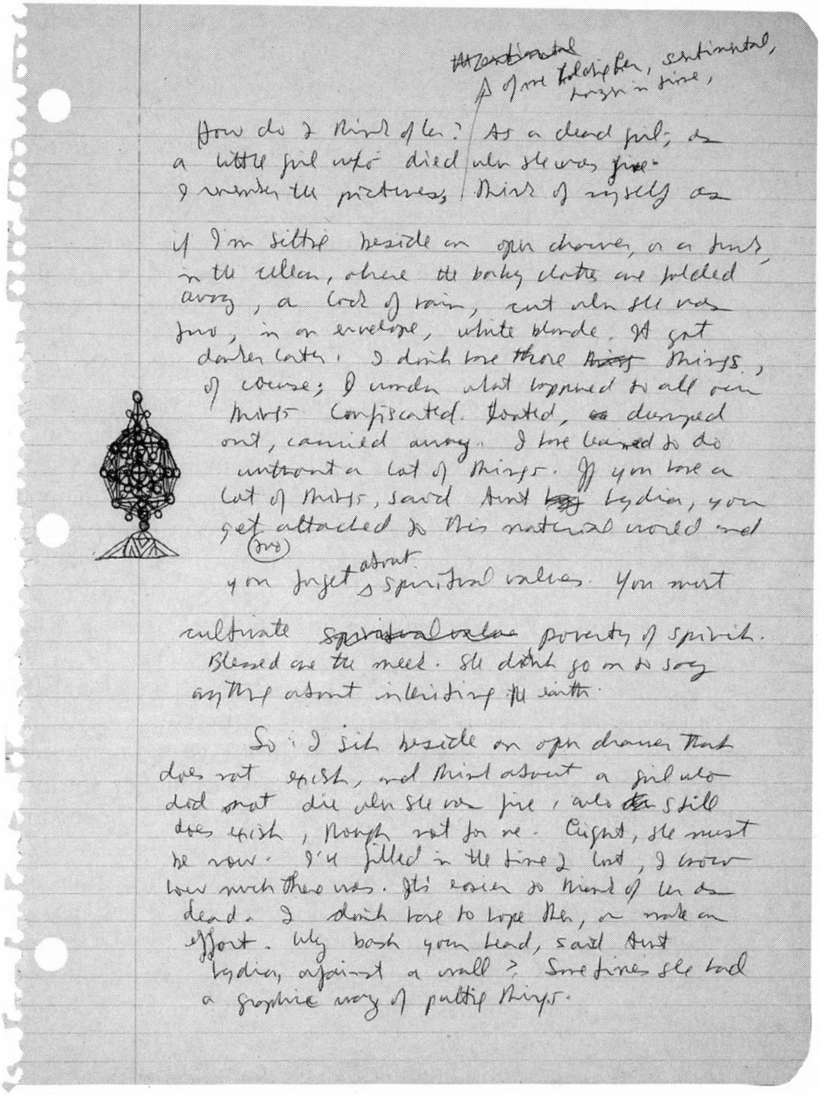

Figure 22. Offred and her Daughter (Fisher Rare Book Library MS Collection 200, box 72, file 1, p. 3: holograph page from Margaret Atwood's handwritten draft of *The Handmaid's Tale*, reprinted by permission of Margaret Atwood. From *The Handmaid's Tale*, Copyright © 1985 O. W. Toad, currently available in Canada in a Vintage Trade edition and in the U.S. in an Anchor Trade edition)

son of her role as enslaved child bearer to a military commander named Fred. She is 'of Fred.' His early-future New England, called Gilead, is ruled by a fascistic male oligarchy that a drastic nationwide drop in the birth rate has vaulted to power. Women are enslaved to breeding, whether as wives (sterile female household heads who raise children), handmaids (fertile young women employed for breeding), aunts (older women who train the handmaids), or servants. Disobedient handmaids face execution, and wives live with as much dignity as possible in abject humiliation. A prostrate wife must hold, between her legs, her husband's handmaid as he lowers himself on the two of them and impregnates the handmaid. Scholars in a distant future have edited Offred's 'tale' from oral confessions that she has recorded on tapes. Atwood satirizes these editors in an epilogue that gives a conference talk by one of them on editing Offred's audio tapes. He writes snidely of Offred's story and thinks of her as a sex-trade worker. Offred's own poignant night-time monologues, presented in a spontaneous style, describe her deeply isolated self in a direct outpouring of speech. Atwood's hugely successful novel was eventually made into both a film and an opera.[8]

The transcription below compares her first holograph version, the first typed version, and any final revisions before publication of one early scene, where Offred remembers her lost, nameless daughter.[9] The manuscript appears to have two paragraphs, although several blank lines appear in them. Sometime after the first draft, Atwood moved this scene to later in the novel, added seven sentences, and shifted the location of Offred's meditation to her bath (1985, 74). The first scene (to be discussed below) has the unnamed Offred-to-be describe the high-school gymnasium where the Aunts house the handmaids-in-training.

There are signs that Atwood wrote this holograph leaf in a state of relaxed cognitive flow. Her writing skirts an urn-like doodle she drew in the lefthand margin of a blank leaf, evidently as she faced the empty page and thought about what she would be writing. The first stage of her writing process, the many months of mental preparation, is about to come to an end. The second paragraph's left margin gradually shifts to the right, despite the vertical rule, as it normally does when a right-handed writer works rapidly. Atwood's cursive script suggests that she wrote this page spontaneously, putting down on paper her inner voice. Another sign of a flow-state is that these two paragraphs share the chunkiness of silent speech or oral conversation. The average clause length – 48 clauses or 'intonation units' in 237 words – is five words, at the upper boundary of the revised 'magical number.' Both Offred's

Second Typed Draft

~~now~~ ₐ as I am now,

First Typed Draft

~~m~~ Maybe I do think of her as a ghost, the ghost of
a dead girl,
a little girl who died when she was five.
I remember the pictures of us I had once, me holding her, ~~a~~ standard poses, mother and baby, ~~fro~~
locked in a frame, for safety. I can see myself now,
sitting beside an open drawer, or a trunk,
in the cellar, where the ~~ab~~ baby clothes are folded
~~away~~, away, a lock of ~~g~~ hair, cut when she was
two, in an envelope, white blonde. It got
darker later. I don't have those things; ₐ ↑any
more↑, the clothes and hair.
I wonder what happened to ~~our~~ all our
things. ~~Confiscated, forfeit.~~ Looted,
dumped out, carried away. Confiscated. ¶ I've
learned to do
without a lot of things. If you have a
lot of things, said Aunt Lydia, you
get too attached to this material world and
you ~~g~~ forget about spiritual values. You must
cultivate poverty of spirit.
Blessed are the meek. She didn't go on to say
anything about inheriting the earth.
I lie, lapped by the water, beside ~~and~~ an open
drawer that
does not exist, and think about a girl who
~~didn~~ did not die ~~we~~ when she was five; who still
does exist, I hope ~~m~~, though not for me. ~~Eight~~
Do I exist for her? Am I a picture somewhere,
~~at the back of~~ in the dark at the back of her mind?

Holograph Draft

1. How do I think of her? As a dead girl, as
2. a little girl who died when she was ~~just~~ five.
   I remember the pictures, ↑sentimental↑ of me holding
   her, sentimental, frozen in time↑ think of myself as
3. if I'm sitting beside an open drawer, or a trunk,
4. in the cellar, where the baby clothes are folded
5. away, a lock of hair, cut when she was
6. two, in an envelope, white blonde. It got
7. darker later. I don't have these ~~thing~~ things,
8. of course; I wonder what happened to all our
9. things. Confiscated , looted, ~~ea~~ dumped
10. out, carried away. I have learned to do
11. without a lot of things. If you have a
12. lot of things, said Aunt ~~Lyg~~ Lydia, you
13. get ↓too↓ ↑too↑ attached to this material world and
14. you forget ↓ₐ ↑about↑ ~~spiritual value~~ spiritual values. You must
15. cultivate ~~spiritual value~~ poverty of spirit.
16. Blessed are the meek. She didn't go on to say
17. anything about inheriting the earth.
18. So I sit beside an open drawer that
19. does not exist, and think about a girl who
20. did not die when she was five, who ~~do~~ still
21. does exist, though not for me. Eight, she must

Holograph Draft

First Typed Draft

Second Typed Draft

First Typed Draft

¶ They must have told her I was dead. ~~They~~ That's what they
would think of doing. They would say it would be
easier for her: to adjust.

¶ Eight, she must be now. I've filled in the time I
lost, I know
how much there's been. They're were right, it's
easier:, to t think of her as
dead. I don't have to hope then, or make a
wasted effort. Why bash your head, said Aunt
Lydia, against a wall? Sometimes ~~she~~ ∆ Aunt Lydia   ~~Aunt Lydia~~ she
had
a graphic way of putting things.

Holograph Draft

22   be now. I've filled in the time I lost, I know

23   how much there was. It's easier to think of her as

24   dead. I don't have to hope then, or make an

25   effort. Why bash your head, said Aunt

26   Lydia, against a wall? Sometimes she had

27   a graphic way of putting things.

voice and Atwood's style look natural. Atwood's schema of Offred's character and speech must already have been very well planted in her long-term memory.

The 5:4 ratio of *currente calamo* changes to editorial, compositional edits that take place after the passage is penned also signifies a flow-state. On-the-move, rapid revisions begin when Atwood overwrites 'just' (I think) as 'five' (2). She crosses out the word 'thing' and adds, right after it, 'things' (7), catches misspelled 'Lyg' mid-word and follows it with 'Lydia' (12), deletes a repetitive 'spiritual value' before writing its final 'S' and replaces it by 'poverty of spirit' (15), and crosses out 'do' and immediately replaces it by 'still does' (20–1). Atwood's cognitive monitor catches these slips before she finishes processing them. They illustrate a writer's mind at work, unattending of itself except as she writes words down on the leaf.

The four editorial changes that Atwood makes after finishing a line or the leaf are editorial or composing ones. They begin with her insertion (in the top margin, marked by a long vertical arrow) of 'sentimental' after 'pictures' (2). This addition must have occurred after she had written some or all of the rest of the line, 'think of myself as.' In her second editorial change, Atwood appears to have immediately crossed out 'sentimental' and written in, under it but still in the top margin, 'of me holding her, sentimental, frozen in time.' I suggest immediately because Atwood left a blank line – which occurs in the middle of a clause – underneath that third line. She might have left that space so that she could further revise that passage later. Next, Atwood adds a circled 'too' underneath and between the two words 'get attached' (13). She revises this as 'get too attached' sometime after she wrote part or all of the rest of the line, 'attached to this material world and'. Because the circled 'too' occupies space below, Atwood leaves the rest of the line behind it empty. The fourth editorial change is Atwood's insertion of 'about' above 'spiritual values' (14). She marks this by a triangle-like caret. It is not clear why Atwood left another blank line under this, between 'You must' (14) and 'cultivate' (15) unless she decided that the triangle got in the way, as her circled 'too' had.

Once finished with the first paragraph (150 words in length), which closes with Aunt Lydia's biblical quotation and Offred's gloss on it, Atwood continues with a shorter second paragraph (89 words; see the transcription below). The first paragraph shows Offred thinking of her daughter as five years old, and the second paragraph as eight years old. Both paragraphs close with one of Aunt Lydia's sayings, and there are a number of verbal echoes.

Addition to Offred and her Daughter

¶ 1		¶ 2	
1	How do I think of her?	20, 24	... think about a girl .... think of her
1	As a dead girl	25	... as dead.
2	... a little girl who died when she was five.	20–21	... a girl who did not die when she was five ...
4	... I'm sitting beside an open drawer	19	... I sit beside an open drawer
12–13	If you have a lot of things, said Aunt Lydia	26–28	... said Aunt Lydia ... Aunt Lydia had a graphic way of putting things.

Once she finished the twelve sentences of the first paragraph, Atwood's creative mind, primed by what it had just uttered (and what she saw, written down by then on the page), repeated it with variations in the second paragraph. It arises as cybertextual feedback from seeing the first paragraph. Each one is not too long to be grasped in one thought. They correspond generally to our cognitive capacity: self-repeating sonnet-sized units appear elsewhere in great writers.

At a later time, Atwood returned to recompose this passage. Her revisions enhance the echoes that link the two paragraphs but also, in a calculated way, alter Offred's character. In the manuscript draft, Offred describes mother-daughter pictures that are 'sentimental,' but in the typed draft of that version they are 'standard poses' (3). Atwood changes Offred's theme from a mother who has lost her child to a child who has lost her mother. The typed draft adds a passage in the second paragraph – beginning 'Do I exist for her?' (22) – in which Offred imagines her daughter in her situation, alive and wondering whether her mother still lives. This addition repeats Offred's earlier thought of a 'picture,' but this time it depicts Offred, not her daughter. Consciously (I believe), Atwood uses verbal echoes in these additions. In the first paragraph, Offred thinks of her daughter 'As a dead girl,' and in the addition she thinks of a daughter who was told 'I was dead'. In the holograph version, Offred finds that 'It's easier to think of her as dead' (24–5), and so in the addition Offred says that 'it would be easier' for her daughter 'to adjust' were she to believe her mother dead. These revisions ascribe a new empathy to Offred: in the manuscript draft, she suffered, like most of us, from an obsession with what she had lost, but Atwood's revisions show her to be newly sympathizing with her own sufferings in others. We might say that Atwood's revisions continue her conversations with herself about what she means to say and are reflected in how Offred responds, cybertextually, to her own sense of loss by projecting it on her daughter.

What should be said about Atwood's composing style, from the little window of opportunity that one leaf offers? Like Offred's, it is minimalist. Atwood keeps faith with her creative mind and its cognitive style: she does not permit external influences and information sources, or a wish to pepper the text with flamboyant vocabulary, to upstage her germinating flow. She reuses, in the additions, Offred's own words from the holograph. Only Atwood's enriched understanding of Offred's character, developing as she writes, require these changes. *How does my child feel?* complicates *How do I feel?* Put cognitively, as the schema in Atwood's long-term memory for Offred grows, Atwood revises her text. This revising process re-engages the same cognitive style that we see in the flow-state uttering that characterizes the first leaf of the holograph. Atwood's reading style is also faithful to her long-term memory. She appears to read the leaf through its chunks and their stitching back to the gist and then only makes editorial changes because the Offred-schema responsible for her original conception has itself changed over time. Atwood's dominant style remains faithful to memory throughout her creative process, from uttering to editing. It is authentic.

The opening scene in the printed book is on leaf 9A of the holograph manuscript (see figs. 23–4). My transcription superimposes at least four writing sessions: the original holograph and its editorial changes; and the first typescript (which revises the holograph text), and its editorial changes. Lineation follows the holograph version where possible. It represents, using superscript, any addition made above the line or in a margin and connected to the text by an arrow or line. Single strikethroughs mark holograph deletions. Words added in the first typescript appear in boldface. Holograph text silently deleted from the typescript appears in an outline font. Double strikethroughs mark editorial deletions in the typescript. If you want to read the holograph version, ignore boldfaced words and passages. If you want to read the first typescript version, ignore the outline words and passages.

~~Here is a story. * about a different room~~

~~In the Red Centre~~ Rachel and Leah Re-education ~~w~~We slept in what had once been the gymnasium. The floor was of varnished wood, with stripes and circles painted on it, for ~~g~~ the games that were **had we**

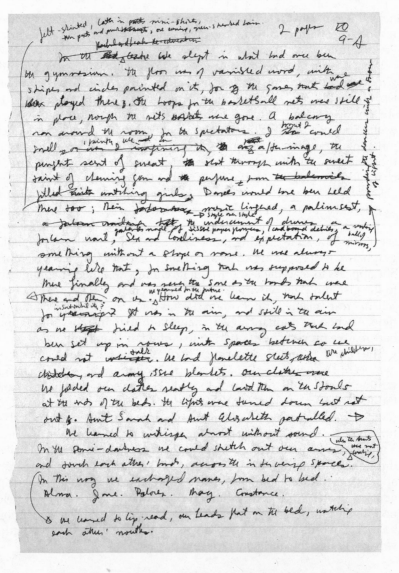

Figure 23. Offred in the Gymnasium (Fisher Rare Book Library MS Collection 200, box 72, file 1, p. 9A, recto: holograph page from Margaret Atwood's handwritten draft of *The Handmaid's Tale*, reprinted by permission of Margaret Atwood. From *The Handmaid's Tale*, Copyright © 1985 O. W. Toad, currently available in Canada in a Vintage Trade edition and in the U.S. in an Anchor Trade edition)

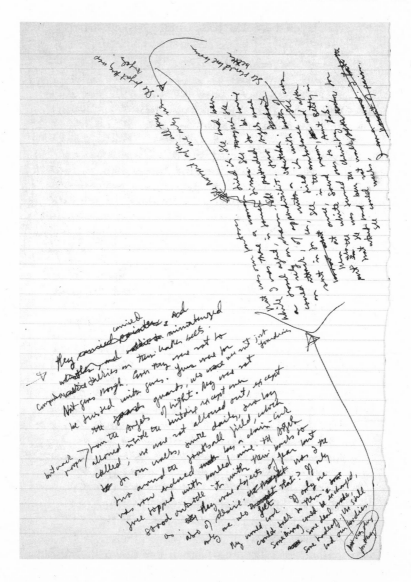

Figure 24. Offred in the Gymnasium (Fisher Rare Book Library MS Collection 200, box 72, file 1, p. 9A, verso: holograph page from Margaret Atwood's handwritten draft of *The Handmaid's Tale*, reprinted by permission of Margaret Atwood. From *The Handmaid's Tale*, Copyright © 1985 O. W. Toad, currently available in Canada in a Vintage Trade edition and in the U.S. in an Anchor Trade edition)

~~been~~ **formerly** played there. The hoops for the basketball nets were still
in place, though the nets ~~baskets~~ were gone. A balcony
ran around the room, for the spectators. **and** I ^thought^ ~~was~~ I could
smell~~, or was I imagining it, an~~ · ^faintly like an^ ~~faint~~ afterimage, the
pungent ~~smell~~ **scent** of sweat, ~~th~~ shot through with the sweet
taint of chewing gum and ~~the~~ perfume, from ~~the balconies
filled with the~~ watching girls. ^felt-skirted,^ **as I knew from pictures,** later in ~~pants~~ mini-skirts,
~~wi~~ **then** pants ~~and punk [????????],~~ **then in** one earring, **spiky** green-streaked hair. Dances would have
been held
there ~~too; their~~ **the** ~~forlornness~~ music lingered, a palimpsest **of
unheard sound,**
~~a fornlorn wailing that~~ → ^style^ ~~over~~ **upon** ^style^ ~~the~~ **an** undercurrent of drums, a
~~fornlorn wail,~~ garlands made of tissue paper flowers, cardboard devils, a revolving hall of mirrors, powdering
the dancers with a snow of ~~coloured~~ light. ¶

    There was old Sex **in the room** and loneliness, and expectation, of
something without a shape or name. ~~We were always~~ **I remember that**
yearning ~~like that,~~ for something that was ~~supposed to be~~
~~there finally~~ **was always about to** ~~arriv~~ **happen** and was never the
same as the hands that were
←－ －－－－ ＼
there and then on us, **in the small of the back,** ~~the~~ **or out back in the
parking lot,** ~~seat or the in the back room,~~ **or in the television** →
**room with the sound turned down and only the pictures flickering
over lifting flesh.** ¶ ^We yearned for the future.^ How did we learn it, that talent
for ~~yearning?~~ ^insatiability?^ It was in the air, and **it was** still in the air, **an
afterthought,**
as we ~~slept~~ tried to sleep, in the army cots that had
been set up in rows, with spaces between so we
could not ^talk^ **whisper.** ~~or whisper.~~ We had flanelette sheets~~, like~~ like
childrens,
~~children,~~ and army issue blankets, **old ones that still said US.** ~~Our
clothes were~~
We folded our clothes neatly and laid them on the stools
at the ends of the beds. The lights were turned down but not
out. Aunt Sarah and Aunt Elizabeth patrolled. →

                [9–A verso]
    →   they ~~carried pointers, and~~ ^carried^ **electric cattle prods, and had**
                ~~whistles, and walkie ta miniaturized~~ **had miniaturized**
                ~~computer walkie talkies~~ **Comptalkies** on their leather belts. ¶
                Not guns though. Even they ~~were not to~~ **could not**

be trusted with guns. Guns were for **the**
~~the guards~~ guards, ~~who were were not just Guardians~~
but crack → **specially picked** ~~from the Angels of Light. They~~ **The**
troops **guards** ~~were not~~
weren't allowed inside the building except when
called; **and** ~~we were not~~ **weren't** allowed out, except
~~to~~ for our walks, twice daily, two by
two around the football field, which
was now enclosed ~~with~~ by a chain-link
fence topped with barbed wire. The Angels
stood outside it with their backs to
us. ~~at~~ they were objects of fear **to us** but
~~also of desire~~ **something us as well.** ~~We thought~~ was I the
only one who [felt] thought that? If only
they would look. If only we
could talk to them. ~~some~~
Something could be exchanged, **we thought,**
some some deal made,
some tradeoff, [that was our] We still
   [fantasy.]

had our bodies.

that was our fantasy.
While I was there a woman tried it. She had been
a travel agent, in former times. She thought she
could rely on charm. She pretended to be having
an attack, of appendicitis. Two Angels were
sent in for her, with a stretcher. I don't
know what She tried it with both of
them at once, in the ambulance. [She should have known better She thought, after all they]
[are only men. She forgot they were Angels.] She was

put [into] in the white sound room, for and after
that she was turned over to Aunt Betty in
what had been the chemistry lab.
She could not walk, after that, for
weeks.

[9–A recto]
We learned to whisper almost without sound.
In the semi-darkness we could stretch out our arms, [when the Aunts were not]

weren't looking,

and touch each others' hands, across the intervening spaces.

We learned to lip-read, our heads flat on the bed, **turned sideways,** watching each others' mouths.

In this way we exchanged names, from bed to bed.
Alma. Jane. Dolores. **Jane. Moira.** May. Constance. **May.**

This section in the holograph falls into five segments, each dominated by a 'compelling' image and a sound: the gymnasium and its dance music (142 words), sex and enforced silence (132 words), the aunts' patrol and wished-for talk with the Angels (136 words), the travel agent and the white sound room (116 words), and the almost-soundless names exchange (60 words). The first four exhibit a sonnet-sized cognitive load. The three segments on the recto page consist of 34 clauses, averaging 9.8 words, and the two additions on the verso have 17 and 18, averaging 8 and 6 words, respectively. Atwood uses about two chunks per clause. Some clauses end in a trail of phrases: the gymnasium includes a sequence of smells (sweat, taint of chewing gum, and perfume), sounds (music, drums, and wail), and room decorations; the sex segment has sheets, blankets, and clothes; the aunts' patrol ends with an exchange, a deal, and a tradeoff; and the last, the exchange of names, a series of five first names. Short clausal and phrasal units are signs of a rapid cognitive flow of chunks.

Echoes and repetitions hold together the three segments on the recto. The novel begins 'We *slept*' but in the second segment the handmaids only 'tried to *sleep*,' and by the end they are wide awake. The gymnasium dance is lit with a 'snow of *light*,' during their bedding, 'The *lights* were turned down but not out,' and the names exchange takes place in '*semi-darkness*.' During the sex segment, the girls have 'an expectation, of something without a shape or *name*' yet cannot '*talk*' as they remember the '*hands*' on them, but at the end they *whisper* their *names* and 'touch each others' *hands*.' The same cluster of lexical concepts informs each of the three segments on the recto because the same schema in long-term memory suggests them to Atwood. She takes care during composing to remove less important word repetitions – 'imagining' (cf. 'afterimage'), 'balconies,' and 'yearning' – but she stresses the core words. Later, when she types the holograph page, Atwood adds expressions that either highlight the associational cluster in her schema characterizing the gymnasium or that the holograph itself suggested. She appends 'of unheard sound' to the palimpsest in the first segment, and 'sound turned down' to the second segment so as to anticipate 'the whisper almost without sound' in the third segment. To echo the 'after-image' in the first segment, she adds the 'afterthought' in the second. Her adjustments during conscious composing strengthen the interrelationships of images and voices among these three segments.

Of the two supplementary passages that Atwood writes on the verso of the holograph and links to the close of the second segment, she only keeps the first. I think that her criterion for deletion is the degree to which it fits in the main associational cluster of lexical concepts, images, and voices. The footfield field, like the gymnasium, is a place where talking is not allowed and where loneliness and expectation replace sexual contact. It belongs in the opening chapter. The travel agent's attempted seduction instead translates sex into an action that destroys yearning and insatiability. Although Atwood does not carry this last segment over into the typescript, she recognizes what suits the original cognitive style with which she unselfconsciously created this opening chapter.

During composition, *The Handmaid's Tale* expanded in every direction, like a balloon in the course of being inflated. Atwood spent more effort amplifying her draft than in revising its minutiae. She trusted her Writer's Own Anonymous to tell the story. She of course worries about the repetitions to which it is prey and removes them, but generally her authorial reading of her drafts of *The Handmaid's Tale* affirms rather than denies the initial flow. This novel may be an exception to her practice – she normally revises her work assiduously for a long time – because her very subject matter, Offred's voice narrative, imitates the process of Atwood's Writer's Own Anonymous. Offred has no name, like Atwood's Anonymous. She tells her story onto tapes without knowing what audience might be listening to it. The novel comes out as auditory dictation by a disembodied voice from the darkness of night. It is 'a story I'm telling, in my head, as I go along' (49): her mind hears itself utter the book – writing does not occur. Offred has no opportunity to revise what she says, just like Atwood's Anonymous. It is Professor Piexoto and his colleague who transcribe, sequence, and interpret Offred's tapes. They can put no name to the woman who produced them and enjoy mocking her as a prostitute. Atwood satirizes the insulting treatment that this pair of reader-centred literary critics give to their author in the text: we recognize the ironical portrayal of these self-important men. Atwood allows her own flow and Offred's dictation to stand. The epilogue, although written by Atwood, describes an authorial reading of Offred's confessions, but it is not Atwood's reading. The writers of the epilogue repress the author's right to be heard just as the author-is-dead movement had discourage interest in affect and intentionality as treasonable fallacies.

*   *   *   *   *

For months I've had just routine requests from you for clear SOVs to replace my wordy fluxes – one of your LEME synonyms for diarrhoea, isn't it? strange what pops up in chunks these days – but I'm glad for a rest after the seven-month romp that left us with an arrhythmia that your cardiologist has treated as if equipping a truck with a speed-governor that really got stress-tested in teaching Shakespeare and authoring to students stuffed with theory and eager to tame me, to Andre, Angela, Elena, James, Jeff, Tesla, and the other guys now somewhere in our LTM who got you to see how driven I am and how lazy you are, how you owe more to my feelings than to the dictionaries you spend so much time on, a bore if you ask me, but the more I reflect (if I do that), the more I guess there's room for all kinds.

IV   Iris Murdoch

Most authors who suffer from dementia do not have work published that was composed while they were declining. Poets Robert Southey and Thomas Moore, mystery writer Ross MacDonald, science-fiction novelist A.E. Van Vogt, man of letters Ralph Waldo Emerson, Claude Shannon (the father of information theory), fantasy writer E.B. White, novelist Somerset Maugham, and diarist Dorothy Wordsworth suffered privately. Many kinds of dementia exist, some occasioned by a sudden lesion to the brain, but Alzheimer's disease and other dementias not caused by a sudden neurological lesion manifest themselves gradually. They can worsen in the middle of writing a book. Then the author finds that the familiar cognitive flow falters and that even composing and editing with writing technologies, cyborgic extentions to memory, do not help because the disease damages reading too. This interruption may seem to be that ancient curse, writer's block, until it begins to affect other kinds of behaviour. English novelist Iris Murdoch was unlucky in this way. Two years after her last novel, *Jackson's Dilemma* (1995), was published, and three years after she finished it, she was diagnosed with Alzheimer's disease. It had profoundly affected her writing of that novel, and no one found out in time.

Cognitive psychologists working with a corpus of spontaneous speech by Alzheimer's sufferers, the Charlotte Narrative and Conversation Collection (some 700 'oral narratives, interviews and conversations'), published their preliminary findings in *Alzheimer Talk* (B. Davis 2005, xiii). Boyd Davis and Cynthia Bernstein report a small galaxy of Alzheimer features in their contribution: 'a decrease both in information content and in coherence' (64), errors in referents (e.g., pronouns without antecedents, things or persons that identified them; also Almor et al. 1999; March et al. 2006), neologisms or novel word forms, 'paraphrasias' (jargon in this field for half-right words and word substitutions), repetitions, 'the replacement of logical conjunctions such as *so* and *because* by *and*' (65), 'empty phrases' (e.g., '*and so on, like that*'), 'indefinite terms ("*thing*"), deictic terms (*that*),' and prefabricated or formulaic phrases in 'utterance-initial' position ('as if ... buying a fraction of time to think'; 67). A dissertation by Susan de Santi (1993) found that 'those sentences which are highly familiar and over-learned remain relatively spared in Alzheimer's disease, whereas those sentences which are new and unfamiliar are difficult to repeat without error' (quoted by B. Davis 2005, 129). In a separate study, Kathy Groves-Wright and her colleagues, reviewing recent literature, confirm the assumed traits that Garrard looked for in Murdoch – 'semantic impairment' from early in the disease, as revealed in tests such as 'confrontational naming and verbal fluency' and in behaviour that exhibits 'word-finding difficulties, circumlocutions, and reduced number of words'; and syntactic degradation at a later stage in the disease (2004, 110). Writing shows 'word substitutions, omissions, and perseverations' (110). In addition, Groves-Wright discovered in tests with forty-two individuals that a drop in word fluency could distinguish between normal persons ('controls') and those with mild Alzheimer's (115). Their word-fluency tests ask individuals to give, quickly, names of things 'within a semantic or phonemic category,' in this case, names for animals (not fish or birds), and words that began with 'f' (113–14). Another language marker is abnormal passive constructions, such as overuse of the 'get'-verb combination (Bates et al. 1995).

The healthily aging elderly experience some of these symptoms, but the deficits do not incapacitate uttering. The elderly find alternate strategies to manage their language production. In any event, challenges of comprehension, reading, and conversation result in delays and simplification rather than panicked scrambling. Near-normal functioning goes on for decades into very old age. What, then, differentiates the healthily aging idiolect from dementia?

Iris Murdoch donated her brain to Optima, an Alzheimer's disease research facility at Radcliffe Hospital in Oxford at her death in February 1999 (Conradi 2001, 592). This generous and quietly heroic act was reciprocated by the loving memoir of her life and dying by her husband, Oxford professor John Bayley. Together, they made public what it was like to suffer from, and tend to, this disease. They set an example in their openness that was appreciated by dementia sufferers, not least professionals like them who live by their wits, have most to lose when they decline, and often avoid its knowledge. Murdoch's own testimony explains how what attacked her differed from becoming elderly.

In *Iris: A Memoir of Iris Murdoch*, John Bayley describes two incidents in spring 1994 that signalled the onset of Murdoch's illness, when she was seventy-four years old. They each spoke at a special conference at the University of the Negrev in Israel, Murdoch choosing to answer questions about her novel-writing. Her responses were atypically sparse and slow in coming, and the audience noticed. Cheerful and encouraging, Bayley made little of the embarrassment that others felt, but afterwards he remembered how she had been complaining at home about difficulties in writing her current novel, published in 1995 as *Jackson's Dilemma*. Of the title character, a servant, Iris had told John, 'It's this man Jackson ... I can't make out who he is, or what he's doing' and 'I don't think he's born yet' (1998, 148). Bayley said that her condition then 'deteriorated steadily' in the eighteen months following the novel's publication (153). Joanna Coles interviewed Iris and John at their home in September 1996, when Murdoch was seventy-seven years old, and she described what was referred to as a writing block as 'a very bad one,' her situation 'a very, very bad, quiet place,' and her experience as 'just falling, falling ... just falling as it were' (Dooley 2003, 246). Her repetition of the same words hints at the problem. In two other expressions, she explains that her memory does not respond to probes: 'At the moment I can't find anything' and 'I'm just wandering. I think of things and then they go away forever' (247). Doctors made a final diagnosis of Alzheimer's disease the next year, in 1997.

Jackson's Dilemma, unlike her previous twenty-five novels, from *Under the Net* in 1954 to *The Green Knight* in 1993, confused the critics. Some, such as Geoffrey Heptonstall, were complimentary: Murdoch was 'at the height of her powers' in a novel that was 'the summation of her talent.' Others, like Valerie Miner, found it 'hard to digest.' A.S.

Byatt thought the novel was 'an Indian Rope Trick ... in which all the people have no selves and therefore there is no story and no novel' (quoted by Garrard 2009, 251). Kate Kelloway judged it to be 'not a perfect novel: the narrative itself is, at times, a little distrait: like Jackson [the eponymous servant], it often moves with scant explanation' (quoted by Spear 2007, 136). Kelloway selects a rare term, 'distrait' (from the French, and often italicized as a foreign word in English), which is only partly explained by the post-colon 'scant explanation.' The term means, 'Having the attention distracted from what is present; absent-minded' (OED). Readers' letters to the reviewing newspapers also pointed out 'small errors and inconsistencies in the narrative' (Bayley 1998, 152). Richard Todd (2001, 679–80) finds several on the same page, two of them inconsistencies in the character and whereabouts of two beloveds, Marion and Rosalind. Was Murdoch distracted?

In interviews from 1964 to 1996 Murdoch helpfully explained her normal creative process. She outlined its three stages about 1988–90. First, she planned a novel mentally for up to a year, making 'scrappy' or 'rough notes'; next, she did a 'very detailed synopsis of every chapter, every conversation, everything that happens'; and last, she wrote the novel out in longhand (Dooley 2003, 222; cf. 14, 27, 38, 57, 126). She had referred to these two writing stages in 1964 as 'two drafts of the whole thing, and maybe three or four of particular scenes' (14) and in 1968 she said that she modified her planned conception 'a great deal in the writing' (27; cf. 14). She described the first, longest stage, mental planning, as reducing one to being 'just a slave of one's unconscious mind' (22) and in 1979 repeated that invention came from 'the unconscious mind,' whose 'force' amply made the 'stuff' was 'something you must thank the Gods for if it is there' (115). Ten years later she acknowledged that this stage was 'agonizing' (221). Things in memory managed to 'sort themselves out in a kind of automatic way' (27). They were 'all strongly related, they all come into being with a kind of necessity in relation to each other' (126). The two writing stages, which took her less time than the first, involved the 'rational intellect': it tempered the creative force, 'preventing it from following patterns which it wants to follow' (115).

At what stage with *Jackson's Dilemma* was Murdoch when she said to her husband in 1994 that she could not 'make out' Jackson and that he had not yet been 'born'? Metaphorically, she suggests that his character is stuck in memory's womb, where his features cannot be discerned consciously. '[T]hings ... go away for-ever,' she told Joanna Coles two years later. This was not the 'agonizing' mental planning, but something new, a problem of retrieving what she thought once, what she had once laid down in memory. After she gave *The Green Knight* to her publisher (before it was published in 1993), Murdoch must have started mulling over *Jackson's Dilemma*. By spring 1994, she would have been writing it. The first seven chapters occupy 188 pages and average 27 pages each, what she usually managed, but then something happened to her last six chapters, which average only ten pages each. These read like a revised synopsis, not a fully developed novel. Characters certainly do things: the ninth chapter begins when Benet changes his mind about wedding Marion and instead proposes to Anne Dunarven, and the tenth chapter opens with a letter from Marion to Benet announcing that his servant Jackson has just arranged a marriage between herself and Cantor. This turn of events alienates Benet, his master, from Jackson for a while. Why these characters change so quickly is not very clear. In the middle of turning a second stage, the synopsis, into a full draft, Murdoch could have begun to experience trouble using her working memory to retrieve character information from schemata previously laid down. Her mind could not give birth to Jackson's character because she could no longer 'find' the cognitive schemata that she had laid down in memory.

Peter Garrard's article on Iris Murdoch as she succumbed to Alzheimer's disease is a uniquely important case study. Late in her life, medical tests detected a mild impairment in her working-memory digit span, 'the sequence length' at which an individual who is asked to recall multi-digit numbers is 'right half the time' (Baddeley 2004, 23). Healthy aging does not affect the digit span (Maxim and Bryan 1994, 32). Then what appeared clearly to be Alzheimer's disease settled in. After her death in 1999, a 'profound bilateral hippocampal shrinkage' turned up at an autopsy: this area, the hippocampus, is the portal that neuroscience has identified as leading from working memory to long-term memory.

These medical results led Garrard and his colleagues to analyse her writings to see if text analysis threw up symptoms of her dementia. They made word-frequency lists from her early, middle, and late novels, *Under the Net* (1954), her mid-career *The Sea, the Sea* (1978), and her last, *Jackson's Dilemma*: and their text-analysis results showed an increasing lexical and semantic 'impoverishment.' Garrard and his colleagues expected to find, by comparing three of Murdoch's novels, increasing evidence of a 'disruption of word and sentence level production and comprehension' and 'disintegration of ... semantic memory' (Garrard et al. 2005, 250). Word-list generation tests routinely show that

Alzheimer's disease sufferers have a 'relative impairment in semantic processing' (Poore et al. 2006, 86). The Nun Study, for example, had discovered both 'reduced syntactic complexity' and lexical impoverishment (Garrard et al. 2005, 251) in writings of members of a religious community, extending over fifty years, where they had developed dementia. Garrard undertook a variety of text-analysis tests after digitizing Murdoch's three works, deleting proper names and dialogue, and running *Concordance* on them. A count of total different word types, taken at 10,000-word cumulative segments through the novels, showed that Murdoch's earliest novel had about 5,600 word types per 40,000 words, but *Jackson's Dilemma*, her final novel, had only 4,500 per 40,000 words. Her vocabulary had suffered a drop of 20 per cent, its 'more restricted vocabulary' leading to a greater rate of lexical repetition (255). The medical tests on Murdoch and her autopsy had turned up a deterioration in one location of the brain that coincided with a reduction in her lexical store and in the information density of her prose. Style and the brain were connected. Neuroscientists had detected her disease in a text that Wimsatt and Beardsley would have us believe no longer had an author to discuss. They used conventional authorship-attribution methods to characterize her idiolect and found ample reason to consider using authored texts as retrospective diagnostic tools (see also Van Velzen and Garrard 2008 and Garrard 2009).

The link between Murdoch's body and mind was her working memory. The hippocampus, its gateway, is involved with the most important part of our mental life, where we directly and self-consciously hear and manipulate, subvocally, our language. In healthy old age, the capacity of working memory for semantic context diminishes, but not its digit span. Sufferers of dementia gradually experience that space shrinking and failing. As they lose the ability to retain new information, and as the amount of language to which they can mentally attend with the inner voice lessens, a major cybertextual channel breaks down. They cannot effectively monitor their speech and writing for errors. The uttering mind eventually resorts to reusing oft-repeated phrases stored in memory as units instead of generating new expressions. Vocabulary thins because neural damage slows words newly learned by means of working memory. Old words are called on again and again, individually and phrasally. Worse, writing loses the complex reasoning and thought that once went into storytelling as schemata, those neural clusters, disintegrate. Binding actions to full-featured characters is no longer possible. Building sentences becomes a frustrating and exhausting exercise as long-used schemata for their construction cannot quickly or wholly be brought into working memory. A terminal writer's block sets in.

A like simplification occurred in Murdoch's syntax: sentences in her last novel became markedly shorter in words, and more sparse in number of clauses. Mean sentence length (in 30-sentence samples from each novel) dropped from 19.7 (with a 11.62 standard deviation) in *Under the Net*, and 22.7 (14.1 s.d.) in *The Sea, the Sea*, to 15.3 (10.8 s.d.) in *Jackson's Dilemma*. Mean clauses per sentence also dropped from 1.5 (1.8 s.d.) and 2.2 (1.0 s.d.) to 0.8 (1.3 s.d.). These results were statistically significant. A third test, the 'mean proportion of repetitions, at intervals of 1–4 words, of the ten most common words in each book' (all of them function words), however, showed that *Jackson's Dilemma* behaved for immediate repetition like *Under the Net*, and for repetitions after three and four words like *The Sea, the Sea* (256). A fourth test also produced a statistically insignificant result: 'the relative proportions of words belonging to different grammatical classes' (257). Murdoch's syntactic structure was 'relatively unchanged' as 'consistent with the predominantly temporal lobe distribution of pathology that was eventually demonstrated' by the autopsy (259).

Semantic impoverishment is not necessarily the best early warning sign of dementia. A diminished idiolect arises from a failure of just one cognitive function out of many. A far more pervasive cognitive disablement is responsible; it affects thinking with long-term memory, not simply the language centres.

Neither Murdoch nor any reviewer of *Jackson's Dilemma* detected its marked lexical impoverishment, although Brad Leithauser (quoted by Todd 2001, 678) says that the 'writing is a mess.' However, they did notice the novel's brevity and the emptiness of the characters. Richard Todd even argues that Murdoch espoused an 'aesthetic of imperfection.' This created 'a numinous mysteriousness,' 'little inward focalization' on the characters, a lead character, Jackson, who has 'no fixed identity,' and a thematic 'unselfing' by them all (679, 681, 684, 691). Todd says that this 'style could not and should not, of course, be held to "foreshadow" Alzheimer's in any meaningful way' and that a bodily explanation for literary effects is a critical 'cul-de-sac' (687). Todd rationalizes the accidental breaking of a carton of eggs by praising the chef's omelette, but he did not have the advantage of Garrard's case study, published four years later. Bran Nicol did know about Murdoch's sense of having lost Jackson: in 2004 Nicol judged him 'one of Murdoch's most successful characters,' a Prospero figure who arranges that everyone, himself included, ends up 'happy' (2009, 39).

How can critics approve of a novel marked by early symptoms of Alzheimer's disease, and of a lead character whom Murdoch admitted she could not find? If readers cannot admit authorial mental illness as a factor in assessing literary quality for fear of reaching a quick dead end, then forms of affective illness too (depression and bipolar disease, known to be endemic in writers) must also be discounted. These sicknesses torment authors and almost certainly present obstacles to healthy readers as they process a book's language and thought. There is, however, one way out of Todd's cul-de-sac: interpret such works as its author's response to and negotiation with illness. The authorial reading is a portal onto that understanding.

If Jackson ends happily, as Nicol says, we should find that feeling in the last scene, when Jackson assesses his state of mind and circumstances, but he admits a diminution of his powers, an incipient madness, grave personal memory loss, and a fear that he cannot comprehend his situation. Inexplicably, this vision of self leads him, at the end, to 'smile' as he walks to Benet's Penndean:

[1] Now Bran had gone, but Jackson continued to **sit** motionless **in the grass**. [2] HE breathed deeply. [3] Sometimes HE had a sudden **loss of** breath, together with a momentary **loss**, or shift, **of** memory. [4] So HE was **to wait**, once more, **forget**fulness, his and theirs. [5] HE thought, **my power has left me, will it** ever **return, will** the indications **return**? [6] No **assign**ment. [7] But punishment? [8] Madness of course always now at hand. [9] HE had **forgott**en where **HE had to** go, and what **HE had to** do. [10] **To the mountains**. [11] If HE went **to the mountains** now HE would find no one there. [12] Stay with Benet – among the rich - seeking the poor? [13] How strange just **now that HE** was able to **sing**. [14] **Assign**ed? [15] HE **remember**ed **now that HE** could **sing**. [16] But **HE had come to** the wrong turning. [17] With Benet, **had HE** finally made a mistake? [18] **Have I simply come to** the end of my tasks? [19] I wish I could say – **'I have** only **to wait.'** [20] **How much** did Uncle Tim **understand**, I wonder. [21] Or, **how much** now will I **understand**. [22] **My powers have left me, will** they **return – have I simply misunderstood**? [23] At least **I had** called Benet to the bridge. [24] Is it all **a dream**, yes, perhaps **a dream** – yet my strength remains, and I can destroy myself at any moment. [25] Death, its closeness. [26] Do I after all fear those who seek me? [27] I have **forgott**en them and no one calls. [28] Was I in prison once? [29] I cannot **remember**. [30] At the end of what is necessary, I have come to a place where there is no road.

This passage has so many repeating phrases and so much syntactic priming (15 instances) that Murdoch either appears to have been desperate to fill out Jackson's ideas or – given that the 14 successive clauses beginning with 'he' are followed by 14 more clauses beginning with 'I' – was suffering from perseveration, a condition of Alzheimer's patients. However, this seamless transition from 'he' to 'I' can be read to show that Murdoch perceives Jackson's symptoms as her own. As he forgets, so does she. As he doubts his powers will return, so does she. The repetitions mark Murdoch's realization that she is Jackson. Her dilemma, having been so useful to so many for so long, is that she, like Jackson at the end of his road, has nowhere to go.

Iris Murdoch's last novel is as much a self-study as was her conversation with her husband about Jackson. When schemata in long-term memory become inaccessible, when working memory constricts, the writer's mind turns in desperation to what it knows from experience: her own increasingly self-unobserved life, preoccupied by happenings that appear disconnected with those they affect. Murdoch created the chief character of *Jackson's Dilemma* in her own image, as if Jackson experienced autobiographical memories of Murdoch's own, mingling with the imaginative 'scene constructions' in her episodic buffer. They faced the same sense of dissolving selfhood. *Jackson's Dilemma*, precisely because it demonstrates a decline that she recognizes and glosses, may be her most remarkable novel.

So it is that Agatha Christie and Iris Murdoch ended their distinguished writing careers with works that had like problems: a vocabulary drop of 20 per cent, simple mistakes in crafting details of the story that readers were quick to point out, an atypically short page count, and a heavy reliance on notebook synopses. *Elephants Can Remember* (1972) and *Jackson's Dilemma* (1995) also both focus on characters – Ariadne and Jackson – that betrayed memory lapses, like the novelists themselves. An elderly writer of detective stories, Ariadne was modelled explicitly on Christie, just as Jackson gave voice to what Murdoch felt of herself.

To see mental decline at work in major writers makes us want to look away. It forces us to recognize that, as Dylan Thomas writes, time holds us 'green and dying,' at once flourishing and perishing. The loss of self that Murdoch endured, the indignity of bad critical reviews, and the public notariety as her health took public attention away from her work qualify the notional 'death of the author in the work.' True, intentionality inheres in text and how an author reads it, but all textual phenomena are cognitive. Poignantly, *Jackson's Dilemma* helps us understand what personal bravery goes into authoring. Cognitively, writers balance on the finest of pin-points when they overcome the mental anxiety that comes of not knowing what they have to say until they say it and at last induce the spontaneous flow of language to begin. For this escape from Plato's cave, authors will give up almost everything. To fall back gradually into the prison of the cave after decades of freedom, as Murdoch did, is no shame; it is a badge of courage in the face of illness. She did more than donate her brain to science – she donated her last book.

*   *   *   *   *

Serves you right for editing my draft and stuffing it with information ... Suzanne grimaced when she saw all the tables and graphs, and hadn't I warned you never to put in anything I didn't make personally, and unlike Ernie I don't do numbers! and so although the seven months had netted us quite a bundle, impressive enough for peer reviewers even when one didn't know what we were up to – is this a memoir (me), or a scholarly tract (you)? – there was a lot of rethinking and rewriting to do, and speaking of that, let me apologize for the draft's errors, inconsistencies, obscurities, and repetitions even if they came honestly, my native mode being talk, and then there's the short attention span, but after all I'm only human and didn't at all mind the feedback, even the obsessive fusion of my larger fragments with your information, and the recent benign neglect, as a result of which, may I say, your muse (your word, not mine), as sure as there is a period at the end of this sentence, is already beginning to forget, despite which ominous concession, I'll catch up with you later if I can.

6 Reading the Writer's Own Anonymous

Yet half a beast is the great god Pan,
To laugh as he sits by the river,
Making a poet out of a man.
                                        (Elizabeth Barrett Browning, 'A Musical Instrument')

Beowulf, The Canterbury Tales, The Winter's Tale, Biographia Literaria, and
Four Quartets have camel-like come through the eye of a cognitive nee-
dle, the alpha and omega values for chunk and load. If the phonological
loop evolved for language learning, as Alan Baddeley believes, then it
is the Procrustean bed on which an author lies down. Syntactic priming and chunking are consequences of the sleep of consciousness in
that bed. Language and storymaking depend on its cognitive infrastructure, however many writing technologies we develop as artificial
memory systems, however cunning we are in devising editing tools.
Authors create the schemata out of which they make characters and
actions over a long period of time by means of subjective experience,
writing technologies, and the language-learning supports of working
memory. As experts, authors know how, within their restricted domain
of knowledge, to shuttle the elements of schemata very quickly in and
out of working memory to enlarge their linguistic conceptual span, and
their consciousness of what they are making. Yet until words become
cognitively phonological, they and the schemata that give them a home
remain blanketed in fog to the author. Finally, the entity that lies down
on this bed, the maker of thought, only reveals itself (and very partially) by means of our senses, hearing, seeing, and touch, which we

employ in language (Crick and Koch 2000). Chaucer astutely addressed the eagle in *The House of Fame* as 'thought.'

All praise, then, to John Milton, who in his blindness composed *Paradise Lost* and waited until morning, day by day, for his daughters or secretaries to come to 'milk' him of his composition (French 1956, 191). His making inverts the conventional classical inspiration, the muses. Milton's ladies emptied, not filled him. He created his poem, line by line, one verse paragraph after another, in his mind as if it were a wax tablet waiting to be inscribed. His cognitive load appears to have been up to 'thirty Verses at a time' (192). He then dictated these segments to his amenuenses. He recalls the example of St Thomas Aquinas, whose secretaries received entire books from his dictation (Carruthers 1990, 203). How could they have done so if authors are always unconscious of how they make language? The astonishing feats of mnemonists answer the sceptics who wonder whether anyone in recent memory has created a substantial utterance, novel-sized, simply with the unaided human memory system. Most of us cannot retain even a mental list of groceries, even though we may be able to use language well enough not to starve, but a few fit minds have exceptional memories.

The ploughman's skill at rote memorization comes in handy even to a great man. Milton authored utterances unselfconsciously, and line by line they flowed into his working memory, but instead of speaking them aloud, or writing them down, he exercised his working memory to save novel expressions in long-term memory. Did he store his works, line by unrhyming pentameter line, in the original long-term holding place of the mind? Walter Ong summarizes what we know about the memory employed by bards from Homer, through Old English and Middle English poets up to modern Yugoslav and Third World bards, who all perform poetry by combining set phrases, expressions, and proverbs:

> In a primary oral culture, to solve effectively the problem of retaining and retrieving carefully articulated thought, you have to do your thinking in mnemonic patterns, shaped for ready oral recurrence. Your thought must come into being in heavily rhythmic, balanced patterns, in repetitions or antitheses, in alliterations and assonances, in epithetic and other formulary expressions, in standard thematic settings (the assembly, the meal, the duel, the hero's 'helper,' and so on), in proverbs which are constantly heard by everyone so that they come to mind readily and which them-

selves are patterned for retention and ready recall, or in other mnemonic form. Serious thought is intertwined with memory systems. (1982, 34)

Milton could also have acted like mnemonists who calculate and store the values of *pi* to many thousands of places by chunking its numbers and assigning a visual tag to each chunk. One technique that they use is the *loci et imagines* (places and icons) method of artificial memory of which Frances Yates wrote in *The Art of Memory* (1966). The image linked to a numeric chunk gives it uniqueness, and the way that those images appear to a speaker mentally walking through a visually mapped and memorized common area gives these chunks their sequence. Milton could have used his episodic buffer in this way, or he could have mapped the contents of his phonological loop to long-term memory. The working-memory executive has a number of slave systems, episodic, phonological, and visual-spatial. Very long productions can be readily authored spontaneously and then stored by one or several such systems. Whichever method Milton used, he could only have committed speech to memory consciously.

This ancient how-to method of artificial memory shows that mnemonists are not necessarily strangers to the constraints that cognitive psychologists have discovered in human cognitive capacity. Silent speech is always chunk delimited and of fragile duration until stored in long-term memory schemata. Once it has been saved as speech or episodic sequence, it can be unwound, each chunk pulling out its successor effortlessly. Like a magpie, a sighted author stores significantly related details, haphazardly collected and not consciously integrated, in one nest over many months and years. A mnemonist like Milton has his fragments all before him in a consciously laid-down sequence.

E.M. Forster attributed literature only to a self-effacing, nameless intelligence who longed for no royalties, copyright, or recognition, and for whom authoring itself was reward enough: his hidden maker named Anonymous: 'there are no names down there, no personality as we understand personality, no marrying or giving in marriage. What there is down there – ah, that is another enquiry, and may the clergyman and the scientists pursue it more successfully in the future than they have in the past' (1925, 23). An author's name – that is, conscious authoring – signs itself, Forster says, only to information. Newspaper facts, reportage, observations, or analysis of texts or data come from the conscious writer-compiler, not the imagination. Paul Auster felt similarly about 'that mysterious other who lives inside me' and signs his works: 'For the author of a novel can never be sure where any of it comes from. The self that exists in the world – the self whose name appears on the covers of books – is finally not the same self who writes the book' (1995, 137). W.H. Auden, however, disagrees with Forster that imaginative authoring comes only from the nameless within us. He says that 'It is true that, when he is writing a poem, it seems to a poet as if there were two people involved, his conscious self and a Muse whom he has to woo or an Angel with whom he has to wrestle, but, as in an ordinary wooing or wrestling match, his role is as important as Hers' (1963, 16). Forster gave credit to the entity called by classical civilizations the Muse, and by cognitive sciences the language production system, by labelling it as a familiar unknown. Auden interpreted authoring as a partnership of conscious and unconscious selves. Their primal author resembles the pre-linguistic thought that Francis Crick, co-discoverer of the structure of DNA, called the invisible homunculus.

Do you have one? Imagine someone sitting at a desk, waiting edgily for delivery, by means of an inner voice, of expressions to write down. This voice becomes so familiar to the sitting figure that he believes it is himself, the one who signs cheques and titlepages. If asked *How did you make those sentences?* he might answer truthfully, 'Well, I don't exactly know, they just came to me naturally,' to which you might object, *Are you the real author of those sentences if you don't know how you made them?* He might then faithfully object, 'But I heard myself utter them, I corrected them as they appeared, and I decided what form they should finally take!' To which you might reply: *While those are no doubt very good things, are you not describing what an editor-publisher does?* Forster felt odd about signing himself as maker of those sentences, or being praised for making them. He did not jump to a conclusion, identifying (like Carl Jung's ghost) the unconscious voice with a collective or (like Joan of Arc) with God. Anonymous does nicely for him, but schizophrenics also hear voices that they believe belong to others, much as we do when we mentally argue with ourselves about the pros and the cons of an issue or action. And then there are dreams. *Are you sure that you – as you understand yourself – authored your own dreams? How is it, then, that you cannot figure out what they mean?*

This questioner does not deny that the authoring voice is Forster's, that he overhears its utterances in working or immediate auditory memory. The Writer's Own Anonymous, however, differs from him who edits and publishes what he hears. That inner voice can surprise and delight us, or it can worry us. Auden quotes Forster approvingly but adds that, only when a poet has 'wooed and won Dame Philology,' can he 'give his entire devotion to the Muse' (1963, 22). She can turn on as requested, like a firefly, and yet, stubbornly resisting pleas, go dark. The subject of an authorial reading is the Writer's Own Anonymous and what his editor thinks of him.

Cognitive stylistics is a tool of authorship-attribution research, a field of enquiry that has few practitioners, it seems to me, because there are so few anonymous works whose authors we want to identify. Anonymous literature is often undistinguished. If great and anonymous, like *Piers Plowman*, thousands of candidates exist, most of whom have left behind them no historical record, so that any attribution attempt is futile. We usually refer to the unknown poet by the title of the work (e.g., 'the *Gawain* poet'), a deft slight of thought that neglects the Anonymous who truly merits study. To attribute authorship of a work universally agreed to be by a known, named writer obliges us to study aspects of the Writer's Own Anonymous. Now that cognitive psychology, neuroscience, text analysis, and corpus linguistics are probing the inner voice, the cognitive style of Anonymous is being clarified.

To make a close reading of Anonymous in the work, to distinguish it from the reader-editor's very self-conscious composed style, we can compare holographs and fair copies or print books. Each processes towards a terminal state, the utterance and the written text. Writ large, the uttered flow is the cybernetic message to which the edited text is the response. Writ small, the cognitive self-monitor okays each segment as it comes out, and the composing editor, an intellect largely freed from memory tasks, crosses out, inserts, rearranges, substitutes, and (sometimes in hope) resubmits a passage to the Writer's Own Anonymous for reinvention.

Every close authorial reading searches for an author's intentions. So difficult is it to distinguish them from the reader's own wishes that most criticism abandoned the attempt some fifty years ago. If authors skilfully, spontaneously uttered their stories in person, and if they were willing to answer questions about them truthfully, we listeners might feel the 'illocutionary force' in stories that Socrates and David Olson believe writing and reading deprive us of. Although long after composing texts, authors tend to forget themselves and, like Coleridge, confabulate what they meant, authorial intent might no longer always be a mystery. Yet when authors die now, they leave their works to publishers rather than to other authors who will recreate them; and we prefer to have stories at our own hours and in our own spaces rather than seeking out the storyteller and the bard in a communally agreed time and place. Literature has become a private experience except in the classroom; and the classroom or reading group teaches us to be alone with texts. Writers thrive, and authors wane.

Cybertextuality explains how to find the bipartite author in the work. Once found, the author's intentions limit the number of reasonable critical readings, although readers these days do not take to constraint kindly. Close authorial readings should not be privileged over all others but assist readers who *intend* to be faithful to the time, place, and circumstances of the author. An ingenious reader can rescue a poor work by advocating a reading inconsistent with the author's intentions. An authorial reading of Agatha Christie's *Elephants Can Remember* finds signs of dementia, but the novel may still be read as Ariadne's (and Agatha's) heroic response to an in-process disaster, as it may be read as one in which dementia in the text is the work's true antagonist. A close authorial reading of Agatha's narrative powers associates the crime of the detective novel, the murders on the hill, with the author's own condition. Her choice of title betrays that possibility. This modern reading, historically unfaithful as it may be, gives *Elephants* an unexpected dignity. Even readers sceptical about close authorial readings may wish to use them.

Close authorial readings attend to both the author's unconscious behaviour in uttering sentences, and the author's deliberate choices in rescuing the work from that behaviour by deleting, rearranging, and adding. The mind's inner voice delivers expertise in a flowing 'trance-like' state. A store of expert schemata in long-term memory issues sequences of chunks (phrases), more often additive than embedded or subordinating. The mind imposes two size constraints. George Miller's 'magical number' (once seven, now three or four) sizes phrases at less than two seconds, as spoken: the alpha value. A simple subject-verb-object sentence could fit in this. An author's cognitive load, the larger constraint, depends on expertise with language and content – a question of how many hours the author has spent with them, and 10,000 hours qualifies most experts – but between 10 and 20 pentameter lines of verse (or in prose an author's average paragraph) is a reasonable guess. At omega-value text boundaries the author may begin to repeat what he has just experienced as spoken or read words. The mind that utters this flow has monitored it before, and during its self-reading has unconsciously reacted to unexpected words with an N400 wave event. Editing and revising raise alarms at a sudden awareness of the flow.

The editor wakes up from the dream of the Writer's Own Anonymous. Only when we understand how cognitive creative processes shape the flow of the writing can we begin to appreciate the reader-editor's reactions. At this juncture, revisions to holograph manuscript drafts reveal choices made to restream the currents of the flow. Authorial choices on how to revise cognitive language production instantiate intentionality.

Associational principles prevail in given, received utterances. Does the author accept them as they come, or does he or she restructure text, using rhetorical or logical strategies of deduction or description to subvert the associative streak that Coleridge came to mistrust? Does the author consciously subvert the alpha and omega constraints, as by multiplying adjectives, dissecting phrases and recombining their pieces, and making noun trains, or embedding passages within passages or deleting syntactic priming and the repetitions that can tie together contiguous thought passages? Does the author increase the abstractness of text, disembodying it, by using more metaphors, or does he or she adhere to Strunk and White's policy of simple concrete diction and so enable readers to relive the experiences of what words denote, even at the risk of trapping them in a solipsistic world?

A few authors (Shakespeare and Eliot) abstain from self-editing, but most authors redraft, sometimes obsessively. Eliot *intended* that associational principles govern his text and that it be natural, unrectified. He gave friends like Ezra Pound the power to wield the knife. For all we know, Shakespeare let his fellow players trim his writings for performance. While imitating a stream or flow of consciousness, Woolf actually dismantles the constraints of chunk size and cognitive load. Her long paragraphs are periodic, and her phrases are reconstructed from disintegrated segments of other given phrases. W.B. Yeats and James Joyce excelled at crafting these disembodied word combinations. Such authors can even draft principles of writing that denature language of its usual cognitive organizational principles. Rather than telling a story, or letting it tell itself, they problematize the business of communication or narrative.

Authors have a basic choice: they can leave well enough alone, or they can interfere with Anonymous. Atwood gives herself freedom to let Offred speak with an unedited inner voice. She revises assiduously, but aside from discarding clunky repetitions Atwood grows her text. Other authors use external language technologies to create a new metalanguage and richly transform their own natural tongue. William Golding did so in *The Inheritors* (1955), a novel about Neanderthals. Russell

Hoban's *Riddley Walker* (1980) uses a hypothetical English developed several thousand years after a nuclear holocaust. Cormac McCarthy's language in novels such as *Blood Meridian* (1985) has a uniquely erudite, syntactically gnarly cast. How contrived it is can be guessed by comparing it to his *The Road* (2006).

In a typical close authorial reading of a work we use an author's comments about her creative process, and her draft versions of that work. With these in hand, we can deduce two kinds of authorial decision. The first takes place during spontaneous flow: *currente calamo* revisions as she becomes fully conscious of what she is saying in writing the text down. These changes respond to problems inside a chunk or a thought passage. The second occurs later, after some period of time, and revises in ways that change how the entire text should be read. They extend or reduce thought passages. These two choices rise directly from the author's feedback to cognitive constraints or limitations I call the alpha and omega values. They open a window on some of the author's intentions in creating the work.

W.H. Auden said that one of six services that a critic could render literature was to 'Throw light upon the process of artistic "Making"' by asking 'fresh and important' questions, even if the answers he gives to them are wrong-headed (1963, 9). An authorial reading asks, what did the reader-editor do when she first saw what her Writer's Own Anonymous produced? The author always gives her creation the first reading it ever gets. Her cognitive monitor finds little whiffs to complain about, but storing the work on paper enables her to become fully conscious of her making and frees her to to analyse and reshape it with machinic tools other than literacy itself. Software can check for grammatical errors, online thesauri propose a word to replace another word, and word processing makes it easy to delete, move, and add phrases, sentences, paragraphs, and chapters.

An authorial reading is feedback to the messages of the Writer's Own Anonymous. The theory that supports it is cybertextuality, which theorizes the becoming of a literary work in unconscious thought and its servant, editing. Cybertextuality begins in what authors say about the creative process, and in the legacy of drafts, workbooks, typescripts, and files that they deposit in libraries for study. Their impressionistic testimony lacks the controls and quantities of scientific experiments on the brain's language-production system, but it has everything else we need. Authors and scientists agree that uttering goes on unconsciously, and authors flow on, unaware of limitations in chunk size and cognitive capacity, or of how one chunk primes the next to which we stitch it. Collocational studies of repeating phrases in authored texts bear out scientific ideas of chunking. Associational mental clusters or schemata in long-term memory, and priming, lead an author to repeat paragraph-sized structures once his mental text enters his external working-memory medium of choice. The author and the scientist both speak of a self-monitor or self-editor. The former unconsciously catches simple errors. During conscious revision, the reader-editor deletes visible repetitions and turns anaphoric stitching into left- and right-branching and embedded syntactic structures. He composes syntactic periods after utterances enter a visual field that can persist in sensory memory.

Cybertextuality observes systemic cybernetic, message-and-response exchanges between the idiolect savant, the Writer's Own Anonymous, and its often indignant, calculating self-editor. It is an intentionalist's theory. Creative process partners two selves in a divided mind, an anonymous cognitive voice, and a conscious reader-editor. The former is our true Muse; the latter is her servant, Auden's Dame Philology. These two have a cybertextual message-feedback relation to one another. The author's idiolect savant leaves traces of intentionality in the edited work, but they are hard to identify except in very close, even tedious, analyses because writing depletes text of so much evidence of its author's purposes that speech delivers: David Olson's interpretation of Austin's 'illocutionary force.' Literary researchers make a good living by teaching how to speculate on and detect what literacy removes. Intentionality shape-shifts during self-monitoring in working memory and during conscious revision when the author's second, copyright-protected self calculates rationally what to add, delete, and rearrange. During an addition, this second self must submit itself to the author's own unconscious again if it is to have anything at all to work with. Two intentionalities are operative. Literature is as much the flow of the idiolect savant as it is the locks, gates, lifts, swing bridges, and dams by which the civil engineer of style constrains it. Who recruits whom, the default mode network or the cognitive control network?

This faith-based interaction between nobody and somebody makes for three kinds of authors, the two-, three-, and four-stage. Most authors mull over their topic for a long time, months and years, laying down mental schemata for their fiction. Some nervous authors add a post-gist stage, writing down what they are growing in schemata. These authors hedge their bets against writer's block and constrain their idiolect savant to flow in prescribed channels. All authors stream the lightly monitored stuff of their Anonymous either into long-term memory or onto page or screen. The two-stage writer absolutely trusts his Own Anonymous. Rarely, a two-stage author leaves the editing to others. Surviving drafts transformed Eliot's *The Waste Land*: what appeared to be an editor's calculated mosaic turns out to be a collaboration of Eliot's idiolect savant and another's editing self, Ezra Pound. Many authors jump-start their work with hope of something nameless taking control as it utters onto the page. Shakespeare, Dickens, Forster, Stephen King, and Atwood candidly place their first trust in their Own Anonymous. With them belong authors who had no choice, being illiterate or blind. Cædmon could not write to make notes, and Milton in *Paradise Lost* could not see to write. Their risky leap into a cognitive unknowing produces authentic work; even they cannot imitate it. Audiences and readers remember Shakespeare's flowing soliloquys by Hamlet far longer than his calculated parallel structuring of supra-plot, subplot, and plot, the superimposed lives of Fortinbras, Laertes, and the prince. Most poets, on the other hand, do not recommend the grip-it-and-rip-it method, which has produced too much teenage verse. The three-stage author edits and revises her work extensively, because she frets about its fallibility: these functions overlap and cycle many times, especially if the reader-editor keeps demanding more copy from her Anonymous. And the four-stage author, who cannot tolerate spontaneity, dislodges himself from primacy in his own creation.

Iris Murdoch and Agatha Christie had three stages. Murdoch kept a notebook for each work-in-progress, and so did Christie. Friends suggested that Murdoch might overcome her block by uttering unprepared, but that was not her way. She had a philosophical mind, accustomed to years of prepared academic lecturing at Oxford on set topics. Home-educated Christie trained as a pianist but shyness deflected her from a career in performance, eventually finding work, and learning about poisoning during the First World War in a hospital dispensary. Her second marriage to a prominent archaeologist, Max Mallowan, enhanced her research skills when she accompanied him to excavations in the Middle East. These authors worked out their ideas on paper long before they started to write. Coleridge had a like temperment, the scholarly edition of his notebooks taking up ten books. He was reluctant to publish 'Kubla Khan,' purportedly a three-stage process, atypical of his custom. Other writers who mistrusted their unchecked muse, used notebooks to keep their own Anonymous within bounds, and revised extensively include George Meredith, George Eliot, and James Joyce, who compiled fifty-five volumes of notes for *Finnegans Wake* alone.

Four-stage authors are a modern phenomenon. B.S. Johnson released his novel *The Unfortunates* (1969) in twenty-seven unbound sections, all but two of which can be read in any order. Interactive fiction allows the reader to choose among various paths through a story. Digital makers are dissatisfied with Anonymous and actively undermine its structures or devise software that gives second parties, such as programmers and readers, co-authoring privileges with it. Espen Aarseth (1997) refers to the works of four-stage authors as cybertexts, which he defines as literature that requires manual work from a reader if it is to be read. A reader's behaviour interactively modifies the work he scans. Computers are an asset but hardly required. Anonymous and the reader-writer can disappear from computer-generated poetry that fills randomly selected syntactic slots with randomly selected words. Everything in the work is, then, feedback to the actions of a procedure that draws on random content. Human-computer co-authorship, however, can be interpreted as a game in which human and computer are players who make three kinds of moves: 'generate draft text ... remove draft text ... or provide the other player with some instructions or intermediate text' (Montfort 2002–3, 213). The nature of instructions to and by the computer will determine to what degree the authored work departs from the *modus operandi* of the Writer's Own Anonymous. Software can mitigate the constraints of unconscious thinking processes just as computer storage relieves our reliance on a long-term memory that cannot be read and a working memory developed to store words and phrases rather than discourse.

Cybertexts are at the mid-point of a spectrum that begins with automatic writing of the kind Gertrude Stein did at the Harvard Psychological Laboratory in the 1890s (Will 2001). Jim Rosenberg (2002–3) describes a typical cybertextual creative process as being three moves that engage a cyborg collaboration between a poet as maker of language and the same poet as programmer: these moves utter, store, and play. The first move is the poet's heard utterance, and the second move his storage of that in the first object as a notebook entry or *texte-auteur* ('requisition') that should act as feedback to the utterer in effecting the third move. In this final stage the poet and the reader play a created 'word object' that sets the stored utterance into interaction with the reader. Between the second and the third moves, someone (preferably the poet) creates this second object, which is an 'object arena' in which the first word object, a 'digital thing,' can run. Rosenberg would discard the second move entirely. He would have the poet store his utterance directly in the poet's own object arena, which then could be played and so give feedback to himself about how to revise his initial utterance. The reader-editor is replaced by a writer-player. Cybertext makers, Rosenberg argues, should not have to use someone else's 'object arena.' The author should be able to create a word-play engine as well as the utterance that runs in it. This engine can leach from a text the chunkiness, syntactic primes, and cognitive constraints inscribed in it by the Writer's Own Anonymous. These may be replaced by other conditions and rules.

Although all literature is the collaborative product of at least two selves in one mind, the unexpected hero of the authoring process is Anonymous. If understanding it were irrelevant, no one would edit holograph manuscripts, foul papers, and notebooks or interview authors about their 'creative process.' This intimate conversation deserves as much study as has been devoted to the reader's interactions with texts partly de-authored. We may not always be able to persuade ourselves that there is an Anonymous, but we still want to find one. We can give a more balanced weighting to authoring and reading than in any previous century because of the cognitive sciences, and the availability of many more drafts (thanks to the value that libraries give them, and to the resulting financial gain that authors reap by saving their papers). Patient science and scholarship unlock the gates of conception and chart the locks and channels of cognitive flow. Interactive concordancers locate and count vocabulary and significantly repeating words and phrases. Usability software such as *Morae* can now archive a writer's every keystroke and word-processing step, together with an audio and video record of the writer's talk and behaviour during a writing session. With this archive, students can watch the idiolect savant and its composing partner at work. If any author speaks aloud his thoughts as he types, he will leave behind a more intimate record of his creative process than we have ever had before. Deriving a history of that process from such vast data pools will challenge future research into authoring.

An authorial reading at times seems to find the same Anonymous at work in all authors. Cædmon's formulae resemble Chaucer's and Christie's repeating phrases in kind, if not in content. Syntactic priming is endemic and so elusive that editor-writers may not even know to look for it. Echoing of previous writing at the boundary of cognitive load happens when authors read what they have just written down at breaks in flow. Everyone's core vocabulary dynamically loses words and phrases and picks up others over several years. We can date Chaucer's work by examining his changing vocabulary profile; we can do the same with any author today whose work extends over four decades, as his did. Shakespeare exhibited semantic networks through collocation, as did James Joyce in *Portrait*. Mental illness affects writers no less than the rest of us. The language of anyone suffering from Alzheimer's disease resembles that of anyone else with the condition at the same stage. Cognitive stylistics finds the species in the individual.

The individual's intentions, on the other hand, can be observed in her response to what her flow-state utters. Coleridge segues from a reverie about an oriental despot into an all-too-typical confession of failure to finish a task. Yeats begins *Responsibilities* with a draft about his male ancestors but revises it, in mid-flow, to apologize for a childlessness occasioned by his long, unrequited obsession with Maud Gonne. Christie writes about elephants who can remember rather than elephants who never forget even as her fictional self loses track of a murderer she knew. Joyce focuses *Portrait* on a poem whose process of creation he would repudiate in *Dubliners* and *Ulysses*. Atwood uses a contemporary worry about falling birth rates, and speculation about a future dystopia, to present one of her own personal obsessions, how she authors. Chaucer (in flight with the eagle), Coleridge, Joyce, Christie, and Atwood each fictionalize an authorial reading of their own work. This is either a very popular topic in canonical authors, or its presence in a work of art primes professional critics to select it for study.

Authorship attribution is the godchild of authorial reading. Like Longfellow's second daughter, 'When she was good, / She was very good indeed, / But when she was bad she was horrid' (1922, 15). How are we to take sides when they are so many different kinds of textual markers, such varied statistical methods, and different conclusions (Juola et al. 2006)? The text interrogations of authorship attribution work if the real author confesses. Alive, he or she can just issue a press release. If not, we have to find the Writer's Own Anonymous of both attributed and unattributed (problem) texts. The old rule of thumb is that, if a stylistic feature looks to be the progeny of the unconscious (e.g., function words), use it in the comparison, but we now realize that any writer can manipulate most surface textual features at will. Parodies such as Henry Reed's 'Chard Whitlow,' vintage T.S. Eliot, thrive on that power. If Jane Austen can vary her function-word usage by character (Burrows 1987), what marker is safe? Attribution must begin with the only truly unconscious text. Only the Writer's Own Anonymous offers that data: combinatorial clusters in stitched chunks, cognitive load, and the number of stages in creative process, that is, how much the reader-editor removes. What the latter leaves unchanged, and deletes from, the work of the former, however, is by no means a fail-safe marker because, unlike Cleopatra, the styles of aging authors do wither. To make an attribution we should have evidence of the unedited flow of both anonymous author and target author, their test works should be close in time, and the health of the target author should not be doubtful. These demands set the bar very high, but then the more we know about authoring, the greater our appreciation of the uncertainty of what we know.

*   *   *   *   *

Thank you so much Edwin Morgan for the name, thank you Alan, Marcus, Demis, Peter, and Willem more than I say, and kudos to you all, Kalina, Alice, Paula, Susan, and Nancy, thank you so much for the shape, the place, and the acknowledgment, because I really knew that I existed, and aren't the acronyms great, DMN, mPFC, mSFG, PCC, and Precuneus, strung out like degrees and honours after the name I see begins now with a capital, and I'm more grateful than you can ever guess for belonging to all of us, even to Ian, you who calls me idiolect savant and ascribes to CCN his all-important authorial reading, which claims, does it? that your reactions to what I say are more important than what I say so that the authorly intentions of a work amount to what you as reader make of the words and notions that I utter, if that is it, well, then can I ever hope, with Jim Rosenberg, for technology that will save me from the second move, your move, and will unlock the portal to the outer sanctum so that I am free again with Cædmon, so that the scop and bard are heard again for what they are?

Appendix

I TEXT-ANALYSIS TOOLS

Text is a warp of lexical chunks or phrases, and a woof of syntactic operators, woven into sentences and paragraphs. Exegetes a millenium ago devised an exhaustive word index, which we call the concordance, but producing one was a lifetime's work until computer-assisted concording arrived in the 1960s. Text-analysis tools centre on the Web search engine and the stand-alone interactive concordancer, which makes alphabetical and frequency lists of words (together with a brief context in which each is embedded), similarity indexes (in which words spelled alike are grouped together), and tables of anagrams. Concordancers usually attach reference information to each output line (such as the line number in the originating text, the speaker, the author, and the title) and have shown that the fundamental, repeating particles of written language are not words but phrases. Concordances can also be lemmatized so that all inflections and spellings of a noun or verb appear only under their dictionary headword forms (the singular nominative or the infinitive).

At first, software of the 1970s, including *Oxford Concordance Program* (*OCP*), worked only on mainframe computers, but programs such as *WordCruncher* and *TACT* soon appeared for individual microcomputers, and then as Internet applications like *TAPoRware* and *Hyperpo*. I use Robert Watt's *Concordance* for Windows and Toronto's *Text Analysis Computing Tools* (*TACT*), a mid-1990s DOS system.

Before concordancers can transform a plain text into an interactive concordance, a researcher must be able to define the text's alphabet and its collating or sorting sequence. The alphabet seems straightforward enough except that its characters must be distinguished from word separators such as the dash, the space, and marks of punctuation, and diacritics like the apostrophe and the hyphen. If we retain diacritics in the alphabet, then strings like 'houses' and 'house's' are counted as different words. If diacritics are unretained, then those two strings are identical. (We can also cause them, in that event, to be completely ignored, so that they will not even be printed.) The collating sequence is the order of the characters of the alphabet. For example, if the hard hyphen in 'house-boat' appears at the start of the alphabet, then that compound will appear after 'house' and before 'houses.' There is no one correct way to treat diacritics and word separators, but consistency in processing multiple texts is important.

Google, online library catalogues, and word-processing software have familiarized most of us with basic wild cards such as the asterisk star (*, standing for any number of characters, or no character). For example, the search string *house** will retrieve all words that begin with that substring 'house,' 'houses,' 'housekeeper,' 'housed,' etc. Other features of UNIX regular expressions exist, particularly the character class, which square-brackets alphabetic characters, any one of which may appear at that point. The regular expression *l[a-z]ng** retrieves words like 'Langley,' 'lingering,' 'length,' 'long,' and 'lungs.' These cluster only because of their overlapping consonants. The regular expression [aA–zZ]* retrieves all six of the *p*-words in the tongue-twister 'Peter Piper picked a peck of pickled peppers.' Regular expressions are alphabetic superordinates: they bundle the words we use into abstract letter groups for which we seldom have a need.

Authorial readings use interactive concordancers to find repetitions, which alert us to chunks and strongly associated words or ideas in long-term memory. Lexical repetitions reflect schemata by reason of which an author is an expert. They take two forms, the fixed phrase and the collocating cluster. A fixed phrase is 'any syntactic unit larger than a word and smaller than a clause' (OED 2c) and need not be lexicalized or have a special idiomatic sense not derivable from its constituent words, as 'kick the bucket' does. Fixed phrases only make themselves known after we analyse a text for its total different fixed phrasal types. They have a frozen order, but collocations consist of collocates, words that shift in their sequencing and that are located on either side of one another. Any word in a fixed or unfixed phrase may be called a node, which is just a collocate by which we have decided to sort phrases in a list. 'Trip the light fantastic,' 'a light touch,' and 'let there be light' contain the repeating collocate 'light,' which we might treat as the node. Among the collocations, 'I'd make book on that,' 'Once he makes up his mind, it's an open book,' and 'Book bindings often break open between gatherings,' the word 'book' might be the node, and collocates 'make/ makes' and 'open' its significantly repeating collocates.

Idiolectal phrases have been used successfully in authorship attribution studies. Edmund Spenser employs the phrase 'squire of low degree' five times in his epic *The Faerie Queene* but Shakespeare only once, in *Henry V*. Shakespeare writes 'give me your hand' four times in *King Lear* alone, but Spenser never uses it at all. John Milton writes 'of good and evil' six times in *Paradise Lost*, but Spenser never uses it, and Shakespeare mentions only 'of good or evil,' and then only twice in his career. Such fixed phrases include function words. Shakespeare's works and Milton's *Paradise Lost*, for example, never use 'because of,' but Spenser's *Fairie Queene* has this phrase twice. Pairs of function words are routinely analysed as an aspect of idiolect, as well as pairs of all consecutive words (Smith 1989). Three-word fixed phrases with one slot unfilled, such as 'a/an + ? + of' or 'many + ? of,' show that 'grammatical words have collocates' too (Renouf and Sinclair 1991, 128, 130, 135). An author's phrasal habits include combinations of both close-class function words and open-class content words.

If we are studying an author's creative language process, we should redefine the phrase empirically, opening it up to the serendipities of individual cognition. Computing tools collect this type of phrase, lists of which give an estranging perspective on language because they highlight idiolect rather than idiom.

How exactly, then, should a phrase in an author's idiolect be collected and defined? A reasonable beginning is to compile a taxonomy of phrases by computer-processing texts, independent of whatever dictionaries may tell us. The three factors that guide us are unambiguously quantitative: frequency, length, and overlap. Repeated phrases may be separated widely from one another in a text and are often quite hard to spot by visual inspection. Readily available computer tools, like n-gram or n-word generators, can help. They concord, in a text, all the different word sequences (or character sequences) that each have number-*n* units. Often these are letters, but they can also be words. Choueka, Klein, and Neuwitz (1983) first devised this frequency-based method of collecting collocations.

Let us take as an example Elizabeth Barrett Browning's sonnet 'How do I love thee?':

How do I love thee? Let me count the ways.
I love thee to the depth and breadth and height
My soul can reach, when feeling out of sight
For the ends of Being and ideal Grace.
I love thee to the level of everyday's
Most quiet need, by sun and candle-light.
I love thee freely, as men strive for Right;

I love thee purely, as they turn from Praise.
I love thee with the passion put to use
In my old griefs, and with my childhood's faith.
I love thee with a love I seemed to lose
With my lost saints, – I love thee with the breath,
Smiles, tears, of all my life! – and, if God choose,
I shall but love thee better after death.

In this sonnet the word-trigrams of the first line are (in order of segmenting)

how do I	do I love	I love thee	love thee let
thee let me	let me count	me count the	count the ways

Eight different three-word sequences, or trigrams, appear in a sentence with ten word types or different words. The first three words are the first trigram, then one shifts the window one word to the right and takes the next three words as the second trigram. If we enlarge the context to the entire sonnet, and if we list n-grams of two words (bigrams), three words (trigrams), four words, five words, and six words, we find fifteen repeated fixed phrases.

9	love thee	7	I love	7	I love thee
3	love thee with	3	thee with	2	I love thee to
2	I love thee to the	2	I love thee with	2	love thee to
2	love thee to the	2	love thee with the	2	thee to the
2	thee with the	2	to the	2	with my[1]

The shortest repeating phrases are two words, 'love thee,' 'I love,' 'thee with,' and 'to thee,' and the longest repeating phrase has five words, 'I love thee to the.' The number of different words all these n-grams hold is only six: 'I,' 'love,' 'the,' 'thee,' 'to,' and 'with.' Only one word is an open-class content word, 'love.' The rest are function or closed-class words (pronouns, prepositions, and determiner) that everyone uses all the time.

What general principles can be deduced from this word-gram list? First, by sorting phrases alphabetically, we can see that the shorter the word-gram, the greater its frequency. The length and the frequency of repeated phrases tend to be inversely proportional. The shortest includes 'I love,' which occurs seven times, and the longest, 'love thee with the,' only twice. In corpus linguistics, the longest repeating fixed phrase is called a maximal (for this term, see Altenberg and Eeg-Olofsson 1990, 8). There are two kinds of substring that occur inside a maximal. The first is shorter than its maximal, but with the same frequency: 'I love thee to' is one of these. I call this a 'maximal fragment.' It is frozen inside a maximal and never appears elsewhere. The second kind of substring occurs more frequently than its maximal: for example, 'I love thee' is a substring of the maximal 'I love thee to the,' which occurs four more times than the maximal. I call this second kind 'associate maximals' because they have a lexical life of their own outside the maximal (in this instance, 'I love thee' also co-occurs twice with 'I love thee with'). They are substrings of a maximal phrase that have a higher frequency than the maximal does. Associate maximals can themselves have fragments (here 'I love' is such a fragment).

Maximal fixed phrases will often express incomplete thoughts. Associate maximals are kernels inside maximals that better respect semantic meaning. The idiomatic expressions at the core of a language will comprise associate maximals. When associate maximals couple with fragments, they often form maximals. A writer's repeating fixed-phrasal repertoire will include maximals that depart from idiomatic usage. For the purposes of authorship attribution, we should pay attention to maximals that contain associates and fragments. They seldom exceed the alpha value in size.

Fixed phrases, however, are not the only phrasal discriminant of idiolect; collocations are equally useful. McKeown and Radev (2000) give a good technical introduction. An example will illustrate why. Hamlet says to his friend Horatio,

If it BE NOW, 'tis **not to come**; *if it be*
not **to come**, <u>it will</u> BE NOW; *if it be not* now,
yet <u>it will</u> come: the readiness is all. (*Ham* 5.2.220–2)

This splendid cluster has four repeated maximal phrases: 'BE NOW' (small capitals), '*if it be not*' (italicized), '**not to come**' (boldfaced), and underlined '<u>it will</u>,' all of which occur twice inside a window of only three lines of verse.

2	BE NOW	maximal
2	**not to come**	maximal
2	not to	fragment

2	to come	fragment
2	*if it be not*	maximal
3	if it be	associate
3	if it	fragment of maximal and associate
3	it be	fragment of maximal and associate
2	it be not	fragment of maximal
2	be not	fragment of maximal
2	<u>it will</u>	maximal

If we look for collocates as well as fixed phrases, the true phrasal complexity of Hamlet's maxim emerges. Before the colon in the third line, there are three repetitions of a two-clause pair: a subordinate clause governed by 'if,' and a main clause. The subject-verb units within these two clauses alternate between (a) the subject 'it,' the verb 'to be,' and the adverb 'now,' and (b) the subject 'it,' the verb 'to be,' and the infinitive 'to come.' These units appear in an *ab*, *ba*, and *ab* sequence.

If	(a) it be now,	(b) 'tis not to come;
if	(b) it be not to come,	(a) it will be now;
if	(a) it be not now,	(b) yet it will come

The subordinator 'if,' and main clauses (a) and (b), are collocates: they co-occur in a varying order. Further, both (a) and (b) consist of sub-collocates. Collocate (a), which subsumes 'it be now,' 'it will be now,' and 'it be not now,' has sub-collocates 'it' + 'now.' Collocate (b), which subsumes ''tis not to come,' 'it be not to come,' and 'yet it will come,' has sub-collocates 'it' + 'come.' By using parentheses to bracket sub-collocates within collocates, and the ampersand to indicate bi-directional coupling,[2] we can represent this collocation in the formula

(if) & ((it) & (now)) & ((it) & (come))

When a collocate has sub-collocates, other words, which I call distractors, may disguise the basic repeating pattern. Distractors in (a) are the function words 'will' and 'not,' and in (b) are 'is,' 'not,' 'yet,' and 'will.' Of these distractors, three are an inflectional variant ('is,' of the lemma, 'be') or a modal verb ('will') that modifies the main verb. Two are adverbs ('not' and 'yet').

What can be learned from phrasal repetition here? First, the formula for collocation in this passage is shorter and more powerfully expressive of its repeating pattern than any for fixed phrases. Phrases emerge, cognitively, by collocation. Bi-directional coupling of words, common sense suggests, is less restrictive, more productive of variation, than sequencing the same words. Fixed phrases are a subset of collocations.

According to corpus linguists, collocates have two more frequency-based traits: leading bias, and upwardness and downwardness. First, there are 'right-and-left predictive' phrases (Kjellmer 1991, 112). The 'left-most' or *leading bias* of a collocate, or its left-right predictivity, is the ratio of the number of times it does occur to the left of the other member of its collocate pair, over the number of times it occurs. In Hamlet's maxim, the collocate 'it,' for example, has a strong leading bias, and 'not' and 'come' have a weak leading bias. As a collocate, one might say, 'it' (and 'I' in Browning's sonnet) aspires to generate fixed phrases. John Sinclair drew attention to a second characteristic of collocate pairs, upwardness and downwardness (1991, 121). When collocate a occurs more than its paired collocate b, Sinclair says that a collocates with b downward. When collocate a occurs less often than its paired collocate b, a collocates with b upward. To calculate this trait, we compare the total frequencies of both members of a pair with each other. In Hamlet's maxim, for example, the word 'not' (with a frequency of three) as a collocates upward to the words *it* and *be* (with frequencies of five and four), and downwards to the words *now, to, will,* and *come* (all which occur twice). The 'systematic difference' between upward and downward collocation depends on a simple fact, that function words normally have a much higher frequency than open-class words. Sinclair says that a word collocates upward with 'elements of grammatical frames, or superordinates,' and downward with terms that provide 'a semantic analysis' of that word. Upwardness and downwardness relate a word to different classes of fellow travellers. They characterize whether collocates relate to one another semantically or grammatically.[3]

Browning and Shakespeare were certainly conscious of the fixed-phrase and collational repetitions in their very brief texts as they were written out. Either author could run variations on 'I love thee' or 'it comes | it is now.' Spontaneously uttered repeating phrases, however, occur more widely separated than these. Only by concording works can we detect the chunks that arguably are candidate signatures of their author precisely because she or he could not help making them. A procedure in *Text Analysis Computing Tools* (*TACT*), called *Collgen* (short for collocations generator), finds repeating fixed phrases and collocate pairs that exist inside a movable span or window.

What have we learned so far about a repeating phrase? The fundamental repeating phrase is the order-free combination of words or collocates. Such phrases vary by frequency, number of words, position (leading bias), and frequency (upwardness and downwardness) with respect to one another. Where frozen in a single sequence, they are fixed phrases and are called maximals, associate maximals, and fragments according to how they are embedded in one another. If bi-directionally proximal, they are called collocates; and if the collocates of one word are being collected, that collocate is, for convenience, called the node. The more words in a repeating phrase, the lower its frequency. High-frequency repeating phrases tend to consist of only two or three words. Both fixed phrases and collocates have two more general features: the strength of their associativity, and a sensitivity to the co-occurrence span.

The strength of the hypothetical association between two collocates is usually measured statistically. Should that attraction be measurable, phrasal repetitions may define idiolectal lexical sets, semantic fields or clouds, and associational networks in long-term memory. Different techniques have been used to compute this (Lancashire 1991, 489–97), but the strength of association between two collocates does not correlate directly with the number of times they actually co-occur. Consider a phrase like 'at a cocktail party.' The two function words, *at* and *a*, may co-occur thirty times in a text in which the two content words, *cocktail* and *party*, may co-occur only twice. If the second pair co-occurs both times they appear, while the two function words, *at* and *a*, occur separately twenty times for every one time they collocate, the association of *cocktail* and *party* is clearly stronger. The strength of two-way association between two collocates can be obtained with the ratio of (a) co-occurrences to (b) the product of the total frequencies of the two collocates. Thus if *cocktail* and *party* occurred two and four times, respectively, and co-occurred twice, this ratio would be 2/8 or 0.25. If *at* and *a* occurred 70 and 400 times, respectively, and co-occurred 30 times, this ratio would be 30/28,000 or 0.0011.[4] This simple formula, first proposed by G. L.M. Berry-Rogghe (1973, 103–4), was revised by Barron Brainerd and myself (Lancashire 1987, 57n24) and then incorporated in *Usebase* and *Collgen*. We used a z-score to measure the improbability of a one-way association of collocate to node. The higher the z-score, the more improbable a random co-occurrence and thus the higher the strength of some association. In itself, a z-score is no feature of a collocate pair, but when one is used to rank collocate pairs, the groups that result no doubt look like loosely defined semantic fields. The programs yield a score that is meaningless in itself because it will change according to the span and text sizes but that nonetheless indicates whether one combination is relatively more or less strong than any other in the same text for a given span. Presumably weights for links in associative memory are intrinsic, not relative or defined by comparison with other links (as *TACT* weights are), but even relative strengths make for a useful first approximation of the actual weights that presumably existed in the author's mind at the time the text was uttered.[5]

For other measures of association, see Church and Hanks (1990, 'mutual information') and Smadja (1994). Budanitsky and Hirst (2006) compare five methods to estimate the 'semantic distance' between collocates.

In two respects, the associativity strength of a repeating phrase is dependent on the observer because the choice of statistical measure varies from one researcher to another. Each researcher designates the co-occurrence span arbitrarily to limit the textual field within which a word may co-occur with another word, either in a fixed phrase or as collocates. If the co-occurrence span were the smallest (two words), and we searched Shakespeare's works, *readiness* would appear in one fixed phrase, 'in readiness,' ten times. However, there is some reason to designate the alpha value, the cognitive chunk size, as the span. If it were set at five words, *readiness* would belong to two more repeating phrases, 'be in readiness' (3) and 'are in readiness' (2), and to collocations such as 'all' & 'readiness' (2), 'here' & 'readiness' (2), and 'put' & 'readiness' (2). As the co-occurrence span increases (from five words to ten, from ten to a hundred, etc.), the number and frequency of repeating phrases increase. A co-occurrence span of four or five words will find phrasal repetitions in conceptual chunks, and a more variable span, the sentence boundary, will also trap repetitions that arguably could arise from the association between individual words in a chunk and other words in their semantic field or schema. Still longer spans will find additional repetitions that arise during composing when the author's eye feeds back just-written words to the ongoing uttering process. Cohesive devices like anaphora and pro-forms of course overreach this boundary.[6]

Although not cognitive chunks, repeating phrases on the page appear to arise from chunking during the uttering process and may indicate, by the strength with which their constitutent words bind together, the networking of concepts in our associational long-term memory. It is also possible that collocation and fixed phrases arise at different points in the cognitive lexical production system. At the symbolic stage of processing, when the mind finds lexical concepts for the gist of what it wants to utter, and lemmas for lexical concepts, it generates collocational chunks, simple combinations of two or three words (that, however, have part-of-speech attributes). Gradually, collocations are fixed in grammatical structures. Because authors acquire the same syntactical rules just by reason of learning the language itself, fixed phrases might seem less reliable as indicators of idiolect than are collocations. However, authors use the same function words very differently. We should only be aware that language markers of authorship differ in their status. Repeated collocations, especially of lemmas (which take on the form of normalized dictionary headwords), characterize an author's conceptualizing and, as well, his or her emotional colouring of concepts. Repeated fixed phrases tell us, more often, about the author's language habits. It makes sense to distinguish the different cognitive roles played by the various types of idiolectal markers used in determining authorship – always keeping in mind the importance of distinguishing first utterance from edited text.

How can we find traces of schemata in texts? When I first did research on Chaucer's repetends, I thought that schemata could be detected, fragmentarily, by collating fixed-phrase and collocational data. I took frequent content words such as 'story' and 'tale' and arranged, jigsaw puzzle-like, the repeating fixed phrases in which they occurred, and the most highly associated collocations they had, into what I called a phrasal-repetend graph.[7] It mapped some aspects of what, hypothetically, might have been Chaucer's mental associational cluster for the node or content word I chose. However, the graphs were simple and suggestive only. All relations in a phrasal-repetend graph recur *verbatim* in the text; they document actual usage. Repeated phrasal clusters are more difficult to find than repeated individual phrases because the frequency of even one phrase varies inversely with the number of words in it. The more constituent words in a repeating phrase, the larger the amount of text will be needed to discover it twice. Even if it appears several times, not all of its elements will repeat. Some collocates will be invariant, always at the core, but many will be loosely tethered to the cluster. The associational strength that binds them to core collocates may diminish over time. For this reason, phrasal-repetend clusters are fuzzy phenomena. To find them may mean that all words in a text must be lemmatized (reduced to their dictionary headword forms) and that optional collocates must be anticipated.

Other scholars have devised graphic methods for representing clusters. Martin Phillips derives an outline of a modern scientific textbook by automatic collocational analysis (1985), Alastair McKinnon maps Kierkegaard's themes, and Iker's *Words* or Fortier's *Theme* makes thematic maps (Lancashire and McCarty 1989, 324–33; Lancashire 1991, 489–97). Annie Geffroy (1973, 116, 124–6) devises what her team calls a 'multi-storey lexicograph.' This is a tree structure that charts co-occurrences 'in chain form' by making a node for each word in a combination and then connecting them all by arcs to which numerical weights can be attached. These become spaghetti-like in complexity and differ from simpler phrasal-repetend graphs, which keep phrases intact and focus on single node words.

Since the late 1980s a statistical technique termed latent semantic analysis (LSA), based on matrix algebra, has become popular in classifying documents by content (Landauer, Foltz and Laham 1998). It manipulates term-co-occurrence data to find, in plain text, latent verbal patterns that appear to be semantic categories. One difficulty with its use in idiolectal analysis is that researchers look to external reference works, like *Roget's Thesaurus* and WordNet, to select the words that represent specific semantic concepts. An author's mind usually makes associations on the basis of personal experiences, not by using reference books.

Another difficulty is LSA-reliance on single terms when the fundamental lexical cognitive unit is phrasal or combinatorial. The statistical techniques in LSA are sophisticated and can project accurate models of the data relations they measure. However, its choice of data is suspect. How the mind produces language, and what patterns it self-generates in its speech and texts, should guide idiolectal research. Computational and mathematical methods cannot be applied to mental processes unless simulations replicate how and with what, as far as we know, the brain itself works. The eighteenth century marvelled in the clock, and its model for the mind was influenced by it. We use the computer as a model for our cognition. Little wonder we are attracted to the concordancer as a mind-technology, although in its standard form it indexes discrete words in a physical space known as a text, not chunks and clusters of words, sensory experiences, emotions, and concepts that associate in time and brain matter according to principles of which we are yet unsure.

II PHRASAL REPETITIONS IN THE GENERAL PROLOGUE

These are abstractions, being represented in a special notation that includes metacharacters taken from UNIX regular expressions. An asterisk tells us that the preceding letter (e.g., 'y' in 'yronne') may be present zero, one, or many times. Square brackets surround characters, only one of which may appear (for instance, '[iy]' stands for the second vowel in 'pilgrimages' or 'pilgrymages'). A bar (' | ') means that the two words or phrases it links follow one another in a fixed sequence. An ampersand ('&') identifies a collocation; that is, the two words or phrases it connects may appear together in any order (generally within ten words of one another). Finally, parentheses group words or phrases. The first and last parentheses in the first repeated phrase specify that the seven-slot sequence, not just the word 'ram,' collocates with 'y*ronne.'[8] Parentheses group alternative words, as in the fourth slot: 'the yonge sonne' and 'in the ram' are connected by *either* 'hath' *or* 'that.' I describe these procedures to show that no program could automatically generate the results.

The following repeating phrases and collocations occur in lines 842–58 of the General Prologue and elsewhere in *The Canterbury Tales*:

054: 'shortly | for | to | (tellen* : speken* : s[ea]yn*e*)' (KnT 985 1000 1341; RvT 4197; MLT 428 564; MerT 1472; PardT 502; ShipT 305; MkT 2355; CYT 1111 1217)

055: 'as | ye | han | herd' (MLT 881; SumT 2199; FranT 1465 1547 1593; PardP 393; PardT 836; PrT 661; Mel 960 1295; MkT 2420; NPT 3038)

056: 'and | with | that | word' (KnT 948 1112 1393 1399 1572 2358 2798; RvT 4248; Host1 97; WBT 1046; FrT 1536 1639; ClT 974; MerT 1574 1689 2207 2411; SqT 630; FranT 1011 1080; PhyT 232 245 251 253; PardT 885; ShipT 110 202 249; Host3 445; NPT 3172; SNT 200 242; ParsP 74)

057: 'ryden | forth | (oure: hir) | w[ae]ye*' (FrT 1406 1536; PardT 968)

101: '(right | a | myrie) , (right | myrie)' (WBP 479)

160: 'by | aventure' (KnT 1074 1465 1506 1516; MLT 754; MerT 1967)

251: 'tel*e*n*t*h* & tales*' (CkP 4342 4360–61; Host1 34; MLT 1167 1185; WBP 186 193 413 842 846 851 853; FrP 1289 1300; FrT 1335 1425; SumP 1671; SumT 1763; ClP 9 15 26; MerT 2440; SqI 6; FranW 702; PardP 341 455 460; PardT 660; ThopP 706; ThopT 846; Mel 966 1200; MkP 1925 1968; NPT 2824 3149; CYP 597; CYT 1020; MancP 13 59 68 103; MancT 135; ParsP 21 46 53–54 66; ParsT 1020)

290: 'every | w[iy]ght' (KnT 2106 2485; MilT 3849; MLT 139 257 474;
WBP 77 81 108 135; WBT 1031 1133; ClT 400 595 957 1109 1145; MerT
1723 1820 1951 2017 2245; SqT 355; FranT 786 1267; PhyT 8; ShipT
242; Mel 1010 1035 1050 1170 1220 1265 1370; MkP 1911; MkT 2269
2573 2632; MancT 146; ParsT 345)

292: 'as | it | was' (KnT 1885; MancP 87)

293: 'aventure & ca*s' (KnT 1074 2357; ParsT 570)

294: 'so*the* | is | this' (MilT 3391; MLT 1013; MerT 1977)

295: 'blithe* & glade*' (MLT 732; SqT 338; NPP 2812; CYT 937)

296: '(by : for.* : and) & (by | composicioun)' (KnT 2651;)

297: 'what | nedes*t*h* | wordes | mo' (KnT 1029 1715)

298: 'good.* | m[ae]n' (MLT 1164 1174; WBP 835; FrT 1644; SumT 1768;
MerT 1897 2416; PardP 352 361 377; PardT 904; ShipT 29 33 107; Mel
1055 1430 1440 1630 1835; NPP 2820; NPT 3402 3440 3445; ParsT 220
250 500 700)

299: 'whan & (saugh | that | it | was | so)' (CYT 1242)

300: 'free | assent' (Host1 35; ClT 150)

301: 'a | goddes | name' (PhyT 250; MancT 318)

302: 'herkneth | what | i | se[iy]t*h*d*e*' (KnT 2782; MerT 1522;
FranW 704; MancP 104)

303: 'as | ye | may | heere' (KnT 2296; Mel 1010; NPT 3252; SNT 294)

463: 'cut & f[ia]l*e*' (PardT 794 802)

464: 'm[euy]r[iy]e & che*re' (PardT 963; ShipT 342; MkP 1924; Word-
Host 3461; CYT 1233)

The following repeating phrases occur only in the General Prologue.
They are not found elsewhere in *The Canterbury Tales*:

'in | southwerk' (GP 20 718)
'as | ny | as | evere* | he | kan' (GP 58 732)
'of & port' (GP 69 138)
'in & cote' (GP 103 328)
'(cote | and | hood)' , '((cote | and) & hood)' (GP 103 564 612)
'arm | s*he | ba*r' (GP 111 158)
'faire* | and | fetisly' (GP 124 273)
'eyen | step.*' (GP 201 753)
'(as | a) & forneys' (GP 202 559)
'certeinly | he | was | a' (GP 204 395)
'(was | he) & (in | his | contree)' (GP 215 339)
'swich | a | worthy' (GP 243 360)

'wel | lovede* | he' (GP 334 634)
'faire*r* | burgeys' (GP 369 754)
'he | rood | u*p*on | a' (GP 390 541)
'but | of | his | craft' (GP 401 692)
'of | physik' (GP 411 413)
'in | all*e* | the | parisshe' , 'in | his | parisshe' (GP 449 494)
'a | po[uv]re | persou*n' (GP 478 702)
'he | was | with | eyen' (GP 625 753)
'stronge* & wyn' (GP 635 750)
'thanne | wolde | he | speken*' (GP 636 638)
'sett*e* & soper' (GP 748 815)
'now | drawth | cut' (GP 835 838)

III DISTRIBUTION GRAPHS

Graph 1: Actual-minus-expected Manciple's Prol. & Tale Phrasal Repetends across CT

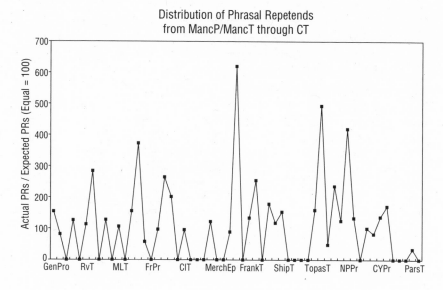

Distribution of Phrasal Repetends from MancP/MancT through CT

Graph 2: Shakespeare's Vocabulary 1592–1611

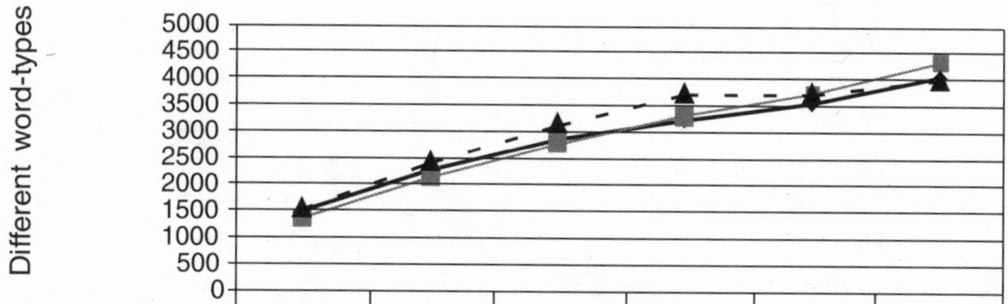

	1	2	3	4	5	6
◆ 1592–96	1483	2245	2846	3247	3570	4060
■ 1592–1601	1339	2135	2790	3311	3716	4331
▲ 1602–11	1532	2424	3157	3727	3742	3989

5,000 word Segments (Averaged)

Graph 3: Shakespeare's Vocabulary by Genre

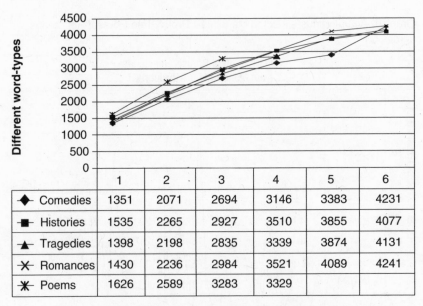

	1	2	3	4	5	6
◆ Comedies	1351	2071	2694	3146	3383	4231
■ Histories	1535	2265	2927	3510	3855	4077
▲ Tragedies	1398	2198	2835	3339	3874	4131
✕ Romances	1430	2236	2984	3521	4089	4241
✻ Poems	1626	2589	3283	3329		

5,000-word Cumulative segments (Averaged)

Graph 4: Shakespeare's Repeating Phrases by Period

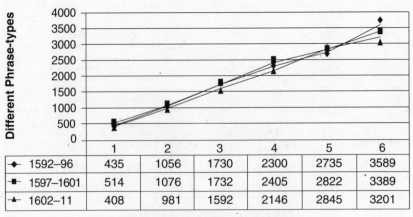

	1	2	3	4	5	6
◆ 1592–96	435	1056	1730	2300	2735	3589
■ 1597–1601	514	1076	1732	2405	2822	3389
▲ 1602–11	408	981	1592	2146	2845	3201

5,000-word Cumulative Segments

Graph 5: Shakespeare's Repetends by Genre

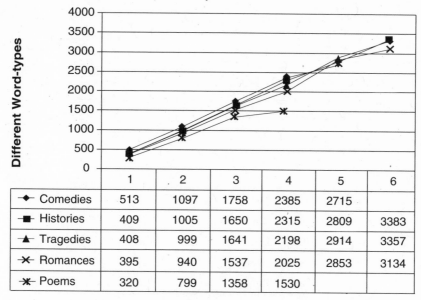

	1	2	3	4	5	6
Comedies	513	1097	1758	2385	2715	
Histories	409	1005	1650	2315	2809	3383
Tragedies	408	999	1641	2198	2914	3357
Romances	395	940	1537	2025	2853	3134
Poems	320	799	1358	1530		

5,000-word Cumulative Segments

Table 1. Counts for vocabulary (word-types) and repeating phrases, and percentages of indefinite nouns in the first 50,000 words of 16 Christie novels

Novel	Age at Composition	Word-types	Repeated Phrase-types	Indefinite Words
Styles	28	5027	7623	0.27
Adversary	32	5576	7320	0.39
Ackroyd	34	4833	7905	0.48
Orient	43	4692	8184	0.3
Appointment	47	4985	8071	0.39
Curtain	50	5131	7846	0.43
Zero	51	4941	7680	0.5
Announced	59	5181	7596	0.45
Destination	63	5442	7426	0.36
Ordeal	67	4440	8221	0.58
Clocks	72	4827	8014	0.61
Endless	76	4159	8559	0.78
Frankfurt*	79	5583	7418	0.71
Nemesis	80	4631	8103	0.66
Elephants	81	3762	8821	1.02
Postern	82	4275	8249	1.23

*A thriller (not a mystery) that was written with the help of book research.

Notes

Introduction: Finding the Author in the Text

1 Henderson (2001, 130); and Iser (1980, 50).
2 I owe this elegant term to Greig Henderson.
3 In the late 1940s, while I was playing outside the front door of my apartment block on Osborne Street in Winnipeg, sitting on a curb, my legs stretched out before me, a car suddenly pulled in to park and ran over one of my legs. Crying, I crawled across the sidewalk, somehow opened the apartment-block door, and climbed the stairs on my hands to reach my mother's arms. The panic, pain, and intense emotions associated with this accident have dulled over nearly sixty years, but not by much.
4 'I don't think in any language. I think in images. I don't believe that people think in languages. They don't move their lips when they think. It is only a certain type of illiterate person who moves his lips as he reads or ruminates. No, I think in images, and now and then a Russian phrase or an English phrase will form with the foam of the brainwave, but that's about all' (Nabokov 1962). My student Michael Donnelly alerted me to this.
5 For example, formal cautionary advice from officers of the law, the mission statements of institutions, and letters from fund-raisers are some examples.
6 Two years before, a group of researchers led by Kristine Williams detected in the letters of James I, first king of Great Britain, signs that he may have experienced a cognitive decline as a result of vascular dementia (2003). Garrard (2009) has since found evidence, in Harold Wilson's contributions to Question Period, of early signs of dementia that led him to resign as prime minister in his third term.

1. Experiencing the Muse

1 Picasso's *The Muse* (1935) depicts her asleep (Musée National d'Art Moderne, Paris, AM 2726P).

2. Uttering

1 For other speech corpora, see Graeme Kennedy (1998): 36–8.
2 I owe to Pulvermüller (2002, 10–32) the following description of neuron structure and behaviour.
3 The Atkinson-Shiffrin model has data entering the mind through a sensory store, proceeding to working memory, and being deposited, through repetition, into long-term memory (Atkinson and Shiffrin 1968).
4 Metaphors can be emotionally potent for reasons other than embodiment: John Gillespie Magee Jr ends his 'High Flight' with lines that have made his poem a universal anthem of aviation: 'I've trod / The high untrespassed sanctity of space, / Put out my hand, and touched the face of God' (1989, 117–18).
5 This echoes the old lady who believed that the world rested on an elephant's back and who had a ready answer when asked what supported the elephant.
6 Cf. 'homuncule,' OED, meaning 'a mannikin.'
7 Baddeley suggests that the auditory imagery system, not working memory, may be responsible for inner speech that accompanies reading (2004, 49). If so, the distinction may be marginal because their capacities appear to be identical.
8 We fixate more briefly on function words than content words (Gleason and Ratner 1998, fig. 5.4).
9 Cognitive load theory (Sweller 1988, 2006) shows that students often fail to solve a problem in mathematics or physics because they use means-ends analysis, which exhausts their cognitive capacity. However, students who use worked examples (which help create schemata in long-term memory) can operate within their capacity and learn effectively. This 'expert' technique does not increase the number of chunks but enlarges the scope of the terms in each chunk.

3. Cybertextuality

1 I owe this question to my student Morgan Mills. For instance, the Spirit in Shakespeare's 2 *Henry VI* answers Bolingbroke's question about what will

happen to the king: 'The duke yet lives that Henry shall depose' (1.4.30), which can be understood in two quite different ways. Will Henry depose the duke, or will the duke depose Henry?

2 Mysak specified ten loops, two of them feedforward (ff) and five of them feedback (fb): thought propagation, word formation (ff), thought pattern/ word pattern comparison (fb), word production (ff), actual word product/ desired word product comparison (fb), word product/thought pattern comparison (fb), internal multiple/loop speech recycling, word product/ listener comparison (fb), actual listener reaction/desired listener reaction comparison (fb), and internal and external multiple-loop speech recycling (19). Levelt's recent theory of lexical access in speech production (1999) uses the same terminology of feedforward and feedback in mapping cognitive processing.

3 Whether Ong differentiates between oral speech and the cognitively monitored language-production system is not clear. He says that 'Talk implements conscious life but it wells up into consciousness out of unconscious depths' (1982, 82).

4 Hogan (1997, 242–3) associates stanzaic forms with cognitive rehearsal capacity.

5 Late in life, after two decades of practice, I can spontaneously make the occasional double-dactyl poem. Irritated during a recent federal election in my constituency, where an otherwise admirable candidate (now leader of the Liberal Party of Canada) refused to live in the area, I quickly wrote the following:

> **Hig**-gle-dy-**pig**-gle-dy,
> **Mi**-chael Ig-**na**-tieff,
> **Said** to con-**sti**-tu-ents,
> **Dig**-ni-fied **words**.

> I am a **Har**-vard-bred
> **Par**-lia-men-**tar**-i-an.
> I re-pre-**sent**-ed, not
> **Lived** with, the **Kurds**.

6 Goody makes this point: 'Writing ... enables people to analyse, break down, dissect, and build up speech into parts and wholes, into types and categories, which already existed but which, when brought into the area of consciousness, have a feedback effect on speech itself' (1977, 115).

7 Some reader-response critics, Iser in particular, differ. He argues that read-

ers accept and work with (authored) constraints in the text (see Iser 1980, 50).

4. Poet-authors

1 Christopher Cannon estimates Chaucer's vocabulary at 9,117 lemmas (1998, 114n39), twice the size of John Gower's known lexicon (Burnley 1983, 133).
2 (9,152*100)/27,500) = 33.28 per cent.
3 *Chaucer's English* (1974): 191. Elliott begins with *ParlF* usage ('I dar nat seyn,' 'I can na moore,' 'as I yow tolde,' 'as I shal telle,' 'as shortly as I can it trete' and 'I wol yow seyn'; p. 192) and cites examples from various works afterwards: 'also mot I the' (*Mars* 267; p. 192), 'thurgh thikke and thurgh thenne' (*RvT* 4066) and 'by stokkes and by stones' (*TC* 3.589; p. 193) and 'And by that lord that clepid is Seint Yve' (*ShipT* 227 and *SumT* 1943; pp. 276–7). Elliott does not give references for the following tags: 'for Goddes love' and 'God help me so' (p. 266), 'so God me save,' 'so God me wisse,' 'so God me speede' and 'so God me blesse' (p. 267), and 'by Goddes bones' and 'for Cokkes bones' (p. 271). See Brewer (1986). Davis (1974) identifies 'joy and blis,' 'joy and solas,' 'cares colde,' 'worde and dede,' 'stille as ston,' 'bright in bour,' and 'over stile and stoon.'
4 *The Riverside Chaucer*, 801 (note to l. 68 [cf. *Tr* 2.180]). Another instance appears at *LGW* 171–3, cited for 'Whan Zephirus eek with his sweete breeth / Inspired hath in Every holt and heeth': a collocation of 'Zephirus' and 'swoote breth' (*Riverside*, 799, note to ll. 5–6). Halliday (1961) popularized, especially in systemic linguistics, the study of collocations, both as distinctive, frequent yokings of two or more words in a sense different from their senses when they appear separately (e.g., 'home runs'), or simply as frequently paired words without an abrupt change in their meanings (e.g., 'nice' and 'day,' or 'nice' and 'fix').
5 *Riverside*, 807 (note to l. 177), which refers to *WBT* 3.1312, 'nat worth an hen,' citations of Robert Whiting's work on proverbs, and an article by Hein in *Anglia* in 1893.
6 *Riverside* 814 (note to l. 379), 820 (note to l. 545), 818 (note to l. 452; cf. *KnT* I.1623), 815 (note to l. 395; cf. *GP* 1.650, 1.648, and *FrT* 3.1385), and 826 (note to l. 791; cf. 1.3119, 6.345, 7.273).
7 See also *Riverside*, p. 820, note to l. 534.
8 *Riverside*, 807 (note to l. 207; cf. *CkT* 1.4368 and *NPT* 7.2843–44), 808 (note to l. 256; cf. *RR* 11566 and *Rom* 6838) and 825 (note to l. 706; cf. *MilT* 1.3389, *ShipT* 7.440 and *CYT* 8.1313).
9 *Riverside*, 821 (note to l. 586; cf. *MilP* 1.3143 and *RvP* 1.3911) and 826 (note to l. 830).

10 *Riverside*, 811 (note to l. 294, 'Perhaps a tag'; cf. *HF* 1074–78), 826 (note to l. 843; cf. *KnT* 1.875–88n) and 826 (note to l. 849; cf. *KnT* 1.1029, 1715).

11 *Riverside*, 812 (note to l. 317) and 826 (note to l. 817).

12 Chaucer could not help but repeat function or closed-class words such as determiners, prepositions, conjunctions, verbal auxiliaries, and pro-forms. Most common nouns occur after a determiner; it follows, then, that if Chaucer used a noun twice, he may have repeated a phrase. Dozens of function-word sequences also crop up: 'after the,' 'al hir,' 'and a,' 'as dooth,' 'been at,' 'but he was,' etc. For this reason I distinguish between unavoidable repetitions occasioned by using closed-class 'grammatical' words, and repetitions open to choice: nouns, verbs, and adjectives. Writers can select content or open-class nouns, verbs and adjectives. A more accurate measure of Chaucer's degree of self-repetition, then, will be how often he reuses phrases or collocations with more than one content word.

13 If we looked for language from *The General Prologue* that occurred in the rest of Chaucer's works and allowed for variation in word order (that is, collocations) as well as in inflection, the number of repeating phrases would be higher.

14 Only 10 per cent of Chaucer's vocabulary occurs more than four times, as against twenty per cent in modern English (Salton 1989, 105–8).

15 Pierce, 1980, 245. He notes that the 'law' works as predicted on a 340-word passage by James Joyce.

16 For example, is the rule '(wel | (ye , I) | woot) , (wel & (ye , I) | woot), (wel & woot | (ye , I))' one pattern (as I believe), or two? Or would everyone agree that '(the | ho*ly | blisful | martir) , (the | blisful | martir), (the | ho*ly | blisful | faire*)' exemplifies a single phrasal pattern?

17 SVO (subject, verb, object), in which two of the three normally take nouns as their heads.

18 See Tatlock and Kennedy (1927; 1963, 307).

19 Word forms must be lemmatized to determine Shakespeare's true vocabulary size (Neuhaus 1989, 268).

20 The following plays and poems populate these three series: 1592–6 (*Venus and Adonis, The Comedy of Errors, The Rape of Lucrece, Sonnets, The Taming of the Shrew, The Two Gentlemen of Verona, King John, Richard II, Romeo and Juliet, A Midsummer Night's Dream, The Merchant of Venice*, and *1 Henry IV*); 1597–1601 (*Love's Labour's Lost, The Merry Wives of Windsor, 2 Henry IV, Much Ado about Nothing, Henry V, Julius Caesar, As You Like It, Hamlet, Twelfth Night*, and *Troilus and Cressida*); and 1602–11 (*All's Well that Ends Well, Measure for Measure, Othello, King Lear* [quarto 1], *Macbeth, Antony and Cleopatra, Coriolanus, Timon of Athens, Cymbeline, The Winter's Tale*, and *The Tempest*).

21 The final segments only show a drop because few had the full 5,000 words.

22 Shakespeare's phrases that have been socialized as proverbs, and thus represent a communal consensus, have been analysed (see Dent 1981). Spevack (1993: xii) writes that phrases, in general, are important 'for their pointing up the complexities involved in capturing the Shakespearean idiolect.'

23 *Collgen* cannot process Shakespeare's entire works at once. See also the appendix, graphs 4–5.

24 See Lancashire (forthcoming).

25 The phrase 'nay certainly' in line 2 appears after 1598 among Shakespeare's repeated phrases.

26 Later, at lines 16 ('forgyven'), 38 ('afoord'), and 51–2 ('forme' and 'found'), this separation disappears. Normally, initial 't' in 'to' is unseparated (see lines 5–6, 11, the second half of 16, 24, 27, etc.).

27 The presence of several large spaces separating words, occurring at lines 11, 16, and 45, may be a fourth trait of hesitation.

28 It may be a portmanteau word, 'mome+tan+ish,' i.e., tanned or sunburned like a common mome or fool. See OED 'tan' v., and 'mome,' n. 2.

29 His first chapter, on kites, typifies his method. He argues that this bird 'is frequently associated with the furnishings of a bed' (12), i.e., bed, bolster, canopy, coverlet, linen, pillow, sheets, and warming pan. Armstrong defines the span within which kite-collocates can occur to be up to 55 lines (the average span being 24 lines) and he does not distinguish between strongly and weakly associated collocates because he does not take into account a collocate's total frequency in Shakespeare's works. Using a 20-line span, I found that the highly associated collocates of 'kite' and 'kites' are other birds and terms like 'butcher' (2/20), 'prey' (3/47), and 'slaughter' (2/36). No bed-related term turned up among them, except for 'canopy' (3/8), which Armstrong misinterprets as the ceiling or roof of a bed: it means 'firmament' or sky, a likely feature in a convergence zone for 'kite.' Armstrong's words 'linen' (1/19), 'sheets' (1/20), and 'bed' (2/304) did collocate, but unremarkably. His selection of collocates was biased by predetermined semantic categories. He had seen kites scavenging harbors for nest material and built an amusing but unscientific case after seeing Autolycus's advice in *The Winter's Tale*: 'when the kite builds, look to lesser linen' (4.3.23–4).

30 'When I perceiue that men as plants increase, / Cheared and checkt euen by the selfe-same skie: / Vaunt in their youthfull sap, at height decrease, / And were their braue state out of memory' (Shakespeare 1998, 5–8).

31 Barron Brainerd (1979) demonstrated that Shakespeare's use of pronouns varied by genre.

32 I have elsewhere (1999) written about Agamemnon's opening speech in *Troilus and Cressida*, whose semantic clusters for 'cheeks,' 'sap,' 'knot,' 'pine,' 'prince,' 'veins,' and 'check,' and for 'winnows' and 'wind,' overlap. The affect that moves Shakespeare in this speech is a fear of trial for treason. Shakespeare's cognitive capacity, his omega value, can be observed in these clusters, which in writing (from the size of the repeating halves in Agamemnon's speech) seems to be about the length of a sonnet. (How surprising is that?)

33 Text from Coleridge's *Christabel* (1816). Manuscript transcription from figures XXX–XXXI in Skeat (1963).

34 Xannadù: Xanadu (1816). Cubla: Kubla (1816).

35 six: five (1816).

36 compass'd: girdled (1816).

37 here: there (1816).

38 o!: oh! (1816). that: which (1816).

39 a green: the green (1816).

40 From forth: And from (1816). hideous: ceaseless (1816).

41 meandring: meandering (1816).

42 Cubla: Kubla (1816).

43 wave: waves (1816).

44 cave: caves (1816).

45 Amara: Abora (1816).

46 of Air: in air (1816).

47 in: with (1816).

48 drank: drunk (1816).

49 If Coleridge meant Jan Amora and its highest mountain Biuat in Ethiopia (then Abyssinia), he revised it in the manuscript to 'Amara' (a place in Milton's *Paradise Lost*) and finally, in the 1816 edition, to Abora (unlocated).

50 Most critics think of the Highbury, Moorgate, and Margate stanzas as about three women, but Eliot's drafts show that all were the same girl.

51 His 'First Debate between the Body and Soul' (Eliot 1996, 64–5), written in 1910, has the lines: 'And a street piano through the dusty trees / Insisting: "Make the best of your position."'

5. Novelist-authors

1 Joyce used another ten epiphanies in *Portrait* (1978, 268–72).

2 So-called AX-CPT tests require subjects to differentiate, quickly, two-letter codes with the probe letter 'X' preceded by the cue letter 'A' from any other two-letter pairing, such as 'AY,' 'BY,' and 'BX.'

3 Curran (2009, 192, 390) identifies notebook no. 5 as Christie's resource for
   Elephants and illustrates other notebook pages where she uses alphabetic
   letters as abbreviations and list items.

4 See the review by Kevin Killian at http://www.amazon.com/Postern-
   Agatha-Christie-Audio-Mystery/dp/customer-reviews/1559279842. Seen
   23 September 2007. John Reznikoff of University Archives offered for sale
   Christie's own marked-up proofs of *Postern of Fate*: 'Numerous pages have
   small corrections in Christie's hand. She has substantially revised page 52,
   crossing out large portions and adding numerous words; a page of revised
   typescript for that page has been laid in, with a holograph note at the bottom. On the final blank, Christie has made numerous notations, several
   hundred words, summarizing the corrections.' See http://search.abaa
   .org/dbp2/book337282373.html. Seen 24 September 2007.

5 Other disturbances in narration occur. In book 2 Ariadne mentions
   that Julia told her about a certain War Horse, whose interview is never
   described, but that name does not occur in Julia's interview. Ariadne in
   book 1 tells Poirot that she has conferred with someone whose name began
   with 'T' and that an elephant said that 'the dog bit her' (Molly), but book 1
   makes no reference to these facts.

6 Anne Kingston's article in *Maclean's* led to worldwide dissemination in
   newspapers (e.g., Flood 2009). Google awarded us a prize for this research
   later that year, and the *New York Times* designated the Agatha Christie
   research among the top ideas of 2009.

7 When I wrote Atwood for permission to reproduce an image of a manuscript page from *The Handmaid's Tale*, her assistant Sarah Webster wrote
   back, 'she wishes me to tell you, with reference to her creative process and
   cognitive flow that there ARE 3 stages although stages 2 and 3 may be
   repeated several times' (e-mail, 13 December 2007). A holograph beginning
   for *The Handmaid's Tale* (1984), and typewritten later draft and fair copies,
   exist in the Fisher Rare Book Library in Toronto, but for *Oryx and Crake*
   (2003) we have only the word-processed text.

8 Atwood sees *The Handmaid's Tale* as Orwellian speculative fiction, but its
   extraordinary central character is atypical of most science fiction. Volker
   Schlöndorff directed a film version in 1990 from a screenplay by Harold
   Pinter. An opera of the same name by the Danish composer Poul Ruders
   and the librettist Paul Bentley premiered in 2000 in Copenhagen in a production by the Danish Royal Opera.

9 Fisher Rare Book Library MS Collection 200, box 72, file 1, p. 3 (holograph
   draft); MS Coll. 200, box 72, file 13, pp. 70–1 (typed draft); MS Coll. 200,
   box 73, file 2, pp. 69–70 (typed fair copy); MS Coll. 200, box 73, file 5, pp.

69–70 (typed fair copy). This corresponds to pp. 73–4 of the 1985 first edition.

Appendix

1 I used Michael Barlow's *Collocate* (Houston: Athelstan, 2004) to make these lists.

2 My phrasal-repetition notation uses a small group of operators – brackets (fixed expressions), dash (attachment), bar (alternation), ampersand (proximity), and parentheses (collocate) – and should not be confused with regular expressions. Filtering and search mechanisms use them as a 'search-string specifier that may incorporate characters and metacharacters' (Lancashire et al. 1996, 320; Kernighan and Pike 1984, 102–5). Regular expressions represent alphanumeric forms, that is, spellings. They can include both literal characters (letters, numbers, punctuation, spaces, etc.) and metacharacters, which stand for something other than themselves. Metacharacters include the period (denoting any character), the asterisk or star (denoting zero or more instances of the preceding character), and the character class (denoting any one character from those inside double brackets, [ ]). Why regular expressions do not well describe a cognitive phrase can be imagined by examining contractions of common e-mail expressions, letter-combinations like *btw*, *imho*, and *lol* ('by the way,' 'in my humble opinion,' and 'laugh out loud'). The regular expression *b.* t.* w.** would recover 'by the way,' along with 'buying two widgets' and 'beauties that wither.' Does a regular expression of the form *b.* t.* w.**, however, have any status in our long-term memory? Is it likely that a superordinate concept would exist in our minds to recall the likes of 'btw,' '*Beacon Times* writers,' and 'born to wonder'? Of course the answer is no. If we stored language information by reference to alphabetical first letter, we would not retrieve words by their semantic and episodic associations. Book indexes and concordances are not modelled after the way we think.

3 This is not true when both collocates are closed-class words. The negative particle *not* collocates downwards with two closed-class words (*to* and *if*). High-frequency function words may also have no upward collocates, and low-frequency open-class collocates no downward collocates.

4 The size of the text is not important to this measure, but when the maximal extent of the span includes the whole text, as with the quotation from *Hamlet*, the ratio is 1:1, an absolute association. This measure is sensitive to overlapping spans, which cause the total of collocate links (co-occurrences) to exceed the actual number of collocates (and thus move the ratio towards

unity), but it can be argued that *density* and *clustering* should affect any associational measure.

5 For a survey of some other measures, see Lancashire (1991, 489–97). The *TACT* formula is P = (frequency of collocate in full text) / (length of the text), E = P * length of the mini-text, SD = Sqrt(length of the mini-text * P * (1 - P)), and Z = (observed frequency of collocate - E)/SD, where P = probability, E = expected (theoretical) frequency, SD = standard deviation, and Z = Z-score. Geffroy and others (1973: 115) use the term 'co-occurrents' to describe 'collocations which are statistically positive and extremely relevant.'

6 Words self-collocate increasingly when the co-occurrence span increases. Self-collocating words cause the total number of collocate links to exceed the actual frequency of the self-collocating word. This is so because *each* instance of the first collocate within a span co-occurs with *each* instance of the second, backwards as well as forwards in each span.

7 A repetend is a 'recurring note, word, or phrase; a refrain' (OED, 2). Shawver (1999) produced an exhaustive analysis of these two semantic networks.

8 If the final parenthesis had been omitted, 'y*ronne' would collocate with just the word 'ram.'

Works Cited

Software

Feinberg, Jonathan. 2008. *Wordle*. URL: http://www.wordle.net/.
Fletcher, William H. 2010. *kfNgram Information & Help*. URL: http://www
.kwicfinder.com/kfNgram/kfNgramHelp.html.
Lancashire, Ian, in collaboration with John Bradley, Willard McCarty, Michael
Stairs, and T.R. Wooldridge. 1996. *Using* TACT *with Electronic Texts: A Guide
to* Text-Analysis. Computing Tools, *Version 2.1 for MS-DOS and PC DOS*.
New York: Modern Language Association of America. URL: http://www
.mla.org/store/CID7/PID236.
Latent Semantic Analysis. See Landauer, Foltz, and Laham (1998). URL:
http://lsa.colorado.edu/
Presutti, Lidio, and Ian Lancashire. 1988. *Micro Text-Analysis System*. Version
2.0. Centre for Computing in the Humanities, University of Toronto.
Scott, Mike. 2008. *WordSmith Tools*. Version 5.0. Liverpool: Lexical Analysis
Software, Oxford. University Press. URL: http://www.lexically.net/word-
smith/index.html.
TechSmith. 2009. *Morae Usability Testing and Market Research Software*. Okemos,
MI. URL: http://www.techsmith.com/morae.asp.
Watt, R.J.C. 1999–. *Concordance*. Dundee, UK. URL: http://www.concordanc-
esoftware.co.uk/.

Articles and Books

Aarseth, Espen J. 1997. *Cybertext: Perspectives on Ergodic Literature*. Baltimore
and London: Johns Hopkins University Press.
Adolphs, Ralph, Daniel Tranel, and Tony W. Buchanan. 2005. 'Amygdala

Damage Impairs Emotional Memory for Gist but not Details of Complex Stimuli.' *Nature Neuroscience* 8, no. 4 (April): 512–18.

Almor, Amit, et al. 1999. 'Why do Alzheimer Patients Have Difficulty with Pronouns? Working Memory, Semantics, and Reference in Comprehension and Production on Alzheimer's Disease.' *Brain and Language* 67, no. 3 (May): 202–27.

Alt, Peter, and Russell K. Alspach, eds. 1965. *The Variorum Edition of the Poems of W.B. Yeats*. New York: Macmillan.

Altenberg, Bengt. 1993. 'Recurrent Verb-Complement Constructions in the London-Lund Corpus.' In *English Language Corpora: Design, Analysis and Exploitation. Papers from the Thirteenth International Conference on English Language Research on Computerized Corpora, Nijmegen 1992*. Edited by Jan Aarts, Pieter de Haan, and Nelleke Oostdijk. Amsterdam and Atlanta: Rodopi. 227–45.

– 1998. 'On the Phraseology of Spoken English: The Evidence of Recurrent Word-Combinations.' In Cowie (1998). 101–22.

Altenberg, Bengt, and Mats Eeg-Olofsson. 1990. 'Phraseology in Spoken English: Presentation of a Project.' In *Theory and Practice in Corpus Linguistics*. Edited by Jan Aarts and Willem Meijs. Amsterdam and Atlanta: Rodolpi. 1–26.

Alzheimer's Disease Facts and Figures. 2009. Alzheimer's Association. http://www.alz.org/alzheimers_disease_alzheimer_statistics.asp. Seen 5 March 2010.

Amis, Martin. 1991. *Time's Arrow*. New York: Harmony Books.

Anderson, A.D. 1984. 'A Collection of Poetry by a Physician with Progressive Neurological Disease.' *Journal of Chronic Diseases* 37, no. 11:863–8.

Andreasen, Nancy C. 1987. 'Creativity and Mental Illness: Prevalence Rates in Writers and their First-degree Relatives.' *American Journal of Psychiatry* 144, no. 10:1288–92.

– 1996. 'Creativity and Mental Illness: A Conceptual and Historical Overview.' In *Depression and the Spiritual in Modern Art: Homage to Miró*. Edited by Joseph J. Schildkraut and Aurora Otero. Oxford: John Wiley. 2–14.

– 2005. *The Creative Brain: The Science of Genius*. New York: Plume.

Armstrong, Edward A. 1946. *Shakespeare's Imagination: A Study of the Psychology of Association and Inspiration*. Lincoln: University of Nebraska Press.

Atkinson, R.C., and R.M. Shiffrin. 1968. 'Human Memory: A Proposed System and its Control Processes.' In *The Psychology of Learning and Motivation*. Edited by K.W. Spence and J.T. Spence, vol. 2. New York: Academic Press. 89–195.

Atwood, Margaret. 1953–. 'Papers.' Thomas Fisher Rare Book Library MS Coll. 200 and 335.

– 1985. *The Handmaid's Tale*. Toronto: McClelland and Stewart.
– 1990. *Conversations*. Edited by Earl G. Ingersoll. Princeton, NJ: Ontario Review Press.
– 2004. '*The Handmaid's Tale* and *Oryx and Crake* in Context.' *PMLA* 119.3 (May): 513–17.
– 2005. *Writing with Intent: Essays, Reviews, Personal Prose: 1983–2005*. New York: Carroll and Graf.
Auden, W.H. 1963. *The Dyer's Hand and Other Essays*. London: Faber and Faber.
– 1991. *Collected Poems*. Edited by Edward Mendelson. London: Faber and Faber.
Auster, Paul. 1988. *In the Country of Last Things*. New York: Penguin.
– 1995. 'Interview with Larry McCaffery and Sinda Gregory.' In *The Red Notebook and Other Writings*. London: Faber and Faber. 116–54.
Austin, J.L. 1975. *How to Do Things with Words*. Edited by J.O. Urmson and Marina Sbisà. Oxford: Clarendon Press.
Baddeley, Alan. 1992. 'Working Memory.' *Science* 255, no. 5044:556–9.
– 1998. 'Recent Developments in Working Memory.' *Current Opinion in Neurobiology* 8, no. 2 (April): 234–8.
– 2000. 'The Episodic Buffer: A New Component of Working Memory?' *Trends in Cognitive Sciences* 4, no. 11 (November): 417–23.
– 2003a. 'Working Memory: Looking Back and Looking Forward.' *Nature Reviews: Neuroscience* 4, no. 10:829–39.
– 2003b. 'Working Memory and Language: An Overview.' *Journal of Communication Disorders* 36, no. 3:189–208.
– 2004. *Your Memory: A User's Guide*. Buffalo: Firefly Books.
Baddeley, Alan, Susan Gathercole, and Costanza Papagno. 1998. 'The Phonological Loop as a Language Learning Device.' *Psychological Review* 105, no. 1:158–73.
Baddeley, Alan, Neil Thomson, and Mary Buchanan. 1975. 'Word Length and the Structure of Short-Term Memory.' *Journal of Verbal Learning and Verbal Behavior* 14, no. 6: 575–89.
Baker, Barbara, ed. 2006. *The Way We Write: Interviews with Award-winning Writers*. London: Continuum.
Barthes, Roland. 1989. 'The Death of the Author.' Trans. Richard Howard. In *The Rustle of Language*. Berkeley and Los Angeles: University of California Press. 49–55.
– 1989. 'From Work to Text.' Ibid. 56–64.
Bartlett, F.C. 1932. *Remembering: A Study in Experimental and Social Psychology*. Cambridge: Cambridge University Press.
Bartlett, John. 1922. *A New and Complete Concordance or Verbal Index to Words, Phrases, and Passages in the Dramatic Works of Shakespeare, with a Supplementary Concordance to the Poems*. London: Macmillan.

Bate, Walter Jackson. 1968. *Coleridge*. New York: Macmillan.

Bates, Elizabeth, et al. 1995. 'Production of Complex Syntax in Normal Aging and Alzheimer's Disease.' *Language and Cognitive Processes* 10, no. 5:487–539.

Bayley, John. 1998. *Iris: A Memoir of Iris Murdoch*. London: Duckworth.

Bede, the Venerable. 1955. *A History of the English Church and People*. Trans. Leo Sherley-Price. Harmondsworth, Middlesex: Penguin Books.

Beer, John. 'Coleridge, Samuel Taylor (1772–1834).' *Oxford Dictionary of National Biography*. Edited by H.C.G. Matthew and Brian Harrison. Oxford: OUP, 2004. Online ed. Edited by Lawrence Goldman. May 2007. 6 March 2010.

Behre, Frank. 1967. *Studies in Agatha Christie's Writings: The Behaviour of A Good (Great) Deal, A Lot, Lots, Much, Plenty, Many, A Good (Great) Many*. Gothenburg Studies in English 19. Göteborg: Acta Universitatis Gothoburgensis.

Bellow, Saul. 2006. 'The Art of Fiction.' Interviewed by Gordon Lloyd Harper (1966). *The Paris Review Interviews*, vol. 1. New York: Picador. 86–110.

Benedikt, Michael. 1977. 'Michael Benedikt.' In *Fifty Contemporary Poets: The Creative Process*. Edited by Alberta T. Turner. New York: David McKay. 46–53.

Benson, Larry D. 1993. *A Glossarial Concordance to the Riverside Chaucer*. 2 vols. New York: Garland.

Berg, Thomas. 2002. 'Slips of the Typewriter Key.' *Applied Psycholinguistics* 23:185–207.

Berry-Rogghe, G.L.M. 1973. 'The Computation of Collocations and Their Relevance in Lexical Studies.' In *The Computer and Literary Studies*. Edited by A.J. Aitken, R.W. Bailey, and N. Hamilton-Smith. Edinburgh: Edinburgh University Press. 103–12.

Besserman, Lawrence L. 1976. 'Merisms in Middle English Poetry.' *Annuale Medievale* 17:58–65.

Bigsby, Christopher, ed. 2000–1. *Writers in Conversation*. 2 vols. Norwich, UK: Arthur Miller Centre for American Studies: EAS.

Birnbaum, Robert. 2004. 'Alice Flaherty.' identitytheory.com. March 10. URL: http://www.identitytheory.com/interviews/birnbaum141.php. Seen 8 March 2009.

Bisht, Raj Kishor, H.S. Dhami, and Neeraj Tiwari. 2006. 'An Evaluation of Different Statistical Techniques of Collocation Extraction Using a Probability Measure to Word Combinations.' *Journal of Quantitative Linguistics* 13, nos. 2–3:161–75.

Biswal, Bharat B., et al. 2010. 'Toward Discovery Science of Human Brain Function.' *Proceedings of the National Academy of Science of the United States of America* 107, no. 10:4734–9.

Blake, William. 1967. *Milton*. London: Trianon Press for the William Blake Trust. Plate 2.

Bock, Kathryn, et al. 2007. 'Persistent Structural Priming from Language Comprehension to Language Production.' *Cognition* 104:437–58.

The book of Sir Thomas Moore, Harleian MSS. 7368, c. 1590–96. Tudor Facsimile Texts, Folio series. [London]: 1910.

The Book of Sir Thomas More. 1911 (1961). Edited by W.W. Greg. Supplement by Harold Jenkins. Oxford: Malone Society.

Booth, Wayne. 1968. 'The Problem of Distance in *A Portrait of the Artist*.' In A Portrait of the Young Man: *Text, Criticism, and Notes*. Edited by Chester G. Anderson. New York: Viking Press. 455–67.

Boston, Bruce. 1991. *Cybertexts*. Beech Grove, IN: Talisman.

Brainerd, Barron. 1979. 'Pronouns and Genre in Shakespeare's Drama.' *Computers and the Humanities* 13:3–16.

Brand, Alice Glarden. 1989. *The Psychology of Writing: The Affective Experience*. New York: Greenwood Press.

Braver, Todd S., et al. 2001. 'Context Processing in Older Adults: Evidence for a Theory Relating Cognitive Control to Neurobiology in Healthy Aging.' *Journal of Experimental Psychology: General* 130, no. 4:746–63.

Brewer, Derek. 1986. 'Chaucer's Poetic Style.' In *The Cambridge Chaucer Companion*. Edited by Piero Boitani and Jill Mann. Cambridge: Cambridge University Press. 229–30.

Browning, Elizabeth Barrett. 1897. 'A Musical Instrument.' In *Poetical Works*. Edited by F.G. Kenyon. London: Smith, Elder. 537–8.

– 1897. 'How Do I Love Thee?' In *Poetical Works*. London: Smith, Elder. 321.

Buckner, R.L., and D.C. Carroll. 2007. 'Self-projection and the Brain.' *Trends in Cognitive Science* 11:49–57.

Budanitsky, Alexander, and Graeme Hirst. 2006. 'Evaluating WordNet-based Measures of Lexical Semantic Relatedness.' *Computational Linguistics* 32, no. 1:13–49.

Burnley, David. 1983. *A Guide to Chaucer's Language*. [London:] Macmillan.

Burns, Robert. 1896. 'Scotch Drink.' In *Poetry*. Edited by William Ernest Henley and Thomas F. Henderson. Edinburgh: T.C. and E.C. Jack. 19–25.

Burrows, John F. 1987. *Computation into Criticism: A Study of Jane Austen's Novels and an Experiment in Method*. Oxford: Clarendon Press.

Butler, Laurie T., and Dianne C. Berry. 2001. 'Implicit Memory: Intention and Awareness Revisited.' *Trends in Cognitive Sciences* 5, no. 5 (May): 192–7.

Callendar, Newgate. 1973. 'Postern of Fate.' *The New York Times Book Review* (16 December): 18.

Cannon, Christopher. 1998. *The Making of Chaucer's English: A Study of Words*. Cambridge: Cambridge University Press.

Carruthers, Mary J. 1990. *The Book of Memory: A Study of Memory in Medieval Culture*. Cambridge: Cambridge University Press.

Chafe, Wallace L. 1998. 'Language and the Flow of Thought.' In *The New Psychology of Language: Cognitive and Functional Approaches to Language Structure*. Edited by Michael Tomasello. 2 vols. Mahwah, NJ: Lawrence Erlbaum. 93–111.

– 1994. *Discourse, Consciousness, and Time: The Flow and Displacement of Conscious Experience in Speaking and Writing*. Chicago: University of Chicago Press.

– 1979. 'The Flow of Thought and the Flow of Language.' In *Discourse and Syntax*. Edited by T. Givón. New York: Academic Press. 159–81.

– 1968. 'Idiomaticity as an Anomaly in the Chomskyan Paradigm.' *Foundations of Language* 4:109–27.

Chambers, E.K. 1930. *William Shakespeare: A Study of Facts and Problems*. Oxford: Clarendon Press.

Chambers, R.W. 1931. 'Some Sequences of Thought in Shakespeare and in the 147 Lines of Sir Thomas More.' *Modern Language Review* 26, no. 3:251–80.

Chang, Franklin, Gary S. Dell, and Kathryn Bock. 2006. 'Becoming Syntactic.' *Psychological Review* 113, no. 2:234–72.

Chang, T. M. 1986. 'Semantic Memory: Facts and Models.' *Psychological Bulletin* 99, no. 2: 199–220.

Chaucer, Geoffrey. 1987. *The Riverside Chaucer*. Edited by Larry D. Benson. 3rd ed. Boston: Houghton Mifflin.

Chaytor, H.J. 1967. *From Script to Print: An Introduction to Medieval Vernacular Literature*. New York: October House.

Chenoweth, N. Ann, and John R. Hayes. 2001. 'Fluency in Writing: Generating Text in L1 and L2.' *Written Communication* 18, no. 1(January): 80–98.

– 2003. 'The Inner Voice in Writing.' *Written Communication* 20, no. 1:99–118.

Chklovskii, D.B., B.W. Mel, and K. Svoboda. 2004. 'Cortical Rewiring and Information Storage.' *Nature* 431 (October 14): 782–8.

Chomsky, Noam. 1957. *Syntactic Structures*. The Hague: Mouton.

Choueka, Y., S.T. Klein, and E. Neuwitz. 1983. 'Automatic Retrieval of Frequent Idiomatic and Collocational Expressions in a Large Corpus.' *ALLC Journal* 4, no. 1:34–8.

Christie, Agatha. 1970. *Passenger to Frankfurt: An Extravaganza*. London: Collins.

– 1972. *Elephants Can Remember*. London: Collins.

– 1973. *Postern of Fate*. London: Collins.

– 1977. *An Autobiography*. London: Collins.

Christoff, Kalina, Alan Gordon, and Rachelle Smith. Forthcoming. 'The Role of Spontaneous Thought in Human Cognition.' In *Neuroscience of Decision Making*. Edited by O. Vartanian and D.R. Mandel. New York: Psychology Press.

Christoff, Kalina, et al. 2009. 'Experience Sampling during fMRI Reveals Default Network and Executive System Contributions to Mind Wandering.'

Proceedings of the National Academy of Sciences of the United States of America 106, no. 21 (May 26): 8719–24.

Church, Kenneth Ward, and Patrick Hanks. 1990. 'Word Association Norms, Mutual Information, and Lexicography.' *Computational Linguistics* 16, no. 1:22–9.

Clanchy, M.T. 1979. *From Memory to Written Record: England, 1066–1307.* Cambridge, MA: Harvard University Press.

Cole, Michael W., and Walter Schneider. 2007. 'The Cognitive Control Network: Integrated Cortical Regions with Dissociable Functions.' *Neuroimage* 37:343–60.

Coleridge, Samuel Taylor. 1817. *Biographia Literaria.* 2 vols. London: Rest Fenner.

– 1816. *Christabel; Kubla Khan, a Vision; The Pains of Sleep.* London: John Murray.

Collins, A.M., and Loftus, E.F. 1975. 'A Spreading Activation Theory of Semantic Processing.' *Psychological Review* 82:407–28.

Conradi, Peter J. 2001. *Iris Murdoch: A Life.* London: HarperCollins.

Cooke, Nathalie. 1998. *Margaret Atwood: A Biography.* Toronto: ECW Press.

Coulthard, Malcolm. 2004. 'Author Identification, Idiolect, and Linguistic Uniqueness.' *Applied Linguistics* 25, no. 4:431–47.

Cowan, Nelson. 2000. 'The Magical Number 4 in Short-term Memory: A Reconsideration of Mental Storage Capacity.' *Behavioral and Brain Sciences* 24:87–185.

Cowie, A.P., ed. 1998. *Phraseology: Theory, Analysis, and Applications.* Oxford: Clarendon Press.

Craik, Fergus, and Robert S. Lockhart. 1972. 'Levels of Processing: A Framework for Memory Research.' *Journal of Verbal Learning and Verbal Behavior* 11, no. 6:671–84.

Crane, Mary Thomas. 2001. *Shakespeare's Brain: Reading with Cognitive Theory.* Princeton, NJ: Princeton University Press.

Crane, Mary Thomas, and Alan Richardson. 1999. 'Literary Studies and Cognitive Science: Toward a New Interdisciplinarity.' *Mosaic* 32, no. 2 (June): 123–40.

Crick, Francis, and Christof Koch. 2000. 'The Unconscious Homunculus.' In *The Neural Correlates of Consciousness: Empirical and Conceptual Questions.* Edited by T. Metzinger. Cambridge, MA: MIT Press. 103–10.

Croft, William, and D. Alan Cruse. 2004. *Cognitive Linguistics.* Cambridge: Cambridge University Press.

Crowder, Robert G., and Richard K. Wagner. 1992. *The Psychology of Reading: An Introduction.* 2nd ed. New York: Oxford University Press.

Csikszentmihalyi, Mihaly. 1996. *Creativity: Flow and the Psychology of Discovery and Invention*. New York: HarperPerennial.

Culpeper, Jonathan, and Merja Kytö. 2002. 'Lexical Bundles in Early Modern English dialogues.' In *Sounds, Words, Texts and Change: Selected Papers from 11 ICEHL, Santiago de Compostela, 7–11 September 2000*. Edited by Teresa Franego, Belén Méndez-Naya, and Elena Seoane. Amsterdam: John Benjamins. 45–63.

Curio, Gabriel, et al. 2000. 'Speaking Modifies Voice-evoked Activity in the Human Auditory Cortex.' *Human Brain Mapping* 9, no. 4 (April): 183–91.

Curran, John. 2009. *Agatha Christie's Secret Notebooks: Fifty Years of Mysteries in the Making*. London: HarperCollins.

Damasio, Antonio R. 1994. *Descartes' Error: Emotion, Reason, and the Human Brain*. New York: Avon Books.

– 1999. *The Feeling of What Happens: Body and Emotion in the Making of Consciousness*. New York: Harcourt Brace.

– 2003. *Looking for Spinoza: Joy, Sorrow and the Feeling Brain*. Orlando, FL: Harcourt.

Damasio, Antonio R., and Hanna Damasio. 1992. 'Brain and Language.' *Scientific American* 267, no. 3:88–95.

Damasio, Antonio R., Daniel Tranel, and Hanna Damasio. 1990. 'Face Agnosia and the Neural Substrates of Memory.' *Annual Review of Neuroscience* 13:89–109.

Daneman, Meredyth, and Patricia A. Carpenter. 1980. 'Individual Differences in Working Memory and Reading.' *Journal of Verbal Learning and Verbal Behavior* 19:450–66.

Davis, Boyd H., ed. 2005. *Alzheimer Talk, Text and Context: Enhancing Communication*. Basingstoke, Hampshire: Palsgrave MacMillan.

Davis, Norman. 1974. 'Chaucer and Fourteenth-Century English.' In *Geoffrey Chaucer*. Edited by Derek Brewer. London: Bell. 58–84.

Day, Robert Adams. 1998. 'The Villanelle Perplex: Reading Joyce.' In *Critical Essays on James Joyce's* A Portrait of the Artist as a Young Man. Edited by Philip Brady and James F. Carens. New York: G.K. Hall. 52–67.

de Beaugrande, Robert. 1989. 'Naïve Respondents and Creative Response.' *Siegener Periodicum zur empirischen Literaturwissenschaft* 8, no. 2:233–54.

Delany, Paul, and George P. Landow, eds. 1991. *Hypermedia and Literary Studies*. Cambridge: MIT Press.

Dent, R.W. 1981. *Shakespeare's Proverbial Language: An Index*. Berkeley: University of California Press.

Deresiewicz, William. 1999. 'His Cigar is Just a Cigar.' *The New York Times on the Web*. 14 November. URL: http://www.nytimes.com/books/99/11/14/reviews/991114.14dersest.html. Seen 18 January 2009.

Dickey, James. 1970. *Self-Interviews*. Edited by Barbara and James Reiss. Garden City, NY: Doubleday.

Diehl, Joanne F. 1978. '"Come Slowly – Eden": An Exploration of Women Poets and Their Muse.' *Signs* 3, no. 3 (Spring): 572–87

Dobbie, Elliott Van Kirk, ed. 1937. *The Manuscripts of Cædmon's Hymn and Bede's Death Song*. New York: Columbia University Press.

Donaldson, Julia. 2006. *The Way We Write: Interviews with Award-winning Writers*. Edited by Barbara Baker. London: Continuum. 49–62.

Dooley, Gillian, ed. 2003. *From a Tiny Corner in the House of Fiction: Conversations with Iris Murdoch*. Columbia: University of South Carolina Press.

Eberhart, Richard. 1977. 'Richard Eberhart.' In *Fifty Contemporary Poets: The Creative Process*. Edited by Alberta T. Turner. New York: David McKay. 85–9.

– 1979. 'An Interview (*Pulse*).' In *Of Poetry and Poets*. Urbana: University of Illinois Press. 249–63.

– 1988. 'The Groundhog.' In *Collected Poems, 1930–1986*. New York: Oxford University Press. 23–4.

– 1987. 'Richard Eberhart.' In *The Poet's Craft: Interviews from* The New York Quarterly. Edited by William Packard. New York: Paragon House. 255–62.

Edson, Russell. 1977. 'Counting Sheep' and 'On *Counting Sheep*.' In *Fifty Contemporary Poets: The Creative Process*. Edited by Alberta T. Turner. New York: David McKay. 90–4.

Eeg-Olofsson, Mats, and Bengt Altenberg. 1996. 'Recurrent Word Combinations in the London-Lund Corpus: Coverage and Use for Word-class Tagging.' In *Synchronic Corpus Linguistics*. Edited by Carol E. Percy, Charles F. Meyer, and Ian Lancashire. Amsterdam: Rodopi. 97–107.

Eliot, T.S. 1951. *Selected Essays*. 3rd ed. London: Faber and Faber.

– 1962. *The Complete Poems and Plays 1909–1950*. New York: Harcourt, Brace, and World.

– 1971. *The Waste Land: A Facsimile and Transcript of the Original Drafts Including the Annotations of Ezra Pound*. Edited by Valerie Eliot. London: Faber and Faber.

– 1996. *Inventions of the March Hare: Poems 1909–1917*. Edited by Christopher Ricks. New York: Harcourt Brace.

– 2005. *The Annotated Waste Land with Eliot's Contemporary Prose*. Edited by Lawrence Rainey. New Haven, CT: Yale University Press.

Eliot, Valerie, ed. 1988. *The Letters of T.S. Eliot*. Vol. 1: 1898–1922. London: Faber and Faber.

Elliott, Ralph W.V. 1974. *Chaucer's English*. London: Andre Deutsch.

Englebert, Douglas C. 1962. *Augmenting Human Intellect: A Conceptual Framework*. SRI Summary Report AFOSR-3223. URL: http://www.dougengelbart.org/pubs/augment-3906.html.

Ericsson, K. Anders, et al. 2004. 'Uncovering the Structure of a Memorist's Superior "Basic" Memory Capacity.' *Cognitive Psychology* 49:191–237.

Ericsson, K. Anders, and Walter Kintsch. 1995. 'Long-term Working Memory.' *Psychological Review* 102, no. 2:211–45.

Evans, G. Blakemore, and J.J.M. Tobin, eds. 1997. 'Sir Thomas More: The Additions Ascribed to Shakespeare.' In *The Riverside Shakespeare*. 2nd ed. Boston: Houghton Mifflin. 1775–94.

Evans, Jonathan St. B.T. 2003. 'In Two Minds: Dual-process Accounts of Reasoning.' *Trends in Cognitive Sciences* 7, no. 10 (October): 454–9.

Fanthorpe, U.A. 2006. *The Way We Write: Interviews with Award-winning Writers*. Edited by Barbara Baker. London: Continuum. 74–82.

Fauconnier, Gilles, and Mark Turner. 2002. *The Way We Think: Conceptual Blending and the Mind's Hidden Complexities*. New York: Basic Books.

Federmeier, Kara D., and Marta Kutas. 1999. 'A Rose by any Other Name: Long-term Memory Structure and Sentence Processing.' *Journal of Memory and Language* 41, no. 4 (November): 469–95.

Feldman, Jerome A. 2006. *From Molecule to Metaphor: A Neural Theory of Language*. Cambridge, MA: MIT Press.

Fifield, William. 1967. '3. Jean Cocteau.' In *Writers at Work: The* Paris Review *Interviews*. 3rd series. Edited by George Plimpton. New York: Viking Press. 57–81.

Finneran, Richard J., ed. 1996. *The Literary Text in the Digital Age*. Ann Arbor: University of Michigan Press.

Flaherty, Alice W. 2005. 'Frontotemporal and Dopaminergic Control of Idea Generation and Creative Drive.' *The Journal of Comparative Neurology* 493, no. 1: 147–53.

– 2004. *The Midnight Disease: The Drive to Write, Writer's Block, and the Creative Brain*. Boston, MA: Houghton Mifflin.

Flood, Alison. 2009. 'Study Claims Agatha Christie had Alzheimer's.' *Guardian* (3 April). URL: http://www.guardian.co.uk/books/2009/apr/03/agatha-christie-alzheimers-research.

Flower, Linda, and John R. Hayes. 1981. 'A Cognitive Process Theory of Writing.' *College Composition and Communication* 32, no. 4:365–87.

Folstein, M.F, S.E. Folstein, and P.R. McHugh. 1975. '"Mini-mental State." A Practical Method for Grading the Cognitive State of Patients for the Clinician.' *Journal of Psychiatric Research* 12, no. 3:189–98.

Forbidden Planet. 1956. Directed by Fred M. Wilcox. Metro-Goldwyn-Mayer.

Forker, Charles R. 1989. 'Webster or Shakespeare? Style, Idiom, Vocabulary, and Spelling in the Additions to *Sir Thomas More*.' In *Shakespeare and Sir Thomas More: essays on the play and its Shakespearian interest*. Edited by T.H. Howard-Hill. Cambridge: Cambridge University Press. 151–70.

Forster, E.M. 1925. *Anonymity: An Enquery*. London: Leonard and Virginia Woolf.

– 1958. 'E.M. Forster.' Edited by P.N. Furbank and F.J.H. Haskell. In *Writers at Work: The* Paris Review *Interviews*. Edited by Malcolm Cowley. London: Secker and Warburg. 25–33.

– 1996. 'Anonymity: An Enquiry.' In *The Anatomy of Memory: An Anthology*. Edited by James McConkey. New York: Oxford University Press. 163–72. [Originally 1925.]

Foster, Donald W. 1997. 'Shaxicon's Designated "Shakespeare Roles."' Online Web document (2 Feb. 1997). URL: vassun.vassar.edu/~foster/shax/roles .html Date seen: 24 April 1998. Retired from Web by 18 March 2010.

Foucault, Michel. 1977. 'What is an Author?' Trans. Donald F. Bouchard and Sherry Simon. In *Language, Counter-Memory, Practice*. Ithaca, NY: Cornell University Press. 124–7.

Fowles, John. 1999. '"Stay alive to everything": An Interview with John Fowles.' In *'Do you consider yourself a postmodern author?' Interviews with Contemporary English Writers*. Edited by Rudolf Freiburg and Jan Schnitker. Münster: Lit. 125–34.

Fox, Michael D., et al. 2005. 'The Human Brain is Intrinsically Organized into Dynamic, Anticorrelated Functional Networks.' In *Proceedings of the National Academy of Sciences of the United States of America* 102, no. 27 (July 5): 9673–8.

Francis, W.N., and H. Kucera. 1964. *Brown Corpus Manual*. Providence, RI: Brown University. Revised 1971, 1979. URL: http://khnt.aksis.uib.no/ icame/manuals/brown/.

French, J. Milton, ed. 1956. *The Life Records of Milton*. Volume 4: 1655–1669. New Brunswick, NJ: Rutgers University Press.

Freud, Sigmund. 2002. *The Psychopathology of Everyday Life*. Trans. Anthea Bell. London: Penguin.

Fulgentius. 1971. *Fulgentius The Mythographer*. Trans. Leslie George Whitbread. Columbus: Ohio State University Press.

Gabrieli, Vittorio, and Giorgio Melchiori, eds. 1990. *Sir Thomas More: A play by Anthony Munday and Others. Revised by Henry Chettle, Thomas Dekker, Thomas Heywood and William Shakespeare*. Manchester: Manchester University Press.

Galison, Peter. 1994. 'The Ontology of the Enemy: Norbert Wiener and the Cybernetic Vision.' *Critical Inquiry* 21:228–66.

Garrard, Peter. 2009. 'Cognitive Archaeology: Uses, Methods, and Results.' *Journal of Neurolinguistics* 22, no. 3 (May): 250–65.

Garrard, Peter, et al. 2005. 'The Effects of Very Early Alzheimer's Disease on the Characteristics of Writing by a Renowned Author.' *Brain* 128, no. 2:250–60.

Gathercole, S.E., and A.D. Baddeley. 1993. *Working Memory and Language*. Hillside, PA: Lawrence Erlbaum.

Geffroy, Annie, et al. 1973. 'Lexicometric Analysis of Co-occurrences.' In *The Computer and Literary Studies*. Edited by A.J. Aitken, Richard W. Bailey, and Neil Hamilton-Smith. Edinburgh: Edinburgh University Press. 113–33.

Geoffrey of Vinsauf. 1967. *Poetria Nova*. Trans. Margaret F. Nims. Toronto: Pontifical Institute of Mediaeval Studies.

Geschwind, Norman. 1979. 'Specializations of the Human Brain.' In *The Brain*. A Scientific American Book. San Francisco: W.H. Freeman. 108–17.

Ghiselin, Brewster, ed. 1952. *The Creative Process: A Symposium*. Mentor.

Gibson, Andrew, ed. 1994. *Reading Joyce's 'Circe.'* Amsterdam: Rodopi.

Gleason, Jean Berko, and Nan Bernstein Ratner, eds. 1998. *Psycholinguistics*. 2nd ed. Fort Worth, TX: Harcourt Brace.

Gobet, Fernand, et al. 2001. 'Chunking Mechanisms in Human Learning.' *Trends in Cognitive Sciences* 5, no. 6 (June): 236–43.

Goldberg, Adele E. 2003. 'Constructions: A New Theoretical Approach to Language.' *Trends in Cognitive Sciences* 7, no. 5 (May): 219–24.

– and Devin Casenhiser. 2006. 'English Constructions.' In *The Handbook of English Linguistics*. Edited by Bas Aarts and April McMahon. Oxford: Blackwell. 343–55.

Goody, Jack. 1977. *The Domestication of the Savage Mind*. Cambridge: Cambridge University Press.

Goody, Jack, and Ian Watt. 1963. 'The Consequences of Literacy.' *Comparative Studies in Society and History* 5, no. 3 (April): 304–45.

Gordon, Lyndall. 1998. *T.S. Eliot: An Imperfect Life*. London: Vintage.

– 1977. *Eliot's Early Years*. Oxford: Oxford University Press.

Gray, Douglas. 2004. 'Chaucer, Geoffrey (*c.*1340–1400).' In *Oxford Dictionary of National Biography*. Edited by H.C.G. Matthew and Brian Harrison. Oxford: OUP. Seen 3 Sept. 2007.

Greg, W.W., ed. 1923. *Shakespeare's Hand in the Play of Sir Thomas More*. Cambridge: Cambridge University Press.

Gries, Stefan Th. 2005. 'Syntactic Priming: A Corpus-based Approach.' *Journal of Psycholinguistic Research* 34, no. 4 (July): 365–99.

Groves-Wright, Kathy, et al. 2004. 'A Comparison of Verbal and Written Language in Alzheimer's Disease.' *Journal of Communication Disorders* 37:109–30.

Guest-Gornall, R. 1973. 'Samuel Taylor Coleridge and the Doctors.' *Medical History* 17, no. 4 (October): 327–42.

Haarman, Henk J., et al. 2005. 'Age-related Declines in Context Maintenance and Semantic Short-term Memory.' *The Quarterly Journal of Experimental Psychology* 58a: 1:34–53.

Halliday, M.A.K. 1961. 'Categories of the Theory of Grammar.' *Word* 17:241–92.

Hampl, Patricia. 1996. 'Memory and Imagination.' In *The Anatomy of Memory:*

An Anthology. Edited by James McConkey. New York: Oxford University Press. 201–11. [Originally 1985.]

Hardman, Phillipa. 1986. 'Chaucer's Muses and His "Art Poetical."' *The Review of English Studies* 37, no. 148:478–94.

Harper, Margaret Mills. 2002. 'Nemo: George Yeats and Her Automatic Script.' *New Literary History* 33:291–314.

Harris, Amanda Jeremin. 2006. 'T. S. Eliot's Mental Hygiene.' *The Journal of Modern Literature* 29, no. 4 (Summer): 44–56.

Hart, Alfred. 1943. 'The Growth of Shakespeare's Vocabulary.' *Review of English Studies* 19:242–54.

Hartsuiker, Robert J., et al., eds. 2005. *Phonological Encoding and Monitoring in Normal and Pathological Speech*. Hove and New York: Psychology Press.

Hartsuiker, Robert J., and Herman H.J. Kolk. 2001. 'Error Monitoring in Speech Production: A Computational Test of the Perceptual Loop Theory.' *Cognitive Psychology* 42, no. 2:113–57.

Hassabis, Demis, and Eleanor A. Maguire. 2009. 'The Construction System of the Brain.' *Philosophical Transactions of the Royal Society* 364:1263–71.

– 2007. 'Deconstructing Episodic Memory with Construction.' *Trends in Cognitive Sciences* 11, no. 7:299–306.

Hayles, N. Katherine. 1999. *How We Became Posthuman: Virtual Bodies in Cybernetics, Literature, and Informatics*. Chicago: University of Chicago Press.

Heaney, Seamus. 1981. 'Seamus Heaney.' In *Viewpoints: Poets in Conversation with John Haffenden*. Edited by John Haffenden. London and Boston: Faber and Faber. 57–75.

Hearle, Noah. 2007. 'Sentence and Word Length.' URL: http://hearle.nahoo.net/Academic/Maths/Sentence.html. Date read: 4 July 2007.

Heighton, Steven. 2002. 'An Interview with the Author.' *The Notebooks: Interviews and New Fiction from Contemporary Writers*. Edited by Michelle Berry and Natalee Caple. Toronto: Anchor. 155–73.

Henderson, Greig. 2001. 'A Rhetoric of Form: The Early Burke and Reader-Response Criticism.' In *Unending Conversations: New Writings by and about Kenneth Burke*. Edited by Greig Henderson and David Cratis Williams. Carbondale: Southern Illinois University Press. 127–42.

Heptonstall, Geoffrey. 1996. 'Jackson's Dilemma.' *Contemporary Review* 268, no. 1560 (January): 51.

Heylighen, Francis, and Cliff Joslyn. 2001. 'Cybernetics and Second-order Cybernetics.' *Encyclopedia of Physical Science and Technology*. 3rd ed. New York: Academe. 1–24.

Hirsch, E.D., Jr. 1960. 'Objective Interpretation.' *PMLA* 75, no. 4 (September): 463–79.

Hoban, Russell. 1987. 'An Interview with Russell Hoban.' In *Alive and Writing: Interviews with American Authors of the 1980s*. Edited by Larry McCaffery and Sinda Gregory. Urbana and Chicago: University of Illinois Press. 126–50.

Hogan, Patrick Colm. 1997. 'Literary Universals.' *Poetics Today* 18, no. 2 (Summer): 223–49.

– 2003. *Cognitive Science, Literature, and the Arts: A Guide for Humanists*. New York: Routledge.

Holland, Norman N. 1988. *The Brain of Robert Frost: A Cognitive Approach to Literature*. New York: Routledge.

Holmes, David I. 1998. 'The Evolution of Stylometry in Humanities Scholarship.' *Literary and Linguistic Computing* 13, no. 3:111–17.

Hoover, David L. 2003. 'Frequent Collocations and Authorial Style.' *Literary and Linguistic Computing* 18, no. 3:261–86.

Hope, Jonathan. 1994. *The Authorship of Shakespeare's Plays: A Socio-linguistic Study*. Cambridge: Cambridge University Press.

Horton, Thomas Bolton. 1987. *The Effectiveness of the Stylometry of Function Words in Discriminating between Shakespeare and Fletcher*. PhD dissertation; Department of Computer Science, University of Edinburgh. December.

– 1994. 'Distinguishing Shakespeare from Fletcher through Function Words.' *Shakespeare Studies* 22:314–35.

Hoy, Cyrus. 1956. 'The Shares of Fletcher and His Collaborators in the Beaumont and Fletcher Canon (I).' *Studies in Bibliography* 8:129–46.

Hughlings Jackson, J. 1932. 'On the Nature of the Duality of the Brain.' In *Selected Writings of John Hughlings Jackson*. Edited by James Taylor. Vol. 2. London: Hodder and Stoughton. 129–45.

Iser, Wolfgang. 1980. 'The Reading Process: A Phenomenological Approach.' In *Reader-response Criticism: From Formalism to Post-structuralism*. Edited by Jane Tompkins. Baltimore: Johns Hopkins University Press. 50–69.

Jackson, James L. 1950. 'Shakespeare's Dog-and-Sugar Imagery and the Friendship Tradition.' *Shakespeare Quarterly* 1, no. 4:260–3.

Jackson, MacDonald P. 1979. *Studies in Attribution: Middleton and Shakespeare*. Salzburg: Institut für Anglistik und Amerikanistik.

Jacquemot, Charlotte, and Sophie K. Scott. 2006. 'What is the Relationship between Phonological Short-term Memory and Speech Processing?' *Trends in Cognitive Sciences* 10, no. 11:480–6.

Jamison, Kay Redfield. 1993. *Touched With Fire: Manic-Depressive Illness and the Artistic Temperament*. New York: Free Press.

Jaynes, Julian. 1976. *The Origin of Consciousness in the Breakdown of the Bicameral Mind*. Boston: Houghton Mifflin.

Jeffares, A. Norman. 1984. *A New Commentary on the Poems of W.B. Yeats*. Stanford, CA: Stanford University Press.

Johnson, Bryan Stanley. 1969. *The Unfortunates*. London: Panther Books and Secker & Warburg.

Joyce, James. 1957. *Letters of James Joyce*. Edited by Stuart Gilbert. London: Faber and Faber.

– 1965. *The Workshop of Daedalus: James Joyce and the Raw Materials for* A Portrait of the Artist as a Young Man. Edited by Robert Scholes and Richard M. Kain. Evanston, IL: Northwestern University Press.

– 1968. A Portrait of the Artist as a Young Man*: Text, Criticism, and Notes*. Edited by Chester G. Anderson. New York: Viking Press.

– 1978. A Portrait of the Artist as a Young Man*: A Facsimile of Epiphanies, Notes, Manuscripts, & Typescripts*. New York: Garland.

Juola, Patrick, John Sofko, and Patrick Brennan. 2006. 'A Prototype for Authorship Attribution Studies.' *Literary and Linguistic Computing* 21, no. 2:169–78.

Just, Marcel A., and Patricia A. Carpenter. 1992. 'A Capacity Theory of Comprehension: Individual Differences in Working Memory.' *Psychological Review* 99, no. 1:122–49.

Kane, Michael J., David Z. Hambrick, and Andrew R.A. Conway. 'Working Memory Capacity and Fluid Intelligence are Strongly Related Constructs: Comment on Ackerman, Beier, and Boyle (2005).' *Psychological Bulletin* 131, no. 1:66–71.

Kelliher, Hilton. 1994. 'The *Kubla Khan* Manuscript and its First Collector.' *British Library Journal* 20, no. 2:184–90.

Kellogg, Ronald T. 2001. 'Long-term Working Memory in Text Production.' *Memory & Cognition* 29, no. 1:43–52.

– 2004. 'Working Memory Components in Written Sentence Generation.' *The American Journal of Psychology* 117, no. 3:341–61.

Kemper, Susan, Ruth Herman, and Cindy Lian. 2003. 'Age Differences in Sentence Production.' *The Journals of Gerontology. Series B, Psychological Sciences and Social Sciences* 58, no. 5 (September): 260–8.

Kemper, Susan, et al. 2001. 'Language Decline across the Life Span: Findings from the Nun Study.' *Psychology and Aging* 16, no. 2 (June): 227–39.

Kennedy, Graeme. 1998. *An Introduction to Corpus Linguistics*. London: Longman.

Kenner, Hugh. 1955. *Dublin's Joyce*. London: Chatto and Windus.

Kernighan, Brian W., and Rob Pike. 1984. *The UNIX Programming Environment*. Englewood Cliffs, NJ: Prentice-Hall.

Kincaid, J. Peter, et al. 1975. *Derivation of New Readability Formulas for Navy Enlisted Personnel*. Millington, TN: Chief of Naval Training.

King, Stephen. 2000. *On Writing: A Memoir of the Craft*. New York: Scribner.

Kingston, Anne. 2009. 'The Ultimate Whodunit: Agatha Christie's Mysteries May Reveal Alzheimer's Clues.' *Maclean's* 122, no. 12 (6 April): 45.

Kintsch, Walter. 1998. *Comprehension: A Paradigm for Cognition*. Cambridge: Cambridge University Press.

Kjellmer, G. 1991. 'A Mint of Phrases.' In *English Corpus Linguistics: Studies in Honour of Jan Svartvik*. Edited by K. Aijmer and B. Altenberg. London: Longman. 111–27.

Knepper, Marty S. 2005. 'The Curtain Falls: Agatha Christie's Last Novels.' *Clues* 23, no. 4 (Summer): 69–84.

Knickerbocker, Conrad. 1967. '7. William Burroughs.' In *Writers at Work: The Paris Review Interviews*. 3rd series. Edited by George Plimpton. New York: Viking Press.

Koch, Christof, and Naotsugu Tsuchiya. 2007. 'Attention and Consciousness: Two Distinct Brain Processes.' *Trends in Cognitive Sciences* 11, no. 1 (Jan.): 16–22.

Koekebakker, J. 1983. 'B.C. Weekly Newspaper Links Micro to Typesetter.' *Canadian Datasystems* 15.2. [Cybertext Corp.]

Kosslyn, Stephen M., and Olivier Koenig. 1992. *Wet Mind: The New Cognitive Neuroscience*. New York: Free Press.

Lake, David J. 1975. *The Canon of Thomas Middleton's Plays: Internal Evidence for the Major Problems of Authorship*. Cambridge: Cambridge University Press.

Lakoff, George. 1987. *Women, Fire, and Dangerous Things: What Categories Reveal about the Mind*. Chicago and London: University of Chicago Press.

Lakoff, George, and Mark Johnson. 1980. *Metaphors We Live By*. Chicago and London: University of Chicago Press.

Lancashire, Ian. 1965. 'Two Poems.' *The Fiddlehead* 64 (Spring): 59.

– 1987. 'Using a Textbase for English-language Research.' In *The Uses of Large Text Databases*. Proceedings of the Third Annual Conference of the UW Centre for the New Oxford English Dictionary. Ed. Donna Lee Berg. Waterloo, ON: UW Centre for the New OED. 728–67.

– 1992. 'Chaucer's Repetends from The General Prologue of the Canterbury Tales.' In *The Centre and its Compass: Studies in Medieval Literature in Honor of Professor John Leyerle*. Edited by R.A. Taylor et al. Kalamazoo: Western Michigan University Press. 315–65.

– 1993a. 'Phrasal Repetends and "The Manciple's Prologue and Tale."' In *Computer-Based Chaucer Studies*. Edited by Ian Lancashire. CCHWP 3. Toronto: Centre for Computing in the Humanities. 99–122.

– 1993b. 'Computer-assisted Critical Analysis: A Case Study of Margaret Atwood's *Handmaid's Tale*.' Edited by George P. Landow and Paul Delany. In *The Digital Word: Text-based Computing in the Humanities*. Cambridge, MA: MIT Press. 293–318.

- 1993c. 'Uttering and Editing: Computational Text Analysis and Cognitive Studies in Authorship,' *Texte: Revue de Critique et de Théorie Littéraire* 13/14:173–218.
- 1996. 'Phrasal Repetends in Literary Stylistics: Shakespeare's *Hamlet* III.1.' In *Research in Humanities Computing* 4. Oxford: Clarendon Press. 34–68.
- 1999. 'Probing Shakespeare's Idiolect in *Troilus and Cressida* I.3.1–29.' *University of Toronto Quarterly* 68, no. 3:728–67.
- 2004a. 'Cognitive Stylistics and the Literary Imagination.' In *A Companion to Digital Humanities*. Edited by Susan Schreibman, Ray Siemens, and John Unsworth. Oxford: Blackwell's. 397–414.
- 2004b. 'Cybertextuality.' *TEXT Technology* no. 2:1–18. URL: http://texttechnology.mcmaster.ca/pdf/vol13_2_01.pdf.
- Forthcoming. 'Cybertextuality by the Numbers.' In *Text and Genre in Reconstruction: Effects of Digitization on Ideas, Behaviours, Products and Institutions.* Edited by Willard McCarty. Cambridge: Open Book Publishers.
- Lancashire, Ian, comp. 1991. *The Humanities Computing Yearbook 1989/1990: A Comprehensive Guide to Software and Other Resources.* Oxford: Clarendon Press.
- Lancashire, Ian, and Graeme Hirst. 2009. 'Vocabulary Changes in Agatha Christie's Mysteries as an Indication of Dementia: A Case Study.' 19th Annual Rotman Research Institute Conference, Cognitive Aging: Research and Practice, 8–10 March 2009, Toronto. URL: http://ftp.cs.toronto.edu/pub/gh/Lancashire+Hirst-extabs-2009.pdf. The poster is at URL: http://ftp.cs.toronto.edu/pub/gh/Lancashire+Hirst-2009–poster.pdf.
- Lancashire, Ian, and Willard McCarty, comps. 1988. *The Humanities Computing Yearbook 1988*. Oxford: Oxford University Press.
- Landauer, Thomas K., P.W. Foltz, and D. Laham. 1998. 'Introduction to Latent Semantic Analysis.' *Discourse Processes* 25:259–84.
- Landow, George P., and Paul Delany, eds. 1993. *The Digital Word: Text-based Computing in the Humanities*. Cambridge, MA: MIT Press.
- Lashley, Karl S. 1958. 'Cerebral Organization and Behavior.' In *Brain and Human Behavior. Proceedings of the Association for Research in Nervous and Mental Diseases* 36:1–18.
- Lessing, Doris. 1988. 'The Art of Fiction No. 102: Doris Lessing.' *Paris Review* 30. no.106:81–105.
- Levelt, Willem J.M. 1989. *Speaking: From Intention to Articulation*. Cambridge, MA: MIT Press.
- 2001. 'Spoken Word Production: A Theory of Lexical Access.' *Proceedings of the National Academy of Sciences of the United States of America* 98, no. 23 (6 Nov.): 13464–71.

Levelt, Willem J.M., Ardi Roelofs, and Antje S. Meyer. 1999. 'A Theory of Lexical Access in Speech Production.' *Behavioral and Brain Sciences* 22:1–75.

Levertov, Denise. 1984. 'Denise Levertov Interviewed by Sybil Estess.' In *American Poetry Observed: Poets on Their Work*. Edited by Joe David Bellamy. Urbana and Chicago: University of Illinois Press. 155–67.

– 1987. 'Denise Levertov.' In *The Poet's Craft: Interviews from* The New York Quarterly. Edited by William Packard. New York: Paragon House. 52–69.

– 1998. *Conversations with Denise Levertov*. Edited by Jewel Spears Brooker. Jackson: University Press of Mississippi.

Lexicon Iconographicum Mythologiae Classicae (*LIMC*). 1992. VI. 1. Zurich and Munich: Artemis.

Le, Xuan. 2010. 'Longitudinal Detection of Dementia through Lexical and Syntactic Changes in Writing.' MSc Paper. Supervisor: Graeme Hirst. University of Toronto: Department of Computer Science (22 January). URL: http://ftp.cs.toronto.edu/pub/gh/Le-MSc-2010.pdf.

Lichtheim, L. 1885. 'On aphasia.' *Brain* 7:433–84.

Lieberman, Philip. 2000. *Human Language and Our Reptilian Brain: The Subcortical Bases of Speech, Syntax, and Thought*. Cambridge, MA: Harvard University Press.

Logan, R.D. 1985. 'From Eros to Thanatos: Condensation and Repetition Compulsion in Coleridge's "Kubla Khan."' *Psychoanalytic Review* 72, no. 4 (Winter): 657–63.

Longfellow, Ernest Wadsworth. 1922. 'There was a little girl.' In *Random Memories*. Boston: Houghton Mifflin. 15.

Lord, John B. 1979. 'Some Solved and Some Unsolved Problems in Prosody.' *Style* 13, no. 4 (Fall): 311–33.

Love, Harold. 2002. *Attributing Authorship: An Introduction*. Cambridge: Cambridge University Press.

Lowes, John Livingston. 1927. *The Road to Xanadu: A Study in the Ways of Imagination*. Boston: Houghton-Mifflin.

Magee, John Gillespie, Jr. 1989. 'High Flight.' In *Respectfully Quoted: A Dictionary of Quotations Requested from the Congressional Research Service*. Edited by Suzy Platt. Washington, DC: Library of Congress.

Magnussen, S., et al. 2006. 'What People Believe about Memory.' *Memory* 14, no. 5: 595–613.

Magoun, Francis P., Jr. 1955. 'Bede's Story of Cædman: The Case History of an Anglo-Saxon Oral Singer.' *Speculum* 30, no. 1:49–63.

Mahon, Bradford Z., and Alfonso Caramazza. 2008. 'A Critical Look at the Embodied Cognition Hypothesis and a New Proposal for Grounding Conceptual Content.' *Journal of Physiology--Paris* 102, nos. 1–3:59–70.

Mallowan, Max E.L. 1977. *Mallowan's Memoirs*. London: Collins.

March, Evrim G., R. Wales, and P. Pattison. 2006. 'The Uses of Nouns and Deixis in Discourse Production in Alzheimer's Disease.' *Journal of Neurolinguistics* 19:311–40.

Marois, René, and Jason Ivanoff. 2005. 'Capacity Limits of Information Processing in the Brain.' *Trends in Cognitive Sciences* 9, no. 6 (June): 296–305.

Martin, A., et al. 1995. 'Discrete Cortical Regions Associated with Knowledge of Color and Knowledge of Action.' *Science* 270, no. 5233:102–5.

Martin, Randi C. 1987. 'Articulatory and Phonological Deficits in Short-term Memory and Their Relation to Syntactic Processing.' *Brain and Language* 32, no. 1:159–92.

Martindale, Colin. 1990. *The Clockwork Muse: The Predictability of Artistic Change*. New York: Basic Books.

Masani, R.P. 1990. *Norbert Wiener 1894–1964*. Basel: Birkhäuser.

Mauriac, François. 1958. 'François Mauriac.' In *Writers at Work: The Paris Review Interviews*. Edited by Malcolm Cowley. London: Secker and Warburg. 37–46.

Maxim, Jane, and Karen Bryan. 1991. *Language of the Elderly: A Clinical Perspective*. London: Whurr.

McCully, C.B., ed. 1991. *The Poet's Voice and Craft*. Manchester: Carcanet.

McGann, Jerome. 2001. *Radiant Textuality: Literature after the World Wide Web*. New York: Palgrave.

McGurk, H., and J. MacDonald. 1976. 'Hearing Lips and Seeing Voices.' *Nature* 263:746–8.

McKenzie, D.F. 2002. 'Speech-Manuscript-Print.' In *Making Meaning: 'Printers of the Mind' and other Essays*. Edited by Peter D. McDonald and Michael F. Suarez. Amherst: University of Massachusetts Press. 237–58.

McKeown, Kathleen R., and Dragomir R. Radev. 2000. 'Collocations.' In *Handbook of Natural Language Processing*. Edited by Robert Dale, Hermann Moisl, and H.L. Somers. Boca Raton, FL: CRC Press. 507–23.

McLuhan, Marshall. 1964. *Understanding Media: The Extensions of Man*. London: Routledge.

– 1962. *The Gutenberg Galaxy: The Making of Typographic Man*. Toronto: University of Toronto Press.

Mel'čuk, Igor. 1998. 'Collocations and Lexical Functions.' In Cowie. 23–53.

Merriam, Thomas V.N. 1993. 'Marlowe's Hand in *Edward III*.' *Literary and Linguistic Computing* 8, no. 2:59–72.

– 1996. 'Marlowe's Hand in *Edward III* Revisited.' *Literary and Linguistic Computing* 11, no. 1 (April): 19–22.

Merwin, W.S. 1984. 'W.S. Merwin.' In *American Poetry Observed: Poets on Their*

Work. Edited by Joe David Bellamy. Urbana and Chicago: University of Illinois Press. 168–80.

Metzing, Charles, and Susan E. Brennan. 2003. 'When Conceptual Pacts Are Broken: Partner-specific Effects on the Comprehension of Referring Expressions.' *Journal of Memory and Language* 49, no. 2:201–13.

Miall, David S., and Don Kuiken. 1998. 'The Form of Reading: Empirical Studies of Literariness.' *Poetics* 25, no. 6:327–41.

Michael Clayton. 2007. Directed by Tony Gilroy. Warner Brothers.

Milic, Louis T. 1971. 'Rhetorical Choice and Stylistic Option: The Conscious and Unconscious Poles.' *Literary Style: A Symposium*. Edited by Seymour Chatman. London and New York: Oxford University Press.

Miller, George A. 1956. 'The Magical Number Seven, plus or minus Two: Some Limits on our Capacity for Processing Information.' *Psychological Review* 63, no. 2:81–97.

Miller, Henry. 1963. '7. Henry Miller.' In *Writers at Work*. Edited by George Plimpton. 2nd series. New York: Viking Press. 165–91.

Milne, A.A. 1924. 'Disobedience.' *When We Were Very Young*. London: Methuen.

Milne, Fred L. 1986. 'Coleridge's "Kubla Khan": A Metaphor for the Creative Process.' *South Atlantic Review* 51, no. 4 (November): 17–29.

Miner, Valerie. 1996. '*Jackson's Dilemma*.' *The Nation* 262, no. 2 (8 January): 32.

Montfort, Nick. 2002–3. 'The Coding and Execution of the Author.' *CyberText Yearbook 2002–2003*. Edited by Markku Eskelinen and Raine Koskimaa. University of Jyväskylä. 201–17. URL: http://cybertext.hum.jyu.fi/articles/117.pdf. Seen 3 July 2009.

Moon, Rosamond. 1998. *Fixed Expressions and Idioms in English: A Corpus-based Approach*. Oxford: Clarendon Press.

Moravec, Hans. 1988. *Mind Children: The Future of Robot and Human Intelligence*. Cambridge: Harvard University Press.

– 2000. 'Robots, Re-evolving Mind.' URL: http://www.frc.ri.cmu.edu/~hpm/project.archive/robot.papers/2000/Cerebrum.html. Seen 8 March 2010.

Morgan, Janet. 1984. *Agatha Christie: A Biography*. London: Collins.

Morpurgo, Michael. 2006. *The Way We Write: Interviews with Award-winning Writers*. Edited by Barbara Baker. London: Continuum. 128–40.

Morsella, Ezequiel, and Michele Miozzo. 2002. 'Evidence for a Cascade Model of Lexical Access in Speech Production.' *Journal of Experimental Psychology: Learning, Memory and Cognition* 28, no. 3:555–63.

Murdoch, Iris. 1996. *Jackson's Dilemma*. New York: Viking.

Mysak, Edward D. 1966. *Speech Pathology and Feedback Theory*. Springfield, IL: Charles C. Thomas.

'Mysterious Affair of Style, A. (Agatha Christie's Centenary).' 1990. *The Economist* 316, no. 7674 (29 September): 101–4.

Nabokov, Vladimir, ed. 1962. BBC Interview of Nabokov by Peter Duval-Smith and Christopher Burstall. URL: http://lib.ru/NABOKOW/Inter02.txt.

Nattinger, J. 1988. 'Some Current Trends in Vocabulary Teaching.' In *Vocabulary and Language Teaching*. Edited by Ronald Carter and Michael McCarthy. London: Longman. 62–82.

Nelson, Theodor H. 1987. *Literary Machines*. South Bend, IN: The Distributors.

Neuhaus, H. Joachim. 1989. 'Shakespeare's Wordforms, a Database View.' In *Anglistentag 1988 Göttingen*. Edited by Heinz-Joachim Müllenbrock and Renate Noll-Wiemann. Tübingen: Max Niemeyer. 264–80.

New York Times. 2009. 'Literary Alzheimer's.' *The Ninth Annual Year in Ideas*. March 17.' [Under 'Arts' and 'Health'] http://www.nytimes.com/projects/magazine/ideas/2009/.

Nicholas, Marjorie, et al. 1985. 'Empty Speech in Alzheimer's Disease and Fluent Aphasia.' *Journal of Speech and Hearing Research* 28, no. 3 (Sept.): 405–10.

Nicol, Bran. 2004. *Iris Murdoch: The Retrospective Fiction*. 2nd ed. Basingstoke: Palgrave Macmillan.

Niedenthal, Paula M. 2007. 'Embodying Emotion.' *Science* 316 (May 18): 1002–5.

Niesz, J. Anthony, and Norman N. Holland. 1984. 'Interactive Fiction.' *Critical Inquiry* 11 (Sept.): 110–29.

Oakley, John H. 1997. *The Achilles Painter*. Mainz am Rhein: Philipp von Zabern.

Oatley, Keith, and Maja Djikic. 2008. 'Writing as Thinking.' *Review of General Psychology* 12, no. 1:9–27.

Oates, Joyce Carol. 2006. 'Joyce Carol Oates.' In *The Way We Write: Interviews with Award-winning Writers*. Edited by Barbara Baker. London: Continuum. 141–9.

O'Donnell, James Joseph. 1998. *Avatars of the Word: From Papyrus to Cyberspace*. Cambridge, MA: Harvard University Press.

O'Donnell, William H., ed. 2003. *Responsibilities: Manuscript Materials by W.B. Yeats*. Ithaca and London: Cornell University Press.

Ojemann, George A. 1991. 'Cortical Organization of Language.' *Journal of Neuroscience* 11, no. 8 (August): 2281–7.

Olson, D.R., N. Torrance, and A. Hildyard, eds. 1985. *Literacy, Language, and Learning: The Nature and Consequences of Reading and Writing*. Cambridge: Cambridge University Press.

Olson, David R. 1994. *The World on Paper: The Conceptual and Cognitive Implications of Writing and Reading*. Cambridge: Cambridge University Press.

Olson, David R., and Nancy Torrance, eds. 1991. *Literacy and Orality*. Cambridge: Cambridge University Press.

Ong, Walter J. 1982. *Orality and Literacy: The Technologizing of the Word*. London: Methuen.

Orchard, Andy. 1996. 'The Making of Cædmon's Hymn.' In *Studies in English Language and Literature: 'Doubt Wisely,'* Papers in Honour of E.G. Stanley. Ed. M.J. Toswell and E.M. Tyler. New York: Routledge. 402–22.

Orr, Gregory. 1989. '"Longing for the Unconditional": A Conversation with Gregory Orr.' In *The Post-Confessionals: Conversations with American Poets of the Eighties*. Edited by Earl G. Ingersoll, Judith Kitchen, and Stan Sanvel Rubin. Rutherford, NJ: Fairleigh Dickinson University Press. 97–107.

Osborne, Charles. 1982. *The Life and Crimes of Agatha Christie*. London: Michael O'Mara Books.

Oxford University Press. 2007. 'Better writing.' AskOxford.com. URL: http://www.askoxford.com/betterwriting/plainenglish/sentencelength/. Seen 10 July 2007.

Paige, D.D., ed. 1951. *The Letters of Ezra Pound, 1907–1941*. London: Faber and Faber.

Palmer, Harold E. 1933. *Second Interim Report on English Collocations*. Tokyo: Institute for Research in English Teaching.

Paterson, Don. 2006. *The Way We Write: Interviews with Award-winning Writers*. Edited by Barbara Baker. London: Continuum. 150–62.

Peacock, Molly. 2002. *Cornucopia: New and Selected Poems 1975–2002*. New York: W.W. Norton.

Pendergast, Bruce. 2004. *Everyman's Guide to the Mysteries of Agatha Christie*. Guelph, ON: Trafford.

Pennebaker, James W. 2000. 'Telling Stories: The Health Benefits of Narrative.' *Literature and Medicine* 19, no. 1:3–18.

Pennebaker, James W., and Sandra Khilr Beall. 1986. 'Confronting a Traumatic Event: Toward an Understanding of Inhibition and Disease.' *Journal of Abnormal Psychology* 95, no. 3:274–81.

Penfield, Wilder, and E. Boldrey. 1937. 'Somatic Motor and Sensory Representation in the Cerebral Cortex of Man as Studied by Electrical Stimulation.' *Brain* 60, no. 4:389–443.

Perry, Susan Karen. 1996. 'When Time Stops: How Creative Writers Experience Entry into the Flow State.' PhD thesis, Fielding Institute. See chapter 2, pp. 11–74.

Persinger, M.A., and Katherine Makarec. 1992. 'The Feeling of a Presence and Verbal Meaningfulness in Context of Temporal Lobe Function: Factor Analytic Verification of the Muses?' *Brain and Cognition* 20, no. 2:217–26.

Peterson, L.R., and M.J. Peterson. 1959. 'Short-term Retention of Individual Verbal Items.' *Journal of Experimental Psychology* 58, no. 3:193–8.

Peterson, Robert R., and Pamela Savoy. 1998. 'Lexical Selection and Phonological Encoding during Language Production: Evidence for Cascaded Processing.' *Journal of Experimental Psychology: Learning, Memory, and Cognition* 24, no. 3:539–57.

Phillips, Martin. 1985. *Aspects of Text Structure: An Investigation of the Lexical Organisation of Text*. Amsterdam: North-Holland.

Pickering, Martin J., and Holly P. Branigan. 1999. 'Syntactic Priming in Language Production.' *Trends in Cognitive Sciences* 3, no. 4:136–41.

Pickering, Martin J., et al. 2000. 'Activation of Syntactic Information During Language Production.' *Journal of Psycholinguistic Research* 29, no. 2:205–16.

Pierce, John R. 1980; 1961. *An Introduction to Information Theory: Symbols, Signals & Noise*. Rev. ed. New York: Dover.

Pinker, Steven. 1994. *The Language Instinct: How the Mind Creates Language*. New York: HarperCollins.

Plath, Sylvia. 1981. 'The Disquieting Muses.' In *Collected Poems*. London: Faber and Faber. 74–6.

Plimpton, George, ed. 1967. *Writers at Work: The* Paris Review *Interviews*. 3rd ser. New York: Viking Press.

– 1988. *Writers at Work: The* Paris Review *Interviews*. 8th ser. New York: Penguin.

– 1992. *The Writer's Chapbook: A Compendium of Fact, Opinion, Wit, and Advice from the 20th Century's Preeminent Writers*. Rev. ed. London: Penguin.

Poe, Edgar Allan. 1846. 'The Philosophy of Composition.' *Graham's Magazine* 28, no. 4 (April): 163–7.

Poore, Quintin E., et al. 2006. 'Word List Generation Performance in Alzheimer's Disease and Vascular Dementia.' *Aging, Neuropsychology, and Cognition* 13, no. 1 (March): 86–94.

Porter, Kevin J. 2000. Review of *Post-process Theory*. *JAC: Rhetoric, Writing, Culture, Politics*. 20, no. 3:710–15.

Posner, Michael I., and Marcus E. Raichle. 1997. *Images of Mind*. New York: Scientific American.

Pratt, Lynda. 2004. 'The "Sad Habits" of Samuel Taylor Coleridge: Unpublished Letters from Joseph Cottle to Robert Southey, 1813–1817.' *Review of English Studies* 55, no. 218 (February): 75–90.

Publishers Weekly. 1977. *The Author Speaks: Selected PW Interviews 1967–1976*. New York and London: R.R. Bowker.

Pulvermüller, Friedemann. 2002. *The Neuroscience of Language: On Brain Circuits of Words and Serial Order*. Cambridge: Cambridge University Press.

– 2001. 'Brain Reflections of Words and their Meaning.' *Trends in Cognitive Sciences* 5, no. 12:517–24.

Purchas, Samuel. 1613. *Purchas his Pilgimage*. London: W. Stansby for H. Featherstone. STC 20505.

Quirk, Randolph, Sidney Greenbaum, Geoffrey Leech, and Jan Svartvik. 1985. *A Comprehensive Grammar of the English Language*. London: Longman.

Raichle, Marcus E., et al. 2001. 'A Default Mode of Brain Function.' In *Proceedings of the National Academy of Sciences of the United States of America* 98, no. 2 (January 16): 676–82.

Rainey, Lawrence. 2005. 'Eliot among the Typists: Writing *The Waste Land*.' *Modernism/Modernity* 12, no. 1:27–84.

– 2005b. *Revisiting* The Waste Land. New Haven, CT: Yale University Press.

Reed, Charlotte M., and Nathaniel I. Durlach. 1998. 'Note on Information Transfer Rates in Human Communication.' *Presence* 7, no. 5 (October): 509–18.

Renouf, Antoinette, and John M. Sinclair. 1991. 'Collocational Networks in English.' In *English Corpus Linguistics: Studies in Honour of Jan Svartvik*. Edited by Karin Aÿmer and Bengt Altenberg. London: Longman. 128–43.

Representative Poetry Online. 1994–. Edited by Ian Lancashire. Toronto: University of Toronto Libraries. URL: http://rpo.library.utoronto.ca.

Revard, Stella P. 1979. 'Milton's Muse and the Daughters of Memory.' *English Literary Renaissance* 9:432–41.

Richardson, Alan. 1997–. 'Literature, Cognition, and the Brain.' Boston College. URL: http://www2.bc.edu/~richarad/lcb/home.html.

– 1999. 'Cognitive Science and the Future of Literary Studies.' *Philosophy and Literature* 23, no. 1: 157–73.

– 2001. *British Romanticism and the Science of the Mind*. Cambridge: Cambridge University Press.

– 2002. 'Literature and the Cognitive Revolution: An Introduction.' *Poetics Today* 23, no. 1 (Spring): 1–8.

Richardson, Alan, and Ellen Spolsky, eds. 2004. *The Work of Fiction: Cognition, Culture, and Complexity*. Aldershot: Ashgate.

Riechers, Maggie. 2001. 'A Labor of Love.' *Humanities* 22, no. 6 (November-December). URL: http://www.neh.gov/news/humanitiesarchive.html. Seen 3 Sept. 2007.

Riegel, Klaus F. 1959. 'A Study of Verbal Achievements of Older Persons.' *Journal of Gerontology* 14, sec. B, no. 4 (October): 453–6.

Robinson-Riegler, Gregory and Bridget. 2004. *Cognitive Psychology: Applying the Science of the Mind*. Boston: Pearson.

Robyns, Gwen. 1978. *The Mystery of Agatha Christie*. Garden City, NY: Doubleday.

Rosenberg, Jim. 2002–3. 'Questions about the Second Move.' In *CyberText Yearbook 2002–2003*. Edited by Markku Eskelinen and Raine Koskimaa. University of Jyväskylä. 83–7. URL: http://cybertext.hum.jyu.fi/articles/107.pdf. Seen 3 July 2009.

Rudman, Joseph. 1998. 'The State of Authorship Attribution Studies: Some Problems and Solutions.' *Computers and the Humanities* 31:351–65.

Rush, Beth K., Deanna M. Barch, and Todd S. Braver. 2006. 'Accounting for Cognitive Aging: Context Processing, Inhibition or Processing Speed?' *Aging, Neuropsychology, and Cognition* 13: 588–610.

Said, Edward W. 2006. *On Late Style: Music and Literature against the Grain*. New York: Pantheon.

Salthouse, Timothy A. 1996. 'The Processing-Speed Theory of Adult Age Differences in Cognition.' *Psychological Review* 103, no. 3:403–28.

Salton, Gerard. 1989. *Automatic Text Processing: The Transformation, Analysis, and Retrieval of Information by Computer*. Reading, MA: Addison-Wesley.

Schneider, Elisabeth. 1953. *Coleridge, Opium, and* Kubla Khan. Chicago: University of Chicago Press.

Scholes, Robert. 1968. 'Stephen Daedalus, Poet or Esthete?' In A Portrait of the Artist as a Young Man: *Text, Criticism, and Notes*. Edited by Chester G. Anderson. New York: Viking Press. 468–80.

Serafine, Mary Louise, Robert G. Crowder, and Bruno H. Repp. 1984. 'Integration of Melody and Text in Memory for Songs.' *Cognition* 16, no. 3:285–303.

Serafine, Mary Louise, et al. 1986. 'On the Nature of Melody-Text Integration in Memory for Songs.' *Journal of Memory and Language* 25, no. 2:123–35.

Shakespeare, William. 1989. *The Complete Works. Electronic Edition for the IBM PC*. Ed. Stanley Wells and Gary Taylor, and W. Montgomery and L. Burnard. Oxford: Oxford Electronic Publishing.

– 1997. *The Riverside Shakespeare*. 2nd ed. Edited by G. Blakemore Evans and J.J.M. Tobin. Boston: Houghton Mifflin.

– 1998. *SHAKE-SPEARES SONNETS (1609)*. Edited by Hardy Cook and Ian Lancashire. Renaissance Electronic Texts 3.1. Toronto: University of Toronto Library. URL: http://www.library.utoronto.ca/utel/ret/shakespeare/1609inti.html.

Shakespeare, William, et al. ca. 1590–96. '*The book of Sir Thomas Moore*.' *British Library Harleian MS 7368*. Tudor Facsimile Texts, Folio series. [London]: 1910.

Shannon, C.E. 1948. 'A Mathematical Theory of Communication.' *The Bell System Technical Journal* 27 (July-October): 379–423, 623–56.

Shawver, Gary. 1999. 'A Chaucerian Narratology: "Storie" and "Tale" in Chaucer's Narrative Practice.' PhD thesis, University of Toronto.

Shelley, Percy Bysshe. 1994. 'Defence of Poetry.' *The Bodleian Shelley Manu-scripts: A Facsimile Edition*, XX. Edited by Michael O'Neill. New York and London: Garland. 20–83. Transcribed in *Representative Poetry Online*. URL: http://rpo.library.utoronto.ca/display/displayprose.cfm?prosenum=6.

Shelton, John. 1966. 'The Autograph Manuscript of "Kubla Khan" and an Interpretation.' *Review of English Literature* 7:31–42.

Shimamura, Arthur P., et al. 1992. 'Intact Implicit Memory in Patients with Frontal Lobe Lesions.' *Neuropsychologia* 30, no. 10:931–7.

Sidney, Sir Philip. 1591. *His Astrophel and Stella*. London: Thomas Newman.

Sigurd, Bengt, Mats Eeg-Olofsson, and Joost van Weijer. 2004. 'Word Length, Sentence Length and Frequency – Zipf Revisited.' *Studia Linguistica* 58, no. 1 (April): 37–52.

Sinclair, John. 1991. *Corpus, Concordance, Collocation*. Oxford University Press.

Skeat, T.C. 1963. '"Kubla Khan."' *British Museum Quarterly* 26, no. 3–4:77–83.

Skipper, Jeremy I., et al. 2007. 'Hearing Lips and Seeing Voices: How Cortical Areas Supporting Speech Production Mediate Audiovisual Speech Percep-tion.' *Cerebral Cortex* 17, no. 10:2387–99.

Sleve, L.R., and V.S. Ferreira. 2006. 'Halting in Single Word Production: A Test of the Perceptual Loop Theory of Speech Monitoring.' *Journal of Memory and Language* 54, no. 4:515–40.

Smadja, Frank. 1993. 'Retrieving Collocations from Text: Xtract.' *Computational Linguistics* 19, no. 1:143–77.

Small, Jeff A., Susan Kemper, and Kelly Lyons. 2000. 'Sentence Repetition and Processing Resources in Alzheimer's Disease.' *Brain and Language* 75, no. 2 (November): 232–58.

Smith, M.W.A. 1989. 'A Procedure to Determine Authorship using Pairs of Consecutive Words: More Evidence for Wilkins's Participation in *Pericles*.' *Computers and the Humanities* 23:113–29.

– 1991. 'The Authorship of *The Raigne of King Edward the Third*.' *Literary and Linguistic Computing* 6, no. 3:166–74.

Smith, Stevie. 1975. 'My Muse.' In *Collected Poems*. London: Penguin. 405.

Smyth, Joshua M., Arthur A. Stone, Adam Hurewitz, and Alan Kaell. 1999. 'Effects of Writing about Stressful Experiences on Symptom Reduction in Patients with Asthma or Rheumatoid Arthritis: A Randomized Trial.' *Journal of the American Medical Association* 281, no. 14 (14 April): 1304–9.

Sorhus, H.B. 1977. 'To Hear Ourselves – Implications for Teaching English as a Second Language.' *English Language Teaching Journal* 31, no. 3:211–21.

Spear, Hilda D. 2007. *Iris Murdoch*. 2nd ed. Basingstoke, Hampshire: Palgrave Macmillan.

Sperduti, Alice. 1950. 'The Divine Nature of Poetry in Antiquity.' In *Transactions and Proceedings of the American Philological Association* 81:209–40.

Spevack, Marvin. 1973. *The Harvard Concordance to Shakespeare*. Cambridge, MA: The Belknap Press of Harvard University Press.

– 1993. *A Shakespeare Thesaurus*. Hildesheim: Georg Olms Verlag.

Spolsky, Ellen. 1993. *Gaps in Nature: Literary Interpretation and the Modular Mind*. Albany: SUNY Press.

– 2002. 'Darwin and Derrida: Cognitive Literary Theory As a Species of Post-Structuralism.' *Poetics Today* 23, no. 1 (Spring): 43–62.

Spurgeon, Caroline. 1930. 'Imagery in the *Sir Thomas More* Fragment.' *Review of English Studies* 6, no. 23:257–70.

– 1935. *Shakespeare's Imagery and What It Tells Us*. Cambridge: Cambridge University Press.

Squire, Larry R. 1987. *Memory and Brain*. Oxford: Oxford University Press.

Stafford, William. 1977. 'William Stafford.' In *Fifty Contemporary Poets: The Creative Process*. Edited by Alberta T. Turner. New York: David McKay. 290–5.

Stevenson, Robert Louis. 1892. *Across the Plains, with Other Memories and Essays*. London: Chatto and Windus.

Strunk, William, Jr. 1918. *The Elements of Style*. Ithaca, New York: privately printed. URL: http://www.crockford.com/wrrrld/style.html. Seen 11 Sept. 2007.

Suddendorf, Thomas, and Michael C. Corballis. 2007. 'The Evolution of Foresight: What Is Mental Time Travel, and Is It Unique to Humans.' *Behavioral and Brain Sciences* 30:299–351.

Suerbaum, Ulrich. 2001. 'Rules of the Game: Agatha Christie's Construction of the Detective Story.' In *Agatha Christie and Archaeology*. Edited by Charlotte Trümpler. Munich: Ruhrlandmuseum Essen and Scherz Verlag Bern. 412–24.

Sweller, John. 1988. 'Cognitive Load during Problem Solving: Effects on Learning.' *Cognitive Science* 12:257–85.

– 2006. 'Commentary: The Worked Example Effect and Human Cognition.' *Learning and Instruction* 16: 165–9.

Svartvik, Jan, ed. 1990. *The London-Lund Corpus of Spoken English. Description and Research*. Lund: Lund University Press.

Takahashi, Masanobu, et al. 2006. 'One Percent Ability and Ninety-Nine Percent Perspiration: A Study of a Japanese Memorist.' *Journal of Experimental Psychology: Learning, Memory, and Cognition* 32, no. 5:1195–1200.

Tannen, Deborah. 2007. *Talking Voices: Repetition, Dialogue, and Imagery in Conversational Discourse*. 2nd ed. Cambridge: Cambridge University Press.

Tatlock, John S.P., and Arthur G. Kennedy. 1927. *A Concordance to the Complete Works of Geoffrey Chaucer, and to the Romaunt of the Rose*. Washington, DC: Carnegie Institution of Washington.

Tennyson, Alfred Lord. 1907–8. *Poems*. Ed. Hallam Lord Tennyson and annotated by Alfred Lord Tennyson. London: Macmillan.

Thompson, Laura. 2007. *Agatha Christie: An English Mystery*. London: Headline Review.

Todd, Richard. 2001. 'Realism Disavowed?: Discourses of Memory and High Incantations in *Jackson's Dilemma*.' *Modern Fiction Studies* 47, no. 3:674–95.

Tomlinson, Barbara. 2005. *Authors on Writing: Metaphors and Intellectual Labor*. Basingstoke, Hampshire: Palgrave Macmillan.

Trosman, H. 1974. 'T.S. Eliot and The Waste Land. Psychopathological Antecedents and Transformations.' *Archives of General Psychiatry* 30, no. 5 (May): 709–17.

Tsur, Reuven, and Christopher L. Heavy. 2006. *'Kubla Khan' – Poetic Structure, Hypnotic Quality and Cognitive Style: A Study in Mental, Vocal and Critical Performance*. Amsterdam: Benjamins.

Tulving, Endel. 1983. *Elements of Episodic Memory*. Oxford: Oxford University Press.

– 2002. 'Episodic Memory: From Mind to Brain.' *Annual Review of Psychology* 53: 1–25.

Turner, Mark. 1991. *Reading Minds: The Study of English in the Age of Cognitive Science*. Princeton, NJ: Princeton University Press.

Turner, Mark, ed. 2006. *The Artful Mind: Cognitive Science and the Riddle of Human Creativity*. Oxford: Oxford University Press.

Van Lancker, Diana. 2001. 'Meaning Is First: A Reply to the Commentaries.' *Aphasiology* 15, no. 4 (April): 396–406.

– 2001b. 'Preserved Formulaic Expressions in a Case of Transcortical Sensory Aphasia Compared to Incidence in Normal Everyday Speech.' *Brain and Language* 79, no. 1:38–41.

– 2004. 'When Novel Sentences Spoken or Heard for the First Time in the History of the Universe are not Enough: Toward a Dual-process Model of Language.' *International Journal of Language and Communication Disorders* 39, no. 1 (Jan.-March): 1–44.

Van Lancker-Sidtis, Diana, and Gail Rallon. 2004. 'Tracking the Incidence of Fomulaic Expressions in Everyday Speech: Methods for Classification and Verification.' *Language and Communication* 24, no. 3 (July): 207–40.

van Merriënboer, Jeroen J.G., and John Sweller. 2005. 'Cognitive Load Theory and Complex Learning: Recent Developments and Future Directions.' *Educational Psychology Review* 17, no. 2:147–77.

Van Velzen, Marjolein, and Peter Garrard. 2008. 'From Hindsight to Insight – Retrospective Analysis of Language Written by a Renowned Alzheimer's Patient.' *Interdisciplinary Science Reviews* 33, no. 4:278–86.

Veit, H.C. 1974. *'Postern of Fate.'* *Library Journal* 99 (January 1): 68.

Velz, John W. 1989. 'Sir Thomas More and the Shakespeare Canon.' In Shakespeare and Sir Thomas More: Essays on the play and its Shakespearian interest. Edited by T.H. Howard-Hill. Cambridge: Cambridge University Press. 171–95.

Wachtel, Eleanor. 1993. Writers & Company. Toronto: Alfred A. Knopf Canada.

Weaver, Constance. 2002. Reading Process and Practice. 3rd ed. Portsmouth, NH: Heinemann.

Webb, J. Barry. 1991. Shakespeare's Imagery of Plants. Hastings, Sussex: Cornwallis Press.

Weich, David. 2000. 'Jonathan Raban.' Powell's Books. URL: http://www.powells.com/authors/raban.html. Seen 18 January 2009.

Weizenbaum, Joseph. 1976. Computer Power and Human Reason: From Judgment to Calculation. San Francisco: W.H. Freeman.

Welters, Linda. 2006. 'Dress.' In Encyclopedia of Ancient Greece. Edited by Nigel Guy Wilson. New York: Routledge. 244–5.

Wentersdorf, Karl P. 2006. 'On "momtanish inhumanyty" in Sir Thomas More.' Studies in Philology 103, no. 2:178–85.

Whiter, Walter. 1972. A Specimen of a Commentary on Shakespeare 1794. Menston, UK: Scolar Press.

Whiting, Bartlett Jere. 1934. Chaucer's Use of Proverbs. Cambridge, MA: Harvard University Press.

Wiener, Norbert. 1961. Cybernetics or Control and Communication in the Animal and the Machine. 2nd ed. Cambridge, MA: MIT Press.

– 1967. The Human Use of Human Beings: Cybernetics and Society. New York: Hearst.

– 1956. I Am a Mathematician: The Later Life of a Prodigy. Cambridge, MA: MIT Press.

– Wilder, Thorton. 1958. 'Thornton Wilder.' Edited by R.H. Goldstone. In Writers at Work: The Paris Review Interviews. Edited by Malcolm Cowley. [1st series.] London: Secker and Warburg. 93–107.

Will, Barbara. 2001. 'Gertrude Stein, Automatic Writing and the Mechanics of Genius.' Forum for Modern Language Studies 37, no. 2: 169–75.

Willems, Roel M., and Peter Hagoort. 2007. 'Neural Evidence for the Interplay between Language, Gesture, and Action: A Review.' Brain and Language 101:278–89.

Williams, Kristine, et al. 2003. 'Written Language Clues to Cognitive Changes of Aging: An Analysis of the Letters of King James VI/I.' The Journals of Gerontology: Series B: Psychological Sciences and Social Sciences 58B.1 (Jan.): 42–4.

Wimsatt, W.K. Jr, and Monroe C. Beardsley. 1946. 'The Intentional Fallacy.' The Sewanee Review 54, no. 3 (July-Sept.): 468–88.

– 1949. 'The Affective Fallacy.' The Sewanee Review 57, no. 1 (Winter): 31–55.

Winter, Nina. 1978. *Interview with the Muse: Remarkable Women Speak on Creativity and Power*. Berkeley, CA: Moon.

Wood, A.B. 1955. *A Textbook of Sound*. 3rd ed. New York: Macmillan.

Wordsworth, William. 1802. *Lyrical Ballads: with Pastoral and Other Poems*. 2 vols. London: T.N. Longman and O. Rees.

Wray, Alison. 2002. *Formulaic Language and the Lexicon*. Cambridge: Cambridge University Press.

Wright, George T. 1981. 'Hendiadys and *Hamlet*,' *PMLA* 96, no. 2 (March): 168–93.

Wyatt-Brown, Anne M. 1988. 'Late Style in the Novels of Barbara Pym and Penelope Mortimer.' *The Gerontologist* 28, no. 6:835–39.

Yates, Frances A. 1966. *The Art of Memory*. Chicago: University of Chicago Press.

Yeats, W.B. 2003. *Responsibilities: Manuscript Materials*. Edited by William H. O'Donnell. Ithaca, NY: Cornell University Press.

Zacks, R.T., and L. Hasher. 1988. 'Capacity Theory and the Processing of Inferences.' In *Language, Memory, and Aging*. Edited by L. Light and D. Burke. New York: Cambridge University Press. 154–70.

Zeki, Semir. 2006. 'The Neurology of Ambiguity.' In *The Artful Mind: Cognitive Science and the Riddle of Human Creativity*. Edited by Mark Turner. Oxford: Oxford University Press. 243–70.

Zwann, Rolf A., et al. 2004. 'Moving Words: Dynamic Representations in Language Comprehension.' *Cognitive Science* 28, no. 4:611–19.

Index

Survey of English Usage (corpus), 55
Svartvik, Jan, 55
Svoboda, K., 61
Sweller, John, 95, 278n9
syntactic priming. *See* cognitive
    constraints
syntax, 208; combinatory nodes,
    82; constructs, 79; operators, 259;
    stitching, 12, 16, 56, 203, 252; struc-
    tures, 58; subject-verb-object, 42,
    208, 281n17. *See* aging, language of;
    Alzheimer's disease, language of;
    Chomsky, Noam; markers, stylistic

Takahashi, Masanobu, 76
Tannen, Deborah, 57, 110
Tatlock, John S.P., 281n18
Taylor, Gary, 138
temporal cortex. *See* brain
Tennyson, Alfred, Lord, 109
text, 105; analysis, 9–10, 13–14, 104,
    127, 238, 248, 259–69; cyborgic, 15;
    dating of, 131–2; denatured, 4, 112;
    mechanical, 12; summarization,
    10. *See also* authoring (products
    of); literary works, analysed
texte-auteur, 254
Thayer, Scofield, 176
Thomas, Dylan, 207, 242
Thompson, Laura, 209–11
Thomson, Neil, 89
thought, 7, 220, 244, 247, 251; as
    natural language, 96; cognitive
    load and, 16, 95–9, 146–7; men-
    talese, 96–9; personified, 117–18,
    126–7, 219, 244; propositions,
    97–8; size of (*see* omega value;
    working memory [capacity]).
    See also conceptualizer; gist;
    homunculus

Todd, Richard, 237, 240–1
Tolkien, J.R.R., 133
Tomlinson, Barbara, 54
Tomoyori, Hideaki, 76
trance, 36, 40, 249
Tranel, Daniel, 70, 77
Tsuchiya, Naotsugu, 63
Tulving, Endel, 65, 194
Turner, Mark, 11, 28–9, 31

unipolar disease. *See* depression
uttering, 8, 12, 53–101, 105, 248. *See
    also* authoring (products of)

Valéry, Paul, 37
Van Lancker (Van Lancker-Sidtis),
    Diana, 56, 58
van Merriënboer, Jeroen J.G., 95
Van Velzen, Marjolein, 239
Van Vogt, A.E., 234
van Weijer, Joost, 97
Veit, H.C., 210
Vidal, Gore, 33
Virgil, 183
visual cortex. *See* brain
visual semantics, 90
visual short-term memory, 91, 100
visual-spatial sketchpad. *See* work-
    ing memory
Vittoz, Roger, 193
vocabulary: Chaucer's, 120–1, 128,
    281n14; Christie's, 213–14, 275;
    Coleridge's, 167–8; counting of,
    255 (*see also* software); drop in,
    17, 255–6; effect of genre on, 138;
    increase in, 255–6; oral formulaic,
    16, 25, 104, 108; paralanguage, 57,
    89; phrasal, 14; terms of art, 121;
    Shakespeare's, 137–9, 153, 273–4.
    See also idiolect; sociolect; words